What
Makes
the
Great
Great

Also by Dennis Kimbro

Think and Grow Rich: A Black Choice

Daily Motivations for African American Success

What Makes the Great Great

Strategies for Extraordinary Achievement

DENNIS P. KIMBRO, PH.D.
DOUBLEDAY   New York London Toronto Sydney Auckland

PUBLISHED BY DOUBLEDAY
a division of Bantam Doubleday Dell Publishing Group, Inc.
1540 Broadway, New York, New York 10036

DOUBLEDAY and the portrayal of an anchor with a
dolphin are trademarks of Doubleday, a division of
Bantam Doubleday Dell Publishing Group, Inc.

Book design by Bonni Leon-Berman

Library of Congress Cataloging-in-Publication Data
Kimbro, Dennis Paul, 1950–
What makes the great great: strategies for
extraordinary achievement / Dennis P. Kimbro.
p.   cm.
1. Afro-Americans—Psychology.   2. Afro-Americans—
Life skills guides.   3. Motivation (Psychology)—
United States.   I. Title.
E185.625.K55 1997
158'.1'08996073—dc20   96-24662
                                                                    CIP
ISBN 0-385-48268-X

To My Students, past and present, at Clark Atlanta University. I've said it before: You're too sharp to fail. To Joseph McCauley, my father-in-law, the role model that we desperately need; and to Pat, officially you are my wife; in reality you're much more: champion, coach, best friend, and the greatest person I've ever known.

Acknowledgments

No effort over time is without roots somewhere else. This book is no exception. In my case, I had the pleasure of working with some real pros. They include: my agents, Carl DeSantis and Jerry Butler, who've been by my side every page of the way. Together, they're the best in the business.

Lori Lipsky and Rob Robertson, my editors, whose appropriate blend of enthusiasm and criticism strengthened the book immensely.

Gloria Gilbert and Pauline Roberson, dear friends, who have been wonderfully supportive.

Without the help of Diane Howell, Linda Keene, Raymond Fears, Amy Hilliard-Jones, Cheri Henderson, and my 1994 MBA class, the Kimbro Executive Profile would not have been possible.

Lisa Oliver, my assistant at Clark Atlanta University, kept me on schedule and allowed me to put my best foot forward. Elizabeth Waters at Nike offered much-needed financial support.

Ruby McCauley, a real gem, and Louise Sims and Alice Hopkins, all experts in life, whose nuggets of wisdom were felt on every page of this book.

My daughters, Kelli, Kim, and MacKenzie, whose love drives me on. They are constantly forced to share my time. I promise to make it up to you.

Contents

Introduction:

The Greatest Discovery

- **The Greatest Discovery**

- **The Power of This Strange Key**

- **Change Your Thoughts and Change Your World**

- **How I Uncovered the Secret**

- **The Nine Principles of Extraordinary Achievement**

- **The Best Medicine**

If you want to be great and successful, you must walk
hand-in-hand, side by side with great and successful people.
—NIDO QUBEIN

People with dreams know no poverty.
Each of us is as rich as our own dreams.
—BENJAMIN E. MAYS

Build it well, whate'er you do;
Build it straight and strong and true;
Build it clean and high and broad;
Build it for the eye of God.
—ANONYMOUS

How much better it is to get wisdom than gold!
And to get understanding is to be chosen rather than silver.
—PROVERBS 16:16

As Bill Pinkney entered his office for the last time, he saw shock in the faces of his coworkers and heard anger in their voices. On most Fridays, friendly greetings echoed the plant. Anticipating the weekend, workers normally waved and smiled across chest-high dividers. This particular morning they clustered in small groups, whispering among themselves as though the world had come to an end. And then the news hit.

"What? I've been fired? You must be joking!"

Pinkney couldn't believe his ears. He went to his office with a sense of dread. A long envelope from personnel lay on the desk with his name typed on it in bold print. That morning, along with several of his coworkers, Pinkney learned that his services, though "valued" by his employer, were no longer required. Imagine, after nearly thirty years of tireless duty for a major Chicago-based cosmetics firm, this fifty-seven-year-old black man was just the latest statistic in the never-ending corporate battle to trim costs and improve efficiency. Though his employer was simply reacting to economic downturns within the health and beauty aids market, Pinkney felt cheated and defeated.

He had struggled up through the ranks—from an hourly worker in research and development with Revlon to a well-paid makeup consultant with Johnson Products, gaining promotions and admiration along the way. What he lacked in terms of formal education, Pinkney more than offset in industry know-how, touting a wide range of experience. It hadn't taken him long to prove his worth. And although he'd heard rumors about layoffs on different occasions, no one really believed the day would come. The industry seemed safe. Pinkney, along with many of his coworkers, felt blessed to have a job that was so secure. He'd felt his position would be around for a long time.

"Then, out of the blue, reality hit me," Pinkney sadly remembers. "After all those years of hard work, they just handed me a pink slip and it was over. I was loyal, talented, and committed to the bottom line. I even took work home to meet deadlines. But none of it seemed to matter. *Dear Mr. Pinkney, we are sorry to inform you that . . .*

By midmorning, Pinkney had said sad good-byes to old friends, collected his belongings and severance check, and boarded the train for the long ride home to face his wife and reorganize his life. He was heartsick with disappointment. *What was he going to tell her? What was he going to do?* Stuck with no job and no income, and with little to tide him over, he could only visualize himself pounding the pavement searching for work. And then it happened!

"I Was Caught in the Mathematics of Life"

As the train neared his stop, Pinkney's life flashed before him. He began to think of lost opportunities gone by; of all the empty dreams he had entertained since childhood. Throughout his adult life, he had never given much thought to his career, or to finding the work for which he was best suited. A job was a job; any work that came by his hand was good enough for him and his family. He reflected, "I was raised that, when you graduated from high school and you got a job at the post office or on the railroad, this would be your lot in life. You couldn't hope for anything more."

But Pinkney wanted more. It all seemed different now. He leaned his head back against his seat and tried to frame the moment. Yes, there had been anxious, unhappy times before, even bad times. Pinkney had lived through a childhood punctuated by poverty. He had been raised by a mother who worked as a domestic until a rheumatic heart forced her family onto welfare. His father was nowhere to be found. His family had moved from place to place in downtown Chicago, searching for any apartment his mother could afford. But he had never lost faith in the future; and now, as he grew older, as far as his dreams were concerned, it was do or die.

"I always wanted to leave a legacy," Pinkney admits. "A sort of benchmark to prove that I could do anything that I set my mind and heart to. Though I never followed through, I've known exactly what I wanted to do since high school. As I shared my dreams with others, I heard all the excuses. I was exposed to all the naysayers who said, 'You're black; you're poor; you didn't go to college; you don't have a father; it's a white man's world.' Here I was forty years later; if I was going to realize my dreams, it was now or never. I was caught in the mathematics of life." As a friendly reminder, he carried with him a poem by Johann von Goethe, the eighteenth-century German writer, given to him by a high school classmate decades ago. Pinkney had committed the verse to memory, not knowing the magic that it held:

Are you in earnest? Seize this very minute;
What you can do, or dream you can, begin it!
Boldness has genius, power and magic in it.
Only engage, and then the mind grows heated;
BEGIN, and then the work will be completed.

There could be no better philosophy for anyone, regardless of what problems or circumstances one may face.

Stunned but not beaten, Pinkney wasted no time with self-pity. By the time he got home, he had decided what he would do with the rest of his life: a solo voyage around the world by sailboat. He would fulfill his high school dream!

THE GREATEST DISCOVERY

Ideas are the most important things on earth. Each of us has his or her own idea mechanism. It comes as standard equipment at birth—it's the mind of all *Homo sapiens.* A baby is born, and we hold in our arms a miraculous living creature whose potential is unknown. What will enter that astonishing brain? And from those ingredients, what kind of life will this child fashion? The greatest discovery is the realization of our own potential. The secret to extraordinary achievement is exploiting that unknown potential.

We become what we think about, but the thinking is up to us. The degree to which people regularly underestimate their capacity for accomplishment is immeasurable. Curiously, we think nothing of the accomplishments of others; that is, what others do we tend to take in stride. But when it comes to setting goals for ourselves, we tend to play it safe and thus remain within limits that are embarrassingly narrow. So if we already have a job, even one with minimal demands, we will usually shun any efforts to prepare ourselves for more attractive opportunities or any sudden emergencies, such as the loss of that job. Each night, we watch the news broadcast the latest corporate cutback or plant closing. Without exception a reporter will ask an unemployed worker, "What are you going to do now that the facility has closed down?" Nine times out of ten the reply is the same: "Well, I guess I'll just have to wait for it to reopen," or, "I've worked in this plant for twenty years. I don't know anything else." Here are men and women behaving like cattle that can graze in only one pasture, and if that pasture is no longer there, they would simply sit down and waste away! In those twenty years, a person could have become a skilled surgeon, a master chef, a fashion designer, or even a rocket scientist. It is totally up to *you!*

PINKNEY SET OUT to capture his dream. His plan was to circumnavigate the globe the hard way—not through the man-made Panama and Suez canals, but by passing below the world's five southernmost capes. There was another angle, too: He wanted to help teach thousands of urban schoolchildren the value of commitment and self-discipline by sharing his voyage with them by radio, computer, and videotape.

Pinkney's journey would require more than character. He would need equipment, supplies, and financing to offset the costs of a journey that would cover 27,000 miles and last two years. The Chicago native worked day and night on a series of part-time jobs. As a manager of a local bakery, his wife, Ina, provided some financial stability. In time, Pinkney began to lure investors. Old Navy buddy Bill Cosby heard of Pinkney's plan and referred him to Armand Hammer, former head of Occidental Petroleum. Hammer was receptive to the idea. The philanthropist gave the project clout and much-needed seed money. Pinkney then launched a massive letter-writing campaign to raise the rest from corporate donors and individuals.

"It was like a political campaign," Pinkney says. Over a five-year period, he raised $400,000 from an array of corporations and individuals that ranged from Motorola, which outfitted his boat with a satellite computer system, to a partnership of investors that included writer Maya Angelou.

Before setting out on his voyage, Pinkney filmed two "just in case" videotapes. One was to be shown to students if he became missing at sea, the other if he was killed during his journey. "I explained that I knew there was an element of danger before I started out," he says, "and that was the price I agreed to pay for pursuing my dream." On August 5, 1990, Pinkney kissed his wife, Ina, untied his forty-seven-foot sailboat, and headed out of Boston Harbor for the world. For the next two years, he and his boat, the *Commitment,* plied the seas, facing ocean hazards he had only read about: gale-force winds, icebergs, and 600,000-ton oil tankers.

But the toughest part of the journey was the solitude. "When there are high waves and strong winds, you've got to act. But when it's quiet, boredom is difficult to fight." During one stretch, Pinkney sailed for sixty-five days without seeing another soul, passing away the hours by reading motivational and inspirational books—mostly the Bible and Shakespeare—150 titles in all. In March 1991, Pinkney had to put in for repairs in Tasmania before continuing on the most harrowing part of the journey. The automatic steering system had broken and he'd stayed awake for six straight nights.

Back in the States, twenty thousand students tracked "Captain Bill" on classroom maps in Chicago and Boston public schools. The *Commit-*

ment docked in five ports around the world so Pinkney could replenish supplies. He sent the schools "video postcards" of himself dancing the toi toi with Zulu tribesmen in South Africa and visiting a Tasmanian devil park in Australia. "Don't let anyone ever set your limitations," he counseled. "Know what your dreams will cost and be willing to pay the price." Inspired by his adventure, students mailed him letters, built model boats, studied navigation, and wrote reports on the countries he visited.

The human spirit, the triumph over fear and doubt, an unshakable determination to succeed, the new dynamics of achievement . . . on June 9, 1992, they all came together in one unforgettable moment. After two years at sea, the *Commitment* docked again in Boston. Pinkney arrived home a hero, cheered by thousands of schoolchildren, teachers, and friends. He became the first African American to sail solo around the world, and only the forty-first sailor ever to complete the journey. In comparison, more people have scaled Mount Everest than have sailed around the five great capes. His voyage made him as lean as an Olympic athlete and spiritually grounded him for good. He has acquired a quiet confidence and a sense of vision.

"When you're out there at sea, your concern is survival," he says. "From that experience, I've learned about leadership, discipline, and perseverance, and not to sweat the small stuff. My horizons are different now." More important, he now knows *what makes the great great.* He knows who succeeds and why. Listen carefully as he describes the process in his own words. "Don't wait! Now is the time to fulfill your destiny. We must act with courage; look forward with hope; and view life through a lens that defines what can be done rather than what cannot be done. If you are willing to work and never, never quit, you can make your dreams come true." What does this message mean to *you?*

Bill Pinkney's personal victory was a triumph of spirit and hope. A win over fear and doubt, frustration and the odds—the new dynamics of human performance. It's an achievement we can all admire. More than that, it's an accomplishment you and I can learn from and use in every area of our lives. What's the secret to discover? It's being able to place yourself in the state of mind that Pinkney achieved as he sailed the seven seas. It's a special place that only peak performers inhabit— where there is no past and no future, only the exhilaration of the moment. Success isn't due to luck or chance. Real success is a matter of finding yourself and building upon what you find. Every person is born to star at something. The point of your life is to discover your purpose. It makes no difference whether it's to be an athlete, a top salesperson in the office, or a provider for your family. Greatness means doing more than you or anyone else thought possible.

What does Pinkney's story mean to you? Will *you* be caught in the mathematics of life? Elbert Hubbard, the old country philosopher, wrote, "Upon every face is written the record of the life the man has led; the prayers, the aspirations, the disappointments, all he hoped to be and was not—all are written there; nothing is hidden, nor indeed can be." Robert Browning, the nineteenth-century English poet, concurred. He stated, "When a man's fight begins within himself, he is worth something." With its beautiful imagery, and its emphasis on improvement, the Bhagavad-Gita states, "A man's own self is his friend, a man's own self is his foe."

What do these messages mean to *you?*

You, who find your life trapped within a sea of hopelessness. You, black man, black woman, who view racism as an insurmountable obstacle. You, who seem chained to a dead-end job, living far beneath your potential and possibilities. You, young student, who struggle for an education in an increasingly violent world. You, single mother, who wish to make your life and home a centerpiece for your children but can't seem to make ends meet. You, absentee father, who have heard the pleas from your wife and children but fail to bear the title of husband and provider. You, the addicted, who stagger beneath the weight of your addiction and life-threatening habits. You, the afflicted, who are burdened with the stress and strain of your disability or "incurable" illness. You, the underclass, who desperately search for meaning and purpose in your life. You, the corporate climber, who, by now, have discovered that the glass ceiling is really cement. You, the entrepreneurial hopeful, who can barely muster the faith to face another day and who continue to pour out your very soul. And you, the misled, who have followed one false prophet after another, preaching his own brand of religion when you should have turned within and worked out your own salvation. What does Pinkney's story mean to you?

The answer should be obvious. It has been a part of your being since inception. After all, you were directed by Earth, Wind, and Fire to "Keep Your Head to the Sky." *Hope:* You could see it in the eyes of Fannie Lou Hamer. You can read it in the words of James Baldwin. You can hear it in the saxophone solos of John Coltrane. You can feel it in the lyrics of Otis Redding's "Try a Little Tenderness." You can sense it in the tender melodies of Babyface. You can recognize it in the comedy of Richard Pryor. You can detect it in the oratory of Maxine Waters. You could perceive it in the command performances of Mahalia Jackson and Kathleen

Battle. And you know it's in the strut of Deion Sanders. What does this story mean to you? *It means there's hope! There's always precious hope.*

TODAY IS JUDGMENT DAY!

Throughout the ages, humanity has been taught to prepare for, and even fear, the day of atonement. In various teachings, our Creator is portrayed as whimsical and changeable. According to tradition, each of us must answer to an omnipotent power who, on the one hand, rewards acts of faith and kindness with eternal bliss, and on the other, punishes less than admirable conduct with wrath and damnation. This day of reckoning has been called, among other things, judgment day.

In the face of religious doctrine and dogma, few have caught the real significance of right and wrong, of good and evil, of judgment day. As we experience life, each of us undertakes a personal quest to uncover greater meaning. In our quest for personal fulfillment, we ascend the ladder of truth regarding our own spirituality and individual possibilities. In the process, we are bombarded with constant choices—choices that only we can make based on our level of understanding that will determine our destiny: "Choose you this day whom ye will serve" (Joshua 24:15). As a result, *every* day is a day of judgment. *Today's* judgment day, for example, is the result of past thoughts. Judgment day, in reality, is the day on which your thoughts become things. Like a living magnet, this is what constantly draws to you people and circumstances in accord with your thinking. What you experience today—judgment day—is a reflection of your consciousness. In essence, if you hope to experience a different judgment day, then *think different thoughts.*

Stated in his own words, Pinkney's story is the saga of a man who decided to seek fulfillment of his dream—a different kind of judgment day. And what a dramatic tale it is! I have related Bill Pinkney's story to emphasize that each of us will one day come face-to-face with the prospect of embarking on our own fantastic voyage. Nearly penniless, and with nothing more to guide him than sheer desire, this powerful soul set out to find true meaning in his life. *Do you really wish to change your life for the better? Are you hoping and praying for a change?* Then realize, regardless of your circumstances, no matter the conditions, all is not lost, life is not hopeless. Never give up, give in, or give out!

Don't wait for that miracle or that break or "the right time." Life is short. Don't wait. *Today is your day!* Choose how you will spend it and whom you will spend it with. Don't put your personal greatness on hold. You are responsible for your own results. You hold within your hands the key to a more meaningful life; a road map to brighter tomorrows; a nugget of truth in the midst of confusion; a valuable blueprint that will enable you to restructure your future. Read it. Study it. *Then get into action!*

For starters, there are some tough questions that you must answer:

- Are you dissatisfied with your present status?
- What new habit must you start that will bring you closer to your goals?
- What must you *stop* doing because this old habit is pulling you away from your goals?
- What must you change in order to move toward where you want to be?

WHAT MAKES THE GREAT GREAT?

There is a quality of personality that many successful people share. No matter how they may differ, there is an attitude, a quiet assurance based on self-knowledge, that says in effect: "I've been tried in some tough situations, and I've passed the test. I know who I am." The successful share a special power. They conduct their affairs with a sense of purpose. Their priorities are clear and they orchestrate the events of their lives with a masterful touch. High achievers move smoothly from one phase of their lives to the next. No motion is wasted.

In the ancient African tradition of sharing oral history, the griot told vivid examples of greatness to which future generations could aspire. They demonstrated the attributes that make men and women heroic. In other words, what makes the great great.

There is a condition or circumstance that has greater bearing upon the happiness of life than any other. What is it? It is one of the most common things in the world and within your reach. If this secret were for sale, oh, how rich you would be! A sunken ship, a buried treasure, an unsolved mystery. Why are these objects so appealing? Because within you is an innate desire to solve the mystery that leads to your own personal hidden treasure. Only the wise can guess its contents. Some might say it is health, or money, or special relationships—but you may possess all of these and still not be content. You may have fame and fortune and yet allow happiness to elude your grasp. Yes, there is *one thing* more necessary to a happy, fulfilling life than any other. What is it? *What makes the great great?*

This secret of wealth and success has remained hidden for thousands of years. Since time began, humanity has searched—mostly in vain—for this precious key. It has been found, only to be lost again, scores of times. The prophets and mystics of all races have had some inkling of its great powers. Every race, group, and culture has had its wise men and philosophers, its men and women of genius and vision who glimpsed the truth that is buried in the spirit. But it remains for those who possess an open heart and an open mind to discover this great truth in its entirety and then to demonstrate to others how they might use it to their benefit. Make no mistake about it: The accomplishments of a few can be achieved by you *if, and only when, you are ready!* It stands to reason that in His name, "The things I do shall ye do also, and greater things than these shall ye do."

What makes the great great? The question was placed before Percy Sutton, owner of New York's famed Apollo Theater. Here is a man who is clearly in charge of the direction of his affairs; an individual who was raised to see himself as one of those blacks whose accomplishments would become symbolic beacons lighting the path for those of his race. He counseled, "If you have but one wish, let it be for an idea."

What makes the great great? Have you found the key? Try asking Robert E. Johnson, founder of Black Entertainment Television, the only black-owned nationwide cable system. Who would know better than he? Johnson is a man whose hopes and dreams have been singed, but he rose again and again to see another day. "Life is a grindstone," he flatly states. "But whether it grinds you down or polishes you up depends upon what you are made of." The Reverend Jesse Jackson concurs. He spoke openly and honestly regarding success and achievement: "You may not be responsible for getting knocked down, but you're certainly responsible for getting back up!"

When the annals of black business history are written, Henry Parks and the Parks Sausage Company will likely be listed as major contributors. To Black America, Parks was a legend, a model of self-initiative and fierce racial pride. Starting with "every nickel I could scrape together," he launched a shoestring operation—grinding out sausage in a converted Baltimore dairy. He couldn't possibly succeed, but he did! At last count, Parks Sausage had more than $20 million a year in sales. Without hesitation, he stood to make his point. "In one hand I have a dream, and in the other I have an obstacle. Tell me, which one grabs your attention?"

No barrier could be erected to shut out Patti LaBelle's voice; she believes she was made for the place that she fills. When asked for *the* secret, LaBelle recalled her father's advice. Since her childhood she could never be caught without a song in her heart or a melody on her lips. " 'Sing loud!' my father always told me, 'just in case someone is listening.' " Talent helps, but greatness has more in common with nerve than it ever will with ability.

What a great lesson Reverend Ike taught his race on that hard, dusty Central Park bench! Toiling in the face of poverty since leaving his native South Carolina, for three months Frederick Eikerenkoetter—Reverend Ike—ate dog food out of cans while reading his Bible and planning for better days. He delved into the book to find precious pearls. He prayed, not to *have* more, but to *be* more; not for fame, but "to be ye transformed." Now, for more than twenty years, his name has been synonymous with spirituality and prosperity. I asked him for the key to greatness, and he took me off in a totally different direction. "Do what I have done," he suggested. "Open up a *can!* The world belongs to those who say *I can.*"

What makes the great great? When asked, Mae Jemison, America's first black female astronaut, was a bit philosophical, choosing just the right metaphor to convey her point. "Greatness can be captured in one word: *lifestyle.* Life is God's gift to you, style is what you make of it." George Halsey maintained a coiled intensity ready to spring into action. A former insurance clerk who now holds the highest pin Amway has to offer, Halsey rendered his thoughts: "Learn to meet hard times with a harder will. If you'll work two years of your life like others won't, you'll spend the rest of your life like others can't."

You can judge how great a people will become by examining the quality of the relationships between its males and its women and children. By this measure alone, a people will either rise or fall. This is the test that predicts fame and fortune. *What makes the great great?* Few people are as qualified as Dr. Alvin Poussaint to discuss the great spirit of the black struggle in America. One of eight children, this noted psychiatrist inherited no opportunities and acquired nothing by luck. His good fortune consisted of untiring perseverance, an acumen for science and medicine, and the Old Testament taught by loving parents who dared to venture past the tenth grade. Dr. Poussaint peered through the window of his Harvard office and established a point of reference. "Morality and values begin at home. If Black America is to continue its greatness, it must take care of its children."

Quincy Jones struck the same note: "Greatness occurs when your children love you, when your critics respect you, and when you have peace of mind." For more than forty years, he has built a remarkable career as a musician, composer, television and film producer, and multimedia entrepreneur. His name is synonymous with talent and genius.

Cornel West, the best-selling author and college professor, when asked for the root of greatness, repeated the question, paused for a moment, and answered in the manner of a man close to his God: "If you want to be great, you must serve willingly and love greatly."

Oseola McCarty's lined, brown hands, now gnarled with arthritis, bear mute testimony to a lifetime spent washing and ironing other people's clothes. Less evident is how this quiet, eighty-seven-year-old black woman managed to donate $150,000 to the University of Southern Mississippi—a school she could never attend. Though faced with poverty and ignorance, she never backed down. "They used to not let colored people go to school there, but now they do, and I think they should have the money." *What makes the great great?* This tiny, gentle woman replied in a barely audible tone: "Do as much as you can for as many as you can." Now McCarty has left a name that can never die.

It's not what the successful *do,* but what their lives promise, that gives hope to our race. Ann Fudge's family is the passion of her life. As the highest-ranking black woman in corporate America, she stands shoulder-to-shoulder with the best and the brightest Wall Street has ever produced. Without batting an eye, Fudge reveals the source of her strength, demonstrating that she is in full possession of the secret. According to this powerhouse, if you're searching for greatness, look no further than your own home. "The first real test of leadership," she says, "is maintenance of the family unit."

Captain Bill Pinkney speaks of faith. "Everyone fears something. Though worry and trepidation may crowd your thoughts, there's always room for faith. So if you attempt something great and you find your knees shaking, try kneeling on them." Death wins no victory over such men.

What makes the great great? Do you know? The overwhelming majority will never recognize the difference between greatness and mediocrity, between happiness and pleasure. They will never sense true fulfillment, nor will they awaken to their highest potential. Greatness is a mosaic composed of very small stones. Each taken by itself may be of little value. But when grouped together, combined, and set, they form a true work of art—the hallmark of achievement. Nine stones, or mental strategies, underlie all success and accomplishment, all greatness. (These stones of greatness, to which I refer, can be found within each chapter of this book.) Fulfillment and personal development come as a result of relating and applying each of these strategies, which in turn will draw you closer to your destiny. A destiny that *you* control.

THE KEY TO SUCCESS

Throughout the ages, humanity has viewed lightning and thunder as the wrath of God, just as the deeply religious look upon poverty, sickness, and lack as visitations of the Almighty. Yet man has learned to harness lightning's electrical power, allowing it to serve him. The laws governing electricity were there all the time, waiting only for the discovery by someone wise enough to show others how to put these forces to good use. Likewise, the power to be and to have lies at your feet. You need only understanding and insight.

Our Creator might have given us our daily bread ready-made. He might have kept us in Eden forever; but He had a grander and nobler plan in mind when He fashioned humanity. There is a divinity within humanity that the paradise of Eden could never develop. There is a blessing in that curse that drove man from the garden and compelled him to earn his bread by the sweat of his brow. It was not by chance that our Maker concealed our highest happiness and greatest good beneath the sternest difficulties. Mahatma Gandhi once wrote that there were seven sins in the world: wealth without work; pleasure without conscience; knowledge without character; commerce without morality; science without humanity; worship without sacrifice; and politics without principle. Ironically, strength grows out of struggle.

At this very moment, you, the reader, possess great capacities for miraculous self-enrichment. You need only exercise these powers as best you can. You need not concern yourself with whether you are proceeding correctly or not. The only prerequisite for this journey is that you are conscious of your own great force. Humanity is designed to be spiritually aware, mentally creative, emotionally and physically alert, happy in all relationships, and continually striving to achieve goals. To settle for only partial fulfillment is a grave mistake. We will never be truly satisfied until we break down all barriers that restrict and limit our soul's aspiration.

What is the key to success? The sick will say health; the poor will guess wealth; the ambitious believe it is power and influence; and the intellectual will offer knowledge. But each misses the mark!

It was out of the richness and the fullness of his own life that the noted black historian Charles Wesley wrote, "How few people realize that success in life depends more upon what they are than upon what they know. It is self-esteem that has brought the race this far."

"God has placed the highest price upon the greatest worth," said

Booker T. Washington to a struggling student overtaken with thoughts of ending his education. The founder of Tuskegee Institute, Washington urged the young man to push forward in spite of his difficulties. Standing in the middle of the historical campus, Washington began to probe the young man, searching for any traces of greatness. "If a man would reach the highest success," Washington explained, "he must pay the price himself. Do you long for an education? Have you the stamina to continue your studies when you're too poor to eat? Will you rise at daybreak and study 'til sunset long after others have retired?

"Will you black boots during the day and quote Latin at night? Do you love learning enough to walk ten miles to borrow a book you cannot afford to buy? And having no money for books, will you borrow the texts and memorize your lessons? Is five years or ten years amid want and woe, too long to spend perfecting your craft?"

The boy stood aghast as Washington continued. "Young man, have you the courage of Nat Turner who laughed in the face of death? Have you the unconquerable will of Harriet Tubman, who said with every fiber of her body *'Thou shalt be free!'* Will you bless your race by paying the price? How much can you endure? It's true, each of us hopes to achieve, but this is not enough. Success is the off-spring of drudgery. *A man must be self-made before he is ever made!"*

Booker T. Washington was hoping to expose the young man to his own greatness—a secret that has unfortunately evaded the grasp of so many. How beautiful the universe is to the man or woman who is at one with the Creator and knows the plan as well as the planner. When an individual realizes that he or she is divine, when he sees that he is a part of the everlasting principle which is the very essence of reality, the goal of our existence, nothing can throw him off balance. He is centered in the everlasting truth and he knows his true potential.

Washington knew this, as do all high-achieving men and women. Washington knew something that average men and women don't know. He knew that *attitude* is everything; that *altitude* is determined by *attitude.* He knew that high achievers shoot for the stars; if they fall short of their mark, at least they come back with stardust in their hands. If achievers fail, they never stay down; they learn from adversity. They learn from their failures what *not to do.*

Washington knew that the road to success is a worthy one to take. He knew that successful people take chances—they walk to the beat of a different drummer. In addition, high achievers come early and stay late; they make the forty-hour workweek look like child's play. Booker T.

Washington knew that those committed to personal excellence dream big dreams and work on making those dreams come true. Achievers know the law of averages; they realize that success is a statistical event. Those bent on success know that if you don't stand for *something,* you will fall for *anything.*

Finally, all high achievers make choices and not excuses; they know that any excuse is a reason for inactivity. They have a strong faith, a belief in Divine power, and respect for their fellow man and woman. They have a smile in their heart as well as on their face. They know that they are responsible for the outcome of their own lives, and, accordingly, they respond with ability. But most important, high achievers know every inch of their road. And now you have the map.

THE POWER OF THIS STRANGE KEY

It was this same key that inspired Aesop, father of the first written word, to influence Western thought and morals. In 560 B.C., the impact of this black man's genius was felt long before other cultures could even read or write. Aesop's writings would be reflected in the thinking of Socrates, Plato, and Shakespeare, as well as every institution of higher learning.

By application of this missing ingredient, Hannibal, the greatest military leader of all time, conquered the Roman Empire. Napoleon ranked him first in daring. Said the French general, "This Hannibal of Africa is the most audacious of them all. He is so bold, so sure, so courageous. At twenty-six, he conceived what was hardly conceivable, and executed what history will truly call impossible. *He refuses to be defeated!*" Hannibal took his mighty army—fifty thousand men and eighty elephants— across the Swiss Alps a thousand years ahead of Napoleon. And it was Hannibal, not the French commander, who said to his troops, *"Beyond the Alps lies Italy!"*

Somewhere, as you read, the key to which I refer will jump from the page and present itself to you. Are you ready for it? When J. Bruce Llewellyn, one of Black America's wealthiest men, was registering for high school, a guidance counselor suggested that he sign up for an auto-repair course. His mother furiously stormed into the school and demanded that her son be placed in an academic class. When the counselor said college was expensive, she exploded: "You do your job and teach him. I'll do my job and see that his tuition gets paid!" Today,

Llewellyn has amassed a fortune in business ventures that include a Coca-Cola bottling plant, a television station, and a major magazine.

Marian Wright Edelman came into possession of this life-changing key when she realized that service is far more important than money. The youngest of five children of a caring mother and a father who was a minister, Marian and her siblings were expected to secure an education and to serve their community. After graduating cum laude from college, Marian refused the comfort and power of a job in corporate law. Instead, she took to the back roads of Mississippi, where she found hunger, neglect, and low self-esteem. Here, she proclaimed, "This is my place!" It was her concern for families, especially for the basic rights of children, that led her to form the Children's Defense Fund. Never too tired to work for justice, never too busy to lend a hand, she pressed forward in public service. When asked for her secret to success, Marian responded, "Give me the man or woman who sees the big picture, who grabs the larger view. Show me the child who has heart and purpose, and stands firm amid ridicule and defeat. It is the homestretch that builds the individual."

"When I was a freshman at Rutgers University," said the remarkably gifted Paul Robeson, "one night I saw in the window of my only competitor for first place on the school's debate team a light burning in the darkness. I sat weary, but resolute to study just a little bit longer. I did so, and the next day recited Herodotus as if I wrote it! I have since learned that it is just such a margin, whether of time or attention or earnestness or power, that wins in every battle, great or small."

Marian Anderson didn't have to use her gift, but she did. Coming from poverty-stricken circumstances in Philadelphia, Pennsylvania, Marian achieved the distinction of being the world's greatest contralto. So much so that, Arturo Toscanini, the great Italian conductor, said that a voice like hers "comes only once in a century."

And who could forget the moving words of Jesse Jackson as he eulogized his long-lost friend. "It took Sammy Davis, Jr., twenty-five years to become an overnight success," Jackson offered as he fought back tears. "And now he's gone. Sammy was not the *first* of his kind . . . nor will he be the *last* of his kind. Sammy will go down as the *only one of his kind!*"

"I did what I could with what I had." With those blunt words uttered as he announced his retirement, Supreme Court Justice Thurgood Marshall summed up his long public life and its impact on American society. These sentiments were true but too modest. During a six-decade career as an attorney and judge, Marshall planned, fought, and won battles abolishing the legal basis of American apartheid, defended black voting rights, expanded women's rights, and championed individual liberties. How was it that Justice Marshall, with all the obstacles placed in his path, and given the immense weight of the responsibility of the highest court in the land, rose to equal the challenge? When a lesser man or woman would have been rendered helpless by the defection and adverse criticism of friend and foe alike, what kept him standing? He knew the key to overcoming barriers and reaching goals and objectives. Overcoming barriers does not make the individual. It only shows the world what the individual has made of himself.

"I was born in poverty," said Dr. Myron Moorehead, Black America's first laser surgeon. "Scarcity and lack were frequent companions. I know what it's like to ask for the necessities of life when my parents had nothing to give." His mother was a domestic, while his father took any job that came by his hand. Nonetheless, as an inquisitive student, Myron was armed with the greatest gift the Creator could ever bestow upon any individual. He went to the nearest library and read stories of the world's greatest physicians, and the rest is history. This once poor, unassuming individual demonstrated to a doubting world that he was ready to clutch his future. In the process, he uncovered the secret of success. Do you know what it is? Listen, as Dr. Moorehead provides a clue: "No books or capital to start with? That didn't phase me. What has been done before can be done again!"

"In what school have you studied?" asked a student at Harvard University.

"I have studied in many schools," replied the guest speaker, who was none other than Malcolm X, the famed Muslim minister. "But the school in which I studied the longest and learned most was the school of adversity."

Two decades prior, a brilliant but impressionable child, then known as Malcolm Little, stood at the door of deceit and hatred. With his heart set on a career within the halls of justice, he stood silent as his dreams were shattered by the one person who mattered most in his life, his English teacher.

"Malcolm," Mr. Ostrowski inquired, "have you given any thought to a career?"

"Yes," Malcolm said proudly. "I want to be a lawyer."

"Nonsense. I will not hear of it," his teacher said disparagingly. "A lawyer—that's no realistic goal for a nigger. Yours is a history of hard labor. I suggest that you lower your sights. You would be wise to consider something more constructive—like carpentry."

Though Malcolm's heart sank, his hopes never dimmed. That night, the tall, gawky boy with a reddish complexion sat on the edge of his bed determined to prove that his teacher was wrong. In Malcolm's mind, Mr. Ostrowski was dead wrong. You see, Mr. Ostrowski couldn't predict the future; Mr. Ostrowski did not have the final authority; Mr. Ostrowski did not understand human nature; Mr. Ostrowski did not want to help; Mr. Ostrowski viewed life through eyes clouded with ignorance; Mr. Ostrowski was a bad judge; Mr. Ostrowski did not recognize the uniqueness of every human being; Mr. Ostrowski was biased; Mr. Ostrowski assumed; Mr. Ostrowski was limited by limited vision; Mr. Ostrowski had a negative mental attitude. But the most dreadful thing about Mr. Ostrowski was that he did not know about the God factor— that a person can change and that *excellence is within everyone's reach!*

Throughout the ages, those who have advanced the cause of humanity have been men and women blinded by a sense of mission: Moses espoused the cause of the Israelites; Martin Luther King guided an oppressed race; and Malcolm X, with neither capital nor influence, held his ground against critics and detractors. All did what was morally right with the power given them by the Creator Himself.

THE GREATEST SECRET ON EARTH

Within the past century, more has been discovered about the great secrets of the universe that shape human life than was known in all the centuries before. It has been said that a contented mind is the first condition of happiness. But what is the first condition of a contented mind? You will not be disappointed when I share with you this all-important ingredient. It is so common and so near, and yet it is overlooked. But without it, mankind cannot reach true happiness.

What caused Benjamin Banneker, a self-taught mathematician, astronomer, author of almanacs and inventor, whose formal education ended before the ninth grade, to chart the constellations and heavens like Michelangelo chiseled his *David?* Banneker's life was a living testament to his ideology. He gave the following words of comfort to a poor black child on the streets of the nation's capital—streets that Banneker helped to design: "The strength of the mind is no way connected with the color of the skin."

Whoever rose to higher influence and admiration in political circles than Frederick Douglass or Sojourner Truth? To what force did George Washington Carver owe his vast influence and great intellectual power? Do you have a clue? As she took the oath of office, Carol Moseley Braun,

America's first black female senator, served notice that she was aware of this power within. She told a reporter, "You cannot blaze forth unless the fire has been smoldering within you." What separates the gold from the dross? If you are ready, the answer is crystal-clear!

CHANGE YOUR THOUGHTS AND CHANGE YOUR WORLD

Have you ever wondered what distinguishes a successful person from the man or woman who is not? A common belief is that success in life is the result of heredity, childhood environment, good luck, or some combination of these. At first glance, there appears to be some basis for such a point of view. On the other hand, there is overwhelming evidence to support the premise that success results more from certain mental traits and personality characteristics known as attitudes than from any other single factor. Attitudes are the result of the choices we make—decisions about what to believe or disbelieve with respect to our lives. Clearly, the achiever is not born. He or she is made.

All too often, those who hunt for happiness never find it. They forget the maxim "the kingdom of heaven is within." Happiness can only thrive within *you*—not in wealth or material possessions, not in fame or fortune. Happiness will not yield up its treasure to the selfish seeker, nor can it be touched by unwashed hands.

"Happiness and depression cannot blossom on the same vine," said Dr. Louis Sullivan, president of Morehouse Medical School. "Some people affirm their woes and beg for sympathy. Others, unfortunately, cast gloom wherever they go. These poor souls were born sick and tired. With them, times are always hard and money is always scarce. But no man is happy who does not think himself so."

"Paradise is here, or nowhere," whispered Lonise Bias to a listless youth, fighting a ceaseless battle with drugs and alcohol. But there was special meaning in her words. And who should know better than Lonise? Her own son, Len, a basketball standout, with a promising career before him, paid the highest price after years of drug abuse. Now this proud black woman grabbed another boy's hands and shook him to his senses. "Son, happiness cannot be found in a bottle or a pill; it can only be discovered in that great spirit that rests deep within. Lord knows, if you can't find it in here, you sure ain't gonna find it out there."

The longer I live, the more I realize the impact of attitude. Attitude, to me, is more important than facts, more important than the past, and even more important than the present. Attitude outweighs education and comes before wealth. It's more important than circumstances, than heartbreak, than success, than what other people think, say, or do. It's more important than appearances, giftedness, or skill. Attitude will make or break an organization, a company, a school, a church, a home, a race, an enterprise, and yes, an individual. Remarkably, we have a choice every day regarding the attitude that we will embrace for that day. We cannot change our past. We cannot change the inevitable. The only thing that we can do is play on the one string we have, and that is our attitude. Life is 10 percent what happens to us and 90 percent how we react. In its simplest form, the key to success and achievement lies in our manner of thinking.

ANY LAW IS YOUR MASTER UNTIL YOU UNDERSTAND IT

You may find this a strange and startling book. I hope you do. You may also find its principles a guide for transforming your life. I wish to give you the key by which you may acquire the true riches of life. Within the course of this book, I will reveal to you the manner by which you will be exposed to your great power. And it is the only manner in which you can come in contact with the individual that you were meant to be. This is the greatest of all gifts!

Each year, approximately 55,000 new books are published. There were probably thousands of different titles in the store where this book was purchased. And yet, of all the books you could be reading at this very moment, you are holding *What Makes the Great Great!* You may call it fate, coincidence, luck, or chance, but I don't believe it is. I am convinced that many times during the course of our lives, our Creator intervenes, challenging us with a golden opportunity, and how we respond determines our future. You and I have been brought together for some special reason. Let's make the most of it.

For whom is this book written? Why is each word on every page so vitally important? Most books are written to entertain or inform; some are composed to motivate the reader into action. This book is written so that it might inspire. It is a book of devotion rather than a volume on psychology or science. It has a humanness which may appeal to aching, troubled hearts. It also has a warm, practical gospel of good cheer which is sorely needed today. By virtue of the fact that you have come into possession of *What Makes the Great Great*, there is the strong suggestion that you are already in the process of searching for your true place. There is also a strong possibility that there is something in your life you would like to change. Perhaps you feel that you are worth more than you are being paid or that your current vocation doesn't fully exploit your abilities and talents. Maybe, at this point in life, you are wrestling with personal problems that have left you bewildered or uncertain. Whatever has driven you to this stage of your life—a moment when you have paused to examine the ideas contained in this book—it would appear that you are deeply in search of answers.

> **Paradise is here, or nowhere. Happiness cannot be found in a bottle or a pill; it can only be discovered in that great spirit that rests deep within. Lord knows, if you can't find it in here, you sure ain't gonna find it out there.**
>
> **—Lonise Bias**

What Makes the Great Great has been written for men and women who are dissatisfied with their circumstances. It is written for those who are receptive to "the still, small voice" that offers hope and a clue that their world could be entirely different. This book is for anyone who is weary of life's roller coaster, which carries them to dizzying heights of bliss and temporary success, only to return them to the very station where they started. Sit back and think, and admit, if you will, that the path on which you have been traveling in your search for happiness, success, peace of mind, wealth, a better life, or some other desire doesn't seem to be leading anywhere, although you seem to be traveling at a faster clip. Ask yourself what you have to lose if you follow other ideas that just might enable you to discover how to achieve your dreams and hopes.

What Makes the Great Great is for those who are willing to challenge their present ideas about life and to alter them when necessary. It is for men and women who are not ready to stand still, individuals who refuse to cease growing. Its purpose is to give you a clearer understanding of your own potential, to show you how to work with it and take advantage of the infinite energy and power of the creative force within you, and to help you transform your life from where and what it is into where and what you desire it to be.

Over the past ten years, I have talked with many men and women about success, wealth, and achievement. Their comments have been invaluable. What they have shown me is a wisdom I now offer to you; one that has helped others advance in their careers, gain greater peace of mind, enjoy harmony where discord had been sown, and reunite families and relationships. This book can awaken the reader to another, more fulfilled way to live.

HOW I UNCOVERED THE SECRET

Throughout the 1970s, W. Clement Stone was easily the wealthiest individual in the world. During the 1920s, Stone took $100—all he had—and took the entrepreneurial plunge selling insurance in downtown Chicago. He managed to survive the Great Depression, perfecting a "can't-miss" sales system in the process. By the 1950s, he expanded his company to include a thousand sales representatives and was heading the largest accident and health insurance company in the nation. Less than twenty years later, Stone's personal fortune was estimated to be one third of a billion dollars.

Every individual has a philosophy. When asked to define his, W. Clement Stone told me, "Inspiration to action and know-how." Stone is a master salesman; but more important, he is a man dedicated to universal principles, delighting especially in sharing the secrets of material and spiritual wealth. In November 1986, I was given the full treatment of his wisdom. The man who had made millionaires of so many approached me with an opportunity to uncover the secret for myself.

On that late fall day, Stone invited me to meet with him at his Chicago office. Surrounded by his lieutenants and secretaries, the elderly tycoon offered to share his immense fortune with me, an unknown writer. However, I later discovered that it was not his material assets that the insurance magnate was willing to share. No, it was something far more valuable and infinitely more enduring. Stone proposed to instruct me on the manner and method in which I, and countless others, could build our own personal successes.

Prior to this fateful meeting, I had dreamed of doing something else.

I had begun to write a book that would document the towering accomplishments of a host of black entrepreneurs who had dramatically molded their destinies while advancing the economic well-being of those around them. Many of the people I interviewed overcame tremendous odds to become highly respected members of the business community.

Meanwhile, my financially comfortable job with a Fortune 500 company had become a daily nightmare. My sales had been impressive and our region continued to lead the firm as it did for a number of years, but my mind was preoccupied with other challenges. My coworkers seemed less than enthusiastic regarding their duties and responsibilities, and my superiors seemed to abandon their sense of vision. They, too, seemed to be playing out the string. I had already started to define the scope of the book, and had identified and interviewed more than a dozen of the entrepreneurs within the study, but I didn't dare tell a soul of my fantasy to become a writer. Mentally, I felt cut off.

Finally, I hit my threshold. I can still remember the letter of resignation I sent the vice-president. In that lengthy and illustrated document, I clearly spelled out my goals and intentions. As I look back, I must have been nuts. What in the world would make me quit? I was thirty-six years old. I had a wife, three healthy children, an equally healthy mortgage, and I was saddled with debt. I had a company car, enviable perks and benefits, and a salary that approached $60,000 a year, not to mention a promotion back to the home office that seemed in the cards. And yet I walked away.

Some people said I was cocky and impatient. Actually, I was frightened. Afraid that I would one day wind up like the majority of people who never ventured into the unknown, who stumbled through their allotted years with hopes and dreams eventually fading from memory, whose lives never made a difference. My letter of resignation was, as Henry Parks, one of Black America's most profiled entrepreneurs, would later tell me, my "declaration of independence." I was intoxicated with ambition. I knew exactly what I wanted and resolved to continue my quest until I found what I was searching for. "The business of philosophy," Oliver Wendell Holmes wrote, "is to show that we are not fools for doing what we want to do." I couldn't agree with him more. And now I found myself in the company of a man who was often called the "world's richest."

In the course of our two-hour meeting, Stone spoke of achievement, wealth, and success. He detailed the rudiments of his philosophy, formed from his experience as one of the world's most successful businessmen. He explained that fortune and fame could be enjoyed by any-one willing to follow a specific formula. In fact, he claimed that no one could achieve great success without utilizing a prescribed set of principles and action steps. "Prosperity and a fulfilling life," Stone said, his hand resting on my shoulder, "lie within the realm of possibilities if we identify and apply the principles of success." I listened intently and asked an occasional question.

Then, dramatically and unexpectedly, Stone pulled out an unfinished manuscript and placed it in my hand. It was a draft of a book that Napoleon Hill, America's most prolific self-help writer and author of the phenomenal best-seller *Think and Grow Rich,* was preparing at the time of his death—two decades before. Hill postulated that it is no more difficult to aim high in life and achieve prosperity than it is to accept and live with poverty and misery. Just as I had studied successful black businesspeople—what made them tick, what traits and qualities accounted for their success—Hill, too, had asked the same question of black Americans: How could black Americans—or any group of people—pull themselves out of poverty and create wealth? Before his death, Hill had written nearly a hundred pages on the subject. Stone proposed that I take Hill's ideas, reinforce them with what I knew of the African American experience, and then update and complete the manuscript. I couldn't believe my ears.

Stone put the question to me squarely: He asked if I would accept the challenge. I told him I would do so if either he or the foundation bearing Hill's name would underwrite the project, since I was deeply in debt and saw no way of easing my financial burden. While those in the room nodded in agreement, Stone paused before deciding against offering me any financial inducement. He knew that if I were to become truly successful, it would be necessary for me to experience the unpredictable and often tempestuous circumstances that all achievers have known. The seasoned businessman placed the ball squarely in my court. I looked him in the eye, took a deep breath, and accepted his challenge.

W. Clement Stone was wonderfully supportive and helpful. He provided a wealth of background information, and he took time from his incredibly busy schedule to clarify points about which I was uncertain. He and his staff reviewed the manuscript and offered constructive suggestions on how it could be improved.

THE NINE PRINCIPLES OF EXTRAORDINARY ACHIEVEMENT

For the next five years, despite monetary hardship and periods of discontent, I saw with my mind's eye a manual that embodied the principles of success and personal achievement and held hopes of presenting Black America with it. *Think and Grow Rich: A Black Choice* offers the same type of advice as the original and most popular self-help book ever written—but with a twist: It is the first self-help book targeted to the African American reader.

W. Clement Stone was right. Within his laboratory, I discovered a simple truth that is not only the core premise of self-help and motivation but an acknowledged fact in the science of human behavior: *Success in any area of life isn't something you do; rather, it's something to see. Success is an understanding, not an activity.* Moreover, I found that high-achieving men and women come in every color, shape, and disposition. Furthermore, they share nine mental strategies—internalized principles, qualities of maximum achievement—that are most in demand. Your greatness will be guaranteed when you begin to incorporate these simple steps and everyday actions into your life. This book will show you how. More important, it will motivate you to try.

1. DEEP-SEATED SPIRITUAL BELIEFS

There is an inner voice that speaks to all humanity. It is the inner urge of the Divine presence in mankind urging you and me to release our talents and express more and more of the God force. Each achiever seemed to say in his or her own unique way: "I am God's child and success and fulfillment is my right." We are not just human beings trying to make it in this world. We are spiritual beings going through a human experience on the way toward complete expression and fulfillment. Therein lies the seed of greatness. Not through religion per se, but by being in tune with the infinite—the imprisoned splendor seeking expression. Do you want to be great? Then know that you are great. Let go of the ego and focus on Truth. Turn to success by turning to the light. Center yourself within the universal flow of all good. It is a feeling similar to what the Reverend Cecil Murray expressed when he said, "I don't *believe* in God. I *know* there is a God!" As Gandhi said, "God comes to the hungry in the form of food."

2. THE "I CAN" CREDO

You are capable of those things you are capable of believing. Or, to put it another way, you should always "act as if you can." With this right mental attitude, you can then find out the truth regarding your innate potential by living out the experience. Far too many of us do the opposite: We decide ahead of time that we can't. We think we're too old, too young, too poor, too hopeless, not blessed with the right parents. The list goes on and on, developing into a litany of negative, limiting language and beliefs. And the outcome is always the same: "I can't!" Negative thinking limits performance. Turn the negative around, and suddenly the impossible becomes possible. When you believe and think "I can," you activate your motivation, commitment, confidence, and concentration, all of which relate directly to maximum achievement. If you think "I can't," on the other hand, you sabotage your chances of achieving your goals.

Over the years, I've interviewed a wide range of high achievers—from Olympic athletes to Nobel Prize honorees—and during those interviews I've noticed one clear and consistent pattern: The most successful people think like winners! The "I can" belief forms the foundation of their approach to all things in life. They refuse to accept "I can't" unless they've collected objective data showing that a goal is beyond their grasp. Even then, they don't say "I can't." They simply reformulate their goals to move them within reach. The same approach will work for you.

3. VISION

The successful man or woman has a guiding vision, a dream, a sense of focus. He or she has a clear idea of what he or she wants to have, do, or accomplish. It is the achiever's divine right to dream. The Almighty provided us with control over the power to shape our own thoughts and the privilege of placing them into any pattern of our choice. Writers like Maya Angelou and Langston Hughes have been labeled geniuses, not because of their poetic prose, but because they show us to ourselves. We can never see in the world what we do not personally possess.

4. PASSION

Chiseled upon the tomb of an inept, disappointed Pharaoh in ancient Egypt is the epitaph: "Here lies a ruler who, with the best intentions, never carried out a single plan." Many of us go through life searching for breakthroughs. We would do better if we went through life backed with the power of a single aim. Some people want success so badly it becomes an all-consuming passion. They wake up every morning and go to bed each evening thinking only of their goals. When asked for the key to achievement, Benjamin Carson, the acclaimed neurosurgeon, said, "I had to become a doctor!" Through symphony and song, Quincy Jones wanted desperately to carve his name on the tablet of success. This he has done. As a black child living in the Northwest, he overcame a life crushed by poverty and despair. But thanks to an unwavering aim, his results can be heard from Piccadilly to Carnegie Hall. Passion is one of the most important ingredients in the recipe for success. Perhaps the biggest break you could ever receive is to find your place and overfill it. "If you set yourself on fire," said the inimitable Don King, "the world will come to see you burn!"

5. COURAGE

Life shrinks or expands in proportion to one's courage. Courage means the willingness to take risks, to accept challenges. Men and women of courage do not worry about failure; they realize the high cost of success. To succeed, everyone must learn to deal with mistakes and failures. All champions realize that the path to personal excellence is cluttered with obstacles. Arriving at the top is a process that involves many setbacks. High achievers accept this process courageously, understanding that you can't stretch your limits without encountering some rough moments along the way.

"Steady, men," shouted P. B. S. Pinchback, a Union army captain fighting for freedom in the all-black Corps d'Afrique. Though outmanned and outnumbered, his last words were: "Before we offer our lives, let's bring back the colors. Faith isn't faith until it's all you're holding on to!" It takes courage to stand firmly while others cower in fear; it takes courage to forsake today for tomorrow; it takes courage to remain in honest poverty when others grow rich by fraud; and it takes great courage to stand alone and fight for what you want.

6. CHARACTER

The successful are always open and honest in all business dealings. Integrity is the basis of trust. Character is the one quality that cannot be acquired, only earned. Character is the poor man's capital. Every thought that enters our mind, every word we utter, every deed we perform, makes its impression upon the innermost fiber of our being, and the result of these impressions is our character. It's been anonymously written: "Fame is a vapor, popularity is an accident, and money takes wings. The only thing that endures is character."

7. COMPETENCE

Sometimes good is not enough. At a final interview with the president of a major corporation, a highly recommended young woman was asked two important questions: "Exactly what can you do for us?" and "What are your specialties?"

"I can do almost anything," the young lady replied.

"Well," said the president, rising to his feet, "I have no use for anyone who can do 'almost' anything. I'm looking for someone who can do one thing to perfection."

Everywhere, we meet men and women who are "almost" successful. Here is a man who is almost a lawyer but not quite. Here is a woman who is almost a doctor but didn't finish medical school. How many people have *almost* mastered a second language? More than once I've read the story of someone who wanted to be great but didn't complete the task. The world is full of well-meaning efforts that end up as half-completed results. There's a great crowd of humanity who can "half do" many things but can't do one thing to perfection. Competence is the difference between excellence and mediocrity.

8. SELF-CONFIDENCE

Experts agree that all of us have deep reservoirs of ability—even genius—that we habitually fail to use. We fail to make use of our talents because we are caught up in the absurd and impossible game of imitating others who, unfortunately, are not worthy of emulation. Since there is no one on earth just like you, how can you be inferior?

Men and women who have made the greatest contributions to humanity were often scorned by ne'er-do-wells. If you find yourself bearing the wrath of others because of your dreams or beliefs, you may be wearing the mark of the achiever. In other words, don't be afraid if you are criticized—you're in good company.

You're in the company of Noah, who was criticized for building a boat in the middle of the desert. You're in the company of Booker T. Washington, who had the audacity to educate southern blacks. You're in the company of George Washington Carver, who was urged not to waste so much time on a tiny peanut. You're in the company of Galileo, who was criticized for postulating that the earth revolved around the sun, and of Moses, who led a group of people from nowhere to somewhere for forty years. You're walking the path blazed by Nelson Mandela, whose unquenchable thirst for freedom liberated a nation. Optimism means expecting the best, but self-confidence means knowing how to handle the worst.

9. DISCIPLINE

"The first and best victory," Plato wrote, "is for a man to conquer himself." Men and women search their entire lives looking for fame and fortune without attaining either. Why? Because they do not understand that the real source of wealth and achievement rests within their own minds and can only be released by the power of strict self-discipline. Discipline is indispensable in all leadership. The mind that is properly disciplined and directed to a clear-cut objective cannot be defeated. The individual who masters himself or herself through self-discipline can never be mastered by others! An old Hindu proverb says, "There is nothing noble in being superior to some other man. True nobility is in being superior to your previous self."

CAREFULLY CONSIDER THESE nine mental strategies. Be open and honest. Question yourself repeatedly about those traits that you already possess and those in which you need to improve. As you develop a vision and manage to say "I can," work at improving your self-discipline, for self-discipline will lead to even greater effectiveness in the areas of passion, courage, character, competence, and self-confidence. Be sure to tap the spiritual force within.

THE BEST MEDICINE

Once upon a time, there was a man who felt he had reached the end of his rope. To him, life was meaningless. All spirit had vanished from his life. Even his family, friends, and his work failed to hold his interest. Finally, nearing the point of desperation and at the end of his rope, he visited his physician. After listening to his story and seeing the depth of his depression, his doctor asked, "When you were a child, what one thing did you like to do best?"

The man took a deep breath, paused for a few moments, then replied, "I enjoyed visiting the seashore."

"Okay," his physician said calmly, "I've got just the remedy. But I must warn you. You must follow my instructions to the letter. Under no circumstances are you to deviate from my treatment." His doctor then pulled a notepad from his rolltop desk and continued.

"Tomorrow, I want you to spend the day at the shore. Find a secluded area on the beach and spend the entire day—from nine in the morning until six o'clock at night. Take nothing to read or anything to divert your attention. I'm going to give you four prescriptions that are guaranteed to cure your ailment. Take the first at nine A.M., the second at noon, the third at three, and the last at six. Do not look at the instructions now. Instead, wait until you arrive at the shore tomorrow morning." With that, the man promised to heed his doctor's orders and left his office.

The following morning, shortly before nine o'clock, he parked his car on a lonely stretch of beach. There was a strong wind blowing in from the sea, and the surf was high and pounding. Depressed and forlorn, he walked to a sand dune near the inviting surf and sat down. As instructed, he took out the first prescription, opened it, and read it. It simply said, "Listen." That's all that was written on the paper—*Listen.* And for three hours that's all he did. He listened to the sound of the buffeting wind. He listened to the lonely cries of the seagulls. He listened to the sound of the rushing surf. He sat motionless and listened.

At noon, he reached into his pocket and took out the second prescription. Just like the first, these instructions were plain and simple. It said, "Reach back." And for the next three hours he did just that: He let his mind wander back as far as it could. He recalled all the incidents of his life that he could remember—the happy times, the bleak times, the triumphs, and the struggles.

At 3:00 P.M. he tore open the third prescription. It said, "Reexamine your motives." This took so much intense thought and concentration that the remaining three hours slipped by quickly as he reexamined his motives—his reasons for living and fulfillment. He clarified and restated his goals.

And at six o'clock, under a gray, darkening sky and with a taste of salt mist in the air, he read the final prescription: "Write your worries in the sand." Pausing for a moment, he knew there was something that seemed to be gnawing inside. With his pants rolled up, he grabbed a stick, walked to the shoreline, and wrote his worry in the sand. Before leaving he stared at what he had written. But as he walked toward his car, he looked back and saw that the incoming tide had already erased his words. A smile eased onto his face as he got into his car and headed for home.

Now is the time for you to ingest these four prescriptions. With *What Makes the Great Great* as a guide, begin to listen, to reach back, to reexamine your motives, and to write your worries in the sand. Begin now to place your troubles, difficulties, and past failures into perspective. Reflect upon the story of Bill Pinkney and each profile to follow. It is a sad day when the curiosity and zest for living slips out of one's life. There is so much to do, so much to give, and so much to enjoy. Now is the time for personal inventory. Now is the time to discover who you are, where you are going, and how and when you will arrive at your destination. If you are not where you wish to be, there is only one reason. Now is the time to find out why. Begin now. Make the best possible use of those talents that you possess, and more will be given to you to use. Remember, what you want also wants you. There are no unanswered requests in the universe. If we do not like what we are receiving, we can learn to ask for something different. Then we will find what we wish.

1

The Greatest Gift:

The Gift of Life

- **The Gift of Life**

- **The Greatest Game**

- **The Goal of Life**

- **Have You Found Your True Purpose?**

- **Finding Your Area of Excellence**

Whatever people may think of you,
do that which you believe to be right.
—PYTHAGORAS

Some are born great, some achieve greatness,
and some have greatness thrust upon them.
—SHAKESPEARE

If you're satisfied with just getting by,
step aside for the person who isn't!
—A. G. GASTON

Surely, there must be somebody who will stand up?
—ROSA PARKS

To you, the reader, I offer these thoughts. To you who have struggled and withstood years of toil and heartache, setback and heartbreak, I offer these words. To you who have been dismayed and downtrodden, held back and overlooked; oppressed, discriminated against, paralyzed by fear and humbled by failure, listen closely. To you who many times have tasted the sweet wine of success only to have its rich nectar wiped clean from your lips. To you who, after years of searching, seeking, and adhering to religious doctrine and dogma, find yourself without peace and fulfillment, and in greater bondage. To you who thought you had found a spiritual sage—a grand master who could restore your soul as well as your affairs, only to expose his own shortcomings, once again leaving you empty and thirsting for more. To you, a member of that tireless generation who searched for success; who traded tired feet for tired souls, having fallen prey to civil rights, equal opportunity, affirmative action, and now, the latest elixir in a long line of proposed remedies, cultural diversity, only to learn that true success finds its way to you through individual effort, singular focus, and relentless faith. To you who hunger in the heart as well as the spirit, read on. *Your time has come!*

Are you ready to take that first step toward a better life? If you are, this "gift" should hold special meaning. No one else can live your life for you. No one else can progress toward greatness for you. This is not an easy world to live in. It is not an easy world to be decent in. It is not an easy world to understand oneself in, or to like oneself in. But it must be lived in, and in the living there is one person you must absolutely believe in. The business you are in, the business we are all in, is the business of living—and the sooner you learn who you are and how you became the person you are, the sooner you will be able to deal with the challenges that may have frustrated you in the past.

There's a spirit that rests within. You can feel it and even see it within those who have mastered the process we call success. You can see it in the manner in which achievers approach their work. There's a flicker in their eyes—a sense of urgency, a zeal to perform. As a young man, S. B. Fuller, entrepreneur extraordinaire, sought the habits of success by dedicating his life to continuous self-improvement. A key factor in his turnaround from poverty to plenty surfaced when he realized that life is a game with laws and regulations.

"Never be content with what you are," Fuller warned, "if you wish to be what you're not! Poverty is a disease of the mind. Everyone is born with a spark of divinity. It's up to you—the individual—to fan that spark." Every morning for more than fifty years, this black cosmetic tycoon would gather his salespeople in a classroom at his corporate headquarters in Chicago and drill them with maxims like these. Moments later, Fuller would unleash them into the marketplace. His lists of virtues included:

- *Salesmanship is statesmanship.* "The only way America recognizes you is for industrial and commercial achievement."
- *Start early and stay late.* "Thank God every morning that you have something to do that day—whether you want to or not."
- *Read.* "Reserve a special time for daily reading and meditation. Ignorance is the root of misfortune."
- *Lead.* "Leadership means initiative, courage, loyalty, integrity, and wisdom."
- *Dare to reach forward.* "It's contrary to the law of nature for humanity to stand still. You either move forward or the eternal march will force you back."

Virtues keep us centered in an imperfect world. Within the nuances of business, people break promises, letters go unanswered, phone calls go unreturned, banks deny credit, applications are lost, and names are forgotten. But the dreamer—the spirit-filled achiever—rises above the clutter and sees that character eventually pays off. Within the game of life the mission is clear: Service and goodness are credited, trustworthiness is an asset. Everything counts. Nothing goes overlooked. The winner gets the cup. "Give till it hurts," Fuller coached. "If people disappoint, it's because they failed to see the bigger picture. Don't worry, your deeds of kindness will come back to you in the end."

The fundamental law of the universe is that every form of life holds within itself every element it needs for growth, maturity, and development. The seed only survives when it casts off all outside support, and places its dependence solely upon the life force that created it. Only then will it draw to itself the vital elements it needs for further growth and maturity. In every individual there is a seed of life, with infinite power to draw to itself whatever it conceives to be necessary to its own expression. It doesn't matter who you are; nor should you be concerned with your present circumstances. The seed of life in you has the same power for good, a power that rests within your hands waiting for you to use it. Will you use it? Only if you value the *greatest gift.*

THE GIFT OF LIFE

If you could have as a gift your most treasured wish fulfilled—the one wish that lies closest to your heart—the thing that you want most in the world, what would you choose? One million dollars? Bounding health? Peace of mind? A devoted family? What one gift would enable you to enjoy life to its fullest? There is such a gift given to you out of sheer love from above. A gift that will bring all the things that you secretly desire; a gift that like magic can clear the congested roadway ahead and set your feet upon the pathway to real happiness. What is this rare, precious gift? The following metaphor may be insightful.

Most of us like receiving presents. We seem to be attracted to special, fancy gifts. During a recent business trip, I stopped in a department store between meetings. There, I noticed a salesclerk wrapping a box of perfumed soap for a customer. Meticulously, each bar of soap was wrapped in tissue paper only to be wrapped again before being placed into a bright, colorful cardboard box. Then a fancy ribbon tied around an artificial flower topped off the box. Quite a package, I thought, for only three bars of soap. Before closing the sale, the clerk presented the package to the customer and asked, "Can I gift-wrap it for you?" I couldn't believe my ears.

Throughout life, all too often we are so concerned with the "outer," the packaging, the wrapping over the gift wrapping, the bows and the ribbons, that we lose sight of the "inner," basic material of life. Too frequently, we become overly concerned with race, culture, gender, the job, the position, the finances, the house, the car, the clothes, that we lose sight of life itself. You see, underneath the tinsel and the tissue paper, you are the living expression of life itself—the *greatest gift!* The gift that should be cherished the most! You are the living expression of the power of creative intelligence. Don't allow thin, cheap veneers to camouflage the real you as well as your hidden powers. Once you cut to the core, you will begin to live life the way you were intended.

THE QUESTIONS CONTINUE

Oh, how little we know of this thing called life. We find ourselves in a confusing world. We go about our daily lives understanding very little of the world around us. We give little thought to the invisible forces that generate life itself and make all success possible. We don't think twice regarding the power of gravity and the spiritual forces that keep us planted to earth instead of spinning off into space. Few of us spend any time wondering where, when, or why. Why is the sky blue? Why is the earth round? Why is day day and night night? Why do we remember the past and not the future? What is this world coming to and where do I come from? Why am I here? Where can I find the answers to life's innermost secrets? The world is crying out. In the midst of floods, hurricanes, earthquakes, riots, wars, and disputes, the world is crying out. When will my dreams come true?

As we try to answer these and other equally perplexing questions, we adhere to some type of worldly view or personal philosophy. We live in a world filled with outside influences which impact our lives. We are influenced by the acts and deeds of others, by the laws and customs designed by our fellow human beings. Everything we do has some effect upon others, as do their actions upon each of us. And yet we must discover how to use our own minds, talents, and unique gifts, and how to live our own lives. "Know thyself," said the ancient Greek philosophers. Socrates believed that "knowledge is the one good; ignorance is the one evil." Shakespeare interpreted the influences of others and demonstrated our responsibility to recognize these influences when, in *Hamlet,* he had Polonius say, "This above all: to thine own self be true." In other words, we should live according to our deep spiritual convictions and our "true self"—the man or woman we were meant to be. Without knowing and being yourself, you cannot truly use the one great secret that gives you the power to mold and shape your destiny.

We all have a desire to be well, prosperous, and fulfilled. The poor wish to become rich. The lonely seek friendship. The ignorant hunt for knowledge. Fulfillment is human nature. But the greatest satisfaction comes with the consciousness that such a power is available if we know it exists, and if we know how to utilize it.

With this awakening and realization, we are brought into complete harmony with the universe—in tune with the infinite. We feel the power and the thrill of life universal. Our intuition becomes keener, our focus sharper. Every step we take is tried-and-true, and the pressures of life disappear from the weight of their own insignificance. We master the habit of viewing life through our inner eye. As a result, abundance replaces lack; health, in time, dismantles disease; and discord is no match for peace of mind. As we respond to the higher impulses of the soul, we become the man or woman we were truly meant to be—true masters of the universe!

LET THERE BE LIGHT!

The process of human conception, 300 million sperm in pursuit of an egg, is still mysterious. Up close, this microscopic contest is as dramatic as the movement of the planets. Imagine the remarkable process that changes a barely visible, single cell into more than 200 million highly specialized cells in just nine months—266 days! Think of the intricate series of events that can transform a single fertilized egg into a fully developed human being that weighs 6 billion times more than the tiny dot from which it grew. It's almost inconceivable that after only forty days into its nine months of growth, an embryo develops a heart that has already been beating for two weeks and a brain and a nervous system capable of sending out impulses. It is even more difficult to fathom that this minute human being is still so small that it can easily fit into a walnut shell. Picturing such a miniature "bundle of potential" and realizing that it has all the vital organs, yet weighs no more than a book of matches, gives us all a glimpse into the remarkable nature of our creation.

When a sperm pierces the egg, it resembles a twisting tornado burrowing into a moon's surface. The sperm head is a mass of genes which merge with the egg's corresponding genes. Each sperm is different. For example, one might carry half the markings of a Marcus Garvey; the next, a Dr. King. Every fertilized egg contains the makings of a child. No matter what the genetic makeup, the potential for greatness is there. Scientifically, this marks a new life. Spiritually, it is the beginning of the beginning: Thought. Consciousness. Unlimited potential. *Light!*

Today Is the Day the Lord Has Made

Events happen quickly. "Take your time, dear. I want you to breathe slowly," says the physician in a calm but assuring manner. "C'mon now, let's do it. Breathe deep!"

The doctor's relaxed manner can be misleading. The process of birth is routine, but nothing is taken for granted. At no other point in life is time so magnified. Everyone in the delivery room is poised. The slightest hesitation, the failure to make a quick decision, a quivering hand—any of these could be fatal. The fetus drops lower into the pelvis. The mother begins to push the baby through the birth canal.

"Okay, you're doing fine. I want you to put your chin on your chest and blow. That's it. Bear down. Push. Push. It's almost over!"

Every living human soul has engaged upon the ride of his or her life.

For nine months, we had lived in a secure world of incomparable close-ness. We had lived within love itself, within our mother's being, sur-rounded by the sounds and sensations of her body, constantly in tune with her energy, her every thought and feeling. But now we journey on a different path. With each contraction, our small body curls into posi-tion, seeking the path that our mother opens to us through her cervix. Remarkably, even now the question begs asking: What does the future hold? But for now, the future must wait. There is still more work to be done.

"Okay, blow, blow!"

By all accounts, this final moment seems both rushed and suspended in time. The physician has now relegated himself or herself to the po-sition of coach, one who is bent on driving his or her players to the breaking point. Now your mother is caught up in the momentum. Sweat is dripping from her forehead. Every part of her body aches but she can't feel a thing. She is more than willing to sacrifice everything for the sake of her child.

"I see the head! C'mon now, let's do it. Keep blowing!"

Your mother's heart pounds faster, and everything around you feels tight and unyielding. The stronger contractions push your sore head against a rigid cervix. What had begun perfectly and lovingly has now heightened all sensitivities in spite of the anesthetic. Both worlds—the mother's womb and the child's world—feel invaded.

"Bear down," the voice prods one last time. "Give it one last push!

"Here it is! Congratulations, you have a healthy . . ."

IN THE BEGINNING

More than 3 million years ago, a tiny female—the oldest living crea-ture known to mankind—slumped to the mud of an East African lakeshore, a land of milk and honey. Here she died, her bones sinking deep into the soft fertile ground. The mud turned to rock and so, grad-ually, did her bones. She might have rested there undisturbed forever but for the roaring geologic forces that ripped the earth apart over the next thirty thousand centuries. To this tiny seed, this "thread of life," you, the reader, as well as every person who ever lived, can claim connec-tion. All human blood flows from this "mother of civilization." Through this thin thread, humanity is interrelated. *Do you know who she is?* It was her dust that fertilized the seven continents.

Look at her face—you should recognize it. *This is the dreamer* who woke up to a new day. Who invented time; who bathed in the Eu-phrates, drank from the Nile and raised pyramids on its banks. *This is the teacher* who charted the constellations, calculated the science of mathematics and engineering, and recited languages other cultures had never seen or heard. Take a good look at her face. *This is the leader,* the African warrior who would never quit; who bolted the gates of despair and cowardice. While others sat motionless contemplating the odds, this conqueror stepped out boldly, believing defeat was impossible. *Do you recognize the face?* You should. *This is the child* stolen from the steamy sands of Sierra Leone and Côte d'Ivoire; whose legacy is dreams deferred and a trail of bones on the floor of the Atlantic; who arrived on these shores reduced to cultivate a foreign land; who remembers the whip and the slaver's track. *Is the face familiar?* Here's another clue.

This is the patriot who would answer the call; who would gladly give his life for freedom though it was denied to him. *Have you seen this face before?* It was seen raising the colors with Francis Scott Key, riding triumphantly down San Juan Hill, flying in formation in Tuskegee, Alabama, and walking the point in Vietnam.

Take a guess. *This is the mother* who cooked and cleaned, who nursed babies and treated beleaguered bodies and tired souls; who raised someone else's child as well as her own; who climbed the back stairs to success; who worked like a dog but in "no ways got tired"; who ate in the kitchen with the rest of the help; who did without while doing within; whose dreams were stolen; who couldn't read or write, but whose advice and wisdom never led anyone astray. This is the woman who stepped back so an entire nation could step forward; who held tightly to the dreams of a race. *Do you know who she is?* You should recognize the face. She's *your* mother, *my* mother, the mother of civilization. This is the stuff that greatness is made of!

YOU ARE MORE THAN ENOUGH

The real question is, Who are *you?* How do you see yourself? Who and what do you think you are? Is life just a strange coincidence, or does it hold some special meaning? As science loves to state, you are a mixture of common chemicals, mostly water, *enough* to fill a small bathtub, and fat, *enough* to produce four to five bars of soap. Furthermore, there's *enough* calcium in your body to make a large piece of chalk, *enough* phosphorus to ignite a pack of matches, *enough* sodium to season a bag of popcorn, *enough* magnesium to spark a flashbulb, *enough* iron to manufacture a three-inch nail, *enough* iodine to make a child seethe in pain, and *enough* sulfur to rid a dog of fleas. In total, you're approximately two dollars' worth of water, fat, and chemicals.

But you're more than *enough!* Closer to the truth is the Bible's poetic and richly moving account of creation, which begins with the most rec-ognizable words in Western history: "In the beginning God created the heavens and the earth . . . in the image of God he created him; male and female he created them . . . the Lord God formed man of dust from the ground, and breathed into his nostrils the breath of life; and man be-came a living being." Moses did not believe that we are an accident of evolution, but someone that our Creator carefully and lovingly created. We are not just another plant or animal or leaf on the vine, for we have received the Divine breath of God, and thus share in our Creator's grand plan and purpose.

In "God's Trombone," James Weldon Johnson's inspiring account of creation, he brings Moses' story to life in his own unique way:

> Up from the bed of the river
> God scooped the clay;
> And by the bank of the river
> He kneeled him down;
> And there the great God Almighty
> Who lit the sun and fixed it in the sky,
> Who flung the stars to the most far corner of the night,
> Who rounded the earth in the middle of his hand;
> This Great God,
> Like a mammy bending over her baby,
> Kneeled down in the dust
> Toiling over a lump of clay
> Till he shaped it in his own image;
>
> Then into it he blew the breath of life,
> And man became a living soul.
> Amen. Amen.

You were created. You're not just a mixture of chemicals and com-pounds. You are a human being made in the very image of our Creator. When you were born, God held you in His arms and whispered, "I cre-ated you, and what I have created is good!" You were created to be, to have, to hold, to become, to do *all things*. And since you possess the only thing that you'll ever need on this holiday of life—the rare gift to dream and aspire—you can achieve. Who are you? *You are more than enough!*

THE GREATEST GAME

Ask the question What is the world's greatest game? and, undoubtedly, you will drum up many answers. Baseball, football, or basketball, to name a few, might be mentioned. Chess, checkers, running, and tennis have their proponents, too. One thing is certain: There has never been a time when men, women, and children across the globe seemed so fascinated and attracted to the world of sports. Each sport can claim a following. Statistically, more people play soccer and golf than any other form of recreation. Spectators who border on the fanatical take in the games of hockey and croquet from its instructional leagues to the thrilling moments of a world championship. Most of these sports provide excellent forms of relaxation and amusement. Each offers some type of balance, a change of pace, and helps to bond friendships that provide the glue in our relationships. You name it, every game seems to strike a common chord within us all.

But none of these contests could wear the mantle of the World's Greatest Game. No. This title can only be reserved for the one game that has an effect on us like no other. It's the only game that keeps score in service and lessons learned. It's a game that deals with the spiritual as well as the material, the earthly and the heavenly: "So run that ye may obtain." It's a game of give-and-take where everyone "suits up" and is given equal opportunity to play; a chance to show our stuff.

For our efforts and benefit, we are given the proper tools and necessary training. To increase our chances of winning, every need is met. For example, do you desire to be a farmer? If so, you will be given soil and seed as well as the plow and the harvest. If you choose to paint, you will be offered a myriad of colors as well as the creative imagination to enhance your talents. Does a woman wish to be a physician? If so, she will be given the sciences, the atom, and the scalpel as well as the gift of compassion. Does a man or woman hope to minister to others? Each will be given the word to inspire, the spirit to guide, and the living souls that seek help to live justly and purely in a less-than-perfect world. What is placed into the beginning of life is placed into the whole of life. What is this game to which each of us must lay claim? *It's the game of life!*

Life is a game. Some people play the game of struggle. Some people play the game of happiness, health, and abundance. Others play the game of sickness. Some play the game of poverty; and there are those who play the game of power. It just helps to understand that each of us plays a game that we set up and, for the most part, feel comfortable while playing. Look at your life. *What game are you playing?* What type of secret satisfaction are you receiving as a participant in your particular game of life? How could anyone enjoy feeling weak, despondent, victimized, poor, helpless, or inadequate? Like similar choices that you make, if this game of life did not bring you some sort of payoff or pleasure, you would cease to play it.

Albert Camus, the French novelist, taught that every man, on the foundation of his own sufferings and joys, builds for all. As I have sought to reach my goals, I've learned that life is a game. It's spiritual, mysterious, fun-filled, and precious, but it is still a game—a game that you have no hope of winning unless you know the rules! Unfortunately, no one ever taught us the rules as we were growing up. Not in elementary school, junior high, high school, or college were we ever instructed with the rudiments—how to handle adversity, how to generate wealth, how to eliminate bad habits, how to eliminate stress, to name just a few, as we traveled through our impressionable years. *Never!* Predictably and sadly, most of us have been relegated to the sidelines as idle spectators in the greatest game of all.

The Creator, or whatever power is behind our existence, did not intend for us to fail or wallow in poverty, self-pity, or mediocrity in any form. Such is not the grand design for mankind. We are blessed with innumerable raw materials necessary for progress, such as imagination, ideas, inspiration, and undeveloped intellectual capacity. The only limitation placed on our abilities is our inability to recognize our unlimited nature. It takes effort to become aware of our staggering and limitless abilities. It takes effort to become enthusiastic over a cause or an opportunity. It takes courage to continue when our results—as well as our friends—tell us to give up. It takes a sense of spirituality to feel right about everything that happens—the joys as well as the sorrows. And it takes a special relationship with our Creator to learn to love ourselves above all others, especially when we are consciously aware of our shortcomings, doubts, and failures.

However, it does not require any virtue to fail. It requires little else than a slowly deteriorating attitude about our present, our future, and ourselves. By our attitude, we decide to read or not to read. By our attitude, we decide to try or to give up. By our attitude, we blame ourselves for our failure, or we foolishly blame others. Our attitude determines whether we love or hate, advance or recede, succeed or fail. How incredibly unique it is that a God who would create the complex and immense universe would create the human race and give to those individuals the free choice that would permit them to select either their own achievement or their own destruction.

This strange but all-knowing God gave to us a delicately balanced sphere called earth, and on it, he placed the human being who would either develop or destroy it. How fascinating that our Creator would leave both projects—earth as well as you and me—*unfinished.* Across the rivers and streams He built no bridges; He left the pictures unpainted, the song unsung, the poem unwritten, the structure unfinished, and space unexplored. To expand upon His grand design, God gave forth the unfinished human soul who, within his heart and mind, had the capacity to do all these things and more. All that we are, and all that we become, has indeed been left to us. At this very moment, as you digest these words, your attitude has determined what you are. Your faith, desire, discipline, courage, patience, character, and childlike excitement about your boundless future are a result of your personal outlook. Our Creator's work is finished, but the work of creating a better you has just begun. For as long as you continue to draw breath, you have the opportunity to complete that work.

THE SECRET OF THE AGES

Most of us have missed the message that all great teachers have known since the beginning of recorded history. The secret of the ages, the one incredible truth that very few understand, rests on the discovery that you are whole, complete, and perfect. Just as a drop of water has all the qualities of the ocean, you and I possess all the qualities of the Creator within. Science, philosophy, and religion all teach in their own way that there's ultimately one power in the universe and that we're one with that power. You and I are individualized expressions of all the power of the universe.

We can never destroy the power within us. We can deny that it's there; we can hide it, we can lie about it, but ultimately, we cannot change the fact that it lies within for our use. What we must do—what *you* must do—is to recognize it and channel its power through your thoughts. You must understand the distinction between who you are and what you do. Who you are is perfect, but what you do is not always perfect. The gap between who you are and what you do is created through ignorance. When you fail to realize your perfection, it follows that your actions will also be less than perfect. But once you know the truth about yourself, you will come to the realization that greatness is your birthright. You were placed on this planet to be successful, and that success requires no apology. If you wish to control your life, it is imperative that you gain a basic understanding of who you are.

There are people who will discourage you if you set ambitious goals, and yet without goals there can be no achievement. There are people who will frown upon you as you seek a better life, and yet it is essential that all of us find our true place if happiness is to be found. There are those who will laugh and ridicule you as you increase your level of knowledge, and yet there is little difference between those who cannot read and those who will not read. There are some who will gossip about you, and yet there can be no cause for rejoicing without overcoming these naysayers. There are those who will despise you when you achieve the improved life, and yet happiness is seldom found in poverty.

ATTRIBUTES OF SUCCESS

Business writer and consultant Brian Tracy has argued that success and human potential are a matter of exploiting talent and attributes. Tracy states that individual potential is contained in an equation, $IA + AA \times MA = HP$, in which HP stands for *human potential*. IA represents *inborn attributes*—qualities that are fixed at birth, including race, gender, parents, and date of birth. No matter how hard we try to change or alter our inborn attributes, it's difficult or nearly impossible, to say the least. You cannot change your race or gender or your mother or father. These elements are determined at birth.

AA represents *acquired attributes,* the knowledge, skills, range of experience, levels of education and wealth, and ability that you have gained or developed as you have matured. Unlike inborn attributes, acquired attributes can be changed over the course of time. For example, to a certain degree, we are all born ignorant. No one is born educated. Understandably, we must seek out knowledge and wisdom on our own. Moreover, no one is born rich. Though our parents or relatives may possess a vast fortune, the fruits of their efforts will only come to us through inheritance or the knowledge of how to utilize these riches. But acquired attributes need not be barriers. A high school dropout can go back to school at a later date to further his or her education. History books are replete with examples of men and women who, though born impoverished, mapped out a life that led them to wealth and abundance. Regardless of your circumstances, poverty and ignorance need not be your lot in life. You can develop, improve, and change your acquired attributes over time through study, patience, and practice. But the process is slow and deliberate, requiring discipline and considerable effort.

The element you control in the equation is *MA, mental attitude,* which is the heart of the issue. Your attitude, whether positive or negative, will impact your level of human potential. Since the quality of your attitude can be improved almost without limit, even a person with average inborn attributes and average acquired attributes can perform at superior levels if he or she possesses a positive mental attitude. And, unlike the other variables in the success equation, your attitude can be improved immediately. According to Tracy, this is why it is your attitude as much as your aptitude that determines how much you will accomplish. Your attitude is the lens through which you view life. It is your general mental state and the outward expression of your thoughts and feelings. Your outer world is an expression of your inner world. You are not what you think you are. Instead, what you *think,* you are. Developing a positive, right mental attitude toward yourself and your life is the first step to unlocking your full potential.

THE GOAL OF LIFE

Who am I? What is my life's purpose? Why was I chosen to experience this thing called life? Perhaps an equally intriguing question is: *Why am I here?* The following story will get you thinking.

During the course of my research, I had the pleasure and the good fortune to hear the legendary T. M. Alexander speak before a group of business students at Morehouse College. Alexander's words were typical of the motivating speeches that he had delivered to similar audiences through the years. His message was brief but stirring. A room full of sharp, ambitious entrepreneurial hopefuls anxiously awaited his remarks. The eighty-eight-year-old black business giant grabbed the edge of the podium and leaned forward. He shot his audience the kind of stare an adult gives a child when he's about to explain one of life's innermost secrets.

"When your outgo exceeds your income," he began, "your upkeep becomes your downfall—that's economic determinism! My father had less than an eighth-grade education," he continued, "but he had a Ph.D. in wisdom and common sense. He told me that if I watched my pennies, the dollars would take care of themselves. I took his advice and decided to go one better by watching them both."

Alexander's story is the American dream made manifest, a plot straight out of Horatio Alger. In 1931—during the bleakest days of the Great Depression—he graduated from the all-black, male school, finishing with honors. John Wesley Dobbs, a self-styled black historian, pillar of the community, and grandfather of Atlanta's first black mayor, Maynard Jackson, used to tease, "I remember when he came out of Morehouse. Here was a black man with a college degree and a briefcase full of ambition. Getting started for T.M. wasn't easy, but success rarely is. Instruments do not become sharp on soap rock; it's difficulties that make men invincible."

To help celebrate his degree, an uncle surprised T.M. with $100, which he used to start the same business that he runs today—Alexander & Associates—one of the nation's oldest and most successful black-owned insurance companies. A black man in business in those days was not only an entrepreneur but also an unwitting crusader. Often isolated and misunderstood, he was a success by any definition, fighting to preserve both space and dignity in a society that wielded racism and discrimination like a sledgehammer. "When I started out, I peddled insurance like produce from door to door, often with no success. However, over time, I was able to gradually build up a loyal clientele, quietly and without fanfare." Sixty years later, Alexander is still at the helm, still climbing and expanding by utilizing the same principles he shared this evening.

His words were fast and breezy, and tinged with his own personal philosophy. "Understanding life is like jumping out of a ten-story building and changing your mind as you pass the fifth floor. The law of gravity will not alter to accommodate your stupidity—neither will the law of success."

Alexander's page in black history was secured when he stepped in to ensure that the Montgomery bus boycott would stay on track. To make the boycott effective, blacks in Montgomery had to find alternate means of transportation to their homes and jobs. Instinctively, they turned to their churches, but the church vehicles used to ferry members across town were not insured. Alexander's attempt to convince his white colleagues to insure the cars met an abrupt end. Word had quickly circulated that no company should provide coverage. A well-connected friend placed Alexander in contact with Lloyds of London, the marquee firm known for assuming any risk. Within hours, Alexander phoned the agency and sold them on his plan. As a result, all church vehicles were insured for liability and property damage, and the boycott bore straight ahead.

Alexander loves to retell the story, adding on his mother's homespun advice. "She always counseled, 'When there is a principle involved, don't compromise. Consequences not withstanding, right is going to win in the end.' "

The Million-Dollar Gift

After the diminutive millionaire concluded his remarks, he started to work the crowd, moving among the students and faculty, kissing a cheek here, grasping a hand there. Amid the centerpieces of bright flowers and platters of cookies and punch, a less tangible element is also present: *hope*. Before he left, he noticed a shy coed, too timid to snake her way through the crowd to meet him. Ever the salesman, Alexander sensed her apprehension and extended his hand. Her face glowed. "Now, here's a young lady I really believe in," the tycoon said with conviction. "You're going to do great things with your life. I just feel it.

"What would you do if you had a million dollars?" he asked, his eyes dancing behind thick glasses.

Almost ashamedly, the young girl turned toward her peers, shrugging her shoulders. "I don't know what I'd do," she replied.

"Well, you better think about it because we all have million-dollar gifts and talents that we never use. Don't make the mistake of not using yours." But Alexander wasn't quite through.

"And what is your most valuable possession?" he asked to all within hearing distance. "The gift that only the Creator can bestow—the gift of a new day. Make it count!"

I stood there and watched him work his magic. Despite this young woman's unease, you could look in her eyes and see her beginning to conquer her fears. She knew that race and poverty were not inescapable burdens, and it began to dawn on her that her future did burn bright and that she controlled her destiny. It was a moving experience.

HAVE YOU FOUND YOUR TRUE PURPOSE?

What would *you* do if you had a million dollars? You may want to recall an old saying that many of us read as children: "I bargained with life for a penny, and life would pay no more." It is worth remembering. Life will pay us—you and me—whatever we bargain for, no more and no less. If we bargain or demand or request peanuts, that's exactly what we—you and I—will receive. This is a simple law with no exceptions.

There's a place for all of us that can only be discovered by finding our true purpose. In doing that which we most enjoy, we will probably make our most significant contribution to society, and the contribution we make will, in turn, determine our reward. As you sow, so shall you reap—cause and effect. For every action there is an equal and opposite reaction. You and I can assess the extent and quality of our sowing by taking stock of our harvest—our possessions—both material and spiritual. Our harvest at any given point in our lives will, with rare exception, reflect the extent and quality of our efforts and service. An unknown author gave the following perspective on life. Read it slowly and analyze your response to each statement.

> What is life?
> Life is a gift... *accept it;*
> life is an adventure... *dare it;*
> life is a mystery... *unfold it;*
> life is a game... *play it;*
> life is a struggle... *face it;*
> life is beauty... *praise it;*
> life is a puzzle... *solve it;*
> life is opportunity... *take it;*
> life is sorrowful... *experience it;*
> life is a song... *sing it;*
> life is a goal... *achieve it;*
> life is a mission... *fulfill it!*

"THIS IS MY CALLING"

When he was a young man, segregation prevented James Lewis from playing tennis in the public parks of Birmingham, Alabama. Undaunted, he would carve a red clay court out of a vacant lot or paint lines on the stained concrete of a dilapidated nightclub. Today, in the parks that once shunned him, Lewis is not only welcome, he's revered. At seventy-five, two knee operations have limited his mobility, but he's still on a variety of courts nearly every day doing what he loves—helping children solve the mysteries of tennis and life. "If anyone wants to learn the game," he beams, "I'm available at no charge. Free!"

A retired steelworker, Lewis taught himself to play tennis more than sixty years ago, developing a wicked backhand. Almost immediately, he began sharing his love of the game with others in his community. Today, for students of all races, he demonstrates the barest fundamentals. "It's a step-by-step process. Forehand, backhand, volley, serve. Once they learn the basics, I let them try to put it all together, just like a jigsaw puzzle."

James Lewis cares about our children. His patience and selflessness are legendary. Besides stressing tennis's "outer" game, he amplifies its "inner" game as well. Qualities such as personal responsibility, sportsmanship, and discipline seem to always find their way into his postworkout conversation. Several of his students have gone on to garner top college scholarships, and all have steered clear of drugs and gangs.

These days, Lewis focuses his missionary zeal on several recreational programs—one of which bears his name—and two local colleges. The U.S. Tennis Association recently honored him with a Community Service Award and $500, which he promptly used to buy balls and rackets for area kids. But this modest man brushes off the accolades. "This is my calling," he proclaims. "It comes straight from my heart. And I'm not through yet. Tennis is the gift the good Lord has given me, so I feel I must pass it along to others. As long as I can still hit the ball, I have work to do."

Think of those whom you label successful. These are men and women who have realized their true purpose: "Make a joyful noise unto the Lord, all ye lands!" If purpose is present, nothing can block the determined soul from his rendezvous with destiny.

"THIS IS MY STORY, THIS IS MY SONG"

A poor woman rummaged through the back shelves of a run down country store searching for something she could use as a paperweight. After finding a beautiful piece of burl wood, she approached the owner and asked its price.

"Let me see," the owner replied, placing the piece of wood on the counter. "Well, it's nearly a pound. I guess that'll be a dollar."

When the woman handed him the dollar, the owner said, "Isn't it funny—that small piece of wood is only worth a dollar. But just think, if you carved it into a chess piece that worthless piece of wood would be worth ten times as much! As a matter of fact," he added, "if that same piece of wood were made into a carved jewelry box, its value would increase another tenfold.

"But most important," he said, "if you took this piece of wood and created a holy cross, the type used by the minister of a church, why, ma'am, your worthless paperweight would indeed be priceless." He said, Isn't it incredible for some to think that our Creator would want them lying in the scrap heap of life? Each of us desperately needs to find ways in which we can be molded and shaped into something more useful. No one ever fails who does his best.

Unfortunately, many view life as a train they board without knowing the itinerary or final destination. Herded like cattle, these passengers take their seats, draw the shades, and close off all faith and any hope for success. So many of us think ourselves into inferiority. We are held back by too much caution. We are timid about venturing. And so we die before we reach middle age, although we will not be lowered into the ground until our bodies catch up to our minds. What happened to the grand dreams of our youth? Struck down by our own caution, our own lack of faith. Opportunities? There were many. But there was always risk. Do we dare? No. We vacillate to and fro. Time beats on and the opportunity is gone. Like a train going nowhere fast, we plod along, giving little thought to rhyme and reason.

But there is a better way! George Eliot wrote over the door of her study, "It's never too late to become the person you could have been." Our moment of rebirth arrives when we recognize our inherent creative value. We are marvelous creatures, microcosms of the universe, perfect in every way. In the creative thinking process we become convinced of our own importance; we discover that life has significance. Though rebirth is a long and difficult task, each of us arrives on earth with an ordained mission. Once you know the truth about yourself, you will come to realize that success is your mission and your birthright. You were placed on this planet to be successful, and success requires no apology.

Finding one's true place does not come without plan or effort. Being born again is no easy task. Technique and training and much hard work are required. And we are always faced with the possibility that it is a destination that we may never reach. Every day we must start anew. Nevertheless, the world has a standing offer over each challenge, every difficulty, every roadblock: "Wanted—the man or woman who knows his or her life's destiny."

HELP WANTED!

Wanted, a woman who does not fear ridicule and humiliation. *Wanted,* a man who clutches his aim with an ironlike grip, who never flinches from unexpected difficulties, who calmly, patiently, and courageously grapples with his fate; who dies, if need be, at his post. *Wanted,* a woman who overfills her place, who is larger than her calling; who sees self-development, education, and diligence as the pillars of success. *Wanted,* a man who mixes common sense with intellectual theories;

who prefers substance to style, who does not allow his sheepskin to spoil his common touch.

Wanted, a woman who is well balanced; who is upright and uplifting, who is firm but fair. *Wanted,* a man who will not lose his individuality in a crowd, a man who has the courage of his convictions, who is not afraid to say yes, though all the world says no. *Wanted,* a woman who is loved and who loves; who walks through life under an umbrella of faith; who knows it is more important to be spiritual and Christ-like than to belong to any particular order or be trapped by religious codes of conduct or beliefs. *Wanted,* a man who is his brother's keeper. *Wanted,* a man who will lead when guided and be humble enough to follow when necessary. *Wanted,* a woman who will compel others to sit up and take notice, who knows how to say "I can." *Wanted,* a man who will live up to his God-given potential. The world waits for such an individual. If you can fill the order, please step forward!

Are you struggling with a sense of fulfillment? Do you have a feeling that you're here on earth for reasons that presently elude you? Perhaps, as you begin to realize that you do have a significant role to play and begin actively to try to discover what it is, you may find your sense of joy. Whenever you find greatness, you will find the man or woman who has mastered the following qualities.

- *Vision.* The ability to grasp the big picture, to anticipate trends and opportunities; to think without limits; to turn fantasy thinking into fantastic thinking. The ability to project yourself into future conditions over long periods of time. A vision is the future that becomes the present, the unreachable that becomes reality.
- *Leadership.* The ability to inspire, to elicit extraordinary performances from ordinary people. Leadership is the challenge to be something more than average. The capability to be strong but not rude; kind but not weak; bold but not insensitive; humble but not timid; proud but not arrogant.
- *Mastery over communications.* The ability to interact effectively, convey your ideas and thoughts in a positive manner in three critical areas: speaking one-on-one, communicating on paper, and speaking before large groups.
- *Common sense.* The wisdom to learn from your mistakes, and the ability to simplify complex subjects by veering straight to the core of what really matters.

FINDING YOUR TRUE PURPOSE

The most important part of this book is not written on its pages but is already in your own mind. Your progress toward success and fulfillment begins with one critical question: *Where are you going?* Finding your true purpose is the starting point of all achievement. Each of us desires the better things in life—love, family, and security—but few go beyond just hoping and wishing for them. If you know what you want, if you are determined to get it to the point that it becomes an obsession, and you back that obsession with continuous effort and sound planning, then you have discovered your true purpose. Once you learn how to harness the unlimited potential of your own mind, you can use this fuel to secure your chief aim. Study and complete the following exercise. As you engage in this effort, do not allow any self-limiting beliefs to cloud your thinking or sabotage this activity.

First, develop a dream list. This list is comprised of everything that you've ever wanted to have, be, or do, written as if there were no limitations. Imagine, for the moment, that you have no limitations with regard to your ability or education; resources or contacts; intelligence or skills; time, money, or other constraints. Allow your mind to roam freely, thinking of those things that you would like to achieve within the next three to five years.

Second, review your list and prioritize each goal with the letter A, B, or C. Next to your *most important* items—those that can make the *greatest difference* in your life and which you *desire intensely*—write the letter A. Next to the items that you would really like to possess or achieve but are not as important or life-changing as the first category, write the letter B. Next to each of the remaining items—things that you wrote that would be nice to accomplish but do not evoke passion— write the letter C.

Third, transfer your A goals to a separate sheet of paper. Again, review each item and write A1 next to your *most important* goal, A2 beside the second most important goal, A3 next to the third most important goal, and so on, until you have organized all of your A goals in order of importance to you. Your A1 goal should be your true purpose—the single most important goal in your life. All highly successful men and women maintain goals in every part of their lives, but they have one clear obsession—the single most important goal that defines and directs their outlook. If properly conducted, this easy but life-changing exercise will cut a path straight and true to the desire of your heart.

SIMPLE ADVICE GAVE SOMEONE'S LIFE NEW MEANING

Percy Sutton, founder of Inner City Broadcasting, and owner of New York's famed Apollo Theater, told me a moving story, one that neither he nor I will ever forget. This tale helps to explain the gift and urgency of life. The story was told to him by his legal client, Malcolm X, the celebrated Muslim minister. Malcolm X became one of the greatest leaders of our time by serving a forgotten people without limit or any thought of financial reward. Throughout America's dark ghettos as well as the most prestigious centers of learning, he drew millions of Black Americans to him with the hope of freedom and the pursuit of happiness.

In 1964, an enlightened Malcolm X left the Nation of Islam to organize people of African descent across the globe. Unfortunately, Malcolm's vision caught his mentor and teacher, Elijah Muhammad, by surprise. After months of staging meetings in a building owned by the Nation of Islam, Malcolm X was sued by the organization. In a much ballyhooed, heated court case, both parties battled bitterly and were geared for the worst. After one particular grueling session, Sutton escorted the storied Muslim minister from a New York courthouse, surrounded by heavily armed bodyguards. Among the turmoil and distress, police and the press squirmed anxiously, as faithful followers on both sides crowded the scene. Sutton and his client were militarily funneled into waiting cars and whisked away, leaving television crews in their wake.

Understandably shaken by the entire ordeal, Sutton caught his breath as he was pressed into the front seat of a black Cadillac, while Malcolm X was seated comfortably in the back. Inside the car sat four dark figures with bulging topcoats. At the time, Sutton admits he was too nervous to look any of them in the face. During the drive back to his office, Sutton sat frozen with his briefcase in his lap, his thoughts and pulse running wild. His client, on the other hand, seemed unaffected by the day's activities. In disbelief, Sutton loosened his tie, slowly turned around and quizzed, "Mr. Minister, doesn't this disturb you?"

"Doesn't *what* disturb me?" Malcolm X shot back.

"You know, all of the guns and bodyguards and stuff," Sutton answered.

"To be truthful, it does. But it really makes those around me feel comfortable. My own philosophy on such matters is gained from a story about an old Arab slave who was afraid of dying. Please allow me to share this fable with you." With his world seemingly closing in from every corner, Malcolm X sat calmly and told an impressionable Percy Sutton the following tale.

One day a slave named Omar said to his master, "Master, O master, give me your fastest horse. I've seen the face of Death and I know it's coming. I've seen it in my dreams. Let me ride in order that I might escape it and survive." Concerned about the slave, his master begrudgingly complied and gave him his fastest charger. Unwittingly, the poor slave had reasoned that if he could ride all day and night, he could live to see yet another day. So Omar mounted the horse and rode. He rode the first and second days without so much as stopping for food or drink. Finally, just before sunset on the third day and at the point of exhaustion, the slave stopped. The road he had traveled had suddenly divided into seven trails, from which he had to choose.

Hoping to choose wisely, Omar rode on. After a few moments, he switched to the trail on his right. From there he progressed for a few hours more, but again pulled his horse up short and switched to the road on his left. This wavering continued until he had ridden six trails. Now, in a last-ditch effort, the slave embarked on the final path, where, less than one hundred yards away, in the center of the road, standing boldly, was the face of Death. Glaring straight ahead, Death cried out, "Omar, Omar, where have you been? For three days I've waited for you. What has taken you so long?"

"You see, Counselor," Minister Malcolm said, "there lies the moral to the story: You can run and you can hide. You can twist and you can turn. You can waste what little precious time you have on this planet but it won't do you any good. Death is something that we cannot escape. You cannot leave this earth alive, so there's no use in worrying about it.

"Each of us should make the most of our lives," Malcolm continued. "We should give life our best—let us use our lives more wisely to chase our dreams, find our true purpose, and be as happy and successful as possible."

When Sutton shared this story with me, I was forced to pause. Even after reading the dozens of books on Malcolm X, the fiery orator, the "by-any-means-necessary black nationalist," I had never pictured him in this light. Imagine his words: "We should give life our best—let us use our lives more wisely to chase our dreams, find our true purpose, and be as happy and successful as possible." I found it refreshing.

YOU HOLD THE KEY!

High achievers live by words like those of Malcolm X—words that wipe out disappointment and embolden the heart for future conquest. Words that encourage and motivate as well as give direction. Peak performers have an internal drive for self-discovery. They operate under a sense of urgency and a passion for accomplishment. Percy Sutton took Malcolm X's words to heart as his career shifted from lawyer to politician to struggling entrepreneur. When I asked him what pursuing the dream meant, he replied, "It means daring to reach, to climb, to crawl, to scratch, to get back up when you've been knocked down, to push forward—ever forward—to forgive. It means sacrificing everything, if necessary, to carve out a place for your own existence. It means *living.*"

Anyone who desires the key to inner peace and abundant riches should clutch Malcolm X's words to his or her heart. By choosing to define life on your own terms, you take the first step toward success. But *you* must *choose.* So many of us awake each morning with dread in our hearts and fear in our minds. We unnecessarily face the monotony of another day with its hopeless toil and ceaseless pressures. More and more of us are being hammered into a lifestyle we cannot endure, cannot afford, and cannot cope with. We have forgotten one of the basic tenets of life: We were given dominion over this world. We each plot our own map. It was never the intention of our Creator to chart a course for us. That would place us all under His bondage. Instead, He bestowed on each of us talent and gifts, and the ability to think and envision our own way in any manner that we choose.

But the key is that we can make our own choices. You have options in your life. We all do. You need not spend another day in poverty, self-pity, or fear. Why is there so much needless pain and grief? Why are there so many unnecessary failures? The answer is obvious. Too many of us have never contemplated the options of a better life. Far too many people have been unaware that they had choices.

Why have we allowed the plague of failure and unhappiness to infect us? Why are we able to conquer dreaded diseases, circle distant planets, view events thousands of miles away, design machines that can tend to our every wish, transplant human organs, even create life in a test tube, and yet make so little progress in elevating our opinion of ourselves and our many talents?

Why is it that in the most prosperous and open society on the face of the earth, more than seven thousand black Americans are senselessly killed each year by other blacks? Why do we, black males, continue to sap our strength and squander our most precious resource—our children—by forcing them to cope in fatherless homes? Why is our community forced to treat thousands of new cases of mental illness each day and stand by helplessly as we witness lives ruined by drug addiction? Why do we, black Americans, shun the benefits of increased economic development by refusing to support black businesses? Why don't more of our children aspire to the professions within their reach that can only come through a quality education? Why aren't more of our race fully functional? Although Black America is 32 million strong, why are nearly 40 percent of us on welfare; why do 32 percent drop out of high school; why are 33 percent of black men aged twenty to twenty-nine in prison, on probation, or on parole; why are 23 percent of black teenage girls unwed mothers; and why do 22 percent of black adolescents aged fourteen to eighteen use drugs? How could it be easier for the South African government to slam the door on its ugly past of apartheid and racial injustice than for scores of black Americans to break free of the infecting plague of helplessness and self-pity?

One of the most important and ageless secrets to greatness that I had to learn is that you cannot begin to turn a hopelessly bruised and battered existence around or sidestep the dreary treadmill of a dead-end job or move toward a better financial destiny until you appreciate the blessings that you already possess.

Blessings? you might ask. That's right, blessings. Begin now to give thanks for those things you *do* have and don't worry about the things that you don't. For example, take a look at your health—you're breathing, aren't you? What's that worth? What's it worth to live in this country—the most free and open society on the face of the earth? What's your career worth? Or, for those of you who are currently unemployed, at least you have the prospects of a career. The rest of the world would give anything—and I mean anything—to walk in your shoes. You are the best and brightest that your ancestors have ever produced. You are what Nat Turner died for; you are what Billie Holiday cried for; you are what A. Philip Randolph strived for; and you are what Nelson Mandela survived for. Regardless of what transpired in your past, you have been blessed. No matter what others may say, think, or do, these are not the worst of times. And granted, these may not be the best of times. But one thing is for certain: This is the only time you have!

There is a maxim that states, "Success in life comes not from holding a good hand, but playing a poor hand well." The easiest thing to do, whenever you fall short of the mark, is to blame your lack of ability or your circumstances for your misfortunes. The easiest thing to forget, especially when fate has been unkind, is that you were *born to succeed*—not fail. Unfortunately, our nation has a growing number of individuals who have already sold themselves on the idea that they just don't measure up, that they just can't cut it. They are already dead in spirit, aimlessly parading through life with no sense of meaning or purpose.

You cannot rise above your level of vision. The man who guides a pushcart through the alley to pick up bottles and rags will remain between the shafts of his rickety cart as long as he believes that he has no talent for anything else.

IS SUCCEEDING EASY?

Only you, the reader, can answer this question. In the long haul, success is far easier than failing. Case in point: A recent National Collegiate Athletic Association survey revealed that black parents are eight times more likely to encourage their children to seek a professional sports career than their white counterparts. Quite naturally, then, 44 percent of black male teenagers believe a pro career is within their realm of possibility, never stopping to consider the odds that only one out of one hundred athletes is offered a scholarship to a four-year institution.

Furthermore, only one out of ten thousand high school basketball, football, or baseball players ever reach the professional ranks and occupy one of the available 2,300 roster slots. To worsen matters, fewer than 30 percent of black athletes receive college degrees, and, not surprisingly, each year thousands of able-minded black males leave schools across the country with no degree, no pro contract, and little hope.

Now consider the safer bet. According to the Bureau of Labor Statistics, in 1992 there were 337,178 black schoolteachers, 68,590 black engineers, 25,704 black lawyers, and 18,975 black physicians plying their trades—many rather successfully—throughout the nation. Now contrast these numbers to the actual figures that blacks constitute in pro sports: National Football League, 789; National Basketball Association, 243; major-league baseball, 163.

From a purely statistical standpoint, numbers of this type seem to lunge off the page. Just think of the thousands—no, millions—of young black males who believed their salvation rested in a $100 pair of gym shoes and came up short of their goal.

What do these numbers imply? Well, the overwhelming majority of black teenagers would have fared much better if they had taken the long-range view. For aspiring young black males, it is far easier and a great deal more realistic to become a Jesse Jackson or a Maynard Jackson than a Bo Jackson or a Reggie Jackson. It might be far easier to become a Charles Drew than a Charles Barkley; a Marcus Garvey than a Marcus Allen; an Earl Graves than an Earl Monroe; a Roy Wilkins than a Dominique Wilkins; a Vernon Jordan than a Michael Jordan; or a David Dinkins than a David Robinson. As a matter of fact, statistics suggest that it is far easier for a black child to hail from "Pinpoint," Georgia, and secure a seat on the Supreme Court than to make it to the NFL Hall of Fame thanks, in part, to his pinpoint passes. It is definitely within the realm of possibility for a young black male to study hard, go to college, and become an engineer who builds rockets that will one day go to the moon than to become another "Rocket" Raghib Ismail or Warren Moon!

How can we save our young people from wasted lives? By helping to direct their paths and by pointing out the truth. For now, let's be content with the solution offered by basketball superstar Isiah Thomas, who, after his sophomore year at Indiana University, left college to lead the Detroit Pistons to a pair of NBA championships. Despite the glamour and glitter that is so often a part of pro stardom, Thomas stood tall in the morass of forbidding statistics and went on to earn his college degree. "At all levels, education is the key to chisel away poverty," Thomas explains. "An education not only affects how you think but how you perceive your world. I always knew I would go back and graduate. And besides, if I didn't finish, my mother would've beat me senseless."

WHY ARE YOU HERE?

Is this our lot in life? Is this how we must live, dreading the pain and horrors of each day, turning *on* each other instead of *to* each other? What's holding you back? Are you afraid to take a chance? What has chance ever done in the world? Has it erected any cities? Has it created any inventions? Has it developed any businesses, any enterprises, any institutions? Was there any chance in Alex Haley's uncovering of his past? Was it chance that bestowed the acclaimed Horatio Alger Award upon Joe Dudley, the founder of the firm that bears his name? What did chance have to do with Angela Bassett's career? Nothing could keep her down. Though she toiled for long hours at low pay in a field that she would eventually master, today, in the cold, calculated, and glitzy world of entertainment her star shines the brightest. Was it chance or luck that built the pyramids? Is it luck that allows men and women to distinguish themselves in education, medicine, and the arts? Has luck ever advanced a cause?

There is hardly a word in the entire English language more abused than the word "luck." For all the faults and failures of men and women, their sins and their errors, luck is made to stand as the sole reason. Is there truth in my words? See for yourself. Go talk with the man or woman who just lost his or her business to bankruptcy. Many times you will find an individual who lost his fortune to wild speculation, extravagant living, lack of energy, refusing to innovate with the times. But the bottom line is clear. You will discover someone who complacently regards himself as the "victim of bad luck."

Go visit the prison inmate, who knows not the consequences of his actions or the ramifications of his thoughts. Here you'll find the man or woman who succumbed to temptations which others have found easy to avoid. This is an individual who shuns personal responsibility, has turned his back on his conscience, and explains away his wrongful acts. He tells everyone—from his prey to the prosecutor—that he is "the victim of circumstances."

Go speak with the weak-spirited individual who, from lack of energy, will, and application, has made little headway in the world. Being outstripped in the race of life by those whom he despises, this person rationalizes why he hasn't done more, achieved more, and attained more. Here, again, you will find traces of the all-potent power of luck. And, as for the success of others, his reason is pure and simple: "They were just lucky."

What is luck? Has any scholar defined it? Has any philosopher explained its nature? Has any scientist shown its composition? If luck is truly luck, why can't it make a fool speak words of wisdom; or the illiterate present mind-boggling lectures? If luck is really luck, why can't those who grope and grovel sleep as beggars and awaken with the wealth of Oprah Winfrey or John Johnson? Has luck ever guided the hands of Ben Carson? Has luck ever directed the steps of Gregory Hines? Even Terry McMillan, one of our most prized writers, wrote the first sentence in her *Waiting to Exhale* a dozen different ways before she thought it worthy of publication. Has luck ever led or controlled her pen?

Young man, young woman, that door ahead of you is probably closed because you have closed it—closed it by lack of training; closed it by lack of ambition, drive, and desire. Though, perhaps, you have been waiting for luck to open it, the determined soul has stepped in ahead of you and opened it himself.

It is not chance or luck. It is *you!* Your efforts, your desires, your thoughts, your actions and deeds—your indomitable will. And yes, though serendipity may play a role, as a rule the best man or woman does win the best place. You alone are great. Greatness does not depend upon where you are now—greatness depends upon where you are going. Success does not depend upon what you are now—success depends upon what you are becoming. Diligence is the procreator of luck. You are not a creature of circumstance, you create your circumstances. You, and you alone, pave the very road on which you run your race!

THERE IS A BETTER WAY!

You're probably living in your own little comfort zone, performing unchallenging tasks where no one will bother you, taking no risks, facing few problems, never concerned about growth or pushing your potential. You call this living? Hopefully, it's hurting you, deep down inside. Why? Because people don't change when they feel good. They change when they're fed up. Pain pushes us to those crucial turning points. And, one day, enough will be enough!

Is there a better way? Yes, there is a better way, and it starts with each of us when we dare to answer the question Why am I here?

How would you answer that question? Why are *you* here? It's been said that if the universe is an accident, then *we* are accidents. But if there's meaning in the universe, then there must be meaning in us, too. Throughout the ages, great men and women have addressed themselves to the purpose of life. Each of us, from time to time, must ask ourselves, Where am I going? Am I living in such a way to bring lasting, important benefits to myself and those who depend on me? Am I honestly proud of the job I'm doing and the manner in which I have been conducting myself?

"What is man anyway?" asked Dr. Benjamin E. Mays of a group of Morehouse students. "Man is flesh and blood, body and mind, bones and muscle, arms and legs, heart and soul, lungs and liver, nerves and veins—all these and more make a man. But man is really what his dreams are. Man is what he aspires to be. He is the ideals that beckon him on. Man is the integrity that keeps him steadfast, honest, and true. If a young man tells me what he aspires to be, I can almost predict his future.

"An individual cannot aspire if he or she looks down," Dr. Mays continued. "The Creator has not molded us with aspirations and longings for heights to which we cannot climb. Look upward. The unattained calls us to climb new mountains. You cannot have too much of that emotion called ambition, for, even though you do not attain your ideal, the efforts you make will bring nothing but blessings. Life should be lived in earnest; it is no idle game, no farce to amuse and be forgotten."

"I once knew a colored boy," said Frederick Douglass, the great abolitionist, "whose mother and father died when he was six years old. He was a slave, and had no one to care for him. He slept on a dirt floor in a hovel. In cold weather he would crawl into a burlap sack resting his feet next to an open-pit hearth. Many times an ear of corn stood between him and starvation. That boy did not wear long pants as you do, but a towel-linen shirt. Schools were unknown to him, and he learned to spell from an old Webster's dictionary. He would then preach and speak, and soon developed a following. He became presidential elector, United States Marshal, United States Recorder, a diplomat, and accumulated great wealth. He wore broadcloth, and didn't have to divide crumbs with dogs under the table. Who was that boy? That child was me—Frederick Douglass!

> **Each of us should make the most of our lives. We should give life our best—let us use our lives more wisely to chase our dreams, find our true purpose, and be as happy and successful as possible.**
>
> **—Malcolm X**

"Don't think because you are colored you can't succeed," Douglass urged on. "Strive earnestly to add to your knowledge. Don't get bitter—get better! What was possible for me is possible for you, but you must have purpose."

"Stand up!" admonished Martin Luther King. Why? "Because a man can't ride your back unless it's bent over."

"Show me a contented slave," explained Nat Turner, a man whose entire life was spent at the end of a chain, "and I'll show you a man without hope or purpose."

Albert Einstein takes a step in a different direction. "The more I study physics," he wrote, "the more I'm drawn to metaphysics. Man is here for the sake of other men only." Dr. Einstein believed that the universe could not have been an accident, and he addressed himself to the purpose of life. Think for a moment. "Man is here for the sake of other men only." Though Einstein belonged to no religious sect or formal ecclesiastical order, the eminent physicist was a deeply spiritual person in the cosmic realm. In this particular case, Einstein used the term "man" in its classical sense to mean human beings—both male and female. Do you agree? Is that the way you answered this question? Do you believe that you are here solely to serve others, and through serving others, you are being served and enjoying life as a result? We are here for the sake of serving others only. And only to the extent that we serve others will we know the purpose of living. It is my sincere desire that you grasp the power of this fundamental principle and the magic that it holds. Each of us needs a settled purpose in life, a target. Then, by doing our very best every day, we will reach this point on which we have set our compass.

FINDING YOUR AREA OF EXCELLENCE

Ralph Waldo Emerson, the nineteenth-century poet and essayist, wrote, "The world makes way for the person who knows where he or she is going." Think what it means to know where you are going. You immediately eliminate all doubts and fears. By identifying your purpose, you cannot be led astray by circumstances or by those who are not yet convinced of the power you possess. Do you lead the pack, or do you blindly follow the path of others? Have you found your area of excellence?

In a 1991 survey, 64 percent of Americans aged twenty-five to forty-nine said they "fantasize about quitting their jobs to live on a desert island, travel around the world, or do something else for enjoyment." Have you ever had that feeling? Do you have that feeling right now? Are you happy in your work? What type of work would be more meaningful for you?

In a 1981 study, 43 percent of Americans polled said "a lot of money" was the key to making a job worth doing. By 1992, a follow-up study revealed that number had jumped to 62 percent. But is it really just money that makes work meaningful, or is there more to it than that? A major university asked thousands of workers to list the most important aspects of meaningful work. Respondents checked the following eight items in order of importance.

1. My job must be interesting.
2. I must receive enough support to get my duties done.

3. I must have enough information to get the job done.
4. I must have enough authority to get the job done.
5. The pay should be good.
6. There must be ample opportunity for me to develop my abilities.
7. There must be some degree of job security.
8. I must be able to see results of my efforts.

What would you add to this list? What would you like to change in order to make your work or even life more meaningful?

I recently addressed a group of students at the Atlanta University complex in Atlanta, Georgia. The AU Center is comprised of four historic black colleges—Clark Atlanta University, Spelman, Morris Brown, and Morehouse. Many of the students were seniors and upper classmen who had grown up in poverty and had experienced tough times. But it was obvious in their earnest faces that they had a positive attitude toward life and that it had already taken them far. Now they were confronting a new, and in many ways more daunting, challenge: the challenge of setting goals based on their desires and unique gifts. For some people, this is no challenge at all. These are the select individuals that the writer and philosopher Earl Nightingale called *goal people.* Goal people, according to Nightingale, are those who seem to be able to do many things with equal facility and equal interest and enjoyment. Nightingale explained that "each of us, because of the way our genetic heritage is stacked, has an area of great interest. And it is that area that we should explore with the patience and assiduity of a paleontologist on an important dig."

This statement both frames and illustrates the very essence of achievement. High-achieving men and women, particularly those who have mastered a chosen field, always attain depth of knowledge in at least one area. Through perseverance and hard work, they may be well versed in a variety of areas, but they are extremely knowledgeable in one key area. This is the process that leads to competence. It begins with an initial discovery—a discovery about what you can excel at doing and what you love to do. This is the key! Throughout my years of research, this one strategy has held true: *Success and wealth can only be secured after you have identified your area of excellence.*

John Rogers, a millionaire investor, delights in his work and it has paid off. As his money-managing ambitions grew, so, too, did his firm. In 1983, he conceived the idea of an investment company, when others viewed his efforts as an unworkable pipe dream. Despite years of hardship and toil, he survived and prospered. What's his secret? A variety of factors enter the picture, but one occupies a dominant position. "I love my work," the young tycoon says ecstatically. "I enjoy the thrills and excitement that the market provides. And I deeply enjoy those moments when I've helped a client increase his or her net worth."

Frank Mingo, the creator of Kentucky Fried Chicken's highly successful pitchline—"We Do Chicken Right!"—told me that he views life as one big marketing campaign. "Whatever I'm doing—whether at home, the office, or socializing among friends—my mind is constantly tossing over new ideas and concepts to test with clients. Sometimes I can't wait to try a new approach."

"Find a field where you can excel," explained *Ebony* magazine publisher John Johnson. "One of the nice things about life is that it affords us a wealth of opportunity. Choose a product or service and set out to be the best in terms of quality or service. Select a market that you can serve better than anyone else. If you can't win the game by preestablished rules, then either change your game or change the rules."

Though her first impulse was to study classical piano, the academic choice for someone who could read music before she could read books, Condoleezza Rice chose instead to follow her *inner* impulse, a love and attraction to different cultures. In high school, a counselor told her she was not "college material." Not only did Condoleezza prove to be college material, but she graduated from the University of Denver at age nineteen and went on to become a leading Soviet scholar—a field that traditionally attracts few blacks.

"I have always been able to follow something that interested me," she explained, "regardless of the risks involved." Here is a black woman, barely forty, who grew up in the face of racial hostility in Birmingham, Alabama; who served on the National Security Council under one U.S. president and translated Russian and Soviet affairs under another. Today, Dr. Rice is the first of her gender and race to occupy the post of provost of Stanford University, a position widely regarded as a stepping-stone to the presidency of a major American university. How did she move with breathtaking acceleration from the round tables of the White House to the lecture halls of academia? Her secret is captured in a nutshell. "There is nothing standing in your way to do whatever you want to do provided you know what you want to do and love to do it. Education is of no value, talent is worthless, unless you have one unwavering aim. Never find yourself without a compass."

I continually encounter the underlying relationship between love of work and success in the marketplace. One of the sad realities of our world is that most people are unhappy in their work. To listen to people talk, it seems as though they believe that if they could just make more money, they would enjoy their work. Actually, the opposite is closer to the truth: If they enjoyed their work more, they probably would earn more money. Aristotle wrote, "Pleasure in the job puts perfection in the work." The secret is to figure out what you really enjoy doing, without regard to the potential financial rewards. And no one can predict what the financial rewards ultimately might be if you possess a passion or love for your work.

FOUR QUESTIONS TO GREATNESS

Before you lies a feast of ideas—strategies that are sure to satisfy your appetite for success and happiness. But during the course of your life, you must answer the four questions of greatness; the answers are the keystone to superior achievement. Finding these answers calls for no special effort. These four questions make no unreasonable demands upon your time or ability. But make no mistake: If you are to experience all that life holds, you must decide *now* upon your purpose! Decide where you are going; begin from where you are. Start with whatever means of attaining your objective might be at hand. Soon, you will discover that, to the extent you make use of these resources, other and better means will reveal themselves to you. Remember, your life's purpose will not be revealed through any one of these answers alone, but your answers are keys to unlocking the secret of your true purpose.

- *What do you love to do?* What occupation fills you with joy? What chosen field could you throw your heart and soul into? A large percentage of today's population do not enjoy their work. This is a tragic fact, considering that work consumes so much of our lives. Successful men and women develop a passion for their work; they love their chosen vocation so much that they choose their endeavor even if it doesn't lead to great financial success. If you had no limitations in terms of time or money, what would you enjoy doing so much that you would choose this area of interest for the indefinite future? The answer to this question is an indication of your labor of love.

- *What would you do for free?* What would you do if no one paid you a dime? Fulfilled men and women are often misunderstood. As we watch them go about their daily routines, we find attitudes and values that contradict much of what we are taught. We are cautioned not to work too hard or too much. Typically, society views work as something done from Monday through Friday—a compartmentalized bit of life void of fun or happiness. The phrases "Thank God it's Friday" and "Stormy Monday" have emerged from the notion that the workweek is filled with toil and drudgery. No matter how impersonal, dull, or tedious the job might seem to others, for successful men and women, their work is their play. And if you're doing what you love to do, your work becomes your play. And if your work becomes your play, you will never work a day in your life.

- *What comes easy to you but difficult to others?* What is your area of unfair competitive advantage? Almost anyone who devotes himself to a given vocation, and who pours his love and energy into that activity, develops a certain talent and genius in that field. Any work can serve this purpose. Whatever it is you choose to do—if done with the right attitude and proper affection—becomes a graceful, joyful activity that leads to a level of proficiency. Examine your current vocation and determine whether it enlists your talents and skills. Each of us has an area of unfair competitive advantage. Seek to identify yours and set out to leave a lasting legacy by investing in your special gift.

- *How do others view your talents and gifts?* As discussed, work can provide us with so much enjoyment that it begins to be experienced as play. However, prior to experiencing work in this most exuberant, almost effortless state, we must first know ourselves well enough to consciously choose the correct path or vocation. This demands not only courage but a type of intuition that separates us from society's expectations and definition of success. Some people are naturally intuitive. Others must seek the support of friends and relatives by asking, "What field am I best suited for?" or, "What career or occupation do you think I would be most effective at?" Check your attitudes and feelings about your work with those whom you respect. Sometimes others can see from a distance what you and I cannot see up close. Significant others can often support self-examination and determine whether a job or position is the right one for us.

These questions represent the final door through which all must pass to attain greatness. Each answer will provide a key that will unlock this door, and the keys will be in your hands when you have prepared yourself to accept them. From this moment on, and for what remains of your life, make a commitment to answer these questions and uncover your life's purpose. Remember, you have but one life to live.

THE POWER OF ONE UNWAVERING AIM!

In the boom years of the late 1970s, the truth had nearly been forgotten. Jake Simmons, Jr., wildcatter, lease broker, oil trader, and outspoken black businessman, made a name for himself in one of America's most hostile arenas—the international oil industry. Jonathan Greenberg, in his book *Staking a Claim,* chronicles the life of the unsung entrepreneur, who not only became the world's first internationally successful black oilman but also managed to integrate into his life a bold career as a civil rights leader.

Simmons was a man who believed that life centered on constant struggle, a challenge to be met by working harder than was necessary and by proving that the power of his potential was greater than any measure of racism which sought to restrain him. "How in hell can a black man stay in bed in the morning when white men rule the world?" Simmons would ask his sons. "I am convinced," he wrote to his eldest son, J. J. Simmons III, "that wisdom is acquired by living purposefully and objectively. One must discipline and control himself. Always keep yourself in a firm position to defend your integrity." Here was a black man who believed in capitalism and the opportunities of the American system, and he was determined to make those opportunities exist for himself and those of his race.

Simmons, part Creek Indian, part African, was raised on his family's 840-acre ranch in Oklahoma. He attended Tuskegee Institute, where Booker T. Washington was to have a profound impact on his life. At a time when contracts were less significant than a man's word, Simmons earned a reputation as honest and trustworthy. During the Depression, he left his home state in lure of business deals in the rough-and-tumble region of East Texas. Blacks owned land there, but few had the resources or connections to produce oil. Simmons found a white lawyer willing to defend their interests and a wealthy oilman willing to buy their leases. He peddled black oil leases around the plains and received percentages and handsome commissions. He used this money to drill for oil near Muskogee, an oil-drenched, eastern Oklahoma town. After numerous dry holes, he struck it big in 1949 and made his first million. With this approach he took on the prohibitive stereotypes of a segregated industry and won the respect of America's oil tycoons.

An unshakable optimist, Simmons's expertise as an articulate and persuasive salesman eventually allowed him to bridge the gap between post-colonial West African nations seeking outside investment and international American mineral companies searching for opportunities in foreign lands. Newborn African states like Nigeria and Ghana had only shaken free from British rule for a few years when Simmons arrived there in the mid-1960s. During the sensitive Nigerian negotiations for what proved to be the most profitable oil deal an American company ever struck in sub-Sahara Africa, Simmons helped solidify the transaction.

Over the next decade, he constructed similar deals in the Ivory Coast and Liberia. Because of his efforts, American multinationals were to invest more than $150 million in Ghana alone. Just three years before his death in 1978, the Ghanian government awarded him its Grand Medal, the nation's highest honor.

Even after his death, Simmons's oil operations continue to thrive. For the past two decades, Simmons Royalty Company, a holding company managed by his youngest son, has expanded throughout Africa's west coast.

This simple story reveals a precious secret that's most effective if uncovered by you, the reader. Jake Simmons, Jr., walked with a specific plan and he conditioned his mind so thoroughly that nothing was going to keep him from making his mark. In his own words, Simmons states that "wisdom is acquired by living purposefully and objectively." The individual who knows where he or she is going and is determined to get there will find a way or create one. There is no grander sight in the world than that of an individual fired up with a great purpose, dominated by one unwavering aim. The man or woman with a resolute purpose, with an overriding passion, is always a minority of one. This once poor black man raised near an Indian reservation in the Southwest had an idea and a plan that neither ridicule, hardship, nor humiliating defeat could conquer. Borne up by this purpose, he pressed steadily toward his goal.

In the entire history of the human race, there has never been, nor will there ever be, anyone just like you. The odds of another human being possessing your unique combination of characteristics and qualities are more than 50 billion to one. This means that you have the potential to do something special or extraordinary with your life; something that no one else can do. However, I must ask: Are you going to do it? It's true that some people are born with rare, unique gifts, but most of us are introduced to life with average talents and abilities. Those individuals that society labels "great" reach high levels of performance by developing their talents to a very high degree in the field of their choice. In other words, your potential lies dormant. It must be identified and developed if you hope to get more out of life. The formula for success is simple: a few simple disciplines practiced every day.

If you truly wish, the revelation in this chapter can mark the turning point of your life. Make your own choices before life makes them for you. If you are going to have a new future, you need a new beginning. If you are going to realize a new destiny, you will need a point of origin. Of all the questions asked by those who dare to succeed, one stands above the rest: "I want to succeed, but how?" Allow me to answer as simply as possible: by utilizing your *greatest gift.* No life ever grows great until it is dedicated, disciplined, and *focused!*

2
The Greatest Question:

"What Does It Take?"

- The Price of Success

- The Four Basic Fears

- The Eight Steps to Greater Courage

- What Does It Take?

The secret of happiness is freedom,
and the secret of freedom is courage.
—PERICLES

You can either stand up and be counted
or lie down and be counted out!
—MAGGIE L. WALKER

Having done all . . . stand!
—EPHESIANS 6:13

What does it take? No one can ask a greater question. Four simple words that stand between you and your moment of decision. If you dare to accomplish anything in this world, if you aspire to the Creator's grand scheme, if your very existence depends upon it, and if you are willing to give up your time, money, and effort for it, then you must confront the eternal question that stands up and looks every would-be achiever in the eye: What does it take? If you dare to walk through the gates of achievement, you must answer this question. It is the way every great success has been won.

You don't believe that prestigious writers, acclaimed artists, revered businessmen and -women were born with the ability to write or paint or lead countless others, do you? Do you think each possessed the latest books or sat before the most rigorous instructors on language, the arts, or finance? On the contrary, their only assets were backbone, shoe leather, and a moral courage best captured by the words of Mary McLeod Bethune, the great educator, who, as she faced her foes, gazed upward and said, "Here I stand, Father. Help me."

If an individual wants to accomplish anything in this world, he or she must not be afraid of running the risks, of assuming the responsibilities. Of course it takes courage to face the possibility of failure, to be subjected to criticism for an unpopular cause, to expose oneself to the shafts of ridicule. But the man or woman who is not true to himself or herself, who cannot carry out the sealed orders placed in his hand at birth, who does not possess the courage to trace the pattern of his own destiny, which no other soul but his own can do, will never know the measure of his own greatness.

WALK THE WALK

All the world loves courage, but how we shrink from courageous acts of our own! We live as others live; we dress as others dress. We conduct our affairs in the manner of other men and women. What does greatness require? It requires the courage not to bend the knee to popular opinion. It calls for courage to refuse to follow customs and rights that run contrary to our own sense of morality. The child who starts out by being afraid to speak what he thinks will usually end by being afraid to think what he wishes. Much of today's unhappiness rests with weakness and indecision. In other words, the lack of courage to stand on your own, to be uncommon within the crowd of conformity. On the walls of the Million Dollar Roundtable can be found the following creed composed by Dean Alfange, Cornell University-trained scholar and businessman:

It is not my right to be common—if I can. I seek opportunity—not security. I want to take the calculated risk; to dream and to build, to fail and to succeed. I refuse to barter incentive for a dole. I prefer the challenges of life to the guaranteed existence; the thrill of fulfillment to the stale calm of utopia. I will not trade freedom for benefice nor my dignity for a handout. I will never cower before any master nor bend to any threat. It is my heritage to stand erect, proud and unafraid; to think and act for myself, enjoy the benefit of my creations and to face the world boldly and say, this I have done. All this is what it means to be an American. I do not choose to be common.

"What a new face courage puts on everything," Emerson wrote. Winston Churchill agreed. "Courage is the finest quality," Churchill explained, "because it guarantees all the others." No truer statement was ever written.

Wherever it appears, courage changes things for the better. Sometimes it's the courage to be silent when a word or phrase comes to mind. It's often the courage to get up on a cold, miserable morning when it's the last thing in the world you want to do. It's the courage to do what needs to be done when it should be done. And it's the courage to follow the silent voice within when it means going against the crowd, standing up for that which you believe is right. It's the courage to stay with something long enough to succeed.

Don't lament and grieve over lost wealth or opportunities. Many an individual has only found himself after he has lost his all. Fear stripped him only to allow him to discover himself. You must toss away the crutches of comfort and stand upon your own two feet, and develop the long-unused muscles of boldness and daring. Within you, God may see a diamond in the rough, which only the hard hits of courage can polish. Execute your resolutions immediately. Does competition trouble you? If so, continue to work. Is your competition an individual? Conquer your place in the world, for all things serve a brave soul. Combat difficulty bravely; sustain misfortune gallantly; endure poverty nobly; and encounter disappointment courageously!

Imagine that you came across a wooden board that measured twelve feet long, twelve inches wide, and four inches thick. You would have little difficulty walking from one end of the plank to the other. But if I stretched that same board between two buildings two hundred feet tall—with nothing but the hustle and bustle of the city traffic below—

could you summon the courage to walk the same board? Just think, same board, same distance, but a new element is introduced—one that alters your mental attitude, considerably—and that element is fear. The fear of what could happen. The fear of what might happen holds us back and keeps us in check. We permit ourselves to fail by default rather than run the risk of failing as a result of having made the effort to succeed. It's not important that we walk the length of the plank whether it's on the ground or suspended in air. But how many things are there at which we succeed that we could succeed at on a much larger scale? It's all a mental game that we picture in our minds. It's here, in our mind—not in actual practice—where we win or lose. As you read the following stories, I hope that you will find the courage to take risks, to fight through life's disasters, and to discover the strength that lies within you beyond the reach of fear.

THE PRICE OF SUCCESS

Society seldom hears of the failures of high achievers perhaps because it wants to think of these men and women in terms of success, not failure. On the other hand, many peak performers often avoid talking about or dwelling on their setbacks. Sometimes their setbacks are too painful to reflect upon. But occasionally, some will expand upon their failures long enough for others to learn practical lessons from their experiences. As it turns out, the clear-cut assessment of many successful individuals anchors around setbacks and rejection. Make no mistake about it: Victories that come easy are cheap. Achievement owes its growth to the striving of the will, the encounter with fear, the ever-present danger of failure. He who has never failed has never succeeded.

By 1983, Michael Hollis, a brilliant young black attorney, calculated his chances for success. It helped that he had a distinctive résumé and a working relationship with some of the nation's most powerful movers and shakers. But he possessed something far more important—a personal knowledge of what was truly possible. Hollis's brainchild, Air Atlanta, took center stage when he stepped boldly to the front and shared his vision: "It's my hope that we can build an airline to service the great multitude of business travelers."

What was it that prompted Hollis to leap into this industry at a time when many carriers were filing for bankruptcy? "I took one look at Atlanta's Hartsfield Airport and saw opportunity," Hollis stated. "Sure, on the surface, it was a risky move. But I've never been one to bow down to a prospect's possible failure. Given my appreciation for mass transportation and the fact that no airline catered exclusively to the business traveler, it was a chance that I had to take." He knew that launching an airline would be an extraordinarily difficult feat. Even without the obvious and prohibitive problems of timing and financing, the technical and managerial challenges alone would be staggering. After all, the public had already witnessed the death of Braniff Airlines and the near collapse of Eastern and Continental. Nonetheless, Hollis watched undeterred. Air Atlanta would be a testimony to its founder's ambition and talent.

Hollis was not the first black to take to the skies. When Warren Wheeler was in his teens, an older sister coaxed him into his first airplane ride. He was immediately sky-struck. Driven by his love of flying, Wheeler became president and principal stockholder of Piedmont Airlines, the nation's first black-owned, regularly scheduled airline. It was a small operation with a fleet of eleven single- and twin-engine props that flew to small North Carolina coastal communities. Wheeler launched his flying service in 1969 on savings and a shoestring. For nearly four years his business floundered until a regional commission sought to expand operations to several seaboard counties. By 1973, Wheeler's company was up and flying, grossing more than $1 million in profits that year.

Hollis was empowered by Wheeler's accomplishments, so much so that he, too, laid plans to blast forward. He was barely twenty-seven, and some people thought he was flying too high. But for all his innocence he would continue to focus on his goals. "I remember the criticism I received for such a lofty goal," Hollis recalled. "But I knew anything was possible."

"If I Were You, I Would Stand for Something"

Michael Hollis attended Dartmouth College and the University of Virginia, where he captured honors and a law degree. At both institutions he cut a path that led to unique experiences. He put the finishing touches on his scholastic career by presiding over the thirty-thousand-member student law section of the American Bar Association—the first black ever to do so.

Hollis later joined Oppenheimer and Company, a Wall Street investment firm, where he became a vice-president at twenty-six, one of the youngest ever. The fact that the youngest child of a Pullman porter and a social worker had come this far was the direct result of an active faith that Hollis acquired from his parents and mostly from his mentor, the late Dr. Benjamin Mays, former president of Morehouse College, who counseled, "If I were you, I'd stand for something."

On the surface, there appeared to be no way he could prevail with the airline. With no industry experience or capital, and starting up during an industrywide recession, Hollis invaded the turf ruled by Delta and Eastern—two carriers that controlled more than 90 percent of the market in the nation's second busiest airport—and bore straight ahead. His first task was to assemble a management team that would include seasoned airline veterans. He picked the pockets of Pan Am and American Airlines, supplying his organization with decades of airline experience. While his team developed most of the marketing and operating strategies, Hollis was free to concentrate on his forte—raising money. He flipped through his Rolodex, which displayed the names and addresses of the most influential men and women in corporate America. He also called upon Atlanta mayor and close friend Maynard Jackson. Jackson provided him with an entrée to the National Alliance of Postal and Federal Employees (NAPFE), the country's largest black industrial union. Convinced with the soundness of Hollis's idea, NAPFE invested $1 million of seed capital. This cash infusion gave Hollis the breathing room to piece together a comprehensive business plan, a tool that would attract the millions of dollars he would eventually need to get Air Atlanta up and running.

Hollis continued his pilgrimage and won financial commitments from the bluest of blue-chip investors. All totaled, the airline had been funded with $90 million; monies that had never before been equaled in black business history.

"It really looked as if we had turned the corner," said Hollis, cheerful, crisp, and openly excited. "But this is a tough business, and contrary to the appearance of things, failure dictates a need to exercise caution." Hollis figured he could create a sizable market niche by going against the grain and attracting the high-end business traveler. Moreover, he would lure prospective customers by offering super frills at coach fares. His tactic ran counter to the industry's trend. "No-frills" airline start-ups, such as People Express, initiated fare wars to lure price-conscious leisure travelers, especially those who didn't mind cramped quarters while toting their own luggage. Instead, Air Atlanta focused on luxury and positioned itself as the "airline born to serve business."

The Wings of Icarus

On paper, it appeared as if Hollis could actually pull it off. But his entrepreneurial overreach did appear, and his dream began to unravel. Air

Atlanta's need for capital caused hemorrhaging throughout the organization. Though the airline was funded with $90 million, it was ill prepared for the capital demands of a deregulated airline industry. From the beginning, the company had to contend with an erratic cash flow. "We never had enough money," Hollis stated privately. "We were never capitalized for more than two months at a time." What had prevented the airline from dissolving earlier was Hollis's ability to secure additional financing again and again. But this hand-to-mouth existence had two effects on his firm: First, the company had to make moves to generate cash for the near term, reducing the airline's prospects for long-term revenues; and second, it gave investors enormous power over the founder.

In the winter of 1985, with Air Atlanta desperately needing Equitable Life's $5-million cash infusion, the insurance giant prodded Hollis to hire former American Airlines executive Harry A. Kimbriel. Kimbriel had spent the past two years acting as an adviser to a federal bankruptcy judge in proceedings involving Continental Airlines. Not only was Continental revived and its creditors paid in full, but Continental became so solvent that its parent company—the Texas Air Corporation—was able to purchase Eastern Airlines, making Texas Air the nation's largest airline holding company. It was during the Continental proceeding that Equitable, which had been a creditor in the case, got its first look at Kimbriel. Weary of Air Atlanta's lackluster performance, Equitable encouraged Hollis to hire Kimbriel as a consultant.

Hollis was convinced that he wouldn't get the badly needed funding from Equitable unless he hired Kimbriel, and he agreed. It was clear that relations between the two men were rocky from the start. Kimbriel was widely seen as having been hired to turn the airline around—a perception that never sat well with Hollis. "I conceived Air Atlanta! I built it, and I'm going to run it," an indignant Hollis told a staffer.

To make matters worse, their differences didn't escape the notice of employees, some of whom began taking sides, further straining relations. In such an atmosphere, supporters of Hollis began circumventing Kimbriel in the chain of command, seeking directives from Hollis. Supporters of Kimbriel, in turn, met with the founder and asked him to step aside as chief executive officer and let Kimbriel take the reins. A petition was circulated and signed by more than one-third of the company's employees challenging Hollis's leadership. In an effort to gain control of the airline, Hollis fired Kimbriel, an act that ended internal dissension but also precluded further investment from the Equitable-led group.

"At Least We Tried"

In March 1986, Air Atlanta encountered rough air. The company faced a $55-million debt. In a fit of frenzy and trying to stave off bankruptcy proceedings, Hollis raised $18 million by selling five of its aircraft to Federal Express. Unfortunately, this proved to be too little too late. Potential investors saw him as a desperate man and withdrew their offers, while once faithful backers began to call in their notes. Consequently, three years of effort and hope came to a screeching halt. Heartbroken, the young entrepreneur with high-flung dreams brooded over his loss. "The problem was simple: The airline wasn't large enough. We managed only eight planes at sixty percent capacity. It cost us damn near every dime. But at least we tried."

What went wrong? Everything was so carefully planned. All the details were meticulously mapped out. Such a major commitment of manpower and financial resources, supported by some of the best management talent. How could this have happened?

As with most business ventures, there is no one simple answer to why the airline failed. The marketplace is complex. Many things contributed to the demise of Air Atlanta, among them poor judgment and volatile egos. Immersed in the brutally competitive world of air travel, Hollis remained oblivious to the tensions and disappointments around him. But even in failure, the Air Atlanta story is instructive. Through it all, Michael Hollis uncovered the central lesson of life: that failure is neither tragedy nor humiliation. Those who have dared have moved the world. The courageous provide an example to the intrepid; their influence is magnetic. People follow them even to their graves. And as Hollis's mentor, Benjamin Mays, was noted to say on occasion: "It must be born in mind that failure to reach your goal is not tragic. The tragedy lies in not having a goal to reach." Nothing is more tragic than encountering a person who believes that his or her life has no meaning, that he or she has no contribution to make. Deep down we all want to know that our lives do make a difference. Though finding a passion is a prelude to finding our purpose, it is the spirit of courage that will transform your life. Courage alone will unlock the gate that leads to the secret power that is stored within you.

THE FOUR BASIC FEARS

Why don't more of us chase our dreams? Why are so many of us reduced to playing out marginal lives of frustration and underachievement? These are lives that fret the future, conceal rare talents, and silence special dreams; lives that indulge in the cowardice of being too careful; lives that supposedly find success by avoiding failure. Why, in heaven's name, do so many find a good alibi far more attractive than actual accomplishment? Why do so few even try to reach their goals? When people are hard-pressed, why do excuses suddenly emerge. But after a decade of research and consultation, I've learned to spot the real reason—fear!—in all its forms and variations: fear of poverty, fear of death, fear of change and uncertainty, and, arguably the most destructive, fear of failure.

Fear is the single greatest obstacle to success. For some, fear blocks the path to the winner's circle. For others, it creates total paralysis. No one enslaved by fear is rich, either materially or spiritually. It is fear that robs us of happiness and freedom. It is fear that steals our peace of mind. It is fear that causes us to settle for far less than we are capable of. Mankind's greatest weakness consists not in the riches he possesses, but in his failure to grab his share. It is fear that is the root cause of negative emotions, unhappiness, and problems in human relationships. The only positive aspect regarding the emotion of fear is that it is learned, and consequently, it can be *un*learned.

Fear is controlled, not overcome. The expression of fear denies men and women the use of the true power of thought—a power so potent that it can enable anyone to overcome any circumstance or setback. Each of us, to some degree, suffers from one or more of the four basic fears of failure. Some people suffer from all of them. The courageous are not men and women who have yet to experience the paralyzing emotions of fear. Courageous people act in spite of their fear. When you face your fears and move toward them, they diminish and recede. But when you back away from the circumstance or person that you fear, those strange powers grow until they can actually dominate your life. You must drive out these negative influences before the positive power of courage can overtake your inhibitions. Franklin Roosevelt's famous words, "The only thing we have to fear is fear itself," are as applicable now as when he offered them during the Depression. Probe deeply into your subconscious and be sure that none of these four costly fears resides within your mind.

FEAR OF POVERTY

Nothing brings humanity so much suffering and humiliation as poverty! Believe it or not, poverty is a state of mind that, if left unchecked, can destroy all chances of progress and achievement. The fear of poverty circulates around the idea that too many people believe they have no value to bring to the world. These individuals are too often infected with the negative consciousness of personal need rather than inspired by the positive consciousness of personal value. As a result, there are more people feeling needy than those who feel valuable. This fear paralyzes the gift of imagination, destroys self-reliance, circumvents enthusiasm and ambition, and breeds the habit of negative expectation. Instead of concentrating on why a particular idea might work, the individual discovers all the reasons why a given plan or concept will not work, and he acts accordingly. Some people are so eager to unlock the shackles of lack and limitation that they will acquire wealth in whatever manner they can—through legal or illegal means.

Since life is an expensive proposition, you will discover that you and I were born to be rich. Wealth is not limited to money, but embraces value—value and potential. We sometimes find ourselves stuck in a rut of mediocrity, and we stagnate not because of *who* we are (our potential), but because of *how* we are (our behavior). You can be rich without being wealthy. The Creator views you and me as pure value or unlimited potential. In other words, you are too *valuable* to be poor; you are too *valuable* to be downtrodden; you are too *valuable* to be lifeless or hopeless. We live in a world that demands value and, in turn, rewards value with money. Once you realize how valuable you are and how much you have going for you, the smiles will return, the sun will break out of the clouds, wealth will find its way to your door, and you will finally be able to live in the manner that your Creator intended.

Whatever may be said in praise of poverty, the fact remains that it is hard to live a complete or successful life unless one feels rich—materially or spiritually. There is nothing wrong with wanting to be rich. We are instructed from above that the love of money is the root of evil. But the desire for wealth is really the desire for a richer, fuller, more abundant life. And that desire is praiseworthy. The person who does not desire to live more abundantly is uncommon. And the individual who does not desire enough money to secure his or her needs will not live to his or her full potential. No one can rise to his full potential in talent or soul development unless he possesses a "prosperity consciousness."

People develop in mind, body, and soul by utilizing rare special gifts. Everything that lives has an inalienable right to all the development it is capable of attaining. Your right to life means that you possess the right to have free and unrestricted use of all things that may be necessary to fulfill your highest mental, physical, and spiritual development—in other words, *your right to be rich!*

FEAR OF DEATH

What is the strongest force known to mankind? What is the power that carries humanity from the waters of doom and destruction to the shores of success? What God-given energy rescues the hope-filled from the hopeless, the up-and-coming from the down-and-out, the strong from the weak? The spiritual power of life itself. Every living thing on earth is given a measure of the life-giving force. All that is required of the lower forms of life—the plant and animal kingdoms—is to "bring forth fruit according to its kind." Of you and me, however, much more is expected. We are sons and daughters of a creator. Therefore, creation is required. You are to spread seeds not merely of humankind but of intellect as well. You are to leave the world a better place than you found it, with more joy, more love, more understanding, more harmony, and more life. The real purpose of life is expression, the constant urge upward and onward. You and I are channels for power. There is no limit to the creative life force that flows to us and through us in this plane of existence and others. As the following story demonstrates, fear not—that which lives can never die. Truth, love, spirit, life—there is no other power!

It happened in the first quarter of a bitterly fought football game. It was homecoming and the stadium was brimming with excitement. Thousands of Ole Miss fans were on their feet screaming as Vanderbilt threatened to score. Vandy's quarterback threw a pass to wide receiver Brad Gaines. In a split second, Chucky Mullins, a free safety, read the play perfectly and tackled Gaines, his helmet crashing into Gaines's back the instant the ball arrived. There was a snap, then a crack. A moment later, Chucky lay sprawled on the field motionless, fully conscious, his neck broken and his spine shattered. He later said that it wasn't the pain that scared him; it was the total absence of it.

On the sidelines, University of Mississippi coach Billy Brewer said a silent prayer. "Please, God, not Chucky. He's had so much pain in his life. Let it be a dislocated shoulder, a pinched nerve—anything but a broken neck." But looking at Chucky, he knew. In his heart he knew. "It was the first time in all my years of coaching that I didn't go out onto the field," the head coach said softly. "I was frozen. I just couldn't."

Chucky was taken by helicopter to Baptist Memorial Hospital in nearby Memphis, where he underwent a three-hour operation in which doctors used wire and a bone graft from his pelvis to fuse four vertebrae in his neck. Carver Phillips, his guardian and closest friend, was heartsick. He knew that Chucky's life was one endless stream of poverty and pain. When he was orphaned at twelve, Chucky phoned Phillips, who was then his basketball coach, and innocently asked if he would take him in. Without batting an eye, Phillips agreed and never looked back. But it was never easy. Phillips's wife, Karen, worked in a sewing-machine factory to help make ends meet. Chucky found a job washing cars at a gas station. One morning, the manager had sent him to clean the rest room and didn't think about him again until lunchtime. Then he went around back, fully expecting to find Chucky asleep. Instead he found him standing tiptoe on a chair, polishing the overhead plumbing pipes. Floor, walls, bowls, mirrors—everything gleamed. "Son, a person could eat off this floor," the stunned manager said. "Why didn't you quit?"

"Quit!" Chucky replied. "Nobody ever told me to quit." That was Chucky Mullins.

> It is not what you have lost but what you have left that counts.
>
> —Chucky Mullins

Karen and Carver Phillips drove to Memphis, heavy-hearted. Doctors told the couple that the force with which Chucky hit the Vanderbilt receiver caused at least four vertebrae to fracture "explosively." There was a danger his lungs could fail; his condition was critical. Later, they rendered the prognosis everyone feared. Chucky was paralyzed. Forever. He'd received a fractured dislocation of the neck's fourth and fifth cervical vertebrae. Not only would he never walk again, he'd be a quadriplegic for the rest of his life.

A month after the tragedy, Chucky had trouble breathing, and doctors performed an emergency tracheotomy. He remained desperately ill, but not disheartened. Teammates who visited found him unable to speak because of the opening in his throat. Chucky brushed off questions about his health. In typical fashion he gestured that he was doing fine. "It is not what you have lost," he reasoned, "but what you have left that counts." What interested him was how *they* were doing.

Ole Miss officials quickly established a Chuck Mullins Trust Fund and invited contributions from students, alumni, and other universities in the Southeast Conference to help meet the staggering medical costs, nearly $10,000 a month. They also decided to take up a collection at an upcoming Louisiana State game. If there were doubts about how Mississippians would respond to an appeal for a black student, they were not voiced. When a call went out for student volunteers to carry plastic buckets soliciting contributions, the needed 150 were signed up in an hour. Hundreds more had to be thanked and sent away. A record 42,354 people turned out for the game, cheering wildly when the Ole Miss Rebels ran onto the field with Chucky's number, 38, on the side of every player's helmet. The next day, in the bursar's office, the money collected was everywhere—checks in trays; ones, fives, tens, and twenties stacked up on chairs and spilling out of fried-chicken buckets. The tally came to $178,168.

Chucky, who was permitted to sit up and listen to part of the LSU game on the radio, was stunned to hear the announcers describe the outpouring of affection for him. Soon his story was being told all over America. Donations arrived from every state in the nation. By mid-November, the total had climbed to $350,000. Later, as the university prepared to elect its "Colonel Rebel," seven standout students, six white, withdrew their candidacies. "It is our hope," they wrote in a joint letter to the dean, "that all students will show their support by voting for Chucky." Three months later, Chucky was moved to the Spain Rehabilitation Center in Birmingham, Alabama. By July, a recurrent bladder infection and related problems required surgery. Still, if there were any dark moments, he kept them to himself.

Against all odds, Chucky returned to classes in January 1991. Some said that was his greatest achievement, but he had an even more breathtaking goal. "I hope to get up out of this chair," he told a reporter. "I know what the doctors say, but I will never quit trying." On Wednesday, May 1, of the same year, as he was preparing for class, Chucky suddenly stopped breathing. A blood clot shut down his lungs. A nurse attending him immediately began artificial respiration, and he was rushed to the hospital. The courageous young man with a heart as big as the world, and who was so easy to love, never regained consciousness and died five days later. The Rebel team was present when Chucky was laid to rest beside his mother in Russellville, Alabama. The entire southeast region was caught up in the moment. Everything ground to a halt. One by one, the Ole Miss players tried to say good-bye, but many could not. Teammate Chris Mitchell summed up everyone's feelings. "God brought Chucky into our lives, and He hasn't taken him away. Some people, like Chucky, are bigger than death; they never die." The special man goes to his grave with a shout!

It is startling to discover how many people acquiesce to the idea of death, and begin to make all sorts of preparations for death, even at a time when they should be enjoying the fullness of life. Life is not simply a journey between two points on an endless highway. Life is eternal, and we are alive in eternity now. Death has no place in the fullness of life, and the individual who holds to the life idea cannot die. What we think of as death is simply the movement of the soul experience of life from one vessel of experience into another vessel.

It may be difficult for most people to interpret death as being anything but an unavoidable tragedy, but this limited view can be broadened by understanding the great plan of the universe: You and I are perfect now—created perfectly—one with our Creator. The will of God is the ceaseless longing of the spirit in you to completely fulfill your potential. It is God seeking to express Himself as you—as radiant health, as eternal youth, as freedom from limitation. It is only the personality—the human ego—that is born and dies, and that seeks and strives to keep us bound to beliefs and opinions of death. It is only when we rise up in the realization of our divine immortality and omnipotence that we can free ourselves from the terrible pangs of the fear of death. Turn away from the appearance of death. "Do not search for the living among the dead." Seek understanding and truth. Know that truth is not something you learn or accumulate, but something you unfold within yourself.

The story is told of the old sage sitting beneath a tree in Egypt. The spirit of the plague went by. "Whither goest thou?" the wise man asked. "I go to Cairo, where I shall slay one hundred Egyptians" was the reply. Three months later, the spirit of the plague again passed the old sage on its journey. "You said you would slay one hundred in Cairo, but travelers tell me you slew ten thousand," said the wise man in disbelief. To which the spirit of the plague replied, "I slew but one hundred. *Fear slew the rest!*" As one learns to be at home in the spiritual and mental world, all of his or her fears lessen and with the easing of fear comes an easing of the effects of fear.

It was September 1994 and now the battle seemed nearly over. Jean Young, lifelong activist and champion of education, was about to end her fight with cancer and everyone knew it. During a book signing featuring her husband's best-seller, a well-wisher approached Andrew Young and inquired about his wife. Without fear or trepidation, the former mayor said, "She's ready," and then added, "I think we're all ready."

None of us have ever been promised a life free of pain or disappointment. Rather, the most any of us has been promised is that we need not be alone in our pain and that we can draw upon a source outside ourselves for strength and courage. Our Creator does not cause our suffering, but rather, helps us by inspiring others to help. Little minds are tamed and subdued by misfortune—great minds rise above it. The Lord is your light and your salvation. Whom shall you fear?

FEAR OF CHANGE AND UNCERTAINTY

Many would-be achievers are stymied by the prospect of forgoing a steady paycheck or facing the unknown. Most simply cannot withstand the risk. But, to be creative, to venture forward, to succeed, one must be willing to *lose* what one has—to embrace uncertainty, to replace security with *in*security. To find true happiness, to be fulfilled, to be at peace with yourself and others, you must learn to take risks.

As the Air Atlanta story suggests, there are instances when circumstances necessitate a gamble or a risk—risk of social displeasure, risk of reputations, even risk of fortune. To paraphrase Michael Hollis's discourse as he pondered his start-up: "I knew it was a risky proposition, but it was a move that I had to take." During the research for this book, I encountered instances when people have been willing to engage in—and have even sought out—the calculated risk. Men and women who have forsaken cushy jobs; people who packed up their belongings and moved beyond the hidden boundaries, mortgaged their homes, and even borrowed money from family and friends to take their shot at a new life.

For example, Thomas Burrell put "every penny into an untried business plan" to launch Burrell Advertising—America's top black advertising firm. Lee Dunham quit his job as a New York cop and gambled $31,000—his entire savings—to market McDonald's hamburgers in the inner city. J. Bruce Llewellyn left one high-level position after another and leveraged everything he owned, just for the opportunity to resurrect a dying urban food chain that could eventually springboard him to greater heights.

"What is success?" I asked Bill White, baseball's National League president. "Success," he replied, "is the ability to close the door on your past, regardless of your failures, and move forward. In other words, if you're not on the way, you're in the way, so it's best that you get out of the way!"

Percy Sutton left politics, including a chance to become New York City's first black mayor, to acquire a string of radio stations located in marginal markets. Henry Parks sold his house and a life insurance policy to raise the necessary capital to market his sausage to a predominantly white clientele. "Don't tell me about the odds," Parks said emphatically. "Hell, you make the odds!"

John H. Johnson pawned his mother's furniture to start *Negro Digest,* a small black magazine with an even smaller readership. "Most people don't really believe in success," Johnson quips. "They feel helpless before they even begin. 'Whitey's' not keeping blacks down. Black America has the power to make it in this society, and so we can't blame the system for everything. Fear gets in the way."

Wayne Dyer, author of the best-seller *Your Erroneous Zones,* discusses the days when we succumb to the power of fear because we fail to live in the present moment. We feel guilty about something that happened yesterday or we are afraid to face something that might happen tomorrow, and we fail to reach total fulfillment today. Fear can keep us from enjoying today.

Wilma Rudolph personified elegance and grace on the track. Off the track, the sprinter who won three gold medals at the 1960 Olympic Games symbolized determination. "Wilma had a great outlook on life," said Ed Temple, who coached Rudolph and several other greats at Tennessee State University. "She could relate to anybody. She would say, 'You'll never know what you can accomplish until you get up and try.' "

The path to success lies within the virtue of courage, taking action, and possessing the flexibility to change until you have reached your objective. C. S. Lewis, the English critic and novelist, wrote, "Courage is not simply one of the virtues, but the form of every virtue at the testing point." In our modern world, with debate over a common sense of morality, we're faced with questions of right and wrong every day. It's not unusual to feel our virtues tested. Mostly, they're small things. But even with a firm system of beliefs, choices can be difficult. It has been said that courage is faith put into action. When a person has faith in himself, his values, and the worth of the goal being pursued, sometimes the simplest of acts can be the most courageous of acts. Courage is acting on what you are.

FEAR OF FAILURE

The fear of failure is the major cause of stress and negativity. Realize there is no such thing as failure. Failure is not a single, earthshaking event. We do not fail overnight. Failure is the inevitable result of an accumulation of poor thinking and poor choices. Simply put, failure is nothing more than a few errors in judgment repeated every day. Keep this in mind and you will achieve all that you can conceive in your mind. You never fail, you simply produce results. Most of us have been programmed to fear this thing we call failure. Yet, all of us can think of times when we wanted one thing but received another. We have all flunked a test, stumbled through a series of relationships, watched a well-thought-out business plan go awry. High-achieving men and women aren't people who do not fail, they're individuals who know that if they try something and it doesn't give them what they want, they simply dismiss it as a learning experience. They use what they have learned and try something else. What is the one asset, the one benefit, you have today over yesterday? The answer, of course, is experience. Those who fear failure compose a mental picture of what might not work or what may go wrong. As a result, this act alone keeps them from taking the very action that could secure their desires.

Many men and women have conquered tough challenges, have fought their way through anguish and defeat to great personal triumph. Many have achieved outstanding success in the arts, literature, science, and medicine—in almost every field of human endeavor—in spite of their fears. They seek the rocky and thorny path. Every hazard is inspiring to them. Every problem is a new adventure. No one can be a failure who is upright and true. No right cause is a failure. There is but one failure, and that is not to be the best that is in us. But what is failure? What must a person do or not do in order to fail or to be designated as a failure?

Maya Angelou grew up in staggering poverty in a small southern town. When she was seven years old, she and her older brother moved to St. Louis, Missouri, to live with their divorced mother. A few months after their arrival, Maya was raped by her mother's boyfriend. The crime was soon discovered, the offender was brought to trial, and Maya was forced to testify. Several days later her assailant was found beaten to death. Shocked by the seeming connection between her testimony at the trial and the death of the accused, Maya vowed to never speak in public again. She kept this dark corner of her life close to her heart for more than thirty years until she wrote her encouraging and metaphysical autobiography, *I Know Why the Caged Bird Sings,* published in 1970. The book sold several thousand copies and won a handful of literary awards but was soon forgotten except by a small number of connoisseurs of creative writing.

From a publisher's point of view, the book experienced only modest success, and critics were less than enthusiastic. At that critical moment in her life, how would *you* measure Maya's success? Failure does not come to a person because he or she is not recognized by the multitudes during his or her crucial moments. Success or failure has nothing to do with the opinions of others. It is only concerned with our opinions of ourselves and what we are doing. When you rely on the opinions of others, the roadblocks and rejections obscure the victories.

For the next twenty-two years, Maya poured herself into a number of artistic activities, mostly poetry and theater, and today, thanks in part to that memorable moment during the inauguration of President Bill Clinton, when Maya Angelou recited the poem she had written for the occasion, "On the Pulse of Morning," sales of her autobiography are into the millions and it has become a literary classic. Though it took more than two decades, *I Know Why the Caged Bird Sings* lives in print, probably forever. And with it, Maya Angelou moves into the company of the literary immortals.

Throughout his schooling, Colin Powell failed many times at New York's City College, but his name will forever be linked with courage and noble character.

Luther Vandross was mocked and ridiculed for eight straight nights when he participated in the Apollo Theater's amateur contests. His audience threw objects and shouted obscenities as promoters dragged him offstage. Yet now no one would think of naming anyone else if asked who is the greatest of the soulful balladeers.

Lani Guinier did not win her cause to serve her country, but she did achieve fame as an orator and apostle of minority and women's rights. Don't poison your future with the pain of the past. Refuse to be intimidated by people or circumstances.

Failure becomes the final test of persistence. It either crushes life or solidifies it. The wounded oyster mends its shell with pearl. "Failure is, in a sense," says William Keats, a nineteenth-century essayist, "the highway to success, inasmuch as every discovery of what is false leads us to seek earnestly after what is true, and every fresh experience points out some form of error which we shall afterward carefully avoid."

Are you afraid of failure? Well, how do you feel about learning? You can learn from every human experience. The critical success question that eliminates all failure is: What can I do better *next* time? If you address this question, you ensure that you will redouble your efforts and try, try, try again until you reach your objective.

I know firsthand about the gifts that can only come by overcoming the fear of failure. After laboring diligently for seven years on what was to become *Think and Grow Rich: A Black Choice,* and with no end in sight, I spent a day with Arthur G. Gaston, the dean of black entrepreneurs. As a twelve-year-old, Gaston picked hundreds of pounds of cotton for pennies a day. But as the decade of the 1990s takes shape, this soft-spoken black man with an eighth-grade education is now board chairman and president of at least ten businesses worth more than $50 million.

I sat in his office firing questions at point-blank range on wealth, achievement, and success. As I concluded the interview, my emotions suddenly became too much to bear. The purpose of my research was to uncover a formula for wealth and achievement that anyone could use. But ironically, I had found myself saddled with debt, called crazy by family and friends, and I could see no way out. With tears in my eyes, I sat before this giant of a man with thoughts of ending this endless search.

I thought about my inability to support my family. Without a dime to my name, overcome with guilt, I struggled with my own self-worth. My spirit had weakened. I was reduced to tears, and I didn't care—I had grown tired. I grew tired of the constant struggle. I was sick and tired of being broke; I grew tired of ducking and dodging creditors; I grew tired of explaining to my family why I wasn't quite making it; I grew tired of the endless streams of rejections from employers and publishers that never seemed to stop. But, mostly, I just grew tired—and this was the day, the hour, the minute, the moment that I said, "To hell with it." And who knows, I might not have written *this* book if Dr. Gaston hadn't shared his thoughts of inspiration. As he lit his pipe, he sensed my uneasiness. He looked me in the eye and said, "Don't tell me it's too hard! Great men and women must be tested in the laboratory of adversity. Fear not, young man, continue to move forward. Greatness takes time. What you can do, you ought to do. But if you are satisfied just to get by, then step aside for the man or woman who isn't!"

YOU MUST REALIZE that all external events lack any emotional component in their makeup. All external events are inherently neutral until you mentally respond and assign an emotional context to them. Nearly all fears are imaginary. They are a product of your mind and do not exist in reality. Unfortunately, you are trampled by forces that you create yourself. The key to eliminating unnecessary fear from your life is to create and hold firmly to positive images. Your fear is real only to the extent that you allow your mind to create it, and then allow your body to feel it.

Throughout the Bible, again and again, the root of inspiration and attainment is stressed: "Prove me now herewith, saith the Lord of hosts, if I will not open you the windows of heaven, and pour you out a blessing, that there shall not be room enough to receive it." Remember, the Creator never consults your past to determine your future.

THE EIGHT STEPS TO GREATER COURAGE

Anyone can develop the quality of courage. But it takes effort and daily practice. Here are some guides.

1. *Raise your level of consciousness.* The basic pattern for acquiring courage must be rooted in conviction and the desire to win. You can apply this pattern to all areas of your life—spiritual, family, and financial. You may want to become rich, happy, and fulfilled. There is no need to sacrifice any of these desires. You can have all of them; it is only a matter of consciousness. Consciousness is made up of awareness, sensitivity, and application. You need to develop assurance, devotion, daring, persistence, and an enthusiastic desire to succeed. Keep your consciousness high with a life-affirming optimism and the expectation of fulfillment. When you open yourself up to abundance, you begin to act in abundant ways. So many times along the way I was told by "experts" how futile my efforts were to tell the world about *Think and Grow Rich: A Black Choice.* But within my heart, I knew that though their advice might be true for them, it only made me more willing to do what I had to do. Success is not arriving there; it is earning the right to be there consciously. You will never reach the palace thinking like a peasant.

2. *You're one of a kind—be creative.* Develop your originality, resourcefulness, and the ability to assert your individuality. Become a self-starter, an independent thinker, able to carry out your own plans. It takes courage to go your own way, ignoring the crowd, the world's opinion. But each act of courage is an option exercised which helps to build a reservoir of energy and faith in your ability

to stick it out and achieve. The more you accomplish, the more you can accomplish. The more challenges you conquer, the more you can conquer.

3. *Stop using the "F" word.* Many achievers would like to see the word "failure" stricken from the dictionary. There is no failure, only feedback. Live and learn. You should not dwell on your mistakes or setbacks, but instead learn from them and then move on. Adopt and apply the success formula: $K + A + C = E$. *K:* Become a sponge for new information and develop *knowledge* in your chosen field of endeavor. *A:* Put this newfound knowledge into *action. C: Commit* yourself to reach your objectives and let nothing deter you. *E:* Use these three keys to achieve *empowerment.* Remember, there is no such thing as failure. You never fail, you simply produce results. "Never look for excuses," Dr. Ben Carson suggests. "Instead of surrendering to failure, find a way to succeed." Failure cannot happen in your life without your permission.

4. *Be prepared.* Help insulate yourself by mapping a plan and then follow through regardless of the circumstances. Do you have talents that could bring in an income if your employer handed you a pink slip? It may be necessary to adapt your plan to shifting conditions or new requirements. But keep your eyes on your goal. With this strategy, you will not only achieve your goals but also find yourself strengthened in the process.

5. *Don't take failure personally.* Those who have experienced a failure tend to view themselves and their failure as one and the same. That's wrong. You and your failure are not identical, and you must learn to view your past circumstances separately. When things go sour, do you label yourself a loser? The language you use to describe yourself can become a powerful reality. Never grumble at your fate, complain, or feel sorry for yourself. Dissolve doubts daily. Work on yourself every day. Shakespeare wrote, "Our doubts are traitors, and make us lose the good we oft might win, by fearing to attempt." Failure is an attitude as well as an outcome. Fears bind us and beget regret. Doubts are destructive. Rout them out as you develop the attitudes that express courage, and never personalize your failures.

6. *Learn how to say "I can!"* Affirm to yourself with energy and conviction, "I can do it! I can do it!" This affirmation short-circuits and cancels out the feeling of "I can't! I can't!" Then do the thing you fear. Confront your fear. Move toward your fear. Use your specific fear as a challenge and instead of backing away from it or avoiding it, confront it and face it head-on.

7. *You'll never march alone.* Spiritual understanding gives you the stamina to stand up, challenge, and change each negative thought and feeling into a positive one. No one walks the road of life alone. One of the most consoling, and truest, assurances given to us is found in the Bible: "Fear not, for I am with you always." Faith in those words will give you spiritual strength to meet any situation or circumstance. Arthur Ashe, tennis star, author, and AIDS activist, called it "winning the match that matters most." The courage of his conviction, blended with tenacity, left behind the stamp of greatness.

8. *Remain centered and meditate.* Clear your mind. Spend twenty minutes at the beginning of every day in silence. Sit quietly and focus on your objectives—not your obstacles. During meditation, your fears will disappear. Tap into the energy that is concentrated in the spaces between your thoughts. Your motivating force should be your goal—not someone else's measure of success. Don't allow chaos to distract you from the task at hand. An African sage said, "Most people spend their lives either in the past or in the future." Live in the present—it's the best way to prepare for a future event. Every few hours, check where you are mentally and relinquish any attachment to the outcome.

Keep these proven action steps for courage in mind at all times. They are involved in every aspect of life. When you practice these steps, you'll never surrender to the dark shadows of fear again. Your spirit wouldn't allow you. You'll discover that success is simply a matter of affirming positive expectations and moving forward. The world seeks those who are willing to throw themselves into battle; who take the unconventional position; who give heart and spirit to terror—the surprise, fear, and exhilaration of the unexplored. The world always stands aside for the courageous soul.

WHAT DOES IT TAKE?

To be beaten, but not broken; to be victorious, but not boastful; to strive and contend for the prize, and to win it honestly or lose it graciously; to use every resource within your disposal, courage lies at the core of success. "The lowest ebb," wrote Henry Wadsworth Longfellow, the nineteenth-century American poet, "is the turn of the tide. Write on the doors the saying wise and old, be bold, be bold, everywhere be bold!" All the great works of the world have been accomplished by courage, and the world's greatest victories are always born in the face of defeat. Failure wins no victory over such men and women.

A great deal of talent is lost in the world for the want of a little courage. Each day men and women go to their graves unnoticed because timidity prevented them from making an honest effort. If only they could have been induced to begin, they would in all probability have gone far in their chosen career. To accomplish anything worthwhile, you must not stand back thinking only of danger and what might have been: "Yea, though I walk through the valley of the shadow of death, I will fear no evil." All achievers have seen their worst fears realized. But, like a prizefighter battered, bloodied, but still fighting, they come to the realization: *I have taken the worst beating the world has to offer, and yet I still stand! I know everything there is to know about the downside of life.* At that moment, they have crossed a line beyond fear. And, freed from fear, they have fought back, furiously, deliberately, without compromise, without hesitation. The winner finds undiscovered reserves of courage within.

The course of history has been changed by men and women willing to dare. And those daring enough to do. Life is a breathtaking adventure—but it is also a struggle. Every winner has scars. Courage requires ambition, audacity, and an unflagging will to succeed. It demands a drive to be different. It means scraping and escaping the barnacles of old ideas. It takes a spirit that welcomes nonconformity, filled with a zeal, an exuberance, and an ardor for the uncertain. Courage is the result of not giving up, of carrying on despite problems of time, place, or circumstance. Courage begets the determination to succeed in a particular area of life despite a mountain of apparently insurmountable obstacles. Courage to accept a difficult and disagreeable circumstance may be the beginning of the breakthrough to freedom.

You hear it all the time, the clang and clatter of those trembling and trepid souls who regularly remind you "It can't be done" and "We've never done it that way!" But you know this to be true: that no great plan is accomplished without overcoming endless obstacles which test the mettle of your determination and the endurance of faith. The man or woman who wins may have been counted out several times, but he or she didn't hear the referee. Suppose Columbus had allowed himself to be disheartened by much "wiser," more "seasoned" sailors; suppose Moses had chosen to be the son of Pharaoh's daughter rather than the liberator of his race; suppose Nat Turner would have turned back in fear; suppose Nelson Mandela had yielded to the threats of apartheid; and suppose 250,000 tireless marchers would have been reluctant to exchange tired feet for tired souls on that 1963 steamy-hot, August day in the nation's capital. Not only would the stream of history have been changed, but what a loss it would have been to the dignity of mankind!

What does it take? You be the judge. It takes the power of an inner force to live life on your terms and not someone else's. It takes a tinge of spirituality to build and forge positive relationships in the face of discouragement, hatred, violence, and despair. It takes the temerity to avoid toxic people—the complainers, the resigners, the shoulder-shruggers—those individuals who would rather ask for help than help themselves. It takes true grit and mettle to end the cycle of poverty and dependence and complacency that occurs too frequently in our inner cities. It takes nerve, black children, to stand and deliver, to excel and surpass, as you turn a deaf ear to poor scholastic expectations. It takes heroism, black male, to stand firm through thick and thin, to keep the family together no matter what and reverse the tide of single-parent households. What does it take? It takes the first peg on the profile of the achiever—it takes a ripple of daring!

Moses found his rod a serpent until he took it by the tail; and, if we face our challenges boldly, our greatest liabilities will become our most cherished assets.

Look at Harriet Tubman reading an advertisement in a southern newspaper: "Five thousand dollars will be paid for the head of a runaway slave woman by the Governor of South Carolina!" Behold her again, a vigilante mob replete with bloodhounds and a hangman's noose is hot on her trail. See her calmly and unflinchingly return to the same state to transport hundreds of slaves to freedom's safe harbor. She was to have said in William Lloyd Garrison's *Liberator:* "Let there be no mistake, for this I will not equivocate. I will not excuse nor will I retreat a single inch until the last slave breathes free." How could fear prevail against such a resolute will? It takes the heart of little David and the faith of Moses—a woman called Black Moses!

With the coming of each new day, John Lucas's life is a testament to the powers of redemption. When he broke into professional basketball in 1976, he was the first college player selected by the National Basketball Association draft. He seemed to have a lock on fame and fortune. Instead, Lucas moved through nine teams in the league and failed two drug tests. The turnaround came in March 1986, when Lucas missed a practice with the Houston Rockets, failed a drug test, and was released by the team. He immediately went on a cocaine binge that left him shoeless and soaked with urine on the streets of Houston. Days later, he checked himself in for treatment for the fifth time. This time it worked!

The former Maryland University great still keeps the red and white tennis shoes he forgot to wear on his last night of drug bingeing. Lucas does not like to be called a role model, yet for many talented athletes who have fallen into the abyss of drug abuse, he is a hero, someone who had the courage to climb back out. During one of his frequent high school talks, he was asked what it takes. "It takes the mental courage to pick up the shattered pieces, hold on, dig deep, and make it through another day."

It took a driving will for Anna Mae Bullock, Tina Turner, to endure the rags-to-riches life of an abused pop idol. On the first leg of a national tour, she finally walked away from a shaky marriage with nothing more than thirty-six cents and a gasoline credit card. Thus began the slow trek back from marital violence to freedom, independence, and worldwide superstardom that only courage could bring.

It took guts for Earleatha "Cookie" Johnson just to stand. To stand by her husband, basketball great Magic Johnson, in his hour of need; to stand in opposition to the medical community with its faithless facts; and to stand up to the tabloids as they tried to splash her with their mud. To this precious black woman, courage is both a gift and a reward that allows you to enjoy because you have fought, rest because you have labored, and reap because you have sown. "I do not fear life without my husband," she explains while fighting back tears. "If God is for you, who can be against you?"

It took "something deep within" for Cornel West to pen the best-seller *Race Matters*. In little more than a hundred pages, the Harvard-trained scholar eloquently challenges black leadership to seek the moral high ground as it searches for answers to the troubled black experience. "The gift desired most in times of peace and in war," he revealed during a Sunday church service, "is a steadfast soul."

A constant struggle, a ceaseless battle to bring success from inhospitable surroundings, is the price of all great achievements. The man or woman who has not fought his or her way up to his own loaf, and who does not bear the scars of desperate conflict, does not know the highest meaning of courage.

At his first meeting with Branch Rickey, Jackie Robinson was lectured by the Brooklyn Dodgers president on the abuse he would face: taunts, beanballs, Jim Crow accommodations. "Are you looking for a Negro who's afraid to fight back?" Robinson asked. "I'm looking for a ballplayer with guts enough *not* to fight back," Rickey replied. Robinson, who had been court-martialed for refusing to move to the back of a segregated army bus, had plenty of guts—and in April 1947 he took the first step toward erasing modern baseball's color line when he joined the Dodgers' minor-league affiliate in Montreal. He was such an accomplished athlete that even if he had been white, this would have rated headlines: This articulate and disciplined infielder was an athletic genius who broke the national junior college broad-jump record, then became UCLA's first four-sport letterman, in baseball, basketball, football, and track. He was playing in the Negro Leagues when one of Rickey's scouts spotted him. Still, as Robinson's first season loomed, the question remained: Could he take the heat and make the majors? Much more than his own career was riding on the answer.

Mary Ann Wright, known to thousands of Oakland, California, residents as Mother Wright, prepares and distributes hundreds of food bags for needy people. Mother Wright says that the Lord's voice woke her up one day and told her to go feed the hungry. Such a simple act of kindness would paralyze others with fear. Using her $236 Social Security check, she bought, cooked, and distributed food to indigent people in a nearby park. Since then, she has served hot meals each Saturday, rain or shine, to Oakland's homeless population. "The Lord has always shown me a way," Mother Wright confesses. "I tell my volunteers to fix plates just like they would for themselves. The homeless are no less than you and me."

As the sculptor thinks only of the dove imprisoned in the marble block, Nature cares only for the soul of the man or woman confined within the human being. The sculptor will chip off the unnecessary pieces of stone to set the bird free. Nature, in turn, will chip away on us unceasingly to bring out our possibilities. Every day of his life William H. Gray III takes blocks of granite and chisels them into fine works of art. As executive director of the United Negro College Fund (UNCF), Gray widens the doors of education for thousands of black college hopefuls. "Wealth is nothing, fame is nothing, character is everything," he exhorts with the fever of a southern preacher. "Through these generous gifts we are in the character-building business." And who should know better than he? At the pinnacle of his career, and in line to become the first black Speaker of the House of Representatives, Gray had to be bold as he shunned both power and prestige to direct the UNCF. If he was apprehensive with his new move, he didn't show it. His parting words to his congressional colleagues: "Knowledge begins when we face our biggest fears."

It takes courage to be outvoted, beaten, laughed at, scoffed, ridiculed, derided, misunderstood, and misjudged. It takes courage to do your duty in silence and obscurity while others prosper and grow famous as they neglect sacred obligations. It takes courage to unmask your true self, to show your blemishes to a condemning world. It takes courage to "march into hell for a heavenly cause." C. Delores Tucker's campaign against vile, violent gangsta rap music offers a clear view of her convictions. At a shareholder's meeting of Time Warner, the world's largest entertainment conglomerate, Tucker, the daughter of a Baptist minister, rose from the audience and challenged the corporation's executives to stop dumping trashy, hateful images and lyrics on the minds of young America. When a senior-level corporate official interrupted her remarks and asked in a condescending tone, "Who invited *you* to this meeting?" Tucker shot back, "Truth and decency did!"

You cannot keep a courageous woman from success. Place stumbling blocks in her path and she will use them as stepping-stones, and using them, she will climb to greatness. Whether you agree with her politics or not, there are no more interesting pages in biography than those that record the life of Joycelyn Elders. Few have come so far from so far back. Surgeon General Elders understood the link between health and poverty like no one else in Washington, D.C. She had seen too many pregnant eleven-year-olds, and too many at age seventeen with two children. She was born in a shack in rural Arkansas and lived, with seven siblings, without running water or electricity. From age six, young Minnie Lee (her name given at birth) slopped hogs, stripped sugarcane, and picked cotton. Her strong work ethic and Christian roots helped her climb from poverty through Arkansas' segregated medical societies. Despite negative accounts, Dr. Elders is an accomplished scientist and professor. As one of the few board-certified pediatric endocrinologists in the South, she has delivered more than twenty thousand babies and authored more than 150 scholarly papers. The words "health care" are emblazoned upon her heart; and neither reputation, ridicule, threats, ostracism, position, nor politics would block her from carrying her message forward.

And where will you find an illustration more impressive than Vanessa Williams? She is the first woman of color to ever adorn the crown of Miss America. Gifted, dignified, and possessing irrepressible good looks, Vanessa was never greater than when she stood face-to-face with the stodgy pageant's executive committee, who asked her to step down in order to preserve the pristine image of the title she bore. A few uncompromising photographs may have scarred her judgment but not her self-respect. "Difficulties call out great qualities and make success possible," she said with her head held high. "Remember, it's a stiff wind that allows the eagle to soar higher."

A mouse that scurried near the home of a magician was kept in such constant distress by its fear of a cat that the magician, taking pity on the tiny creature, turned it into a cat itself. Immediately, it began to suffer from its fear of a dog, so the magician transformed it into a dog. Then it began to suffer from fear of a tiger. Consequently, the magician turned it into a tiger. Then it began to suffer from fear of a hunter. Finally, the magician said in disgust: "Be a mouse again. As long as you think like a mouse and act like a mouse, it's impossible for you to be anything more noble!"

These are turbulent economic times. Layoffs, mergers and acquisitions, cutbacks, downsizing—our mental outlook vacillates daily between hope and frustration. What will it take for you to find your special place and fill it? What will it take for you to pick through the smoldering ruins of your dreams? How much of your talent is being wasted for want of a little boldness? When crestfallen and infected with the disease of self-pity, what will it take for you to "rise, take up your bed and walk"?

Samuel Smiles, who wrote the first success book, entitled *Self-Help,* in 1859, said that we always learn more from our failures than from our successes. We often discover what will do by finding out what will not do, and he who never made a mistake has never known the thrill of turning apparent loss into a gain. Never hide your talents. If you remain silent, you will be forgotten. If you fail to advance, you will fall back. If you bow before a challenge, your self-esteem will forever be scarred. And if you cease to grow, death is inevitable. Be certain: Nothing will happen to you that you are not equipped to handle. Just as any gem is polished by friction, you will become more valuable through your adversities. If one door is closed, another will be made available.

What will it take for you to lead when you are used to being led? The race does not always favor the swift, the battle does not always reward the strong. So, too, in the race of life, distance alone does not determine the prize. We must take into account the roadblocks, the challenges, the inequities, the circumstances. What will it take to shun yesterday's failure; to turn your back on hatred and animosity no matter how much injustice you have tasted; to finally unlock the door to fortune and success? It will take the "C" word—that gift of a word that separates the victor from the victim. It takes *courage!*

"THEY TOLD ME, 'YOU'RE NOT GOING TO MAKE IT' "

For Bessie Pender, this day in late August figured to be much like every other day she had spent at Larrymore Elementary School in Norfolk, Virginia, over the past seventeen years: The floors had to be mopped, shelves dusted, and more than a dozen offices cleaned. She opened a classroom door and was shocked by what she saw: chairs turned upside down; desks upended; books, papers, pencils, and glue spilled everywhere. Bessie threw up her hands and said to herself, "Lord—enough! I can't take it anymore." And then the question begged asking: "Do I want to clean these rooms, or do I want to teach in these rooms?" This was the day that Bessie Pender would change her life forever; she would become a teacher.

Two months later, Bessie applied to Old Dominion University in her hometown seeking a degree in education. She was thirty-eight years old and strapped for cash. Once accepted, she began a killer schedule that lasted seven years: morning classwork at ODU, and then, that afternoon, she would change into her green custodian uniform, grab a mop, bucket, and rags, and start her eight-hour shift. Nearly exhausted, she would return to her red brick, single-story home, where she would feed and tend to her husband, Ben, and their eighteen-year-old daughter. Many times Bessie heated meals that had been prepared the previous weekend. Each night, it seemed, her books became her pillow. And during finals she would go without sleep.

After an instructor told her she would make a terrible teacher, Bessie entertained thoughts of quitting. "In college, some of my professors told me, 'You're not going to make it,' " she recalled. "I got a D in geography in my first semester, and I felt like a loser." But the love and encouragement of family and friends kept her on course.

"My mom and dad were so supportive, especially my father. He drove me to school and to work every day until his health began to decline. Sometimes he would sacrifice his entire Social Security check to pay for my tuition." With only a semester to go before graduation, Bessie's fortitude would be tested one last time. A bout with emphysema left her father too weak to attend her graduation. She bought her cap and gown two weeks before the ceremony and, carrying a rolled-up fake diploma, wore the outfit on a visit to his sickbed. In a twist of fate, he died a month after she graduated—she was the first in her family of six to do so.

It was Bessie's stubborn refusal to surrender her dream and rocklike courage that most impressed recruiters. Coleman Place Elementary School principal Jeanne Tomlinson interviewed three teachers for the same job. All were fresh out of college. But, in Tomlinson's eyes, Bessie had the enthusiasm and determination to achieve. "Anyone who works that hard to get something," her principal suggests, "is going to make it."

And Bessie still works hard. Each morning at eight, she arrives at Coleman Place, half an hour earlier than required. By nine-thirty, as the children start to file in, Bessie is waiting in the doorway ready to give each a hug. Though she now earns more than twice her custodian's salary of $10,650, she hasn't forgotten where she came from. At the end of the day, she has her fifth-grade class wash the blackboard, empty the wastebaskets, and place their chairs on their desks. Nor is she likely to forget what she learned on the way to becoming a teacher, a lesson she now passes on to her pupils. "I tell them, 'Greatness is buried within their hearts but they must muster the courage to mine it out.' "

JUST CUT IT OUT!

The inspirational writer Napoleon Hill devoted his life to sharing the philosophy of individual achievement with millions of aspiring men and women. As a young man he had the ambition to become a writer. Toward that end, Hill saved his money and bought the finest, most complete dictionary available. All the words he would ever need were in that book and Hill meant to master them all. But he did something quite strange. He turned to the word "impossible" and with his penknife clipped it out of the dictionary and threw it away. As he stated on several occasions, he then had a reference book that was void of any negative concepts. Thereafter, Hill built his entire career on the premise that nothing is impossible to the man or woman who wants to succeed in a big way. I am not suggesting that you cut the word "impossible" out of your dictionary. But I certainly suggest that you cut it out of your mind. Eliminate it from your conversation, drop it from your thoughts, erase it from your attitude. Remember these words instead: "Nothing is impossible for he that believes."

Rise above fear! Aim high when pursuing the riches that life has to offer. Remember that you live in a land of opportunities where no one is limited in either scope or nature as to the wealth he or she may acquire, provided he or she is willing to give adequate value in return. Successful people do not bargain with life for poverty, death, uncertainty, or failure. They know there is a force through which life may be made to pay off on their terms. This power is known to all achievers. The next time you get hung up on being needlessly stifled by fear, reconsider the stories within this lesson. Success will knock at your door when you display the courage to be honest, the courage to resist temptation, the courage to speak the truth, the courage to be who you really are, and the courage to live honestly within your means and not dishonestly upon the means of others.

Free yourself of the chains stamped "I can't!" and you will be able to achieve the desires of your heart. You can do anything—if you believe you can. Easy? Of course not. Nothing in life worth achieving is easy. Can you pull it off? Yes, but you'll never know unless you try, and *keep* trying. Those who are willing to lose rarely do.

Here are twelve essential elements that have guided the success of General Colin Powell. Use them as a daily guide. They will fuel your ability to stand courageously in the face of all obstacles. Pay close attention to his final rule.

Colin Powell's Rules

1. It ain't as bad as you think. Things will look better in the morning.
2. Get mad, then get over it.
3. Avoid having your ego so close to your position that when your position falls, your ego goes with it.
4. It can be done!
5. Be careful what you choose. You may get it.
6. Don't allow adverse facts to stand in the way of a good decision.
7. Check small things.
8. Share the credit.
9. You can't make someone else's choices. You shouldn't allow someone else to make yours.
10. Remain calm. Be kind.
11. Develop a vision. Be demanding.
12. Don't take the counsel of your fears or naysayers.

3

The Greatest Journey:

The Journey into Your Mind!

- • Ideas and the Imagination
- • The Subconscious: Gold in Your Cellar
- • The Rich Get Richer
- • Mental Laws
- • How to Attain the Greatest Idea in the World

It was just my imagination, running away with me.
—EDDIE KENDRICKS AND THE TEMPTATIONS

'Tis the mind that makes the body rich.
—SHAKESPEARE

Yes, you have a gold mine between your ears;
your mind and your imagination.
—EARL NIGHTINGALE

A mind is a terrible thing to waste.
—THE UNITED NEGRO COLLEGE FUND

Have you ever given much thought to the value of ideas? From less than worthless, they run the gamut all the way into the hundreds of billions of dollars. From the wheel to the zipper, the bow and arrow to the H-bomb, electricity to the computer—each has been drawn from that bottomless gold mine: the mind of mankind! Everything that you and I will ever possess will come to us as the result of the way we use our minds. The one thing that we possess that makes us different from every other creature that walks the earth, and the highest function of which our minds are capable, is the ability to think creatively.

Remember Henry David Thoreau's admonition in his classic *Walden?* He told us that if we have built castles in the air, our work need not be lost, for that is where they should be. Then he urged us to put foundations under them. I am going to share with you some powerful tools that you can use, not only to construct your castles in the air but also to erect them in concrete. You are about to learn how to turn many of your dreams into reality. But you must listen with an open mind and an open heart and then be prepared to act. All the noble thoughts, magnificent dreams, and secrets of achievement are of little value unless and until they are placed into action.

Ideas move faster than speeding bullets and penetrate more swiftly and deeply than laser beams. Ideas can change the direction of life and move the consciousness from despair to hope to upward flight. Nothing can enslave an idea or the imagination. No matter where we live, there is no poverty-stricken domain on the face of the earth where the Almighty will not perform his miracles right before our eyes. No spot is so barren that ideas will not grow: "For as he thinks in his heart, so is he." Each of us has the opportunity to draw upon our inner resources, which foster all ideas, dreams, and hopes.

Can you accept the notion that your imagination rules your world? Pay careful attention to this amazing man who learned the power of ideas.

Ed Gardner is a man you wouldn't notice in a crowd—a deep-rooted midwesterner, perennially dressed in a white button-down shirt and conservative suit. Nonetheless, the secret to his success is his passionate commitment to ideas. Gardner has built a $95-million hair-care company, Soft Sheen Products, by outsmarting the competition—carefully, always backed up by months of arduous planning geared to snatch opportunity at every turn.

Gardner's story began in the West Chesterfield section of Chicago. His father was a self-taught electrician who plied his trade when he wasn't sweeping floors for a local furniture company. His mother, a sharp-witted and forceful woman, cared for him and an older brother. Theirs was a home of ample love and plenty of direction. As a child, Gardner held a string of jobs. But by far the most memorable was hawking newspapers for the *Pittsburgh Courier* and *Chicago Defender.* "I was eight years old when my mother finally gave in to my pleas. I asked her several times for permission to sell newspapers but was always rebuffed. I guess you could say this was a sign of things to come. I wanted to sell papers, not for the measly two dollars a week that I would earn, but because the paper route would be mine. These would be my customers!"

After high school and a stint in the army, Gardner continued to act on that ambition. He graduated from college with a degree in education and had planned to work himself up the bureaucratic ladder within Chicago's public schools. Though the security of teaching clearly took care of a mortgage, his wife, and four small children, Gardner found few outlets for his business talent and ideas. To fill the void, he began selling beauty supply products for a regional chain after hours. Gardner recalls the days when he would load up his Hillman-Huskie and head for Chicago's 47th Street.

"I peddled products out of a cardboard box on Chicago's South Side. Each day after school I would head home, grab a quick shower and a bite to eat, and then head off to push my products. Back then, working ten-hour days was neither easy nor glamorous. But I was developing a certain feel for the marketplace. I could see the immediate effect of my ideas." More important, Gardner got a glimpse of the big picture. He saw a world made up of people selling themselves and realized that desire and initiative, when properly applied, lead to growth and development. He also learned the central rule of riches: *Wealth is the unpredictable result of individual faith, diligence, and ingenuity.* Gardner's hard work and determination began to lead to modest success.

The Dream Takes Hold

By the start of the 1960s, Gardner had been promoted to assistant principal and began to wade deeper into entrepreneurial waters. With the help of his family, he began mixing and packaging his own hair preparations in the basement of his home. Soft Sheen's first product was a light hair and scalp conditioner that was in direct contrast to the heavy pomades used by black beauticians. The tiny firm grabbed a toehold on the competition and chiseled out a corner of the market. For the next six years, Gardner cautiously added to his line and stayed out of the way of larger black manufacturers.

But with his success came an agonizing decision. Gardner was no longer able to manufacture his now widely accepted product and perform his duties as a principal. This was no ordinary midlife crisis. He and his wife, Bettiann, weren't blind to the security of the school system; yet he believed he could make a go of it on his own. He mulled over the decision for months. "I had just been promoted on my job while the demands of my business were expanding. When I decided to take the plunge—something that I had hoped to do—my friends and relatives thought I had lost my mind. I remember a neighbor asking my wife, 'You mean Ed's going to leave that job to sell hair oil?' I couldn't explain it to them. They never realized the power of my dream."

Initially, the going was tough. Everything seemed to be in a constant state of flux. Sales on his most profitable product had flattened. It was already 1978, a full five years since he had decided to go full-time, when Gardner began to suffer from all the guilt and anxieties that achievers report when telling of their crucial moves. Soft Sheen was in the third year of a four-year slide and struggling. That year, the company had sales of less than $2 million and a handful of employees, and Gardner saw nothing on the horizon. For the first time his spirits began to wane.

By the start of the new year, Gardner seemed to be searching for opportunities that didn't exist. He was traveling at a frenetic pace, trying to shore up sales. For a man who seemed to live his life in advance with well-timed moves, he had no new products, nothing to anticipate. The days seemed to slide by unnoticed. And then it happened!

One Life-Changing Idea

During a trip to the West Coast to help gather his thoughts, Gardner noticed the sporty hairstyles among active Californians. Willie Barrow, a local cosmetologist, developed a method that would moderately curl naturally straight hair, a process that was gaining momentum among both whites and Hispanics. Unlike other bothersome styles or permanents, "the curl," as it was aptly called, required little maintenance and seemed perfectly suited for the fast-paced, carefree lifestyle. The wet-look craze was a fad that attracted both genders and all age groups as well as an inquisitive Ed Gardner. In his accustomed fashion, he began to think of the possibilities. This was a groundbreaking opportunity, and nobody saw it clearer than he.

But the process was fraught with problems; it took beauticians six to eight hours to create the hairstyle, and the cost ran as high as a hundred dollars. But Gardner wouldn't be stopped. He realized this could be his chance to propel Soft Sheen into the big leagues. He toyed with an idea: What if I could reduce both time and cost?

Lacking a scientific background, Gardner had a team of chemists plug away until they found the right formula for the product. With typical élan, he took a financial beating, pouring in time and money on an untried, untested product. Meanwhile, Gardner and his staff searched tirelessly for the niche that would allow Soft Sheen to restructure the market. The magic moment finally arrived one year later when the first batch came down the assembly line.

Long since convinced of the product's viability, an ecstatic Gardner loaded a truck and immediately dashed to trade shows in Michigan and Missouri. It wasn't until he got to Detroit, buttoned his shirt and straightened his tie, and sold $4,000 worth of "curly perm" that he realized the product lacked a name and a label. "Once beauticians saw the results," he says excitedly, "they gobbled up the product right out of unmarked jars." Arriving back in Chicago, Gardner found little time to gloat in his success. Instead he focused on developing a marketing concept, one that would include the distribution of Care Free Curl—so named by his son—and a supplemental line of products that would transform his fragile, family-owned enterprise into a $95-million monolith.

FORMULA FOR SUCCESS

Today, Soft Sheen has continued to ride the crest of almost uncontrollable growth. It's now the largest minority-owned manufacturing firm in the United States and is one of *Black Enterprise* magazine's top ten black-owned companies for 1994.

Ed Gardner and Soft Sheen were highly successful in executing pathbreaking ideas. What can you learn from this example? Gardner quickly points out the key: "What will it take to succeed? Hard work, determination, of course. The support of friends and family, without a doubt. Those are all a part of it, but what's most important is your ability to utilize your imagination; to tap into your inner reserve, the source of all achievement."

There's an erroneous theory that surfaces again and again: that chances for success continue to erode and dwindle. That fewer opportunities exist today than were available in the past. That our nation has reached its plateau, that the world is dominated by those who have already capitalized on all prevailing ideas, and that success is a finite realm already filled to capacity. This is nothing more than conjecture. There is no scarcity of opportunity—there is only a shortage of ideas. Countless individuals gain new wealth every year, whether the economy is on the upswing or ailing. The only limits are those established within their own minds.

Psychologist and best-selling author Charles Garfield says ideas are the "primary tools needed in constructing a powerful mission. Great accomplishments are always the result of the imagination translated through words and action plans."

Abraham Maslow, founder of third-force psychology, believed there is a tendency in everyone's life for "self-actualization." Maslow described self-actualization as "the clamoring of capacities to be used, a restlessness for self-development, accomplishment and esteem." One's full potential emerges not just from developing skills, but from first unlocking the door to the internal resources of the mind waiting to be tapped. The key to unlocking that door comes from envisioning a mission—maintaining a dream.

Albert Einstein stated that "imagination is more important than knowledge." Einstein claimed that he had only two original ideas during his entire life, and that these were the products of his reasoning plus intuition. A human acts, feels, and performs in accordance with what he imagines to be true about himself and his environment. This is the fundamental law of mind. It is the way in which humans are structured. Man is, for the most part, "teleological," always moving in the direction of his most dominant impulse.

Maxwell Maltz, the renowned plastic surgeon, theorized that imagination—the dream—plays a far more crucial role in life than one is led to believe. "Creative imagination," according to Maltz, "is not something reserved for the artistic or atunely creative. Imagination sets the goal picture that our automatic mechanism relies upon. One acts, or fails to act, not because of will, as is commonly believed, but because of imagination."

Scientists at the Brain Institute at the University of California at Los Angeles believe that the creative capacity of the human brain approaches infinity. Your brain can store, combine, and create more bits of information and imagery than thousands of videotape recorders, tens of thousands of computers, and millions of microfilm cartridges. There are no limits other than the self-imposed. So don't censor your dreams. Give them free rein. Dream big! Visualize the possibilities of becoming president of your firm, running your own business, or achieving great success in your line of work.

IDEAS AND THE IMAGINATION

An idea is a target that beckons. Ideas animate, inspire, grab, and transform purpose into action. Ideas, especially the good ones, are fragile and mercuric. They often stun us with their brilliance and perfection. They can force their way into our minds at moments of leisure—while bathing, exercising, swinging in a hammock, or driving to work—or can vanish as quickly as they came, disappearing into the forest of our minds never to be conjured up again. Whenever and wherever they enter, I've come to learn that ideas—the product of the human mind—are the world's most valuable things.

People tend to underestimate their own ideas simply because they've formed the habit of underestimating themselves. Amazingly, even within the top echelons of business and industry, high-paid executives have developed the tendency to devalue their own ideas. Throughout society, we tend to give others credit for being "smarter" or "more creative." Experts point out that most people don't receive many ideas because they've never recognized their importance or the means of developing them. To develop good ideas, we need an active, inquiring, creative mind. We need to develop the habit of questioning everything, realizing that nothing is as good as it will be and that we live in a state of constant change. Ideas are aesthetic and moral as well as emotionally idealistic.

Keep in mind that the idea we are searching for is never beyond our reach. One nineteenth-century inventor wrote, "We have had our solutions for a long time, yet we don't know how we are to arrive at them." George Washington Carver knew what he was looking for when he decided to find multiple uses for the peanut. Once that decision was reached, he was able to find the ideas he needed, as difficult as it was. You might say that not everyone is able to do what Dr. Carver did. Well, you're right! Because not everyone is searching for three hundred uses for the peanut. In fact, most people are quite content with the life they already lead, as unimaginative as that may be. The point I wish to emphasize is that, once you know what you want to do—what you want to accomplish—you will reach your goal if you dare to unleash your imagination. The process is not difficult to understand.

Just imagine Saint Paul, a man of enormous ability, who might have led the Sanhedrin but, for the sake of his idea, was forced to sew tents for his daily bread. Picture him condemned to the gallows at Caesarea, incarcerated a year later in Rome, beaten by his oppressors, despised by his own. Yet the grand idea of the unity of humanity that consumed his soul enabled him to master his circumstances and turn from despair to hope in the process.

When Peter Bynoe set a goal to own a professional basketball team and when Percy Sutton sought to acquire a string of radio stations, they were focusing on worthwhile and attainable objectives. "I always keep my creative forces at work by keeping my eyes open," says Sutton, founder and president of Inner City Broadcasting.

Peter Bynoe, onetime co-owner of the Denver Nuggets basketball team, says, "Everything that I achieved began with an idea. The secret of my success involves being able to distinguish good ideas from bad ones."

During my visit to the headquarters of Joshua Smith, founder of the Maxima Corporation, one of his associates said of him, "The vision inside of his head is crystal-clear. That he cannot be turned from it or be corrupted by outside influences is the key to his success." And Clarence O. Smith, cofounder and president of *Essence* magazine, concurs. "The key to success," he says, "is not what you have, but what you look forward to."

There are plenty of good ideas left to be forged in our world. Everything has not been discovered, uncovered, or invented. All good things have not been created; there are endless opportunities—enough to challenge the most creative soul: "Most assuredly, I say to you, he who believes in me, the works that I do he will do also; and greater works than these he will do." But we observe, study, think, and, finally, *act*. A philosopher once wrote, "There's not much to do but bury a man when the last of his dreams is dead." Why? Because thousands of men and women have made vast sums of money from ideas that others casually dismissed. Victor Hugo, the French poet and playwright, was correct. He wrote more than a century ago, "Nothing in this world is so powerful as an idea whose time has come." And it's equally true that there's nothing in this world of *less* value than an idea about which nothing is done. The greatest fortune that anyone could lay claim to is one good idea!

Creative thinking puts a fresh, new face on our world. All of our progress has come, now comes, and will come as a result of creative thinking—using our brains creatively. But what is a brain? It's a priceless resource that is given to each of us free at birth. It's as though the Creator said, "Here you are! You now have a copy of the creative agent that produced the plays of Shakespeare, bridged San Francisco Bay, choreographed the dance steps of Katherine Graham, inspired Maya Angelou to write an inauguration poem, and harnessed the energy of the sun. I put it into your keeping for the span of your life. Do with it what you will." Yes, you have a gold mine between your ears—in your mind and your imagination. But for most of us, owning this greatest of all earthly possessions is like owning some complex, unsolvable puzzle containing at its heart a jewel of great value. To use it effectively, we must tap the power within that will enable us to solve the puzzle and find its treasure.

A GIFT AT BIRTH

Imagination, the personal search for truth and ideas, is the element that separates us from everything else in nature. Our very existence is derived from the power that exists in our minds. Most of the earth's creatures have been given the gift of concealment through protective coloring. In fact, throughout the animal kingdom, those that need concealment blend in so well with their natural surroundings that when they lie motionless, they become virtually invisible. This quality protects them from their predators or their quarry. These creatures, through the endless ages of evolution, have conformed to their environment and copied the appearance of their natural surroundings.

But what of mankind? He is among the weakest, physically, of all creatures. He can be killed by a leopard one-fourth his weight or by a virus that is invisible. He has no protective coloring at all but can easily be seen in any type of environment. He can't run fast enough to escape any animal bent on catching him; he can't swim very far; and he has no claws or sharp teeth, has weak vision, and can hardly climb a tree. He can't even catch a kitten that doesn't want to be caught.

But he was given a priceless treasure—a fortune! He was armed with the ability to reason, the capacity to *think,* and the use of his imagination. Because he can think, he doesn't need to blend in with his environment. He can make his environment change to match him. In fact, just as you can tell the type of country an animal comes from by looking at the pattern of its coloring, you can often tell the type of ideas a person has by observing his or her surroundings. Environment fits the person just as an animal fits its environment. The extent to which an individual uses the gift of imagination will determine the kind of environment in which he or she will live. Only mankind can alter the scenery to match his needs, his desires. By changing himself, he changes his surroundings and is thereby ruler over everything. Thanks to this concept, he solves the riddle of life-shortening diseases; travels at the speed of sound; swims to the bottom of the sea; and will one day visit the farthest planets of the universe.

Yet this is the source of the most disturbing paradox: With the greatest treasure within their grasp, the majority of people neither know they possess it nor use it, but spend the bulk of their time criticizing and mimicking others, playing a worthless game of conformity. No two of them are exactly alike, yet they pretend they are by allowing others to do their thinking. They have in their possession the most precious treasure on earth, and they don't even open the box.

PARADISE LOST

In John Milton's *Paradise Lost,* Satan tells us, "The mind is its own place, and in itself can make a heaven of hell, a hell of heaven." No one knows or can even guess the uncounted millions who are living in a virtual heaven of opportunity in every area of their lives, and yet, turn it instead into a living hell. So many people have every opportunity to love, yet they hate; they have every opportunity to trust, yet they distrust; they have every opportunity to work and give of themselves, yet they hold back in the suspicious dread that they're being cheated. They have every opportunity to share in the wealth of the richest society since the beginning of the world, yet they sit and grumble because it's not simply given to them. They're ignorant, though they're surrounded on every side with a free and abundant opportunity to learn to their full capacity. The public libraries in their towns and cities are half-empty, waiting in vain for all to enter and learn. Their schools and parents beg them to continue their education to qualify themselves for a fast-changing world, but they drop out. In every walk of life, in every stratum of society, you can see their bitter, desolate expressions, the hollow eyes and listless hands of those whose minds have been condemned to experience a "hell of heaven."

Seneca, the Roman philosopher and dramatist, wrote, "A great, a good, and a right mind is a kind of divinity lodged in flesh, and may be the blessing of a slave as well as a prince. It came from heaven, and to heaven it must return; it's a kind of heavenly felicity which a pure and virtuous mind enjoys, in some degree, even on earth."

Geoffrey Chaucer, the fourteenth-century English poet, wrote, "My mind to me a kingdom is; such present joys therein I find that it excels all other bliss that earth affords." Every person's mind is his kingdom and he is the reigning monarch that decides what kind of a kingdom it is to be—bleak or bountiful, rich or poor, interesting or dull, happy or unhappy." The most important moment of our lives occurs when we understand that we can fashion our lives by shaping our imagination. What digging, plowing, and cultivating are to land, thinking, reflecting, and dreaming are to the imagination. We know the soil is rich; the harvest is up to us.

DISCOVER THE POWER WITHIN

Wouldn't it be nice to own a master key that could unlock *everything?* That could unlock the doors to success, relationships, wealth, health, wisdom, and more important, every problem that you've ever confronted? Well, prepare yourself, for you are about to receive your master key to life.

Imagine that you're standing on a platform facing a crowd of prominent leaders, well-wishers, and everyone that you've grown to respect and admire throughout your life. Standing next to you is a stately-looking gentleman, splendidly dressed in business attire. His presence is commanding; his face is lined with compassion. His eyes sparkle like nuggets of gold. In his hands he holds a large, brass key. The man turns to you and says, "It is my profound pleasure to present to you the Official Key to Life. Please accept it with our congratulations and best wishes. Use this key to unlock every door that is closed to you." He then hands you the key and a booklet entitled *Official Key to Life Manual: 1001 Uses.* As he does, the crowd of well-wishers breaks into enthusiastic applause.

You receive the key gladly, holding it firmly with both hands. You notice that your name is engraved on the shaft in elegant italicized letters. The key radiates the same forceful presence as the elder statesman. As you descend the platform steps, your sense of anticipation builds. You hurry to your seat and sit down, placing the key in your lap. Although you're not usually one to read instructions, this time you do. The *Official Key to Life Manual* suggests that you keep this key with you at all times. It explains that the key has two unique properties: One, it automatically changes size to solve any problem, large or small; and two, it eventually unlocks any kind of challenge or difficulty, so that no door can prevent you from experiencing your true destiny. The manual lists a number of ways in which the key can be used. Here are a few of them:

- *To unlock success,* picture either a closed door marked "success" or your main desire. Place the key into the lock and turn. The door swings open and now you are in possession of your heart's desire.
- *To unlock love,* picture a heart that has been abandoned or a relationship gone sour. Maybe it's boarded-up and dark. The lock is rusty, but your key unlocks it. Love and light pour out.
- *To unlock wealth,* picture abundance, feel prosperity. Set a specific dollar figure you intend to acquire and visualize yourself in posses-

sion of these riches. Become a clear thinker. Insert the key and turn. As you do, you will unlock the door to your personal fortune and lock out all thoughts of poverty and failure.

• *To unlock health,* picture a sound body and firm heart. Every day visualize the level of fitness that you desire locked behind a glass cabinet door. Your key unlocks your fountain of youth.

These are only a few ways in which your key to life can unlock any problem. You'll think of many other uses. Carry your key with you at all times—use it anytime a problem or challenge arises. Your master key can help set you free.

This lesson centers on a discovery I made that has brought me a more-than-satisfactory share of the good things in life. When properly used, this same gift will help you gain a greater abundance of whatever it is that you deeply desire. I know you will be able to gain your goals of love, success in your field, fame, fortune, and vibrant good health. You won't have to use the trial-and-error methods I used, for I have outlined the route that you can quickly and easily follow to reach your goals. You see, within every human being is an infinite, unlimited, and powerful force that works better than the most sophisticated modern computer. That infinite, unlimited source of supply is the *subconscious mind*—the center of all creative activity!

THE SUBCONSCIOUS: GOLD IN YOUR CELLAR

What would you say if I told you that down in the basement of your house sat a box full of gold coins? After you got over the initial shock you might mention many things—but there is one thing you wouldn't do, and that would be to ignore it. You would immediately go down to the cellar, amid all the junk and clutter, and retrieve the box and put it to good use. And yet, has it ever occurred to you that most of us live out our entire lives with a box of gold in the basement of our minds that we rarely use? Deep down below the surface of our thought lies that powerful component of our mind that we call the subconscious. Our subconscious mind is the storehouse of our memory, the guiding light of our life. It is a source of energy stronger than any electrical current, more powerful than any explosive. Nothing can approach the powerful capabilities of the subconscious mind. But to be successful, we must make greater use of it. Unfortunately, most of us go through life without ever realizing how to use this wellspring of power. Only a small percentage of people discover the subconscious mind, understand it, and subsequently learn how to guide its hidden powers to achieve complete success in whatever they set out to do. We tend to live like famished paupers sitting at a bare table in a cold, damp room, not knowing there's food in the cupboard and a warm fire in the hearth.

When you know how to use the hidden power of your subconscious mind, you can attain riches beyond your wildest dreams. Your subconscious mind can activate your imagination and inspire you with new thoughts and fresh ideas. You can use this power to gain the financial prosperity that will offer you a new level of freedom to be whatever you want, do whatever you want, and experience your heart's desire. Your subconscious mind can help you locate your true place. It will help you determine what you are best suited to do so you may utilize your innate talents and gifts. Through this power source, you'll be able to find the right position or vocation that will eventually lead you to your labor of love.

You can use your subconscious mind to rid yourself of frustration, anger, and resentment. This hidden guide will help you solve your most pressing problems and lead you to make the right decisions. You can also use the power of the subconscious mind to free yourself from fear, anxiety, and worry forever, as well as to deactivate and defuse failure attitudes and replace them with a more positive outlook. Furthermore, when you use the power of your subconscious mind, you will be able to enjoy abundant and radiant health. Just releasing frustration, worry, and stress will improve your quality of health. You'll bubble over with vitality, energy, and a zest for living. Life will truly become worthwhile; each day will be meaningful, filled to the brim with the sheer joy of being alive.

Your subconscious mind is lying there dormant within you, just waiting to be placed into action. Your subconscious mind is unlimited, infinite, and inexhaustible. It never rests; it keeps working every moment of life. You need only to activate it and put its marvelous power to use.

SEVEN STEPS TO ACTIVATE YOUR SUBCONSCIOUS MIND

One of the principles many high achievers use is: *Find a need and fill it.* The same principle applies to your subconscious mind. Unless there is a need for it to work, it never will. You must give it a goal to reach, an objective to achieve, before it will go into action. Here is a seven-step procedure that will help activate the power of the subconscious mind:

1. Your subconscious mind operates best in a mental climate of faith and acceptance. Confidently expecting that your problems will be solved, obstacles removed, and your goals achieved is the mental state that intensifies thought and causes the subconscious mind to function at its best.
2. Know exactly what it is you want to accomplish. Be specific about the goal you want to reach, the objective you want to attain.
3. Believe in your heart that your subconscious mind will deliver the answer you want and need.
4. Separate fact from opinion. Do your homework and gather all available facts on the subject.
5. Feed those facts into your subconscious mind with your request for an answer.
6. Relax. Wait patiently and watch diligently for the answer to your question or the solution to your problem. In due course it will come.
7. Take immediate action when your answer arrives. The first six steps are critically important, but unless you follow through and take action, all the preceding work will have been wasted. You'll soon discover that if you fail to act, your subconscious mind will reach the conclusion that you are not serious about your requests for help.

Scientific breakthroughs, great musical compositions, inspiring books, and all other ideas for original accomplishment are born within the subconscious mind. The subconscious mind is the source of all inspiration, all motivation, and the excitement that rushes over you when aroused by a new idea or possibility. It is the source of hunches, intuition, and flashes of brilliance. It is "the still, small voice" within. From this great within comes the power to perform immortal deeds. We are conscious that there is something in us—but not of us—that is never sick, never tired, and that never goes wrong. All principle, truth, love, lives in this great within. Here is the home of beauty and justice. Here abides "the peace which passeth all understanding," and here shines "the light that was never on sea or land."

We are conscious of something within that is deathless, something immortal, divine. We all feel this, the living Christ, this silent messenger which accompanies us through life, directing our moves, advising us, warning us, protecting us, no matter where we go, no matter how far we fall. Many feel just as sure of this blessed mothering presence, this messenger of peace and goodwill, as though they could see it with their own eyes. There is something within that tells us we are at one with the power that made all things and that, once we drink at the fountain of the spirit, we shall never know thirst or want again. No life can be poor when enfolded in the infinite arms and living in the very midst of abundance, the source of all supply.

Many great people have stood before this power in awe, calling it different names. The Reverend Calvin Butts, pastor of New York's Abyssinian Baptist Church, calls it "the power within our lives." Oprah Winfrey, America's number one talk-show host, labels it "the force for good." Napoleon Hill referred to this source as "infinite intelligence," calling it the universal storehouse of knowledge. In the great race of life, divine authority has the right-of-way. "There's a higher being in all of us that keeps us balanced," says Ann Fudge, Black America's highest-ranking corporate executive. "Believe in it. Use it. This is the secret to my success." And Johnnie Colemon, founder of Chicago's Christ Universal Temple, simply calls it *spirit.* "It works if you work it," she attests. Each day she implores her congregation to set this power free in their lives. The history of the human race is replete with incidents that bear unmistakable testimony to the validity of spiritual perception. For example, so much of Western civilization was molded and shaped by the whisperings of the still, small voice to Saul of Tarsus.

Call this power by whatever name you wish, but you cannot deny its existence. Humanity need not look far for the source of this power. It lies in everything the physical senses can perceive: from the smallest grain of sand to the largest star that makes its appointed rounds in the universe. It appears in the balanced forces of energy in the atom. It is the all-pervading medium we call space and, therefore, it surrounds us as an ocean of potential power which we may consciously contact and direct to our own worthy ends. There is almost no limit to what you can accomplish when you set it free on a regular basis.

You may not be an inventor, or compose fine musical arrangements, or author unforgettable stories, but you can still use the hidden power of the subconscious to discover new and more efficient ways of doing things in your vocation or personal life. No one possesses a lock on all creativity. This power has been placed at your disposal by divine decree. The only condition that is required is to commence. Give your subconscious mind the reason or the raw material it needs to release its powers, and keep it going with a deep-rooted desire for successful accomplishment. When you do, yours will become a master mind!

TAP INTO IT!

There is an old story of a boilermaker who was hired to repair a huge malfunctioning steamship boiler system. After listening to the engineer's description of the problems and asking a few questions, he went to the boiler room. He gazed at the maze of twisting pipes, listened to the thump of the boiler and the hiss of escaping steam for a few minutes. Next, he felt the cold pipes with his hands. Then he hummed softly to himself, reached into his overalls, took out a small hammer, and tapped a bright red valve. Immediately, the entire system began working perfectly, and the boilermaker went home. When the steamship owner received a bill for $2,000, he complained that the boilermaker had only been in the engine room for five minutes, and requested an itemized bill. Here's a copy of the boilermaker's invoice:

For tapping with hammer	$ 1.00
For knowing where to tap	1,999.00
Total	$2,000.00

Success is a matter of knowing how to use the power of our subconscious minds to transform the quality of our lives. When you use your subconscious mind correctly—"knowing where to tap"—you will be able to solve any problem, overcome any obstacle, and achieve any goal you sincerely desire. Each of us can tap into the source of all personal greatness and individual achievement by knowing when and where to tap into this source of all creativity.

If aroused, this force could carry you to heights of achievement such as you have never imagined. It is a power that has brought forth great leaders in every walk of life and in every generation; men and women of vision and ideas who have pushed back the frontiers of fear, ignorance, and poverty. The power is clothed in no mystery, and it will perform its miracles for anyone who will work its daily deeds. It is called by a myriad of names, but its nature never changes. It works through but one medium, and that is the mind. It expresses itself in thoughts, ideas, and dreams, and it is as free as the air we breathe and as abundant as the scope of the universe. It is not a newfound philosophy that the world craves, but the utilization of the unerring power from within which moves mountains.

Just as a skilled musician can take hold of a violin and cause that instrument to pour forth the most stirring and moving strains of music, so is there a power that can lay hold of your mind and cause you to go forth into the field of your chosen vocation and play a glorious symphony of success. No one knows the extent of the hidden forces that lie within. Though you cannot gauge your capacity for greatness, this one great truth remains constant: Any desire that you plant deeply in your subconscious will eventually seek expression through the physical world. Where imagination prevails, power may be found. *If you want more out of life, be sure to demand more of your imagination!*

THE CHICKEN AND THE EAGLE

There was an eagle who lost an egg one day, and as fate would have it, the tiny eagle egg was found by a hen. She took the egg home to the chicken coop and sat on it with all the loving patience of an incipient mother. A few weeks later the egg was hatched, and out stepped a tiny eagle. The tiny bird had an eagle history, eagle genes, eagle chromosomes, eagle power, and eagle potential. But because he was born into a chicken environment, he grew up thinking he was a chicken. He grew up dreaming chicken dreams and thinking chicken thoughts and playing chicken games and entertaining chicken ambitions.

In fact, he was even made to feel ashamed of his eagle features. You see, even though he didn't know who he was, the other birds in the barnyard did. They met among themselves and said, "We've got to keep this bird thinking that he's a chicken, because if he ever finds out that he's an eagle, he'll rule over us."

As a result, the little bird became ashamed of his eagle heritage and eagle features. The other birds made fun of his mighty eagle beak, because they had little thin, narrow, weak chicken beaks. They also made fun of his mighty eagle talons, because they possessed weak, tiny, scrawny chicken feet. And he became ashamed of the richness of his deep, dark eagle feathers. At one point in his life, he even considered cosmetic surgery. He thought about cutting off half of his eagle beak and he thought about dyeing his dark eagle feathers, so he could look more like the chickens. Ironically, his greatest ambition in life was to one day hop, skip, and jump up on the fence post to cockle-doodle-do at daybreak like the rooster.

But one day, when this confused bird was playing in the barnyard, he saw the deep dark contours of a mighty shadow swim across the ground. For the first time in his life, this little lost bird looked higher than the fence post, higher than the tree line, and saw the remarkable sight of an adult eagle in full flight—with all of its majesty, grace, and power. The little lost bird was transfixed. He said to himself, "Wow! I sure wish I could be like that."

The adult eagle perceived the dilemma of the little lost bird and swooped down from the stratospheric heights and said, "Boy, you ain't no chicken. You're an eagle! Your mighty talons were not meant to rake and scrape on the ground for worms and feed, but to snatch the craggy side of yonder mountain of achievement.

"Boy," he repeated, "you ain't no chicken. You're an eagle! Your eagle eye was not meant to be limited to the narrow confines of the barnyard but to seek out the distant horizon of your own unfulfilled potential, and spread your wings as you catch the lofty winds of your immeasurable genius. You ain't no chicken—you're an eagle!"

Each of us could benefit from this tale. Success lies with the man or woman who is undisturbed by appearances or circumstances. An individual never reaches heights above his or her habitual thought. It is not enough, now and then, to mount on wings and soar into the infinite. We must habitually dwell there. Greatness rests easily at the pinnacle of the mount of achievement where others dare to rise. Negative conditions begin to melt once we make statements of truth regarding our potential. A sudden flash of realization propels us into a new environment. In other words, it is of little consequence what has transpired in your past. Neither the universe nor this author cares what you've failed to accomplish. It is of small value if you were raised in a chicken home in the heart of a chicken neighborhood and associated with chicken friends. It really doesn't matter if, during your childhood, you attended chicken schools and were taught by chicken teachers who shared chicken lessons. I see no reason to worry if you completed your studies and now tout a chicken degree that helped you land a chicken job, where you report to a chicken supervisor. Remember, don't think chicken thoughts and don't dream chicken dreams. You're an eagle!

Creativity is an ability given to us at birth, and thankfully, it cannot be lost. Creativity only goes into hiding and lies dormant from lack of use. It can be tapped and revitalized upon demand. You need only accept the idea that you still possess what you were given at birth—the inherent wisdom, intelligence, and creativity that constitute your particular brand of genius. Creative genius is the forging of the new, or the rearranging of the old in a novel and exciting way. It represents the actualization of human potential and the creative energy of your subconscious mind. It contains the wisdom of the past, the understanding of the present, and the vision of the future. If you wish to explore your full potential and identify new opportunities for high achievement, you must challenge your creative powers; you must stretch to new limits and explore the possibilities.

THE RICH GET RICHER

There is a science to producing great wealth—wealth in all its forms: financial, personal, and spiritual. It is an exact science, just as physics and mathematics are precisely exact. There are certain laws that govern the process of acquiring wealth, and once we learn and adhere to these laws of wealth and success, we will gain riches in all its varied forms. Wealth is not something that we produce, but something that we accept and tune into.

Several years ago I had an experience that shows how this process works. In 1991 I had the pleasure of teaching the Napoleon Hill Science of Success course at the Georgia State Correctional Facility in Forsyth, Georgia. During a luncheon, I was seated with two correctional officers who were a part of the program. As we finished our meals, an inmate gathered our dishes and cleared our table. Outside of his white and blue prison garb, he made quite an impression—at least on the surface. His uniform was neat, his shoes polished, his demeanor warm and courteous. He seemed to be a young man that would be welcomed anywhere. Outside of the circumstances surrounding our encounter, one would think this young man would have every chance in the world to succeed. We exchanged pleasantries—though visitors were discouraged from speaking to inmates—and I introduced myself. After he noticed a copy of my book *Think and Grow Rich: A Black Choice,* I discovered the cause of his troubles. Without having the slightest idea of what the book was about, he looked down and said, "Oh, the rich get richer and the poor get poorer."

Against my better judgment, I pursued his line of reasoning. I asked him how he had come to such a conclusion. He related the circumstances of his birth. His father had deserted his mother before he was born. Life in the projects was the only life he had known. "Ditching school" in turn led to "snatching candy at the corner drugstore," which was followed by gang activity and, finally, drugs. He was filled with envious hatred and a resentment of achievement aimed at anyone who excelled. "Why try?" he reasoned. "The rich get richer and the poor get poorer. What chance do I have anyway?"

Ironically, I agreed with the inmate, pointing out that the Master also agreed with him. Jesus once said, "Unto every one that hath shall be given, but from him that hath not shall be taken away even that which he hath." Like many biblical expressions, this seems to be a bit harsh, but nevertheless it illustrates the truth Jesus was trying to teach humanity. He had tried to demonstrate that thought has power; that it was the alpha and the omega—the beginning and the end—of our experience. In this verse he was saying that those who gather more of this world's goods have evidenced more of a wealth consciousness. At this point, the Master did not debate whether wealth was good or bad, or whether those who acquired it did so wrongfully. Jesus merely professed a mental law of mind by which one draws anything into his experience.

Compare this young man's outlook with that of Wally "Famous" Amos, the chocolate chip cookie tycoon. Here are two people with similar backgrounds and experiences, but vastly different results, proving that it is not what life does to us but how we react that matters. One used his talents, thereby releasing the creative forces of the master mind. The other, confined within a state of faulty consciousness, gave in to envy, hatred, and feelings of persecution. These emotions, in turn, drained his consciousness even more and robbed him of his true value. A maligned fate diminished even the little worth that he had—but it was his own state of mind that was the thief in the night. It is no disgrace to be born in poverty, but it is most decidedly a disgrace for anyone to accept the condition permanently. He had tried to play the game of life—as so many do—without taking the time to learn the rules. And now he was about to pay the price for his ignorance. This young man was, and is, poor in material possessions as well as in spirit; many of his wounds are self-inflicted.

THE HIGHER THE THOUGHT, THE CLEARER THE VISION

There are those who have broken away from poverty and tough circumstances, who have never allowed these negative influences to infiltrate their souls. Throughout Wally Amos's life, he courageously stripped away all thoughts of futility and refused to allow society to set its measure upon him. The law of truth written upon his heart made him determined to break the bars of lack and limitation as he programmed his mind to master any outer condition. Few names in the upscale cookie industry are larger or more well known than "Famous Amos." Thanks to a perceptive quality of sight, Famous Amos cookie crunchers have satisfied their sweet tooth the world over. As a matter of fact, his is the only chocolate chip cookie to achieve "star power" since he baked the first batch in 1975. While several gourmet cookie firms are more profitable than the company generally considered the pioneer, no one has come so far or encountered as many difficulties as this one's founder, Wally Amos.

Two decades ago, Amos was unproven. Starting from scratch, he walked the streets of Southern California with hundreds of samples of his tasty cookies, searching for backers. He found that raising capital was difficult. Conventional financing sources were closed and several private investors didn't pan out. With few options left, he knew where to tap. A talent agent to the core, Amos gave his product celebrity status by calling it Famous Amos and then turned to his friends, who bankrolled his chancy dream with several thousand dollars.

Despite the risks and his own apprehension, Amos opened his first store in March 1975. "I now realize that I was grossly undercapitalized," he recalled in an interview. "With no funds for advertising, I had to gather all of my creative forces. I was too naive to consider the possibility of failure. I worked eighteen-hour days baking cookies, handling interviews, and promoting my product. I once exchanged a day's worth of product—$750—for advertising time on a local radio station. I had employees offer cookies to passersby in neighboring Beverly Hills and Hollywood. If I wasn't so blinded by my vision, I would have easily talked myself out of it."

After hesitating for a moment, Amos searched for the right words and then continued. "In 1974, my life was in financial ruin. Nonetheless, I managed to prosper. People often ask, 'How do you unleash the entrepreneurial spirit?' The answer is simple: faith, insight, and openness to the creative flow."

Great accomplishments are always the result of images translated through words and action plans. The interplay between ideas and the action steps that follow can constitute an achiever's working life. Upon close examination, it usually turns out that ideas do not originate in the outer circumstances of one's life, but within his or her mind's eye. To prove this point, Amos used an apt analogy.

"What do you see?" he asked of me as we gazed out of a twenty-second-floor window in a plush Atlanta hotel.

"I see little cars and little people," I innocently replied.

"No!" he retorted. "Tell me what do you *really* see."

At this point, I began to measure my words, uneasy as to what would be his response if I answered incorrectly. Sheepishly, I said, "Wally, I still see little cars and little people." He then placed his hand on my shoulder and whispered, "My goodness, that's opportunity down there. It exists everywhere. All you need to do to see it is to raise your level of consciousness and tap into the master mind. You can only receive what you see yourself receiving."

Black America—no, all of America—is currently living in the middle of a revolution. It is as earthshaking and radical as was the Industrial Revolution, in which society shifted from horse-drawn carriage to supersonic travel. But what lies at the core of this revolution is not brute force or physical labor. Creative thinking rests at the nucleus—riches of the mind and spirit—the marriage of truth and the miracle power of the master mind.

YES, THE RICH GET RICHER AND THE POOR GET POORER!

Ideologies and philosophies have rested on the misinterpretation of this fact of life. So many lives have been wasted because millions have believed that the rich were lucky and the poor were underprivileged. Leaders of all colors and ethnic backgrounds have wrestled power away from the weak, exploiting this lie for their own benefit, pitting race against race, brother against sister, and class against class. Encouraged to seek handouts, the underclass and downtrodden are kept in spiritual darkness because they do not know where to tap. Their reaction to life is much like that of the young inmate who said, "Why try? The rich get richer and the poor get poorer." They live far beneath their power as persons and their possibilities as inhabitants of our great planet. As the great philosophers pondered and speculated upon society, they became deeply convinced that it is our natural destiny to grow, to develop, to succeed, to prosper, and to find our portion of happiness. In a nation where opportunity abounds, each of us is commissioned to find within our lives a personal realization of the very best that exists—including personal wealth.

Contrary to many religions and teachings, wealth is *not* an evil. Poverty, on the other hand, represses the individual spirit and drains all initiative. Yes, it has been written, "the meek shall inherit the earth." But where is it written that in order to be "meek," one must be poor? Here lies the argument used by those to justify their lack of progress: those who relinquish their dreams and hopes in the face of difficulty; those who make less than a total commitment to any cause or calling; those who never attempt; those who never try to advance their circumstances through an honest effort. But the time has come to break this deadly cycle. The moment of truth has arrived; each of us must assume complete responsibility and accept the blame. We must lay the burden of guilt where it truly belongs—at the feet of you, me, the individual. It is time to take up our beds and walk!

Each of us must realize that we are the product of our thoughts. We can only garner that which is the reproduction of our own consciousness. All achievers claim there is a principle flowing through us and acting upon us. But because it is an intelligent and creative principle, it can only act upon us in the way in which we act within it: "That it is done unto him according to his own belief." No leader, no ruler, no one can give us more than our own individual consciousness can attract. This idea alone spells the difference between success and failure; between the person who is master of his or her fate and the one who sees himself as a victim of uncontrollable forces. The reason there is still poverty in this land of abundance is that many do not understand this basic law of life; they do not realize that they must radiate in order to attract and that what they do radiate they constantly attract. Many people have yet to learn that you cannot get something for nothing, that you must give in order to receive. You must sow before you can reap. When you do not give or sow in terms of effort or service or higher consciousness, you make no contact with the Creator's lavish abundance. Therefore, there is no channel through which the universe can pour forth its riches, in all its forms. If we are not thriving, if we are not flourishing, if we are not successful, we have lessons yet to learn.

We must know where to tap by learning to express this creative force that life feels in us, thinks in us, and streams to us and through us, by knowing who we truly are. You and I are much greater than we think. This is the law of life—the law of the universe, the law of destiny. It is the law of creation working through us, individually. We must learn how to become receptive to this flow of good. We must be open to the good, the true, the beautiful, and initiate the action that will bring these mental treasures into physical manifestation.

The rich get richer and the poor get poorer. Truer words were never spoken. But it is a statement of mental law—not an edict of the Creator. Creative thought is the only power that can produce wealth from a formless substance. Wealth is the result of riches within our consciousness.

MENTAL LAWS

Throughout the ages, man has attempted to make sense of the universe; to unravel mysteries that have challenged his intellect and seek solutions to seemingly unsolvable problems. In searching for the truth and often questioning it, scholars, thinkers, philosophers, and scientists have immeasurably influenced our world. Their medical breakthroughs, scientific discoveries, physical laws, and mathematical principles have imposed order, coherence, and clarity on what once seemed a random, indiscriminate, and lawless world. The driving force behind these great thinkers was their innate desire to succeed, to focus their minds on a question and to strive relentlessly until they found an answer. And in their wealth of wisdom, we now find mental laws of personal success and achievement that each of us can use to maximize our own potential. The mental laws are as timeless and immutable as the natural and physical laws that govern the universe. They hold true for everyone that abides by them and are applicable in every area of life. Whenever you see an individual who is not achieving his or her full potential, you see a violation of these mental laws that is both sad and unnecessary.

Just as there are basic laws and principles that control our physical world, there are basic laws and principles that control our mental world as well. Before we can hope to operate our human success system, we need to know the basic laws that determine our behavior and affect our very being. In this regard, we have no choice. We cannot bypass these laws in an attempt to negate their application. They are present in all mental workings and operate successfully to bring about the results that you desire. Mental laws are similar to physical laws in one respect: They are in effect 100 percent of the time. For example, the law of gravity is constantly in force. Our knowledge level or our awareness of the subject of gravity doesn't matter. The law is neutral. What does matter, however, is that the law is in force all of the time, whether it is convenient for us or not.

Mental laws also work 100 percent of the time. A life that is going well is a clear signal that our thoughts and activities are aligned and in harmony with these spiritual principles. Conversely, whenever we experience challenges or moments of despair, we might be violating one or more of these laws—whether we recognize them or not. These mental laws have been known for centuries. Unfortunately, only a few of us understand them or apply them in our daily lives. Deepak Chopra, the physician and author of works on mind-body medicine and human potential, defines law as "the process by which the unmanifest becomes manifest; the observer becomes the observed; the seer becomes the scenery; and the avenue through which the dreamer manifests the dream." Because they are central to our happiness and prosperity, it is essential that we become familiar with these laws and integrate them into everything we do.

LAW OF PRACTICE

Practice makes perfect. This familiar proverb embodies one of the great laws of human nature. There is simply no achievement without practice, and the more practice, provided it is done intelligently, the greater the proficiency and the sooner our goals will be realized. This maxim is true in every branch of human endeavor. Success, growth, and achievement are spiritual ideas of excellence. And, like any form of excellence or superiority, they require patience, effort, and practice. Excellence means investing in yourself. Excellence means real work. But those who set their sights high and are willing to reach for the laurel wreath in life are those who become great and true champions. They are the special people who ennoble the entire race, those who ultimately accomplish the most and leave an enduring legacy. Excellence requires effort; and effort demands practice.

A famous concert pianist applied this principle of repetition to his musical talents. He maintained a rigorous eight-hour-a-day practice schedule throughout his career. Asked why he persisted in practicing even after he had become world-renowned for his musical excellence, he replied, "If I miss practice for one day, I notice. If I miss practice for two days, my critics notice. But if I miss practice for three days, my audience notices." Practice is the price of proficiency.

LAW OF MENTAL EQUIVALENCY

Simply defined, the law of mental equivalency states that thoughts objectify themselves. Your thoughts, vividly imagined and charged with emotion, become your reality. Nearly every circumstance in your life—either for better or for worse—has been created by your thinking. Everything that occurs in your life begins in the form of thought. Thoughts become things. They take on a life of their own. First you have them, then they have you. To alter your life requires a transformation of your thinking: "Be ye transformed by the renewing of your mind." Change your thinking and you will change your life. Thought is the mental equivalent of what you wish to experience in your reality.

LAW OF CONTROL

The law of control states that you feel positive about yourself to the degree that you feel you are in control of your life; and conversely, you feel negative about yourself to the degree that you feel you are not in control—or that you are controlled by others or some external force. Your locus of control can be either internal or external. That is, you can feel that you are in charge of your life—happy, free, and fulfilled—or you can feel controlled by others—helpless, trapped, harboring a victim mentality. You will find that the areas in which you experience the greatest peace of mind and satisfaction are those areas in which you feel you have the greatest amount of control. You will also discover that the areas in which you are most unhappy or experience the highest levels of stress are those in which you feel you are not in control.

Gaining control of your life requires accepting responsibility for your thoughts and actions: "Choose this day who you will serve." In the Old Testament, the book of Leviticus tells of a sacred custom called the "escaped goat." When the troubles of the people became too much to bear, a healthy male goat was brought into the temple. In a solemn ceremony, the highest priest of the tribe placed his hands on the goat and recited the list of woes. The problems were then transferred onto the goat and the animal was set free, taking the troubles of the village away with it. That was nearly four thousand years ago, but we still use "scapegoats" today. We frequently use other people or other things in our lives to avoid accepting the responsibility of who we are and what we do. Instead of working on what is going on inside us, we try to blame that which is around us. It is always easier and more convenient to assume the answer lies elsewhere or with others. But this offers us only a false sense of hope. There is no way that you can gain control over your thoughts and actions without accepting full responsibility.

In this sense, control and responsibility are necessary companions on the road to positive thinking and living. Responsibility, control, and a sense of freedom go hand in hand. Whenever you see the word "responsibility," its true meaning is synonymous with "freedom." In other words: *control = responsibility = freedom:* "Ye shall know the truth, and the truth shall make you free." Regardless of the depth of your convictions or the height of your logic, it is impossible for any individual, group, or people to be free without accepting total responsibility for their lives!

Perhaps an effective mental conditioner would be to verbally affirm the following.

> *"Today I accept responsibility for my life. I direct the law*
> *of control to produce a new quality of life. I allow myself*
> *no regrets about the past. My consciousness is open to the*

*present. Therefore, I only express goodwill and perfect
harmony. These ideas are instantly reflected back into my
experience. I am happy living my life."*

Failure to accept full responsibility for your thinking will bring continued frustration and unhappiness. The law of control is essential in maintaining a high level of energy, peace of mind, self-confidence, and positive emotions. Success lies in waiting for those who master this law. Control begins with your thoughts, the only thing over which you do have complete control. Make sure they're rock-solid.

LAW OF EXPECTATION

The law of expectation states that whatever you expect with confidence becomes your own self-fulfilling prophecy. This means that what you get is not necessarily what you *want* in life, but what you *expect.* Your expectations exert a powerful influence that causes people to behave and situations to work out as you anticipated. Successful men and women have an attitude of confident, positive expectancy. They expect to be successful, they expect to reach their objectives. They expect to win, and they anticipate achievement as a reward for their creativity. Seldom are they disappointed.

There's a power in enthusiastic expectation to an ideal! What are hardships, slander, ridicule, persecution, and toil to a soul throbbing with the expectation of mastering a purpose? The desire for success and the expectation for failure rarely reside in the same breast. Anger begets anger; and hate, hate. Expect success and forget the rest.

Clarence Smith and Edward Lewis are not the men they thought they would be. Unforeseen changes converged on them from every side, but they rode them out by adhering to the law of expectation. In the late 1960s, the two met in Manhattan, almost by accident. At the time, both had clearly defined careers—Lewis was a financial planner for Citibank, and Smith sold insurance for Prudential. Smith sensed Lewis was a prime prospect for his company's many services and pitched him over lunch. Lewis said the timing was wrong but promised to stay in touch. From that first encounter, a friendship grew that would later develop into a relationship of enormous importance.

In due course, the two would meet again, this time at a Harlem seminar sponsored by Shearson Hamill in the latter part of 1968. The brokerage firm invited a cross section of black professionals to explore ideas for possible businesses. Among those present were Lewis and Smith, Cecil Hollingsworth, a printer, and Jonathan Blount, an energetic twenty-four-year-old ad salesman for Bell Telephone. Within this forum, these would-be capitalists fumbled with a number of ideas, none of which seemed to stick. Blount took center stage when he shared a conversation that he had had with his foster mother a few months before. "Why isn't there a magazine for black women?" she had asked. At the time, Blount shrugged his shoulders and his mother either lost interest or lost track of her idea. But the young man asked the question again— this time to a group of entrepreneurial upstarts. Hoping for a more favorable response, he supplemented his query with sparsely documented data.

"What do you think?" Smith asked Lewis as they left the meeting. Lewis shook his head and grabbed his coat. "It makes sense," he answered. What he thought was that it was all very exciting. That maybe, just maybe, this seed of an idea could take root. But what he *really* thought was that he finally saw a way for him to parlay his fund-raising skills and tenacity into something worthwhile; a way in which he could make a difference. He saw a path in which he could march to his own music.

Smith also felt the magic in the moment. Ironically, his career was finally on track. He was thirty-five years old, earning $30,000 a year as a top-notch salesman of insurance. He had a handsome family and a cozy suburban home. By any definition of success, Smith had made it. But his lifestyle also meant a slide into obscurity. Smith had come to the point where he dared to try his wings for something new. He felt one step closer after that fateful meeting. Lewis and Smith had the itch. They returned to their jobs silently renewed and began to chase their dreams. Almost indignantly, the question struck their collective nerves: Why wasn't there a magazine for black women?

In 1969, the itch turned into a rash. Lewis and Smith met with Blount and Hollingsworth to discuss the concept further. Each seemed sincere and willing to take the leap into entrepreneurship. Together, they formed a partnership, the Hollingsworth Group, a name taken from stationery Cecil Hollingsworth had left over from his graphics consulting firm. A banker proposed, and the group concurred, that it would be wise for them to try and piece together what little data they could find on black readership and black female consumer preference.

When all was said and done, the four brash young men with no publishing experience found themselves in agreement on one key point: The magazine industry—virtually unchanged since the Depression— was about to take on a new group of fastly emerging consumers: women of color of varying ages who believed in self-development. The industry was about to confront a new magazine responding to the desires of this overlooked market. What the group found was a red carpet to their future. It soon became apparent—at least to Lewis and Smith—that they could no longer continue their jobs and still push their idea forward. Each spent all his time and effort entirely on spec, with no assurance the concept would fly. Besides investing their own money, they poured in staggering amounts of their most cherished capital—hope and positive expectation—and continued to lean into their dream. Although Lewis and Smith were committed to leaving corporate America, leaving the security of a job was a step that some of their partners could not take. When asked to cross the bridge of faith, the Hollingsworth Group was pared down to a party of two.

The result was a new publication, *Essence,* the first lifestyle magazine for black women. With an initial printing of 150,000 copies, the magazine made its debut in May 1970. Today, Lewis and Smith jointly conduct the affairs of one of Black America's top twenty privately owned companies.

However, the birth of any magazine is always a struggle against the odds, and *Essence* was no exception. Warned that any special-interest venture would have at best a "shaky future," the two mavericks were bent on making the project a success. "As you can imagine, it was not easy then—nor is it easy now," Lewis says. "We were undercapitalized and forced to operate on a tight budget. But through it all we persevered, never losing our sense of mission." During those periods when he felt overburdened, he'd recite his mother's words: "The road to freedom is rocky and steep."

But Clarence Smith touched upon a key principle of achievement as he discussed the components of success: "From our initial projections, we thought that our break-even point would be three years. But hell, we were in business *six* years before we ever made a profit. Within the first year alone, there were at least four different times I thought we might go under. Experts told us that we didn't have a chance. The only thing that kept us going was that we *expected* success."

As you read these lines, keep in mind the basic crux of the law of expectation: *Whatever you expect with confidence becomes a self-fulfilling prophecy.* Success is not difficult to achieve once you make practical use of positive expectancy. As this story points out, Lewis and Smith subconsciously triggered this law by confidently expecting the realization of their goals. Anyone with sufficient initiative and ability can duplicate the fortunes of these achievers if he or she adheres to the fundamental requirements of this principle. Both failure and mistakes can be converted into assets of priceless value when you *expect* to succeed.

LAW OF RECIPROCITY

All relationships are based upon the law of reciprocity. This law states that people are internally driven to reciprocate for anything done either to them or for them. Friends and associates will be willing to help you achieve your goals only when you have demonstrated a willingness to help others achieve their goals. In other words, people don't care about *you* until they know how much you care about *them.*

The most successful men and women in our society are those who have helped the greatest number of people achieve their objectives: "He that will be great among you, let him serve." They build a vast reservoir of goodwill and, in turn, will be compensated for having aided others. For example, the direction of Joe Dudley's life was drastically altered when he mastered this law. Living under the thumb of poverty for the majority of his life, Dudley turned his focus to supporting others. As a result, he built a multimillion-dollar hair-care business in the process. Today, he instructs others that service will always be a welcome commodity. "You can have anything that you want," he proclaims, "if you only help enough people get what they want." Your returns in life are the result of your contributions to others. Shakespeare wrote, "The fragrance of the rose lingers on the hand that casts it." If you give hard work, helpfulness, and honesty, you will receive riches, rewards, and the respect of others. Under this law, you, and you only, will determine just how much you will receive.

LAW OF HABIT

Virtually everything we do is the result of our habits. You are a bundle of habits. The way you walk, talk, think, act, and deal with the important people in your life is largely habitual. We are creatures of habit. Life is habit—a succession of unconscious responses that become more or less automatic. Since your thinking and behavior are subject to the same principle, your habits will make or break you. Habits can be either stepping-stones or roadblocks to success or failure, happiness or unhappiness. In the absence of an outside force or a definitive decision on your part, you'll continue to act in accordance with these patterns, ad infinitum. You'll work in the same job, associate with the same people, eat the same foods, take the same route to work, and engage in the same activities for the remainder of your life.

Changing habits that are no longer consistent with your objectives will be one of the most challenging steps that you will ever take. Good habits are hard to form but easy to live with; and bad habits are easy to form but hard to live with. The toughest things to change are bad habits that run counter to the goals that you want to achieve. If a habit isn't helpful, it is hurtful. If a habit is not leading you toward success, it's probably leading you to failure. Habits aren't instincts; they're acquired reactions. They don't "just happen," they are caused. Once you've determined the original cause of a habit, it is within your power to either accept or reject it.

It takes approximately three to four weeks to break a habit. It takes the same amount of time to develop a new one. After this brief period, the habit becomes "rooted." In other words, an automatic response. Remember, we first form habits; then habits form us. In the individual drive toward achievement, if we do not consciously form good habits, we will unconsciously form bad ones. Successful men and women have simply formed the habit of doing things that failures will not do. It is just as easy to form the habit of succeeding as it is to succumb to the habit of failure. Perhaps now is the appropriate time to ask: What habits would I like to change or alter?

LAW OF FORGIVENESS

The vital importance of forgiveness may not be obvious at first, but you may be sure that it is not by chance that every great spiritual teacher has insisted strongly upon it. The law of forgiveness states that you are mentally healthy to the degree that you can freely *forgive* and *forget* offenses done against you. You must forgive injustices—not just in words, but in your heart. This is required, not for someone else's sake, but for yours. Failure to carry out this basic act gives control of your life to those whom you have judged to have wronged you. Forgiveness means changing any misperceptions. When we forgive another for anything that he or she may have done to us, we are really saying, "I no longer give you the power to control who I am, how I think, and how I will behave in the future. I take full responsibility for my life." Forgiveness is the most liberating act of life.

The inability to forgive lies at the root of all negative emotions—resentment, condemnation, hatred, and guilt. Medical science has proved that holding a grudge or harboring anger toward those who you feel have hurt you is a major cause of illness. To fulfill your potential, to develop your full spiritual capacity, you must let go, and cut the cord to anger and resentment. You must forgive!

Nearly fifty years ago, Dr. Frederic Loomis, an old country physician, wrote a short but memorable article entitled "The Best Medicine." Though the author died a short time after publishing his moving piece, he still lives on in the minds of thousands of people. Dr. Loomis wrote, "It's but little good you'll do watering last year's crops. Yet that's exactly what I've seen hundreds of my patients do over the past twenty-five years—*watering last year's crops.* Watering with freely flowing tears things of the irrevocable past. Not the bittersweet memories of loved ones but things done which should not have been done. And things left undone which should have been done. . . .

"Each of us can lighten our own load by forgiving or perform some small deed for someone else. In this manner we can make the past recede as the present and future will again take on their true challenge and perspective. As a doctor I've seen it tried many times, and nearly always it's been a far more successful prescription than anything I could have ordered from the drugstore."

One of the most difficult things for any individual to do is to forget his or her past mistakes or the mistakes of others; to let bygones be gone. This small stroke of maturity is easy to say, but difficult to do. We all know people who sit and play with the tragedies of the past—like children in a sandbox—refusing to forgive those who have wronged them in any way. They should instead think long and hard on the words of Shakespeare: "Things without remedy should be without regard." In other words, what is done is done. It's time to forgive and forget. It's time to turn to the future with the wisdom brought by past pain and begin to consider the needs and desires of our fellowman.

One of the most memorable covers of a national magazine appeared nearly two years ago. It was a picture of Nelson Mandela embracing F. W. de Klerk, South African President—the man and the symbol of the unjust society that incarcerated him for twenty-seven years of his life. That portrait of forgiveness left a lasting impression on me. Thirty years prior, that same picture was drawn featuring Malcolm X, the famed Muslim minister, after he made his last pilgrimage to the Holy Land. Malcolm X returned a new man, completely transformed. People whom we consider reverent or spiritual or role models of decency are always able to forgive without qualification or doubt. They do not cloud their consciousness with thoughts of anger or vengeance directed toward those who have attempted to wrong them. Rather, they provide society with a model of forgiveness that we can use in our daily lives. To be forgiven, we must forgive. Forgiving brings forgiveness. Failure to forgive creates hell for the unforgiver, not the unforgiven. Practice forgiveness. It is the greatest act!

I am your constant companion. I am your greatest helper or heaviest burden. I will push you onward or drag you down to failure. I am completely at your command. Half the things you do you might just as well turn over to me and I will be able to do them quickly and correctly. I am easily managed—you must merely be firm with me. Show me exactly how you want something done and after a few lessons I will do it automatically. I am the servant of all great men; and alas, of all failures, as well. Those who are great, I have made great. Those who are failures, I have made failures. I am not a machine, though I work with all the precision of a machine plus the intelligence of a man. You may run me for profit or run me for ruin—it makes no difference to me. Take me, train me, be firm with me, and I will place the world at your feet. Be easy with me and I will destroy you. Who am I? I am habit!

—Anonymous

.   .   .

THESE MENTAL LAWS are the most powerful forces ever discovered. Each law enables you to begin unlocking the powers of your subconscious mind. Use these principles in a positive and systematic way. In any attempt to improve your current circumstances, never allow yourself to drift from those time-proven principles that have flowed from generation to generation in a steady stream to serve as the fundamentals for finding, developing, and living the good life. In the simplest terms, success begins by exercising your power of choice to take direct control over your thoughts. By disciplining yourself to think and talk and act in accordance with these mental laws, you begin to live life on purpose. You begin to develop what writer and lecturer Brian Tracy terms a "sense of destiny," which is the hallmark of true success.

HOW TO ATTAIN THE GREATEST IDEA
IN THE WORLD

Processionary caterpillars travel in long, undulating lines, one creature behind another. Jean-Henri Fabre, the French naturalist who died in 1915, once led a group of these caterpillars onto the rim of a large flowerpot, so that the lead caterpillar actually touched the last caterpillar in the procession, forming a complete circle. In the center of the flowerpot Fabre placed pine needles, a main source of food for such creatures. With an ample supply of food close at hand and plainly visible, for seven days and nights the caterpillars circled the flowerpot until they died from exhaustion and starvation. Why? Because these mentally programmed creatures refused to veer off the beaten path.

People often behave in a similar way. Habitual patterns and ways of thinking become deeply established, and it seems easier and more comforting to continue these thought patterns than to cope with change—even when change represents freedom and achievement. With regard to success, so many people miss the boat because it's less tedious to "follow the follower" and question the qualifications of those "leaders" just ahead than it is to take the road less traveled and engage in independent, constructive thinking. The toughest thing for people to fathom is that individuals in such large numbers can be so wrong—just like those caterpillars who traveled in circles to their death, with food and life just a short distance away. If most people are living that way, they contend, it must be right. At one time or another, most of us have fallen prey to this type of thinking. But a little checking will reveal that throughout recorded history, when it comes to the subject of achievement and progress, this one idea holds true: *The crowd is always wrong!* Experts have pointed out that the average individual conjures up at least four ideas a year, any of which would lead to a modest fortune. Unfortunately, only a few turn their dreams into reality. But for those men and women who do, they come to share common traits and qualities: They determine the agenda; they set the pace; and they dominate the field of play.

> **You can have anything that you want if you only help enough people get what they want.**
>
> **—Joe Dudley**

Do you realize that nothing has yet been done perfectly? Everything in the world remains to be done or done over. A major magazine recently reported that one out of every four products advertised in a particular issue was little more than an idea or an experimental laboratory project ten years ago. Today, more money is invested in research and development in a single year than was spent during the first 150 years of our nation's history. No one product has ever been manufactured, distributed, advertised, or sold as efficiently as it might be or someday will be. As we comb the globe, there isn't a perfectly managed business, organization, institution, or government. The greatest picture has yet to be painted. The most touching poem has not been written. The best way to train salespeople, an easy way to stay slim, a cure for baldness, a better mousetrap—all of these problems are still unsolved. Psychology, sociology, and economics are still being revised. Physics, mathematics, and chemistry await another Einstein or George Washington Carver. Languages and the arts await another Ralph Ellison and Romare Bearden. Nothing is known completely and positively—nothing has been done finally and right—everything changes. So the world waits, and then moves forward in surges as here a man and there a woman makes a fresh and daring discovery or proposes some bold new idea. Most of these contributions to social and scientific progress come from creative individuals who have the courage and strength to challenge and break the bonds of conventional, routine thinking. In this swift-moving world, there is tremendous opportunity for the man or woman who will use more of his or her mental powers.

Begin now to use your mind to think about those things that can be done or need to be done. Ask yourself the following critical questions:

- How can I improve myself so that I can become a better person?
- How can I get along better with my customers, colleagues, friends, and family?
- What can I do to increase my value and advance faster in my organization?
- How can I generate new ideas for advancing my profession or improving my business or industry?

By asking these questions you're taking the vital early steps in the creative process. You're beginning to exercise your mind and put your creative powers to work. As you search for new answers, you begin to add zest and interest to your life. You'll feel transformed, revitalized, and renewed with a newfound energy. Yes, you have a gold mine between your ears, but you must dig out that rarest of all precious gems—your creative genius.

FREE YOURSELF FROM ERRONEOUS THINKING

Several years ago, during a leadership conference held on the campus of Purdue University, I addressed nearly two hundred students on the topic of business and success. Throughout my remarks, I intentionally underscored the role that vision and imagination play in the process of growing a business. My presentation was well received and the audience was most inquisitive. I was delighted to field a host of questions from many bright students who seemed bent on hitting their stride in today's business world. After my talk, I weaved my way through the crowd, pausing briefly to autograph books. I had nearly reached the exit when a young, smartly dressed black woman approached me with a look of consternation. From all outward appearances, she looked as if success were a foregone conclusion.

As I handed a book to a well-wisher, she broke through the crowd and blurted within earshot of everyone, "Dr. Kimbro, I don't believe a word you said. Everyone knows that it takes money to make money, and without adequate start-up capital, no one stands a chance!"

Needless to say, I, as well as those who heard her remarks, was stunned. A hush fell over the group, and those nearest to me squirmed in embarrassment. All eyes shifted in my direction in anticipation of my response. As I continued to greet people, I flashed a warm smile and told my critic that I would address her comments in a few moments. I signed the last book and then began to share my thoughts—principles and spiritual concepts—that I had uncovered in more than a decade of research.

"Tell me something about yourself," I asked the young skeptic. In the moments that followed, she told me that she had read of my visit through a flyer that she kept neatly folded in her purse. She had debated whether or not to attend. Nearly three years ago, brimming with desire and determination, she had graduated from Purdue with a degree in engineering. Upon graduation, she had agonized over the prospects of accepting a job in corporate America, hoping instead to launch a business. Her rationale was to work for a few years, save her money, then break out on her own. She really wanted to be her own boss; to be free and in control; to call her own shots. It all seemed easy enough. But somewhere over the course of three years, her dream vanished. First came the rent for a well-adorned apartment. Then car payments. Shortly after, bills and more bills, mostly credit-card debt to maintain a stylish image. Though she landed a great job—the pay was decent, the work was relatively easy, and the promotions had come in a timely fashion—there was one hitch: She hated every minute of it. At age twenty-four, she was snared by golden handcuffs and began to doubt her abilities. And now I was the recipient of her frustration as she questioned one of the spiritual laws of prosperity.

To demonstrate the true cause of wealth and prosperity, I asked a series of questions. First I asked, "Over the course of one year, if you sold your possessions—your car, clothing, and furnishings—could you raise fifteen thousand dollars?" She studied me for a few seconds, then shifted her feet to look at those around her.

"You mean *every*thing?" she quizzed.

I nodded. "Yes, everything."

"I guess I could," she finally replied.

"Good," I shot back. "That was the same position that Bob Johnson found himself in when he dared to start Black Entertainment Television ten years ago." To carry my point further, I asked, "If you sold everything, could you raise ten thousand dollars in nine months?"

Again, she paused before responding. "Ten thousand dollars in nine months? Yeah, I guess so."

"Great," I said. "That's the dilemma that Wally 'Famous' Amos faced when he held hopes of launching a cookie empire."

I continued my discourse. "Could you raise five hundred dollars in six months?" Her response was that she could. I brought it to her attention that John Johnson was in the same predicament when a lack of financing nearly brought *Ebony* magazine to a grinding halt.

By now the crowd was leaning on every word. Some bystanders were taking notes. I looked her straight in the eyes. "If left with no possible way of retreat, could you raise two hundred and fifty dollars in ninety days?" Her answers were coming much quicker: "Yes," she said.

"I'm glad," I informed her. "Because Earl Graves was faced with the same question when he brought *Black Enterprise* magazine to newsstands across the country."

"Could you come up with thirty dollars in thirty days?" Meekly, she said yes. "That's what it took for George Halsey to purchase an Amway sales kit that led him to riches that only a few can comprehend."

And to bring this exercise to closure, I asked, "If left with nothing, could you raise two dollars?" By then, the once assertive young woman was too shy to make eye contact.

"Two dollars?" someone in the crowd heckled.

"Yes, two dollars," I said to no one in particular. "That's all Madame C.J. Walker [America's first black millionaire] possessed when she was raised from the rank of menial worker to millionaire! Her imagination allowed her to see the big picture."

Prosperity, wealth, and abundance are normal, a way of life. They are an active way of thinking and living in accordance with the spiritual and mental laws of abundance and supply. Wealth consciousness is a state of mind. Empty pockets never held anyone back. It's only empty heads and hearts that can do that! If you are constantly concerned about how much money you need, then irrespective of your net worth, you are really poor. Our most precious natural resource is not our mineral deposits or our bountiful majestic landscape. It is the mental attitude and the imagination of every generation that has combined experience with education to deliver goods and services that improve the quality of life of humanity worldwide.

Each of us was created with all that is necessary for fulfillment. We need only to learn to open ourselves to receive the good that is around us and within us. And where can this good be found? Within our imagination! Prosperity is a spiritual idea. It has nothing to do with the materialistic display of affluence. Although in the physical realm it may take money to make money, in truth, wealth and abundance require much more. They require a dream, a goal, a purpose, a vision, a mission, visualization, foresight, an idea, thought, but most important, a *prosperity consciousness.*

Begin now to control your thoughts and move beyond the limits of form. Turn a deaf ear to scarcity and lack. Let the dead bury the dead. Turn to the dreams of the future rather than the history of the past. Tap into the invisible part of your powers that holds the key to future growth and development—the imagination.

HOW TO TURN YOUR DREAMS INTO REALITY

Have you ever considered the possibilities of thinking in different ways? Think about how you can create something, in your work and in your life. Remember, nothing is done to perfection; nothing is final or complete. No matter what you desire, if it is within the realm of reality, you can obtain it through imagination and creativity applied to your work. Today, throughout the field of enterprise, nothing is being done the way it can be or will be. Change will be the norm. In the future, everything can and will be done much better as the result of our applied creativity. People who resist change will be impediments to progress. Yet the first words the new employee often hears is the familiar refrain, "This is the way it's done around here." A. Barry Rand, a senior-level executive with Xerox, once remarked, "If we're doing anything this year the way it was done last year, we're obsolete." This comment may seem extreme, but in most cases it's true. In order to generate original ideas, society will need a way to create new sets of mental patterns. When you can master this skill, you will produce ideas where none existed. Here are seven new, bold ways to *THINK.*

• *Think association.* The creative person is forever associating ideas and concepts and continually searches for relationships. Your brain cannot deliberately concentrate on two separate objects or ideas without eventually forming a connection between them. No two inputs can remain separate in your mind no matter how remote they are from each other. The key is to hold both of them in your attention and to look for relationships and connections between the two. Through association we can remember places, persons, and things. An association list is used by memory experts to recall lengthy lists of articles by associating each item with another article in a previously memorized list. Once you become aware, you'll routinely see connections between dissimilar objects, leading you to greater creativity.

• *Think combination.* Almost everything in nature, including you, is a combination of elements. Water is a combination of hydrogen and oxygen. A simple pencil is a combination of wood, carbon, rubber, paint, and metal. Other examples include: ham and eggs, pie a la mode, franks and beans, the mobile phone. Imagine, someone conceived the idea of combining music and comedy, and as a result the musical comedy was born. As African Americans, we are a combination of two of the greatest countries and cultures known to mankind. By uniting the mundane or common into a new product or service, you can create a number of useful ideas. Everything you see, hear, touch, taste, or smell offers opportunity to consider new combinations.

- *Think adaptation.* Somebody thought creatively when either he or she adapted airplane seat belts for use in the automobile. The phonograph record and motion picture, originally developed for entertainment, have been adapted for teaching and education. Throughout the remainder of the decade and beyond, we will see the result of individuals thinking adaptation and coming up with ideas worth millions of dollars. Why couldn't one of these people be you? The only limit to what you can achieve by adapting old products to new uses, and old methods to new applications, is the limit to your own creativity.

- *Think substitution.* When you think substitution, ask yourself how you might substitute a different material or procedure for the one currently being used. For example, within many industries, plastic is substituted for wood and metal. Stainless steel is a substitute for other metals. At one time, the transistor replaced the vacuum tube, and now the computer chip replaces them both. In short, don't assume that anything is indispensable—feel free to substitute. Just because something has been used in the past doesn't mean society will continue to use it in the future. Take a look at everyday products and services. Perhaps there is a substitute that will work better or last longer, or cost less or be more durable, and so forth. Think substitution.

- *Think big.* Think bold, think no limits, think *big!* Picture a skyscraper, jumbo jets, giant soft drinks, large economy-size products—what do they have in common? They're of greater benefit because they were made larger. By increasing size, you add value as well as possibilities. On the other hand:

- *Think small.* Consider the solar battery, the transistor, the compact car, the palm-top computer, or a Sony Walkman. What do you work with that could benefit others if it were made smaller?

- *Think rearrangement.* That is, shift things around. Turn products or concepts upside down, inside out, reverse order—rearrange things.

For example, just imagine when fashion designers had the audacity to place mink on the inside of coats. All the warmth, luxury, and status of a full-length mink in a casual coat. Consider the "running" shoe: In a world that values its leisure time and relaxation, people now wear a shoe specifically geared for physical activity, effort, and sweat. Think rearrangement. What ideas, services, or industries could benefit from this type of thinking? What can you turn around, shift, alter, modify, revolutionize, or rearrange? Salespeople use these creative techniques to discover new applications for products and new ways of emphasizing customer benefits. The opportunities are endless.

If you want to spur your mind in a new direction, think association, combination, adaptation, substitution, magnification, minification, and rearrangement. If you force yourself to think in these seven creative ways, you will be amazed by the ideas you develop. This type of thinking increases the scope of your mind power, enabling you to move closer to realizing your full potential. Your mind has an infinite variety of things it can do and an infinite capacity for work. Allow the master mind to help you conceive the greatest idea in the world!

4

The Greatest Asset:

"Right"-eousness

- **Integrity: The Magic Word**

- **What Do You Value Most?**

- **How to Develop Integrity**

If honesty did not exist, we ought to invent it
as the best means of getting rich.
—GABRIEL RIQUETI MIRABEAU

One falsehood spoils a thousand truths.
—ASHANTI PROVERB

The opposite of compromise is character.
—FREDERICK DOUGLASS

Do the right thing.
—SPIKE LEE

There are men and women throughout society who conquer before they speak and who exert an influence out of proportion to their ability. People wonder about the secret of their power. What is the key to their success? The world, it is said, is always searching for men and women who are not for sale; men and women who are honest, sound from center to circumference, true to the heart's core. Men and women who will stand for right even if the heavens quake and the earth moves; who can tell the truth regardless of the outcome; who neither boast nor flinch; in whom the hope of everlasting life runs strong and deep; who know their message and tell it; who know their place and fill it; who are willing to eat what they have earned and ask for help only when they deserve it; who, if given a choice, would ask for a strong back rather than a light burden; who are not too proud to humble themselves in the company of others and say, "Thank you, Father."

CHARACTER IS WHAT YOU ARE IN THE DARK

Have you ever watched an icicle form? Did you notice how the dripping water froze, one drop at a time, until the icicle was a foot long or more? If the water was clean, the icicle remained clear and sparkled brightly in the sun; but if the water was dirty, the icicle appeared cloudy, its beauty spoiled. In the same manner our character is formed. Each thought and action adds to its shape. Each decision we make—about matters great and small—contributes. Every bit that we absorb into our minds and souls, be they impressions, experiences, or the words of others, helps create our character. We must remain concerned at all times regarding the "droplets" that we allow to drip through our lives. Acts that develop habits of love, truth, and goodness silently shape and mold us into the image of the Creator—just as habits born of jealousy, hatred, and evil mar and eventually destroy us.

All of the above is true. One powerful virtue can revolutionize your life, as it has done for so many. Single-handedly, this quality can set you on the path of prosperity, or it can trap you in bondage—both mentally and physically. If you incorporate this trait into your personal philosophy, this value alone will solve life's true riddles. Each new day the soul meets itself. Inscribed over the portals of Spelman College is the inscription: "Our whole school for Christ." Handsomely framed on the walls of its New York headquarters, the United Negro College Fund displays a statement by the Reverend Jesse Jackson that captures the essence of its mission: "The Black college has a special calling . . . to reach the unreachable, to teach the unteachable, to embrace the rejected and be patient with the late bloomers." And, finally, carved into the weather-beaten stone steps of a small southern church is this advice: "There are only two ways to read the Bible: One, read it with your mind made up; or two, read to allow it to make up your mind."

Our character is forming daily. It is a low standard of greatness that measures an individual by his or her employment or by possessions alone. The mason may stagger under the bricks of the millionaire who employs him, but the manner in which the mason lives may be as far above the lifestyle of his employer as heaven is to hell.

What a shock to the aristocratic board of trustees of Spelman College when Johnetta Cole interrupted their meeting to single out and embrace an elderly black woman who had prepared their food. "God bless you, Miss Johnetta," the little woman said adoringly, unable to make eye contact.

When the life-size bust of football legend Eddie Robinson was unveiled during a moving ceremony in Atlanta, Georgia, the sculptor, Robert Ilg, was asked to address the audience. He simply ran his hands across the lifelike bronze image and said, "This is my speech." What could be more eloquent?

The character of Arthur Ashe was mightier than his affliction, and it banished the fear and sting of death. Who can estimate the power of a well-lived life? A strong, true character is not the result of mere physical condition. It involves the living spirit. Just as the water reveals the springs from which it comes; just as the mind reveals its teachers, so, too, the words we speak and the actions we take reveal what is behind our character. Character is a noble pattern cut into fine cloth.

When asked at his retirement party what he intended to do with the rest of his life, basketball Hall of Famer Julius Erving replied, "I think it's time to focus on being a good husband and father. If I can't succeed in this mission, I can't succeed in anything." Nothing so strengthens the heart and enlarges the soul as the constant effort to measure up to a high ideal.

INTEGRITY: THE MAGIC WORD

How can you make your life yield to its fullest? How can you uncover the real secret of power? How can you attain a true and lasting greatness? How can your life be filled with happiness, peace of mind, and a rich, abiding satisfaction that never decreases? The answers to these tough questions have been sought throughout the ages. And there is an answer!

Follow closely. Take issue with me if you must. Every day we witness men and women who fail to measure up to the power of this quality. Examine it closely—see if it will stand every test. But tell me, finally, if this key is not true or complete. There is one simple principle, which, if firmly laid hold of and, if made the central creed of one's life, will make that life truly great and blessed.

Of all the qualities that parents can instill in their children, which would you say is the most important? Several years ago, the editors of a business magazine conducted a survey on what qualities it takes to be successful. Although they didn't bother to indicate what they meant by success, the term was nevertheless construed to mean successful in life. Oddly enough, the same quality surfaced among fathers, mothers, teachers, and businesspeople alike. The one word that was mentioned above others was *integrity.*

There are millions today who dismiss this important concept, but the odds are good that those who do so or their children are not doing very well. Children who are taught the importance of integrity never seem to lose it. It becomes a part of their being—their way of doing things. More than anything else, this simple key will guarantee success in life. Integrity is an individual's greatest asset. It will remain when everything else is taken away. You cannot lose integrity. It will stay when your money is gone; it will be there when friends have forsaken you. Though your ideal is what you *wish* you were, and your reputation is what people *say* you are, integrity is *what* you are!

Thomas Macaulay, the nineteenth-century British historian, professed, "The measure of a man's real character is what he would do if he would never be found out." Would he be totally honest and aboveboard with others? Would he cheat or steal? If what is done in secret stays a secret, what would *you* do, how would *you* live? If you found a wallet stuffed with money, would you return it to the owner? Our conscience nudges us when we contemplate doing something wrong. Those who ignore their conscience forsake their best friend and lifetime guide.

If the measure of an individual's real character is determined by what he would do if he weren't found out, the only person capable of judging his actions is the person himself and his God. If he can look at himself in the mirror each day and know he's living as honestly as he can, that, too, will be reflected. The essence of his character is written on his face, and he can read between the lines. "By their fruits you shall know them."

Integrity is what a husband wants in his wife, and she in him. Integrity is what we look for and hope to find in a doctor, a dentist, the individual who designs and builds our home, those whom we work for as well as the people who work under us. It's what we want more than anything else in a politician or an appointed official; in a judge and a jury. Even the criminal respects the justice who pronounces his sentence. Integrity is the world's most valuable quality in a service, a product, or a person. Integrity goes beyond honesty. It means facing life as it is, not as you wish it could be. Integrity means having the courage to admit your mistakes. It means listening to your intuition; trusting the still, small voice within and going with the flow of your own nature. It is much more than the superficial virtues that keep a person from cheating or stealing. The real test of the value of integrity is when it costs you money, emotion, or time to live up to it. Integrity, or the lack of it, is generally taught in the home. It is a state of mind and character that is found at the very core, and in every fiber of peak-performing men and women. Integrity is the greatest gift in the world—a gift that only you can give yourself. Demand it from yourself and reward it in others.

THE BIG ONE

Everything seemed normal on that Sunday evening, January 16, 1994, at California State University at Northridge. The next day—Martin Luther King Day—was a national holiday and nearly everyone had the day off. Although the university was in the midst of its spring registration, parking lots were empty, buildings were bare; all was quiet, though the silence was almost deafening. Then, at 4:31 A.M. Monday, it happened! The earth began to tremble, then shake violently. People were thrown from their beds. Furniture crashed to the floor. Those who were fortunate enough to survive and make it to their rooms—two were not—heard glass shattering everywhere. When the shaking stopped, in that frozen instant of silence before car alarms went off and police and fire sirens broke the silence, it seemed to be the "Big One"! And California State University at Northridge was the epicenter.

The quake dismantled communication and computer systems, halted registration, and rendered all major facilities, files, and records inaccessible. Transcript production and application processes were shut down, and valuable research was lost. The school's new logo, created the year before, was attached to the library's towering columns. School officials chose the location because they wanted to display a symbol of power and strength. Ironically, pieces of the building are now missing, the columns have cracked, and disaster relief officials are weighing the prospects of whether the structure can be saved at all. But the price was much more costly. Two promising Cal-Northridge students lost their lives under the rubble of their collapsed apartment. By the time the news reached the campus, everyone was shaken to the core. Never before had a college or university been hit with such a natural disaster.

The earthquake registered 6.8 on the Richter scale, enough to rattle the nerves of everyone throughout the state, including the school's pillar of strength, President Blenda J. Wilson. "I knew I was in for a tremendous challenge when I took this job," Dr. Wilson admits, "but I didn't think it would be this big of a challenge. After the quake I was told that, considering the circumstances and the amount of loss and devastation, our school would be closed for the balance of the year. I couldn't believe my ears!" Blenda Wilson bore the unenviable title by faculty and students alike as the commander in chief of a university campus that looked more like a war zone. When the final numbers came in and the destruction was assessed, she was informed that the Northridge earthquake caused more damage to the facility—$300 million—than any other disaster in U.S. history. The next day she toured her quake-ravaged school, stopping frequently to console victims. However, it was Blenda who needed a tender shoulder to cry on when she received the news from disaster officials that it would take nearly a year to piece her campus back together.

A headlong pace has become Blenda Wilson's operating mode since the day the California State University board of trustees named her to the post, making her the first black and first female to direct the largest system—350 acres, twenty-seven thousand students—within the state of California. Her credentials for the post were remarkably complete. A nationally known speaker on higher education policy, she holds both master's and Ph.D. degrees in educational administration. Wilson became the first woman of color to serve as chancellor of the University of Michigan, and by age forty, she was an associate dean at Harvard University's Graduate School of Education. However, her new assignment would fully tax her abilities.

For example, in her new post she has had to confront massive layoffs within faculty and staff due to declining revenues, sagging morale, and a fiscal budget seemingly out of control. Nonetheless, this tiny woman with the smooth bronze complexion stood tall in her moment of crisis and quickly snapped into action.

"Several buildings were severely damaged, including our new library and administration building," President Wilson explained. "We were told that, dependent upon our ability to expedite contracts for repair work, favorable weather conditions, and timely delivery of materials and supplies, our school could be in a state of repair for three to four years. I just shook my head and told my staff, 'We will be back in *one month*. And not just back, but better!' "

For the next four weeks, clad in a sweater, jeans, and tennis shoes, Wilson and members of her staff huddled in makeshift tents to discuss strategy and reassure doubters that their school would indeed be back. But it would take a taxing commitment from all involved. Her first move was to reestablish communications. Unable to enter any campus buildings, the administration set up shop in a complex of eight tents. Water had to be trucked in. For two days, the only link to the outside world was a single cellular phone. Emergency information phone lines were established for those who had questions about the quake as well as class registration and schedules. Volunteers manned the lines around the clock. Mail service was reestablished, but the backlog was immense. Student loans and financial aid checks exceeding $7 million had to be retrieved and accounted for.

Next, Wilson ordered four hundred temporary, single-story buildings—not nearly enough to accommodate the school's heavy class load—to be placed on every available open space to serve as classrooms and offices. She even asked high-level administrators, who were used to spacious offices, to sidestep their egos and work from card tables outside trailers. Class schedules were redesigned to provide continuous instruction from 7:00 A.M. to 10:00 P.M. weekdays and extended hours on weekends. Night school professors were told to bring flashlights because many of the portable rooms had not been wired. New parking lots were surfaced and shuttle buses were scheduled to run to and from the lots to the newly configured campus. Dr. Wilson then convinced both students and her fellow university presidents to use the facilities at UCLA and Cal-Lutheran, area schools with vast resources but nearly an hour's drive away. Sandwiched between these activities was the endless task of fund-raising to offset unexpected costs. This she conducted with remarkable ease, raising hundreds of thousands of dollars.

All too fast, the day finally arrived—February 14, 1994. Twenty-seven thousand students and three thousand faculty and staff converged on the campus—many for the first time since the earthquake. They were faced with a campus that resembled a trailer park, with some classes meeting under trees while their trailer classrooms were being assembled. Chaotic as this day seemed, everyone was elated to be back—especially juniors and seniors. Despite the enormity of problems—the loss of two precious lives; the countless aftershocks that had everyone wondering when it would end; a skeletal communications system; reassembling student files; and a campus-wide cleanup of hazardous chemicals that kept workers away and cost the university nearly $50,000 per day—their president had kept her word.

Blenda Wilson spared no pains and considered no chore too burdensome. Sixteen-, eighteen-, and twenty-hour days would not rob her of her objective. Whenever she found anything to be done, she did it; whenever anything had to be investigated, she investigated it; and if anything had to be repaired, she made sure that someone repaired it. All under the backdrop of personal integrity. She was never spoiled by flattery or soured by disappointment. "I didn't pull off any miracles," she said. "If anyone pulled off any miracles, it was our faculty, staff, and students. They're the ones who did it." Amid the confusion, busted freeways, and severed phone lines, Dr. Wilson stayed true to her word: "Not just back, but better!"

THE MARK OF INTEGRITY

Blenda Wilson's story doesn't end here. The purpose of sharing her message is not to discuss the tragedy that ravaged this sprawling California campus. No, her story goes far deeper than just a few pages. There is a valuable secret that you should know. Somewhere in her experience you will find yourself. This truth, sublime in its simplicity and powerful in its beauty, is the highest lesson of human relations—the first character trait that children should learn and the last that humanity should forget. It is a virtue that Dr. Wilson would rather not live without. It is, perhaps, the most striking phrase uttered by one individual to another: *I gave my word.*

Society needs more heart. It needs more of the spirit of Blenda Wilson. Keeping your word—honesty and trustworthiness—is the straightest, surest path to respect and success. It pays to be on good terms with your conscience. The secret of integrity is an absolute surrender of self to all that is better and purer. Before a consuming zeal for all that is fair and noble, the barriers to our goals and desires recede and are diminished. Settle it with yourself that no matter the circumstances or the adversities, you will never lie, cheat, steal, injure, or deceive *anyone.* Whatever you do, *keep your word.*

If keeping your word brings pain and difficulties, bear it like a champion—this is the quickest way to *become* a champion. If keeping your word brings stress and strain, hold on to your integrity and face the consequences. If keeping your word causes others to scoff and discount, don't take the easy way out. Maintain your upright demeanor and remember this maxim: "All that troubles is but for a moment." Let others lead small lives, but not you. Let others argue over small things, but not you. Let others cry over small hurts, but not you. Let others forsake their honesty, character, and integrity—but not you!

The most valuable asset that you will ever have is how you are known to others: your reputation for honesty and fair dealing. As Shakespeare wrote, "He who steals my purse steals trash, but he who steals my good name, steals all." Never allow anyone or anything to cast aspersions on your character. You must guard your good name and your reputation above all things; you must never compromise your integrity or peace of mind for anything or anyone. On several occasions I have witnessed people who chose to concede their integrity and peace of mind—for money, their career, fame, or a relationship. Unfortunately, they ended with nothing. The individual of upright character radiates an influence for good wherever he or she goes. Goodness of mind reflects itself in the face and manner so that it can be clearly read by others. A genuinely good person is a constant guide and inspiration to those about him.

For example, during one of the most difficult days of her ordeal, a young student sat in Dr. Wilson's makeshift "office" preparing for class. Anyone else would have felt compromised, certainly slighted, but not this rock of integrity. Blenda Wilson just stepped aside, smiled intently upon her young visitor, cleared a space, and told the coed to continue. To this famed educator it was but one incident in a crowded day, a mere example of compassion soon lost under the weight of more trying moments. But to the impressionable undergraduate it was an experience never to be forgotten. When asked later did she feel imposed upon, true to form, Dr. Wilson demonstrated the power of integrity that frames her life. Listen to her words; the proof is complete. "Throughout this tragedy," she said, "so many people made sacrifices. My staff and faculty gave of themselves; from working long hours to even holding meetings in their cars. This was no imposition at all. Besides, when it comes to leading people, you never ask others to do what you are not prepared to do." Sum it up as you will, integrity is the great desideratum of life.

MAKE YOUR MARK

Keep your word. Never ask others to do what you are not prepared to do. These are two ideas worth discussing. When you keep your word, you and your word become very powerful. Living up to your promises will bring great inner strength. To say you are going to do something and then not do it weakens your integrity and, like the boy who cried wolf, makes us and others question if you are telling the truth.

The most important part of this lesson will not be found within these pages, but will be discovered in your heart. Open your dictionary and turn to the word "integrity." Write its meaning in your soul. For if you are ever to overfill your place in this world, you will have to approach your fellowman in the spirit of complete integrity. Blenda Wilson's story illustrates a key component of this virtue: having the courage of your convictions—doing what you believe is right—and then doing the right thing. Search where you will, whenever you find an individual who has attained the higher brackets of success, you can be sure that his or her good fortune was fueled by integrity. You will never know your capacity for achievement until you learn how to combine your efforts with truth and integrity. The products and services of your hands will yield you only a small return. But those same products and services, when properly guided by your heart, will render a fortune in material well-being and peace of mind.

Such actions are sorely needed today, in a world where so much emphasis is placed on expediency and the quick fix. Do not take the world's estimate of success as your own. Look for the underlying strength in each individual. The real height of the pyramids is not measured between the base and the capstone, but includes the hundreds of feet of solid masonry below. Many of the most successful lives are lived in accord with these great structures. Those that reach to the heavens are held firmly in place by the strength of their foundation. The greatest worth of an individual is never fully measured unless you look below the surface—that which is unseen and unheard—to the very foundation of integrity. Some people label it conscience, but I prefer to call it God's voice in mankind: "Blessings are on the head of the righteous." It is the still, small voice that whispers "right" or "wrong" to every act; it is the priceless gem that the Creator dropped into the dust when He fashioned us in His own image. The Almighty has whispered into the ear of all creation, "Look up!"

Black America is ripe for a return to integrity. We need to witness a reemergence of this quality as one of the predominant values in the collective human character. Those who do have integrity and consistently try to exercise it have discovered something the rest of society ought to know: Integrity makes life easier as well as more joyful and meaningful. When wealth is lost, nothing is lost; when health is lost, *something* is lost. But when integrity is lost, *all* is lost!

Robert Louis Stevenson wrote, "Anyone can carry his burden, however hard, until nightfall. Anyone can do his work, however hard, for one day. Anyone can live sweetly, patiently, lovingly, purely, for twenty-four hours."

Samuel Smiles, the Scottish philosopher, taught, "There are many persons of whom it may be said that they have no other possession in the world but their character, and yet they stand as firmly upon it as any crowned king." At the turn of the twentieth century, theologian and essayist Grenville Kleiser concurred: "It is well to mingle freely with good men, but it is still better to be a good man. Goodness has a power all its own to instruct, persuade and inspire."

Shakespeare wrote, "The purest treasure mortal times afford is spotless reputation; that away, men are but gilded loam, or painted clay."

"Never forget," explained Cunningham Geikie, a distinguished nineteenth-century writer, "that wrong-doing cannot repay in the end. It may promise pleasure or profit, but it is the old story of Eve's apple over again in every case. Shame, danger, self-reproach and loss follow it, as Hell follows death in the Apocalypse."

Best-selling author Steven Covey brings us even closer. "Integrity is the foundation of trust which is essential to cooperation and long-term personal and interpersonal growth."

Benjamin Elijah Mays, the last of the great schoolmasters, would exert his influence for generations to come. He preached, "It will not be sufficient for Morehouse College, for any college for that matter, to produce clever graduates, men fluent in speech and able to argue their way through; but rather honest men, men who can be trusted in public and private—who are sensitive to the wrongs, the suffering, and the injustices of society and who are willing to accept responsibility for correcting the ills."

We are instructed in the book of Matthew: "Blessed are those who hunger and thirst for righteousness, for they shall be filled . . . blessed are the pure in heart, for they shall see God."

What star ever shone with purer light or commanded more admiration than Booker T. Washington? Whoever rose to higher respect in political circles during nineteenth-century America? One day, as Washington and a friend strolled down a southern street, a passerby deliberately bumped into Washington and uttered a racial slur. His friend was livid. "Dr. Washington," he questioned, "aren't you going to retaliate? You should give him a tongue-lashing!"

Washington smiled as he removed a piece of lint from his jacket. "No," he said calmly. "I refuse to give anyone a cause for me to hate."

And finally, the noted black historian Charles Wesley wrote, "You preach a better sermon with your deeds than with your lips." *Integrity is power!* Hang this motto in every home, in every office, in every school. Plant it within the hearts of men and women. Mothers, engrave it on every child's heart. Today is judgment day!

THROUGH IT ALL, THEY MAINTAINED THEIR INTEGRITY

In the back rooms of the Department of Agriculture in Washington, D.C., a slender middle-aged woman worked diligently for nine dollars a week. Traces of refinement and culture distinguished her from her colleagues. She was thankful to have the job, a position bestowed upon her by then Agriculture Secretary J. M. Rusk, in response to the following letter:

Cedar Hill Anacostia, D.C.,
November 26, 1891.

Hon. J. M. Rusk, Secretary of Agriculture:
Sir,—I have the honor to remind you, as requested, of the case of Miss _____, a member of the family in which I was formerly a slave. Circumstances have reduced the fortune of that branch of the family to which Miss _____ belongs, and hence she seeks, through my intercession, some employment by which she may assist herself and family in this, their hour of need. It is a strange reversal of human relations that brings myself, the slave, and this lady, brought up in the lap of luxury and ease, now to seek the humble employment I ask for her. Miss _____ will, I am sure, if given the place she seeks, prove herself a useful member of the Agricultural service, and grateful for the appointment. Hoping that no obstacle will be found to her getting the place she seeks, I am, sir, very truly, your obedient servant.

Frederick Douglass

Power is the great goal of ambition, and it is only through integrity that one can arrive at a personality strong enough to move humanity and nations. In 1968, a young sanitation worker from Memphis, Tennessee, wrote to Dr. King. He stated in part, "The fate of an entire race centers on you." Mentally exhausted, his speeches increasingly alluding to his possible death, Dr. King answered the call and preached his most stirring sermon. There was no other individual in the world that could stand against his integrity. By comparison, what are the millions of the Rockefellers or the Kennedys compared to Martin Luther King's true worth? What are the works of Michelangelo or Van Gogh compared to the righteousness and moral fiber of Dr. King's shining example? Few people have ever been the foundation that has prevented society from crumbling.

In athletics, Jackie Joyner-Kersee is born to wear a crown; always dashing, racing, jumping, hurdling, heaving a six-pound shot, slinging spears. She has at last reached the station her grandmother foretold nearly three decades ago in naming her after a former First Lady. But her chances had seemed so slender. Jackie was born in East St. Louis, Illinois, the second of four children, born to children. Her mother and father were sixteen and fourteen the day they wed. The young couple took up residence in both the coldest and warmest house in the neighborhood, across the street from a tavern, down the block from a pool hall, and around the corner—blessedly—from a playground. Her father shined shoes and mowed lawns before finding more stable work on the railroad, which unfortunately carried him far from home for considerable stretches of time. But it was Jackie's mother who set the moral and spiritual tone in the house. "She applied discipline just for discipline's sake," Jackie remembers, "like making us wear the same outfits two days in a row. 'Why the same clothes back-to-back?' I'd ask. 'Can't I stagger them?' 'No,' she'd say. 'This is the rule of the house.' "

The son of postal workers, Danny Glover, movie producer and screen star, is a rare bird in a business that often breeds huge egos and distrust. The talented actor, one of the more bankable personalities in Hollywood, long ago decided not to live among the glitz and glitter. Instead, he chose to remain with his wife and daughter in San Francisco's modest Haight-Ashbury section. Glover's idea of time well spent is to visit schools across the country, encouraging literacy and discouraging drug use. "I must be a part of something real," he confessed. "Fame is fleeting. I'm going to be the guy next door long after I'm a celebrity, and I try to keep that in sight." No one goes unnoticed, no matter how ordinary. Humility and honesty tell the story of our lives.

The main business of life is not to do, but *to become.* You cannot help trusting such individuals who believe this; their very presence gives confidence. Hazel O'Leary was a senior-level executive for the Northern States Power Company in Minneapolis, Minnesota, when she was nominated for the position of Secretary of Energy. Former National Urban League CEO and White House transition team leader Vernon Jordan made frequent calls to Minnesota inquiring about her candidacy. Among others questioned was O'Leary's superior. "She is the very person for the position," her boss replied. "But we can't spare her."

"Sir," Jordan replied, "we don't want someone who can be spared."

Integrity is the end and aim of the highest life. It is infinitely more precious to be nobly remembered than to be nobly born. In 1947, Walker Smith, better known as Sugar Ray Robinson, bested a talented Jimmy Doyle in a championship fight. Robinson never looked better. In the middle rounds, a thundering right hand came crashing to Doyle's head. The young fighter died the next day. Unknown to anyone, including his fans and close friends, Robinson established a trust fund to care for the fallen fighter's wife and children.

With fewer than five professional games under his belt, Bob Bass, general manager of professional basketball's San Antonio Spurs, was asked by a sportswriter what he liked best about the team's newest member, David Robinson. "Is it the way he attacks the boards, or his ball-handling skills? How about his inside game?" Bass kept his eyes fixed on his prize recruit and said without emotion, "The thing I like best about David is the way he stands during the national anthem." Character lies at the root of all virtues.

Few women married to powerful men have been able to hold on to their identity as well as Jean Young. The wife of Ambassador Andrew Young never flaunted her beliefs or her values—she simply lived them. While Andrew Young headed the U.S. Mission to the United Nations, the couple lived in a ritzy penthouse in New York's Waldorf-Astoria Towers. But after only a few days under such royal conditions, Jean Young fired her maid and her butler. She did it because each time her children requested something to drink, they were served in a silver goblet on a doily-lined tray. She realized this form of luxury was sending her children the wrong message. "Be not simply good," she counseled her children. "Be good for something."

If integrity is your thing, you can find a lot to love about Joe Clark, former principal of Eastside High in Paterson, New Jersey. Bullhorn cradled under one arm, a stack of books and papers resting in the other, Clark inspired, motivated, and expected nothing short of personal excellence from his school. He embraced his students, slapped high fives, and stared down anyone who thought his efforts to educate poor blacks and Hispanics were a waste of time. Many times in his battle for principle and truth, he stood alone fighting ignorance and racial bigotry. In his book there was no middle ground, no compromise between right and wrong or success and failure. Clark never pandered for public favor or sought applause. In the end he received both in abundance. Character and wholeness were his goals, and he went straight to his mark. Though many educators shunned his methods, Joe Clark was too

vocal to be censored, too broad for narrowness, and too focused for re-
venge.

Bob Greene, a columnist for the *Chicago Tribune,* relates that one
cold night after a game, Chicago Bulls superstar Michael Jordan headed
through a large crowd of fans toward his car. As he opened the car door,
Jordan saw a youngster in a wheelchair some twenty feet away. The
boy's neck was bent at an unusual angle; his eyes could not look directly
forward. Jordan walked over to the boy and knelt beside him. The
youngster was so excited that he began to rise out of the wheelchair.
Michael comforted him, talked softly, and placed his arm around the
boy's frail shoulder.

The child's father tried to snap a picture, but the camera didn't work
at first. Jordan noticed. Without being asked, he continued to kneel at
the boy's side until the father was able to take the picture. Only then did
the superstar return to his car. The boy's eye were glistening with tears
of joy. His dad was already replaying the moment with his son. If nothing good ever happens again for that little boy, he will always know that
on one night Michael Jordan cared enough to include him in his world.

Life finds its noblest spring of excellence in the hidden impulse to do
the right thing. Oprah Winfrey once displayed her integrity and made
life richer without ever using any of her millions. Though forced to
stand alone, she endeared herself to all of her viewers when she called
a press conference to state the obvious: The talk-show format—the very
industry that she helped to create—had played a major role in wresting
America away from its spiritual and moral codes of conduct, and she
would now change it. Nothing is more important than lifting a life to a
plane worth living.

Thirteen years after he enrolled as a freshman at Auburn University,
Vincent "Bo" Jackson finally returned home. This former Heisman Tro-
phy winner would find fame and fortune as a two-sport idol, earning
millions in the process. But his most heroic act occurred on a late fall
day before one thousand well-wishers who watched him walk across
the stage to receive his degree. What made him do it? Why did he scram-
ble and struggle to lay possession to something he surely did not need?
Listen closely—his answer is worth noting. "Five years ago," Bo confessed, "I promised my dying mother that I would complete my degree.
I had more than thirty credit hours to go but I have always been a man
of my word."

What a person *does* is the real test of who a person *is.* In his last public address as he resigned his post as Chairman of the Joint Chiefs of
Staff, General Colin Powell broke the code to success. He left his lasting

legacy with three simple words: *duty, honor, country.* No individual ever entered into General Powell's company who did not feel himself uplifted and enlightened when he left. The real value of a people must be weighed on scales more delicate than the balance of trade. The real measure of a nation's worth is the amount it has contributed to the spiritual hope and moral conduct of all mankind.

No other treasure in the world commands such a price as the jewel of integrity. Jesse Jackson recalls his first lesson in family values. As a six-year-old on Christmas Eve in his native Greenville, South Carolina, he and an older brother helped their father clean the offices of a prominent judge. Charles Jackson, the building custodian, gave his boys a quick lesson in the art of mopping, dusting, and polishing furniture. But his instructions went a bit further. "As you tend your duties," he pointed out, "if by chance you happen to find a ten-dollar bill lying around, don't touch it. It was left there to test your character." He continued, "Boys, you should never risk your integrity or your soul for any amount of money."

If there is one quality that will make itself felt, it is integrity! You may have little education, slender abilities, meager resources, and no influence. Yet if you possess impeccable integrity, this trait alone will demand influence and secure respect. Do you see this quality, greater than courage and leadership, in Moses at the Red Sea, Paul in every village and hamlet, Crispus Attucks at Boston Harbor, Sojourner Truth in her prayer closet, Nat Turner on the slaver's track, Johnetta Cole at Spelman, Arthur Ashe at center court, Naylor Fitzhugh in the boardroom, Ralph Bunche on the General Assembly floor, Booker T. Washington at Tuskegee, Sybil Mobley at Florida A&M, Clara Hale in the nursery, Roberto Clemente in right field, Bernard Shaw on the evening news, Walter Massey in his laboratory, or in scores of others who have achieved greatness? Integrity is to greatness as perfume is to the flower.

"If we work upon marble, it will perish," wrote Daniel Webster, the nineteenth-century American statesman. "If upon brass, time will efface it; if we rear temples, they will crumble into dust. But if we work upon our mortal minds—if we imbue them with principles, with the just fear of God and love for our fellowman—we engrave on those tablets something which will brighten through all eternity."

If we want the deepest level of fulfillment, we can achieve it in only one way, and that is by doing what all high-achieving men and women do: by deciding what we value most in life and then committing to live by those values every single day.

WHAT DO YOU VALUE MOST?

Perhaps now is a good time to ask, Where do you stand? What lies at the center of your life? What do you value most—what are your highest values? These questions and their answers play an important role in your personal development. All of us maintain some type of value system that is uniquely our own. As we seek to further understand our behavior and motivation, it is of great importance to clarify our values. Values may be defined as the standards of desirability by which the individual chooses between alternative behaviors. Values have been defined as something regarded as desirable, worthy, or right. Values are not attitudes, but are standards by which attitudes are formed. Values are not behavior traits, nor are they needs. A need is a lack of something desirable. But a value is highly regarded. Research has indicated twenty basic values that are important, in varying degrees, throughout society. Those who know their values and live by them make their mark on the world.

> You should never risk your integrity or your soul for any amount of money.
>
> —Charles Jackson

In any serious study of achievement, the merit of such values becomes obvious. These values are proven, enduring guidelines for human conduct. All values govern personal effectiveness. People may argue about how they are to be defined, interpreted, and applied in real-life situations, but they generally agree about their intrinsic worth. Values surface time and again, and the degree to which we recognize and live in harmony with them moves us toward success and survival. To make sure your philosophy of personal achievement is firmly grounded, it's important to have an inviolate set of ethical standards. Such firm guidelines not only provide the ethical framework within which you live your life but also help you make difficult decisions. A behavior either meets your standards or it doesn't. Below are society's most commonly cited values as defined by the W. Clement & Jessie V. Stone Foundation.

Achievement.
To accomplish, win or attain; do successfully

Compassion.
Pity, with the desire to help

Courage.
A quality of spirit that enables one to face danger

Creativity.
Having the power or the ability to create; to cause to come to existence

Faith.
Belief without need or certain proof; confidence in or dependence on a person or thing as trustworthy

Health.
Freedom from defect or disease

Honesty.
Fairness or straightforwardness of conduct; integrity; uprightness of character

Justice.
The quality of being impartial or fair; righteousness; conformity to truth, fact, or reason

Knowledge.
A result or product of knowing; information or understanding acquired through experience. Learning; erudition

Loyalty.
Fidelity, allegiance; the state, quality, or fact of being loyal

Morality.
Virtuous conduct; a system of principles of right and wrong conduct; a code of ethics

Physical appearance.
Concern for the beauty of one's own body

Pleasure.
An agreeable or delightful sensation; enjoyment; one's preference, choice

Power.
Ability to act; capability; potential capacity; possession of control, authority, or influence over others

Recognition.
Acknowledgment of a fact or claim; made to feel significant and important

Responsibility.
The state of being accountable; answerable legally or morally for the discharge of a duty, trust, or debt

Self-discipline.
To train to obedience or subjection; a system or rules or method of practice

Wealth.
Affluence; abundance of valuable material possessions or resources

Wisdom.
Knowledge; learning; practical judgment; insight; common sense

Work.
Continued exertion directed to some end; labor; toil; a feat or deed

   Now list these values in order of their importance to *you.*

1. _____   7. _____

2. _____   8. _____

3. _____   9. _____

4. _____   10. _____

5. _____   11. _____

6. _____   12. _____

13. _____   17. _____

14. _____   18. _____

15. _____   19. _____

16. _____   20. _____

What do you stand for? What do you believe in as unchanging principles? What are the things that you will do or will not do in pursuit of your goals? Goal attainment begins by defining your core values. Your basic values, in turn, become the foundation upon which you can build and define your life. Your choice of the values that you will live by is one of the most important things that you will ever undertake. A value, once chosen, is carved in stone; you cannot practice a value only when it's convenient. When you choose and commit yourself to a value, you are making a firm decision to live by that value without compromise, no matter the circumstances, no matter the temptations. Once you've selected your core values—usually three or four—you can then organize the remainder in order of importance, from the "most" important to the "least" important. Think of examples where you have been able to put these values into practice.

Not only are your values important but so is their order. Each higher-order value will take precedence over any lower-order value. For example, if your three basic values in order are wealth, responsibility, and self-discipline, then you would sacrifice responsibility and self-discipline to wealth, and you would sacrifice self-discipline to wealth and responsibility. In my research, I have discovered that high-achieving men and women succeed in part because they've established clearly articulated values. Many have selected honesty and morality as the basic operating values to govern their personal and business lives.

OUR PROBLEMS ARE NOT INSURMOUNTABLE

There are many problems facing Black America—teenage pregnancies, a soaring divorce rate, a declining number of college students, a growing number of black males within the penal system, chronic unemployment, an expanding underclass, and yes, the residual effects of racism. Moreover, within one generation, the social fabric of the black family unit—which had survived Middle Passage, slavery, reconstruction, Jim Crow laws, and segregation—has ventured precariously close to decimation. Far too many of our children grow up in a world torn by violence, destroyed by poverty, decimated by despair, and devastated by insensitivity. Many social programs have answered the call for more government involvement. Typically, both political parties have spent enormous energy blaming each other and pointing their collective fingers at a host of external factors. But the underlying cause of the ills facing Black America have nothing to do with external factors. The root cause and *solution* can be found in the heart and soul of Black America itself.

A nation of children without fathers is not going to outcompete Japan or western Europe. A nation unable to distinguish between right and wrong won't raise our standard of living. A nation of moral misfits will eventually become a nation of economic misfits. As a race, neither our means nor our worth is measured by money alone. If we possess a hefty purse and a lean heart, broad estates and a narrow understanding, what will we gain? What a dreadful sight to see: an old man who has spent his entire life getting instead of growing. The spiritual and moral well-being of a people is forever linked to the spiritual and material riches of a people. Clearly, what is needed at this hour is the one quality that is greater than wealth; the one trait that would make anyone rich beyond his or her means; the one virtue that is above all others. Try as we might to stifle the voice of the mysterious angel within, she always says yes to right actions and no to wrong ones.

The power of character lies within the soul of its people. Truth strikes a common chord that can be felt throughout the universe. A book or work of art puts us in the mood or train of thought of the person who produced it. Is Billie Holiday dead? Ask the thousands of struggling young artists who sing her songs and mimic her style in jazz clubs the world over. Colin Powell read of the Buffalo soldiers only once before their story inspired his entire life. John Rogers, the black financial whiz kid of the 1980s, was inspired to his glory by the success of his idol—John H. Johnson. Mae Jemison was about to complete high school when she caught wind of the exploits of Benjamin Banneker, and from that day forward, she was branded with ambition. During the darkest period of slavery, Nat Turner's name was the watchword of the Deep South. While the conscience of many a slave echoed the words of Washington and Jefferson and Lincoln, subconsciously, each slave spoke Turner, thought Turner, and prayed Turner. What heart and soul doesn't enshrine the power of character?

HE KNOWS THE ANSWER

John Thompson knows. That's the secret of his success. Even as he strides along the sidelines of a Georgetown University basketball game with his trademark white towel draped over his right shoulder, his six-foot ten-inch frame dwarfing players and fans, coach Thompson is always in the game—challenging an official, benching a player, or encouraging and hugging another. He knows what he wants and uses a deep sense of values to guide his life. Told that he couldn't make it in grade school, Thompson earned a degree in economics from Providence College before occupying a seat on the board of Nike.

A black man from a poor neighborhood in segregated Washington, D.C., Thompson had one huge asset—his family. Though illiterate, his father woke up each morning at five to earn what he could. Despite her education, the only work Thompson's mother could find was house-cleaning. Determined to give their son a better start in life, John's parents sent him to Catholic school. But hampered by poor vision that made it difficult for him to read, he fell behind. By the fifth grade, the frustrated nuns had decided that Thompson was a slow learner and asked him not to come back. His parents were not about to let someone else write off their son. A determined public school teacher got him glasses and made sure John caught up. His mother inspired him to meet his challenges head-on and to find a way to win. She gave him the following poem:

> You can do anything you think you can.
> It's all in the way you view it.
> It's all in the start you make, young man.
> You must feel that you're going to do it.

In 1980, every major college coach in America had his eyes on one skinny, seven-foot Jamaican-born center. With his electrifying play, coach after coach offered Patrick Ewing every inducement under the sun. But not Thompson. Instead of brandishing titles, money, or special perks, he allowed his mother's character to direct his actions. He told the high school senior, "Education is about change—if you have the potential. It is my job to make you reach that potential." Ewing rose to the challenge, with his coach's help. The basketball superstar now lectures others on the responsibility of reaching one's full potential—through discipline and hard work—in sports, business, or life.

But the high-profile motivator is clearly at his best when coping with defeat. Anyone can rack up a win or two. But only the greatest can turn a devastating loss into an even greater victory. For example, in 1983, Georgetown was clearly one of the best teams in the country. Ewing, later to be a perennial all-star for the New York Knicks, was already being compared to basketball immortals. Thompson put everything he had into the Georgetown Hoyas, who cruised through the early rounds of the NCAA tournament, playing the best basketball their coach had ever seen. The final game pitted Georgetown against the North Carolina University Tarheels.

Carolina had an awesome team featuring two future NBA Hall of Famers, James Worthy and Michael Jordan. The lead changed hands several times in the final minutes until, with only seventeen seconds in the game, Jordan hit a jump shot that gave Carolina a 63–62 lead. Now the game, the season, and the championship were in the hands of Georgetown's play-making guard Fred Brown. In the heat of the moment, Brown made a terrible mistake. He inadvertently threw the ball to his opponent Worthy, giving North Carolina the crown. As millions watched in disbelief on television, all eyes turned toward the crestfallen player and his coach. Some fans were incensed; others were beside themselves. Jeers and taunts came from the stands. How could a player make such a mistake, people wondered, in the biggest game of the season? Instead of throwing a tantrum as most Georgetown faithfuls wanted him to do, Thompson was forced to answer to a higher calling by displaying the one virtue that directs his soul. He wiped his brow, walked slowly over to the young man, and hugged him. The gesture changed Brown's life.

"I was really down on myself," Brown told a reporter weeks later. "Coach Thompson's actions made me realize that it wasn't the end of the world. Thanks to him, I'll never be the same."

Still, the defeat was a terrible blow for Thompson, who wants to win but won't allow himself to be fooled by one triumph or disaster. The next season, 1984, was Ewing's last. For the third time in his four years, Georgetown made it to the NCAA finals. This time they won easily, beating future all-star Hakeem Olajuwon's Houston Cougars, 84–75. As the final seconds ticked off, Thompson remembered what had transpired a year before. In the waning moments, he walked over to Fred Brown and hugged him again. "We've got it, baby," the coach exclaimed. "Never give in or give up." The championship that eluded Thompson's grasp the previous year had been secured.

Who is the greatest among you? It is the man or woman who liberates you from your surroundings, who unlocks the floodgates of your possibilities; who, through character and tone, raises your consciousness and helps you to see circumstances in a broader light. These individuals of integrity are the conscience of a society. Small things become great when a great soul sees them. Thank God for those men and women who would rather be right than rich!

SET THE HIGHEST STANDARDS

A junior high school student had survived all the preliminary rounds of a national spelling bee. But in the final round, she misspelled a word. The judges, however, failed to hear her correctly and gave her the nod. The contestant, realizing that she had misspelled the word, eliminated herself from the competition.

A woman walking along New York's Fifth Avenue stopped a stranger to ask for directions to a well-known museum. The gentleman said, "Go two blocks to the right and then turn left." When the woman had walked nearly a block and a half, she heard the stranger calling her. She turned around as he approached.

"I'm glad I caught you," he said while attempting to catch his breath. "After you ventured off, I realized that I had given you the wrong directions. I didn't want you to get lost."

As Dr. King phrased it in a way that is as heartfelt as it is beautiful: "I have a dream that my four little children will one day live in a nation where they will not be judged by the color of their skin but by the content of their character." One hundred years from now, what difference will it make whether you were rich or poor, prince or pauper? But what a difference it makes whether you did what was right or fell prey to what was wrong.

The great aims of your life must be to develop the virtue of integrity. Integrity entails pursuing the truth wherever and whenever we find it, standing our ground even if no one else follows. It means avoiding the little white lie, shunning the status quo, and turning a cold shoulder to the unsubstantiated rumor. Each of us must set living greatly as our highest goal. With integrity as our guide, we need to set the highest standards for ourselves and dedicate our lives to achieving those standards. Strength of character is the ability to choose integrity under all conditions. Even when we talk about the importance of courage, we are referring to the ability to do what is right, irrespective of the situation in which we find ourselves. If you wish to improve your sense of integrity, strive for fidelity in your relationships. In other words, keep your word, adhere to your commitments, accept complete responsibility, and associate with others who maintain their integrity.

Integrity is like an engraving: Its image is stamped upon the soul. The marks of integrity are deep and indelible, and can be read by those around you from the way you live and act. Integrity is intimately related to your moral values and your deepest spiritual beliefs:"All things whatsoever ye would that men should do to you, do ye even so to them."

HOW TO DEVELOP INTEGRITY

Here are seven tips that will aid in your development of integrity.
1. *Always live in truth; never violate universal laws.* Never tell a lie; refuse to live a lie; refuse to participate in a lie.
2. *Look for the divinity in mankind.* Treat everyone the same. Be kind, straightforward, and honest with every person you meet. As you operate in truth, you'll come to the realization that each of us is interconnected—we are all one. Life begins with a progression from self-centeredness to understanding relationships with others. We aren't mature until we have both the ability and the willingness to see ourselves interconnected, as one among others. You may deal with others as you wish, but if you understand the law upon which this principle is based, you will know that its application spells success. You can compensate for any shortcomings by stating a simple affirmation:"There is only one God, and we are all children of God!"
3. *Never engage in work or a vocation that you do not believe in.* Never sell or recommend or work with a product or service that you do not believe in or use, or that doesn't warrant your trust.
4. *Always decide what's right before you worry about what's possible.* In all your dealings, resolve to do whatever is right regardless of outcome. Never allow money or relationships to cloud your decisions.
5. *Never look for or expect to get more than what you've put in.* Never expect something for nothing. Everything has a price; everything requires an investment of some kind. Never expect "easy" money, wealth without working, or to "get rich quick." So much time, money, and effort are wasted searching for a fast, easy scheme to make a lot of money. It takes years of hard work and discipline to produce financial success. Integrity means being willing to pay the full price of success in advance, before tasting the fruits of your labor.
6. *Accept total responsibility for your life.* A person of character looks

to himself or herself as the cause of his or her life. Everything that happens to you is the result of your own thinking, your own conduct, and your own behavior. The development of integrity—being true to yourself and others, living up to the very best that is within you, and setting a standard that everyone can follow—these are the giant steps to the development of your full potential as a human being. Resolve now to change those areas of your life that are not consistent with high integrity and greatness of character. Allow peace of mind to be your barometer of what is right and what is wrong. Don't wish for fewer problems; *wish for more skills.* Don't wish for fewer challenges; *wish for more wisdom.* And don't wish it were easier; *wish you were better.*

7. *Develop your own code of ethics.* We need to realize that the direction of our lives is controlled by the magnetic pull of our most valued principles—our ethics. They are the force in front of us, consistently leading us to make decisions that create the direction and ultimate destination of our lives. This is true not only for us as individuals but also for the organizations, institutions, and the company that we keep.

Demonstrate the highest standard of personal integrity, honesty, and trustworthiness in all social activities and throughout your personal life.

Discourage all forms of discrimination, racism, and sexism. Maintain the courage of your convictions, but respect and honor the opinions of others.

Accountability. Accept full responsibility for both the failures and successes in your life. You are accountable to life—life is not accountable to you.

Kindness. Don't criticize, condemn, or complain. It takes character and self-control to be forgiving. Instead of condemning others, try to understand them.

Wisdom. Seek to take in new information each day. Become a sponge for knowledge. It isn't what the book costs; it's what it will cost if you don't read it. Formal education will make you a living. Self-education will make you a fortune.

Happiness is a well-lived life and filled with people of substance. Learn how to be happy with what you have while you pursue all that you want.

Appreciation. The measure of mental health is the disposition to find good everywhere. Be generous with kind statements, and thank others when they least expect it.

Strive for personal and professional excellence. Whether you stay six weeks, six months, or six years, always leave it better than you found it.

Work, which many people call a curse, is really the salvation of the race. The few who do are the envy of the many who only watch.

Humility. Study and enhance spiritual progress. Every step toward truth is a step toward progress. Each day we should seek to find and fulfill God's purpose. Humility is a virtue; timidity is an illness.

Continue in this process until the peace that passes all understanding pervades every area of your life. Seek truth in everything you do; nothing can match its power. When you stand for truth, you are fully integrated, whole and firm. You can walk amid any darkness and despair, totally protected and assured of safety. You can "march into hell for a heavenly cause." When you remain true to integrity, you are aligned with the force of the universe. When you walk with integrity, you walk with God Almighty.

5
The Greatest Advice:

Work!

- What the Whole World Is Seeking

- Your Life's Work

- Seven Criteria for Choosing the Correct Vocation

- Who Makes It Up the Corporate Ladder and Why

The harvest is plentiful, but the laborers are few.
—MATTHEW 9:37

When you work, you fulfill a part of earth's furthest dream.
—KAHLIL GIBRAN

If anyone will not work, let him not eat.
—2 THESSALONIANS 3:10

None of the secrets of success will work unless you do.
—A FORTUNE COOKIE

An accomplished pianist gave a performance before a large group. After the recital a woman rushed to the virtuoso and said, "I'd do anything to play as you do."

The artist who had given the concert began to collect her belongings but stopped long enough to give her admirer a brief stare. Then she said, "Oh no you wouldn't." A hush fell over the room and the woman stood in sudden embarrassment. Looking at the pianist, she repeated her original statement. "I would, too, do anything to play the piano as you do!"

The virtuoso shook her head and replied again, "No, you wouldn't. If you would, you could play as well as I do, possibly better. You'd do anything to play as I do except what is really required. You wouldn't sit and practice, hour after hour, day after day." She then flashed a warm smile. "Please understand," she said, "I'm not criticizing. I'm just telling you that when you say you'd do anything to play as I do—if you really meant it, you would do it!"

In the pause that followed, everyone in the room realized that this talented artist had spoken the truth. They would love to have her talent now, fully matured and developed, but as for putting in the twenty years of unremitting toil that perfected her craft—no, that was a different matter.

Remember that:

- Greatness comes to those who develop a burning desire to succeed.
- Success is achieved and maintained by those who try—and keep trying. There's no future in saying it can't be done. Real success—doing your best—is not in the stars or the luck of the draw. It lies within persistent, daily effort.
- Concentrate your energies and intensity on the successful completion of your goals.
- Apply the words of Booker T. Washington, who advised, "Start where you are with what you have, knowing that what you have is plenty enough." The quickest way to the top is to start at the bottom.
- The *worst* days of those who enjoy what they do are better than the *best* days of those who don't. Find something you like to do and make it pay. Competency begins when you begin to enjoy your work. Unless you learn to do at least one thing well, perhaps a bit better than others, there's little chance of attaining your objective.
- Assume that opportunity knocks often, not just once. But if you knock on opportunity's door, be sure your bags are packed.
- In all things pursue perfection because in the pursuit of perfection, you will surpass excellence.

- Promise yourself you will never give up. Any of the achievers profiled within these pages would have never been heard of had they been content to stay at a thankless job and blindly put in their time.

Myra Evans is part of the new breed of black business class—ambitious, educated, and no stranger to hard work—and she wanted to introduce gelato, an Italian frozen treat, to upscale New Yorkers. Evans got the idea of launching an Italian gelateria after vacationing in San Francisco. There, an older brother introduced her to an Americanized version of gelato and sorboreto, an Italian parfait resembling sherbet. "I guess it was love at first lick." Evans returned to her East Coast home to discover that sophisticated New Yorkers had never experienced the delicacy. She approached a seasoned council of retired Small Business Association (SBA) veterans with a smartly packaged business plan and poured out her heart. With neither the time nor the temperament to learn of her affection for Italian ices, the SBA rudely dismissed her and discouraged her from pursuing her dream. She remembers the terse details of that humbling meeting.

"They weren't optimistic at all. They told me that New York was a haven for ice cream outlets, and that many fold each year. In addition, they also asked if I had any experience in the food business. When I said no, they laughed. 'You obviously don't know how demanding the food business can be,' they smirked." As Evans walked out from that depressing meeting, she blurted, "I'll get experience, all right—by capturing the market!"

A JOURNEY OF A THOUSAND MILES BEGINS WITH THE FIRST STEP

Compared with the quest for a winning recipe, which had taken months, seizing the market and attracting investors would be relatively easy. Evans wrote a business plan as part of an offering circular. The plan highlighted marketing and advertising strategies as well as the finer points of management responsibilities. To gain a handle on the market, she interviewed a number of gourmet restaurateurs and probed many of New York's more frequented ice cream parlors. To verify all that she had heard, a close friend supplied additional data gathered by a local advertising agency. Her research led to the following conclusion, which she rattled off like a young MBA in a corporate briefing: "The majority of ice cream lovers are women," Evans explained. "Age thirty-five to fifty. The business is not as seasonal as one might suspect."

Having completed her homework, Evans's investment and money

management training served her well. With the aid of an attorney, she wrote her own prospectus and raced about to line up the financing. The document outlined the initial offering and was circulated among friends and coworkers. Evans covered some of her financial exposure by selling small pieces of her company, although she maintained a majority of the equity. Within one week, she raised $15,000; after a month, the figure shot up to $50,000. Sensing victory and within a few shares of her projected $500,000 goal, Evans invited potential backers to a taste test. The palates of these seasoned financial types were no match for the "out-of-this-world taste" that distinguishes true gelato. The plan worked, and she was fully subscribed by the time her doors opened. In all, each of more than thirty people committed a minimum investment of $5,000. Gelato-Modo, Inc., was capitalized at more than $1 million, with Evans maintaining 51 percent ownership.

Equipped with the necessary funding, her creative sparks flew. Evans chose the former site of an Upper West Side dry cleaner as the location of her first unit. The area was upwardly mobile and full of trendy, young professionals. To further substantiate her target group, she acquired Census Bureau data on the area's demographics. Evans thought some of the ease with which she attracted investors had something to do with her plan to make the business authentically Italian. "Italian gelaterias emphasize elegant cuisine with spacious café-like surroundings. The environment has to be one in which customers can enjoy the cosmopolitan ambience while savoring their meal." Evans was so keen on introducing an Italian product in a uniquely European setting that she flew in three gelatieri to "run the shop through its initial paces, ensuring that it had the look and feel of those in Florence and Milan." Today, this petite, young woman who adorns little or no makeup has traded her traditional Wall Street attire for blue jeans and faded sweatshirts. At last count, Evans manages four gelaterias, with hopes of further expansion.

THE QUICKEST WAY TO THE TOP IS TO START AT THE BOTTOM

Labor is the great teacher of the race. It calls us away from hapless instructors and meaningless theories and enrolls us in the school of hard knocks. It teaches patience, perseverance, discipline, and application. It offers reward and punishment; it imparts the power of quick decision. Labor instructs: Do what you are told to do and then some. It's the "then some" that will raise your salary. Greatness never comes because it is craved; it is the result of unceasing effort. Make no mistake—labor is the only legal tender. The gods will sell everything for it, nothing without it. You will never find success "marked down."

Born in an age and country in which knowledge and opportunity abound, how can you sit with folded hands asking God's help in work that He has already given you the necessary tools? Even when the chosen people had their progress checked by the Red Sea, and their leader paused for Divine help, the Lord said, "Wherefore criest thou unto me?" In other words, use what you have and work!

When Dominique Dawes was nine years old, she visualized winning upcoming gymnastic events by taking a crayon and writing the same word over and over again on the mirror in her bedroom. The word that she wrote with such studied tenacity was "determination." A decade later, she has endured the daily grind of a seven-hour training schedule. Her youthful drive is paying off. Dominique Dawes is the odds-on favorite to capture the gold in the 1996 Olympic Games. It is work more so than determination that has delivered the goods.

Whoopi Goldberg's a comic, but she's no joke in the entertainment industry. As her movies continue their far-ranging appeal, Whoopi has positioned herself as one of the highest-paid talents in Hollywood. It's a distinction that earns her nearly $10 million per film, not bad for a child who grew up in a New York City housing project. By age twenty-one, Whoopi had been a wife, a mother, a divorcée, and a welfare recipient. But today, this Academy Award–winning actress with her signature dreadlocks attributes her success to one special gift: In the world of the silver screen, action is power. There is no one, great or small, that cannot make his or her life better by work.

The scoreboard read: Atlanta Hawks 112, Washington Bullets 90. More than twelve thousand beaming fans seated at the Omni in Atlanta, Georgia, had witnessed history. The Hawks victory was coach Lenny Wilkens's 939th career win, placing him ahead of the legendary Red Auerbach as the winningest coach in National Basketball Association history. Over the course of a professional career that began in 1960, Wilkens played fifteen seasons, made the all-star team nine times, ranked sixth in assists in NBA history, and was the league's second black head coach. He has participated in more games as a player and/or coach than anyone else. Known for his graceful intensity, Wilkens may not have been the best coach or the most skilled player. When Red Auerbach unrolled his program, his presence was commanded by power. When Michael Jordan soared to the basket, everyone stood up to take notice. But when all is said and done, you will find the name Wilkens under the win column before any of his competitors. Why? Because he was committed to outwork them!

What star shone brighter or demanded more admiration throughout the halls of education and commerce than the plain but cultivated Dr. Reatha Clark King? The barriers are not yet erected that can say to this aspiring talent, "Thus far and no farther." Born in the teeth of poverty in South Georgia, to a mother who didn't make it past the third grade and a father who couldn't read his name, Reatha's road to success ran uphill. As a senior at tiny Clark College, she sat in the dean's office holding a tearstained copy of her grades. Though her performance in the classroom was stellar, she was unable to pay her tuition. Her hopes of an education would have been dashed had it not been for her grandmother's wisdom. "She taught me the value of work," Reatha recounted. "I had to work extra hard, I had a weight to carry that was different from my peers."

Reatha would apply all that she had learned, working night and day, taking any job that came by her hand. One of the tops in her class, she toiled as a maid as well as a menial laborer. No position was beneath her. Endurance is a much better test of character than genius. Soon, her commitment caught the eye of the school's president. He instructed her professors to allow her to complete her exams even if her payments fell short. And what is the result of her tireless energy? Thanks in part to her strong work ethic, Reatha's résumé includes a fair share of "firsts": first of her race and gender to preside over a predominantly white university, Metropolitan State in Minneapolis, Minnesota; first African American female to be named president and executive director of the prestigious General Mills Foundation; and one of the first black women in the country to earn a doctorate degree in chemistry. The darkest shadows of life are those that an individual makes when he or she stands in his or her own light. The hopes and dreams of a people will only be realized through concentrated energy. Work is the remedy—the magic potion. It is the answer to whatever ails you.

ONE MORE HILL TO CLIMB

There's a steep hill in a Chicago suburb that was an important element in the personal development of one of pro football's greatest players. During the off-season, *every* season, he would run up the tough slope no matter the weather, regardless of the conditions. Over and over again, he would charge up that hill. Sometimes teammates would join him. Even rival players from other teams would try to match him, step for step, only to quit near the peak, dropping out in total exhaustion in the summer sun. Few could believe that anyone could be that obsessed with conquering a hill. There were times when he, too, had had enough. And when these moments surfaced, he rallied again and charged one last time. When the football season arrived, bruised and battered, he fought for every yard, every inch, every breath. Near the end of the games, when victory and defeat hung in the balance, that hill provided the critical difference. While others faded, this Hall of Fame running back seemed to get stronger. There was little question that he was talented. But all professional players have talent. Walter Payton also had that hill. It wasn't easy, it wasn't newsworthy, it was backbreaking work!

WHAT THE WHOLE WORLD IS SEEKING

What the age wants are men and women who have the nerve and the grit to work and wait, whether the world applauds or jeers. It wants a Walter Turnbull, who can spend eighteen years of his life guiding the Harlem Boys Choir before ever producing a record; a Muddy Waters, who can devote four decades of his life in dusty Mississippi towns sharing his version of the blues; a Madame C. J. Walker, who can struggle on for ten long years before she built her hair-care empire; a Stevie Wonder, visualizing love and compassion in a world he could not see; a Toni Morrison, who plodded on cheerfully after numerous rejections for her novel *The Bluest Eye;* a Barbara Jordan, who decided at age ten that she would make her mark in politics. She laid no claim to genius; she said her success was only a matter of hard work.

Naomi Sims, author, lecturer, and business executive, is a picture of sublime determination and grit. Tall, dark, and stately, Sims rose through the ranks to become one of the nation's most sophisticated couture models. See her raised in poverty in Oxford, Mississippi; dry your eyes as this tiny black child is shuffled between too many foster homes to count; hold your breath as she is dismissed as an idle dreamer who dared to challenge the social barriers of beauty; empathize as she pawns her clothes to pay her college tuition; and stick your chest out proudly as you watch her face grace the covers of *Vogue, Ladies' Home Journal, Life,* and *Cosmopolitan.* It seemed as if nature worked for ages to bring this beautiful flower to perfection!

And finally, consider Francis Cardinal Arinze, the archbishop from Nigeria: A convert to Catholicism at the age of nine, with Bible in hand, he spent fifty long years walking the back roads of West Africa searching for life's true meaning. Thanks to his tireless effort, a black man is now heir apparent to the papacy. How did he do it? Some have said the archbishop loves what is honest, true, whole, just, and spiritual. But mostly, he loves his God and his work. The world wants men and women *who can work!*

YOUR WORK PAINTS A SELF-PORTRAIT

A young man once made an appointment to interview a well-known author. As he began the conversation, the author interrupted and asked, "Why did you want to see me?"

The young man paused, then replied, "Well, I'm a writer, too. I was hoping you could share your keys for success."

"What have you written?" the author quizzed.

"Nothing," his visitor replied. "At least nothing that is complete."

The writer stood up before asking another question. "Well, if you haven't written anything, what are you writing?"

His guest responded, "Well, I'm currently in school and I'm hoping to find the time to pen a few thoughts."

As the author walked toward the door, he fired one final question before cutting the interview short. "So why do you call yourself a writer?" Writers write; composers compose; painters paint; and workers work. What you do to a great extent defines what you become, and, in turn, what you *are* gives rise to what you *do.* When what you do externally matches with what you are internally, greatness will not be denied!

THOSE WHO SUCCEED MUST PAY THE PRICE

Who are you, young man, young woman, in the prime of your life? Why should you, able-bodied and fit, be exempt from society's burdens and duties, and eat bread earned by the sweat of another's brow? Who are you to lay down your tools when you have not added one iota to the coffers of the world? Why sit idle? Is there no way in which you can utilize each passing moment? Are all the opportunities gone? Are all the positions filled? Are all the seats taken? Is the competition so fierce that you must be content with just sneaking by? Neither heaven nor earth reserves a place for the lazy. *Nature* demands that you labor first, then experience the reward of rest. *Success* demands that you allow no moment to pass until you've extracted every possibility. *Opportunity* has the uncanny habit of favoring those who have paid the price with years of preparation. The man and woman of the hour has spent many days and nights getting there. No one has climbed the ladder of success with his hands in his pockets. Whoever succeeds must hold his or her ground and push hard. Whoever attempts to pass through the door to success will find it labeled "Push!"

The soul of each of us is a gallery. In it we can hang works of art. We can enhance it with beauty; decorate it with detail; adorn it with faithfulness; embellish it with caring; trim it with passion; and dress it with desire. We can make it a place of radiance that can inspire and elevate, that can render humanity to a greater purpose. Or we can fill the studio with hideous images which will haunt our souls forever. We can mar the walls with indifference; stain them with apathy; blot them with carelessness; tarnish them with laziness; and blemish them with negligence. No matter how hard we try, we cannot leave the walls blank; for if we are idle, the walls will grow dusty and dingy. The canvas is given to each of us, the brush is placed in our hands by the Creator as we enter life. We cannot change or erase our efforts. Each indifferent or careless stroke will remain there forever—a testament to the level of our commitment.

DO NOT BE DECEIVED

A young boy, carving out an existence in the heart of the inner city, was arrested for snatching a woman's purse containing less than ten dollars. Weeks later, when asked by a judge why he stole the money, the boy responded, "Because the world owes me a living." No doubt the child had heard this many times from those he had grown to respect. A vast number of people seem to think that the world is under great obligation to them. Mistakenly, they believe that the Creator as well as society owes them a living. More than once I have heard seemingly well educated men and women say that they were brought into this world without their consent and they had hoped to get their share of life's rewards without giving anything in return.

How foolish can one be? I wonder, did they ever think what they really owe the world just for the privilege of living? Did they ever consider that humanity has been trudging since time immemorial on their behalf, and that they are reaping the harvest of those who have gone before? Can they look the tireless workers of the world in the eye and tell them that they intend to enjoy the benefits of their labor, the fruits of their efforts, without rendering anything in return? Everything that has gone before us, at some point, enters into our life and time. You and I enjoy the sum of the past each moment of our lives. Think of the untold millions who have laid down their lives in order to make our generation more comfortable, to minister to our convenience and peace. Think of the river of blood that has been shed, of the millions who have perished in misery and gloom, to purchase the freedoms you and I savor. Wherever we go, millions have paved the way. Generations have planned for our reception upon earth; countless others have prepared a table before us, getting things ready, guarding against danger, saving us toil and drudgery. How dare we say the world owes us a living!

The child who believes he or she can tiptoe through this world on the back of what somebody else has produced and still develop the highest character and moral standards fights against his Maker. I have heard the well-to-do boast that necessity was the mold that shaped them into something far more useful; which gave them the foresight, the stamina, the shrewdness, the creative power, the ability, to make and protect their fortune. And yet they turn around and leave a fortune to their children, which will likely sap their energy, snatch their ambition, and rob them of their enthusiasm and zest for living. They have placed a crutch into the hands of their children instead of a staff. They have taken away from their children the incentive to self-development, self-elevation, self-discipline, and self-help, without which no real success, no true happiness, is possible. So many well-meaning parents think to spare their sons and daughters the drudgery, the hardships, the deprivations, the lack of opportunities, that fueled the hopes of their elders. Instead, they have created grown weaklings who are unable to fend for themselves. Once they go down, they are as helpless as capsized turtles, or unhorsed men in armor.

Do not deceive yourself by thinking that you will get something for nothing. All the laws of the universe fight against such a theory. When you were born, civilization opened an account on your behalf. You, personally, must make each journal entry. No one else can pay the debt you owe. The law of the universe recognizes only one legal tender: personal service.

YOU ARE RESPONSIBLE

You might ask, "These requisites for success are unreasonable. How am I to adhere to them?" And I answer, any individual can acquire the habit of making an effort once given the chance. Your higher challenge is to engage in the present moment of your experience. To attach yourself to your duties and assignments, fully extended. To take a good mental approach to your calling and to make your best effort on a continuous basis. You are instructed in 2 Timothy: "Work hard so God can say to you, 'Well done.' Be a good workman, one who does not need to be ashamed when God examines your work."

Each of us has more talent than we will ever use. So, when you hammer a nail, feel each strike; when you sell a product or service, sell yourself first. If you are called upon to sweep the streets, do so in the manner that Dr. King suggested: "If a man is called to be a streetsweeper, he should sweep streets even as Michelangelo painted, or as Beethoven composed music, or as Shakespeare wrote poetry. He should sweep streets so well that all the hosts of heaven and earth will pause to say, 'Here lived a great streetsweeper who did his job well.' "

Be ready and willing to stand by your work. The world does not demand that you become a physician, a lawyer, or a merchant. But it does demand that whatever you undertake, you do it to the best of your ability. You are only one; but still, *you are one.* You cannot do everything, but *you can do something.* Do not refuse to embrace the something that you can do. Life owes you only the chance to be something. It will give you that and nothing more. If your vocation is simple or mundane, elevate it with diligence and caring. Broaden it with originality. Master every detail. Study it as you would any profession. Learn everything that is to be known about it. Go to the bottom of your business if you would climb to the top. This is your responsibility to life.

A FATHER'S ADVICE TO HIS CHILDREN

Never be satisfied with "fairly good," "pretty good," or "good enough." Accept nothing less of yourself than your best. This is the law of the universe. Nature completes every little leaf, its edges and stem, as exactly and perfectly as though it were the only leaf to blossom. Even the flower that blooms in the mountain dell, where no human eye will ever behold it, is made with the same perfection and exactness of form and outline, with the same delicate shade of color, with the same completeness of beauty, as though it were intended for royalty. Put such a quality into your work, so that anyone who comes across your efforts will see character in it, individuality in it, your trademark of superiority upon it. Your reputation is at stake in everything you do—and your reputation is your capital. It is just a small difference between good and the best, and it makes the difference between the artist and the artisan. It is the added touch after the average man or woman would quit that makes the master's fame.

Percy Sutton is quite blasé about his break into the business world, though his eventual rise to the top of the cable broadcasting industry is one of the implausible, yet routinely repeated sagas of ,individual achievement. His father, a hard-bitten jack-of-all-trades, including principal of his hometown's "colored" high school, was five years old when the Civil War came to a close. Sutton's family grew up with the state of Texas, acquiring land six blocks from the Alamo, in what is now downtown San Antonio. By the time Percy was born in 1920, the family had reached the middle class. As the youngest of fifteen children, and born to a father who was then sixty, he received the best of his father's wisdom. And that wisdom was a collection of thoughts, philosophies, and dreams that grew out of a confining past: "He wanted to make us independent persons," Sutton reflects, "to walk down the corridors of power, where he had never been able to walk."

As a parent, Sutton's father was both firm and kind. While rearing his children in an all-black section of town, he never allowed them to get away with poor grammar, and wouldn't allow it among their friends either. "Scholastically, my father was hard to impress. He had a philosophy that every Sutton was going to achieve. A C should have been a B, and a B should have been an A; and if it was an A, why wasn't it an A before this? Needless to say, I was highly motivated."

In the twenties and thirties, the Sutton house was not only a home but a way station for eastern black intellectuals heading west. No hotel would accept them, no matter how high their accomplishments, and by the time they got to San Antonio, bitterness had settled upon them like dust. As they sat around and discussed remedies to America's racist treatment, young Percy would sit at his father's feet, absorbing every word.

His father wanted his children to be different, to be pioneers, "firsts." He called them smart and inflated their fragile, developing egos, and, until his death, he would, like some latter-day Polonius, lecture them on the vicissitudes of life and law.

" 'Strive!' " Sutton says with assertion, mimicking his father's mannerisms. " 'Wait. Pray. Be proud. Try to find your outer limits, and don't worry about falling on your face.' This comes from my father. He taught us to get up and wipe ourselves off, and try again." As crucial as his father's skills were to his own personal development, they are even more important to his own children. "Attitude, discipline, and ambition," he stresses, "are the clay in which success and progress will be molded."

Strive. Wait. Pray. Be proud. Try to find your outer limits, and don't worry about falling on your face.

—Percy Sutton

There can be no richer man or woman than the individual who has found his or her labor of love. Personal fulfillment through the virtue of work is the highest form of desire. Work is the conduit between the supply and the demand of all human needs, the forerunner of human progress, and the medium by which the imagination is given the wings of action. A labor of love is exalted because it provides joy and self-expression to those who perform it.

THE BEST SERMON

One day a woman was working in the garden outside of her house when a traveling minister stopped by. "What a lovely garden," he exclaimed, getting out of his horse-drawn buggy. Full of roses, orchids, and other beautiful flowers, the garden was bordered by sculpted hedges and stood out from the other gardens in the neighborhood.

"My good woman. God has certainly blessed you with an extraordinary garden."

The woman stood up and wiped her brow.

"Yes, and I am very grateful. But you should've seen this place when He had it all to Himself!"

As he rode away, the traveling minister realized that every gardener along this road had been blessed with the same soil, the same opportunity, and that each garden was a reflection of the people who created it. What someone does with their garden is their business. While each gardener had similar materials to work with, this woman had done something truly extraordinary, for her garden had far surpassed her neighbors'. The woman was grateful for what she had been given, but she knew that what she did with it was the difference between success and failure. Good fortune may help you get to the top, but it takes hard work to stay there. Though many philosophers have made the statement that man is the master of his destiny, most have failed to say why. Man may be the master of himself and his destiny because it is he who can taste the fruit of his own labor. To a world that requires service, measures discipline and patience, demands a fair day's wages for an honest day's effort, and values the time and commitment that excellence demands, the road to greatness is spit-polished with sweat. Work is the shortest path to success.

YOUR LIFE'S WORK

Finding and creating your life's work, even if it is entirely different from what you have done most of your life, will bring you more happiness and wealth than any other action you can take. If your primary responsibility in life is being true to yourself, that can only be accomplished by carrying out what you are called to do—your unique and special vocation. The true American dream not only provides the freedom to use your gifts and talents to achieve your highest goal but also gives you the freedom to fulfill your purpose in life. You are meant to work in ways that suit you, drawing on your natural talents and gifts. This work, when you find it and commit to it—even if only as a hobby—is the key to happiness. Your life's work involves *doing what you love* and *loving what you do.*

Now, what is that work? Usually, something that excites you and makes you feel a strong emotion whenever you think about it. It is the career you were undoubtedly *meant* to have; something that is "right" for you. Finding and creating your life's work will require that you listen to your inner voice and follow your instincts. Whatever you are seeking, it is seeking you. A life's work inspires passion. It sustains energy. It seduces you. It trails your every move. And, as a result, you will be well compensated for working effortlessly on a job that you would gladly perform for free. Wealth is the by-product of doing anything well.

LABOR IS LIFE!

It has been said that we need reminding as much as we need educating. Individuals have the most perverse tendency to take the best things in life for granted. In fact, a human being has the capacity to take anything, no matter how great, for granted—once he or she becomes used to it. The actor in front of the cameras, the captain at the helm of an ocean liner, the writer in her study, the painter in front of his canvas—all seem to allow the charm and excitement of their work to fade like the noonday sun. Their careers have grown cold and stale, as mundane as brushing teeth.

Our Maker did not give us minds of our own and free wills so that we could drift aimlessly, without a sense of purpose and direction. We must control and use our talents to their fullest in ways that each of us sees best. To do otherwise is to waste our lives. The hopeless plodders—those who insist upon the mundane life—know too well the banality of waste: a human life rich with potential reduced to mere existence. These individuals are prisoners of work. They conform to low standards, they limit their growth. Each of us has seen these prisons of mediocrity in all walks of society: Executives who clamor for the "golden handcuffs" that will keep them in their gilded cages of unfulfillment; laborers who go on strike for contracts that bind them to low productivity; and office workers who oppose anything that challenges the status quo.

You and I were not created to be chained. We were not designed to follow, but to achieve, to strive, and to build. Imagination is the key. When we fail to use our imagination, our work becomes routine. Routine leads to the rut of mediocrity. Mediocrity is the farthest point possible from creativity. Imagination discovers possibilities where none existed before.

Great men and women know the real value of work—not just the inherent value to those who benefit from it, but its greater value to the person performing it. Those who dare to succeed seem to have the capacity for never taking their work for granted. However, most people must search and listen for their calling. You can begin by knowing that you are someone who has a rare gift within you. In fact, you came to this planet with that special, unique talent. You can start by looking into opportunities of interest. Believe that it is never too late to begin your life's work.

HOW ONE MAN FOUND HIS CALLING

Even as a twelve-year-old, Herman Russell was careful with what little money he had. A string of odd jobs and a demeanor that was deadpan and businesslike belied his years. By sixteen, he had learned to earn money and he decided to open his first bank account. Creating wealth seemed to be foremost in his mind. Somehow, he knew even then that the fortunes of youth could quickly wither.

Herman J. Russell grew up with the gritty taste of plaster dust in his mouth and a hunger to help shape the long shadows that Atlanta's skyline cast over his poor South Side neighborhood. At an age when his peers were discovering carburetors and the opposite sex, Russell was seething with the spirit of enterprise and built his first duplex. The income from the monthly rent would help finance a college education at Tuskegee Institute. By twenty-nine, he was helping white developers transform the city's downtown skyscrapers. Thirty years later, he rested at the helm of a $145-million conglomerate, not to mention a personal fortune estimated between $40 million and $100 million. Russell's success is the story of the son of a poor plasterer maneuvering his struggling firm in a race-based environment that both penalized and rewarded his efforts.

The construction industry provides an excellent example: The road to opportunity is paved with effort. On the surface, Russell seems remarkably calm despite a schedule that includes sixteen-hour workdays. At 6:00 A.M., he can usually be found on a construction site conferring with staff and officials. By ten o'clock, he's huddled around a conference table at the office of the Department of Housing and Urban Development (HUD), authorizing documents for upcoming projects. At noon, he must forgo an Atlanta Chamber of Commerce luncheon (though he is a board member and past president) to host an unscheduled meeting with Olympic Committee officials and city staffers. He's also missing a committee meeting to nominate a local college president and a 1:30 appointment with a developer—not to mention the failure to return several important phone calls, including one from the White House. By early evening, he's entertaining business associates in a private box at an Atlanta Hawks basketball game. The next day—and the next week—follow a similar schedule.

"Opportunity Always Comes Dressed in Work Clothes"

Herman Russell's philosophy reflects his own hardscrabble upbringing. Raised in a family of workaholics, Russell outpaces all but a few. The youngest of eight children, he grew up on the crumbling streets of Summerhill, the poorest of a series of impoverished black neighborhoods in Atlanta. His father, a proponent of Booker T. Washington's philosophy of self-reliance, put his son to work at the age of ten, and he has been working ever since. "My father believed in land, and that has obviously rubbed off. He was a plasterer who struggled to feed his family. He learned the trade from his father and passed it on to me. Under his guidance I worked at different jobs—laborer, hod carrier, and mortar mixer. At twelve, I was one of the best plasterers around. I could make anything out of plaster. But more important, he taught me the basic principles of success—discipline, punctuality, thrift—and that opportunity always comes dressed in work clothes."

After college Russell moved back to Atlanta and bought a ragtag pickup truck for $150. He set up his own firm by combing the city and doing small, residential plastering. By the 1960s, Russell had successfully expanded into small-scale, residential development, the market to which most black contractors were then confined. His big opportunity came with the civil rights movement. By middecade, Atlanta's leading developers were under intense pressure to invite black businesses to participate in the city's rapidly expanding economy. By 1970, Russell was building 400-plus-unit apartment complexes and had become a millionaire. But he hungered for more, which meant he would have to cross the color line that traditionally separated the Atlanta business community. He got help when newly elected Maynard Jackson, Atlanta's first black mayor, issued a bold initiative requiring contractors doing business with the city to either institute affirmative action programs or enter into joint ventures with minority firms. Russell, and other struggling black contractors, felt the windfall.

"Booker T. Washington was right," Russell points out. "There's no victory without labor. No race can prosper until it learns there is as much dignity in tilling a field as in writing a poem. This is the foundation of wealth." The sweeping nature of Russell's ideas cannot be overemphasized. Good ideas—even great ones—are not rare. But getting them listened to, believed in, or acted upon is rare indeed. Gifts are not rare either. In fact, we all have them. Moreover, the world welcomes them. What the world won't welcome, however, is idleness. It remains for us as individuals to accept the drudgery, the toil, and to overcome eminent discouragement to cultivate our gifts. So while gifts are not rare, people who refine them are. The meaning of life does not come from skimming its surface, but plunging headlong into the depths of a great task. Christ did not say, "Come unto me, all ye pleasure hunters, indolent and lazy"; but he did instruct, "Come unto me all that labor and are heavy laden." Never feel above hard work. Effort, sweat, and commitment will lift anyone into respectability.

SEVEN CRITERIA FOR CHOOSING THE CORRECT VOCATION

A poet once wrote, "Blessed is the man who has found his work." For the man or woman who has found an unending area of interest, the future is indeed a happy prospect. And let me add, such work exists for each of us. If we have not yet found it, we can do no better than to continue our journey until we do discover it. Latch onto the full message of Dean Briggs, one of America's foremost business educators, who taught, "Do your work. Not just your work and no more, but a little more for the lavishing's sake. That little more which is worth all the rest. And if you doubt as you must; and if you suffer as you must—do your work. Put your heart into it and the sky will clear. And then out of your very doubt and suffering will be born the supreme joy of life."

Imagine you have just received a diploma and you are about to walk into your dream job. What is the work that you will perform? What is your level of compensation? Who are your coworkers? Describe your work environment. What does it look like, feel like, sound like? How do you feel in this setting? What do people say to you, ask of you, or report to you? What rewards do you experience?

Have you found that work—your correct vocation? You need to ask two key questions as you approach the following exercise relating to your professional life: First, is my current professional career the one best suited to me? Second, if I am in the career best suited to me, am I using my talent to its full potential? If you haven't discovered your true vocation, you may benefit from the following guidelines for choosing the correct vocation, stipulated in part by inspirational writer Mark Victor Hansen.

1. *The position must be self-chosen.* You must choose it. Not your mother, father, or significant other. Did somebody encourage you to pursue this field? The successful employ the secret of preparation as a way of achieving goals and sidestepping obstacles. They adhere to the words of Whitney M. Young, founder of the Urban League, who taught, "It's better to be prepared for an opportunity and not have one than to have an opportunity and not be prepared."

2. *The position or occupation must be something that excites you.* Passion is the keyword. The successful select work suited to their education and temperaments—they engage in labors of love.

3. *There must be ample opportunity for unlimited personal and professional growth.* What each of us must do is to progress in our professions; to strive for constant improvement; to become effective and efficient in the career of our choice. In education as well as in business, we must not only strike while the iron is hot, but we must strike it until it becomes hot.

4. *Creative thinking must be required.* Successful men and women possess the ability to turn nothing into something. They transform weeds into gardens and pennies into fortunes by combining the blessings of work and imagination.

5. *You cannot watch the clock in a level of compensation.* Trading hours for dollars is the lowest form of compensation. Peak performers do not evaluate their work by the number of hours it takes. They never equate what they earn with the work they perform. Time is a tool, not an end. Those who master greatness don't complain about long hours; they complain that the hours aren't long enough

to accomplish everything they want. How long does the successful man or woman work? *Until.*

6. ***All work must be beneficial to humanity.*** Successful people view work as a giving process: serving for the sake of serving; giving for the sake of giving. In other words, their work is seen as a calling. Collectively, they've adopted the motto "Only the best will do!" They hang this dictum in their office, in their home; they weave it into the texture of everything they do. Achievers see work as a means to better their world.

7. ***The vocation must allow you to associate with those you choose.*** You have the ability to surround yourself with others like you.

Those who fall short of the mark can trace their failure to the demand of the hour—laboring under the correct vocation. The giants of the race have been men and women of concentration, of high energy, who have hammered their blows in one place until they have accomplished their purpose. And that one place was the *right* place! Mankind was designed for labor. "Thou shall live by the sweat of thy brow" was written centuries ago, and the immutable destiny of humanity will never change. The true doctrine is that labor—systematic, industrious, congenial—is not only a necessity but the source of our highest enjoyment if chosen correctly.

WORK WITH ALL YOUR MIGHT

Beautiful lives have blossomed in the darkest of places, like colorful lilies full of fragrance springing from the most stagnant waters. One man will evoke harmony and beauty from the toughest surroundings, while another will turn fame and fortune into poverty and despair. The noblest sight the world offers is of a young man or woman bent upon making the most of his or her life. He who puts his soul into his work, however lowly that work may be, turns meaningless words into poetry. Man is not merely the architect of his own fortune; he must lay the bricks himself.

WILLIE GARY'S HOME, though poor and small, was big on values. His parents, two migrant workers who followed the crops—picking beans in Florida, peaches in Georgia, and apples in North Carolina—shared scripture each day, using the Bible as the reference point in their lives. There was no church nearby, but each Sunday an aunt would set up wooden boxes like pews under a shade tree and seat all eleven children. "God gave His only begotten son so we could live," she taught. "So we must give ourselves to him. And one way is being of use to others."

"You know what *that* means, son," his father said later as they worked in their garden. *"Work!* Work joyfully even if you're not paid for it."

The boy's eyes lit up, staring in disbelief. "You mean work for nothing?"

His father explained. "It's better than sitting around doing nothing." The old man set out to make his point. He stopped digging long enough to wipe off his garden fork, making it shine in the Florida sun. Then he ducked into the toolshed and grabbed another fork, this one much older with a broken handle. "See the difference?" he asked. "The shiny tool is working. The dull one is useless just rusting away." His father tapped the rusty fork and said, "Nature has a way of doing away with anything that's not being used." Though his father had only a grade-school education, he possessed wisdom beyond his years. No one could be more grateful for this invaluable lesson than his impressionable son.

Despite their nomadic existence, Willie Gary's parents strove to keep their children in school. Education would one day provide an escape from the hopeless camps. But it was difficult. Migrant children attended classes only in the morning. By noon, buses roared into the schoolyard, waiting to rush them back to the hot, steamy fields. Crawling on his hands and knees under a blowtorch sun, wincing at mosquitoes, Willie picked beans from midday to sundown, dreaming of better days.

At age twenty, he left home with the hope of playing football at Bethune-Cookman College in Daytona Beach. The local paper hailed him as a hero: the town's first black male to enter college. But once arriving on campus, Willie discovered that he was one of 125 hopefuls trying out for only forty positions. He had to make the team or he would be sent packing. Day after day the roster was whittled down. Finally, on the last day of practice, the coach summoned him into his office. "I'm sorry, son . . ." he began. Tearfully, Willie didn't stay long enough to hear the rest of the coach's words. He cleaned out his locker and left for the bus station.

Crestfallen and disappointed, the next morning he phoned his high school football coach explaining his circumstances. His coach paused for a moment and replied, "Willie, there's a small school in Raleigh, North Carolina—Shaw College. Their coach is a personal friend. I'll give him a call and see if I can arrange a tryout. He's a little guy like you— maybe he'll give you a chance."

That Sunday evening, Willie boarded a Greyhound bus and rode all night to Raleigh. He arrived on campus carrying his possessions in a worn-out suitcase held together by string. Too excited to sleep, he headed for the coach's office.

"I'm Willie Gary," he blurted.

The coach looked up from his desk, puzzled. "What can I do for you?"

"Well—I—uh, I want to play football," he stammered. "I'll do anything to make the team."

The coach leaned back in his chair and said, "I'm terribly sorry. I don't have any openings. Our squad is full."

"*Every* position?" Willie asked.

The coach stood and put a consoling arm around the boy's shoulder. "Yes, every position. I'm afraid you'll have to go home."

He Used This Principle to Give Away $10 Million

Willie left the coach's office knowing this time he couldn't go home. Outside the athletic department, he slumped on a bench holding his head in his hands. Several players passed by, rendering a sympathetic ear. They suggested he spend the night on a sofa in the lounge of the football dorm. The following morning, he recalled his father's admonition: Work even if you're not paid for it. But what could he do? He kept his eyes open, mixing with other players as they walked to the locker room to suit up for practice. As they set out for the field, they left the locker room in a shambles. Willie searched for a broom and mop and began cleaning up. After the players showered and left, he cleaned the room again. An assistant coach casually remarked, "You really want to go to school, don't you?"

To further make his case, Willie visited the admissions office, completed an application, and, embarrassed, told the director that he didn't have the ten-dollar fee. It all seemed so hopeless. A day later the coach spotted him on campus and remarked, "I heard you're doing a good job in the locker room. I'll give you a meal ticket for the remainder of the week."

One step, Willie thought.

The coach added, "Maybe you can bring the first-aid kit to the field. And our trainer could use a hand."

Another step.

The coach paused long enough to ask, "Where are you sleeping?"

"Well, I've got a place," Willie said less than convincingly.

"No, you haven't," the coach said sternly. He adjusted his cap and said, "I'll get you a bed until Friday. Then you've got to go."

As the coach walked away, Willie was fraught with worry. Friday? That's only two days away. Everything appeared hopeless.

Friday afternoon, the assistant coach called, "Hey, Willie. The coach wants to see you."

The boy with the big heart forced a smile, expecting the worst. He entered the office hesitantly. The coach met him at the door. "I thought I told you to go home," he said slyly.

"Well—I—uh—" Willie couldn't speak.

The coach broke into a grin. "I'm glad you didn't," he said. "One of our linebackers was hurt during practice. We have a place for you *if* you still want it."

Willie couldn't believe his ears. He nearly jumped through the ceiling. Before replying, he slipped into a jersey and pads two sizes too big and ran onto the football field. For the next four years, Willie Gary would not only shine on the gridiron for Shaw College, but would turn in a stellar performance in the classroom as well, earning a degree in business. In 1975, with his law degree in hand, he drove back to his home state of Florida to launch a practice. In one of his first cases, an elderly woman tottered into his office. She was having trouble with the utility company regarding her bill.

"I'm sorry, Mr. Gary," she trembled, dabbing her eyes with a handkerchief, "but I must tell you I can't afford to pay you." Willie never forgot that precious lesson taught to him in the bean fields twenty-five miles away. He looked down at his desk for a moment, thinking of his father.

"Don't worry, ma'am," he said. "I'll take your case." The look on her face was ample reimbursement. One phone call took care of her problem. But this was only the beginning. Impressed, the old woman recommended his firm to another family whose dilemma involved major litigation. Again, Gary's firm won. But this time they shared a $100-million judgment!

Today, Gary, Williams, Parenti, Finney & Lewis, Gary's firm, represents clients where millions of dollars hang in the balance. Over the past fifteen years, Willie Gary has never lost a case. In an effort to give back and support the institution that supported him, Gary has pledged to donate $10 million to Shaw University, making his gift the largest contribution any black college alum has ever made. In addition, he openly shares his keys to success with young people and church groups across the country. Everyone is always eager to hear the story of how he won a spot on the football team. He gladly shares that tale, but he also tells listeners how to win at life. "Just remember two simple rules," he teaches. "Trust in God and be willing to work!"

Listen closely. Two crucial points stand out in Willie Gary's rise to prominence. First, the circumstances surrounding his childhood might have discouraged a lesser man or woman from pursuing his or her dreams. And second, through hard work he was able to withstand the forces that tried to keep him back. There are two types of people who never seem to get ahead: those who wait to be told what to do, and those who do nothing more than what they are told to do. There's nothing new about the "greatest advice." It may be applied by anyone who possesses the untiring desire to seize it and make the most of the moment.

MESSAGE FROM A MASTER

Dante Gabriel Rossetti, the nineteenth-century poet and artist, was once approached by an elderly man. The old fellow had some sketches and drawings that he wanted Rossetti to review and suggest if they were any good or if they displayed any talent. Rossetti took a look and immediately knew the paintings were worthless, showing not the least sign of talent. The artistic master was a kind man, and he told this elderly man, as gently as possible, that the pictures were of little value. He was sorry, but he could not lie. Though openly disappointed, his visitor seemed to expect Rossetti's judgment. He then apologized for taking up the artist's time but asked one final question: Would he please look at another batch of paintings—these done by a young art student?

With one look at the paintings, Rossetti's face lit up. "These," he said, "are very good. It's obvious this young artist has a great deal of skill. He should be encouraged to develop his talent."

Rossetti could see that the old fellow was deeply moved. "Who is this fine artist?" he asked. "Your son?"

"No," the old man said sadly. "It was me—forty years ago. If only I had heard your words then, I might have been encouraged to paint." How can you and I help anyone reach his or her objectives? By passing down the greatest advice.

"Blessed is he who has found his work," wrote Thomas Carlyle, the nineteenth-century English essayist. Perhaps nothing Carlyle ever wrote is so well known, so widely quoted, as the eight words that express his lifelong philosophy. For more than one hundred years, this familiar sentence has emphasized the dignity of a life's work and a life's purpose. "There is a perennial nobleness, and even sacredness, in work," he continues. "There is always hope in a man that actually and earnestly works. In idleness alone is there perpetual despair."

James Russell Lowell, the American poet, concurs. He wrote nearly one hundred years ago, "No man is born into the world whose work is not born in him. There is always work and tools to work with for those who will."

"The crowning fortune of a man," Ralph Waldo Emerson professed, "is to be born to some pursuit which finds him in employment and happiness, whether it be to make baskets, or broadswords, or canals, or statues or song. The world is no longer clay, but rather iron in the hands of its workers, and men have got to hammer out a place for themselves by steady and rugged blows."

Michelangelo states, "It is only well with me when I have a chisel in my hand."

And Samuel Smiles writes, "All that is great in man comes through hard work, and civilization is its product."

Dorothea Brande's *Wake Up and Live!* was published in 1936, during the very depths of the Depression. It was a life preserver to a nation drowning in despair, and its message is as meaningful today as it was during those dark years. She states, "In the long run it makes little difference how cleverly others are deceived; if we are not doing what we are best equipped to do, or doing well what we have undertaken as our personal contribution to the world's work, at least by way of an earnestly followed avocation, there will be a core of unhappiness in our lives which will be more and more difficult to ignore as the years pass."

"Work or starve" is nature's motto. It is an inexorable law of nature that whatever is not used, dies. "Nothing for nothing" is her maxim. If we are idle and shiftless by choice, we shall be limited and powerless by necessity. We are the sum of our endeavors. Our reward is in the race we run, not in the prize. Success is the child of effort and perseverance. It cannot be coaxed or bribed. Pay the price and it is yours.

More than just a shrewd observer of the early American Asian immigrant, Marcus Garvey, the 1920s African nationalist, pointed out his Asian counterpart as a demonstration to his race of what is possible:

> *No sooner does he place his foot upon this soil than he*
> *begins to work. No position is too menial, no task is too*
> *trivial. He has come to make money; his needs are few. He*
> *barely lives, but he saves what he gets. He commences*
> *trade in the smallest possible way, and he continually*
> *adds to his lot. Others scorn drudgery and remain poor—*
> *this newcomer toils patiently, and grows rich. A few years*
> *pass by, and he secures warehouses; becomes a contractor*
> *for produce; buys foreign goods and employs his newly*

*imported countrymen, who have come to seek their
fortune as he did. He is not particularly scrupulous in
matters of opinion. He never meddles with politics, for
they are dangerous and not profitable. He holds his own
with other groups, and works while they sleep. He is
diligent, temperate, and uncomplaining. He keeps the
word he pledges, pays his debts, and is capable of noble
and generous acts. Speak lightly of him if you would
speak at all.*

"Black America has been led to believe that it has absolutely no
power over its economic future," says Henry Parks. "We overemphasize
the power of racism and discrimination, and downplay our potential
and freedom of choice. The formula has been laid bare: *Ethnic pride
and hard work lead to wealth and success.* There's no need to write a
book to teach others how to make money. The key has been there for
anyone to use. Just look in the kitchen of any Chinese restaurant and
you'll find the answer. Let's not reinvent the wheel!"

If your health is threatened, work. If disappointments surface, work.
If your faith falters, work. If you inherit riches, continue to work. If your
dreams are shattered, and the star of hope begins to darken your horizon, work. If sorrow overwhelms you, or your friends prove untrue or
desert you, work. If you are happy, keep right on working. No matter
what ails you, work. Work as if your life depended on it, *because it does!*

HOW TO ADVANCE IN YOUR CAREER

There is a question you must ask: Where is the source of your income? A job? Investments? Inheritance? On this matter you need to be
crystal-clear. Many people falsely claim their income lies within a title or
a particular position. They fail to realize that the source of all wealth
lies, not within any position, occupation, or range of investments, but
within the spiritual nature to embody the best that rests within each of
us. This is an earthshaking revelation. Work is, and should be considered
by all, a giving process. The Master instructed, "Let not the left hand
know what the right hand is doing." In other words, don't get trapped
in the error of equating what you *earn* with what you *do.* How easy
and, yet, how mistaken we are to be influenced by the "another day, another dollar" syndrome. Let your work, whatever it may involve, be a
demonstration of the creative flow. What do you think about your
work? How well do you perform your job? Is it tedious labor or meaningful activity? Do you have significant professional skills that are not

being used? Examine your work and question whether it enlists your talents and capabilities. Check your attitudes and feelings about the work you do. Is it right for you? Are you utilizing your education, training, and range of experiences? If not, you may need to consider changing your job or even your career. If you view your daily tasks as a steady grind, perhaps now is the time to analyze your career and seek a more fulfilling vocation. Perhaps you are due for a career change. Or maybe you need a change in attitude regarding your work, your company, the people involved, and its products. Remember, a *job* is something you do for money, but a *career* is something you do out of love. Chase your passion, not your pension!

There is an answer, a solution, a rule that has never failed for those who have truly applied it. When it comes to improving career choices, one of the greatest secrets of success was delivered to us from the mountaintop nearly two thousand years ago: "And whoever compels you to go one, go with him two." Go the extra mile. If you begin today to give more of yourself, to do more, to serve more, to put out more on your job and in your career than you're getting paid to do, miracles will begin to occur in your life. Whatever your occupation—salesperson, teacher, accountant, executive, janitor—if, each day, you do more than what is expected, your life will change for the better. When you give more each day, every day, not only will you promote yourself, but by being indispensable, new and existing opportunities will discover you. Resolve today that nothing great was ever achieved without enthusiasm. To do anything that is truly worth doing, jump in with gusto. Take off your coat and embrace the day's most difficult tasks. Remember, the busier you are, the sweeter your sleep, the tastier your food, the greater your reward, and the more satisfied you will be with your place in the world. Work as though you would live forever, and live as though you would die today. Go the extra mile.

ANATOMY OF THE GREAT EXECUTIVE

Everyone needs to master something. Whatever you do in life, be greater than your calling. Choose one profession, and master it in all details. Sleep by it, swear by it, and by all means, work for it, and success will add glory to your labor. Corporate executives, for example, choose and master careers in business with the thought that, all things considered, corporate life offers the greatest opportunity for personal satisfaction. They come to the corporate world hoping to have their full range of talents and abilities tested and utilized. Business schools of yesteryear summed up the philosophy that presupposes individual success: Go to the bottom of your business if you would climb to the top. Do that which is assigned, and more will be added unto you.

These ideas are not new, but are they enough? What of the black corporate executive—those men and women who risk resources and reputations to reach the highest rung on the corporate ladder; those individuals armed with the latest management techniques who also have felt the tug of ambition? Do the same traits apply? Is hard work enough? If not, what are the core skills and values? Time and again, high-achieving men and women have been subjected to intense examination to reveal their inner secrets to success. Volumes of research have pinpointed certain traits that are common among peak performers. These characteristics have often emerged from self-appraisals and personal accounts as corporate climbers try to piece those factors together that repeatedly earmark business success. However, little is known of the skills of those remarkably successful black, senior-level executives who, like their white counterparts, continue to encounter a changing environment, stiff competition, ever-shrinking markets, as well as racial bias. What is known of these men and women who take on the odds and continue to pursue their objectives?

Achieving corporate success and remaining competitive through the ups and downs of an unstable economy has never been easy. The wave of restructuring, spin-offs, mergers, and acquisitions is no fluke. There are some costs. Failure is frequent. Adjustments and midcourse corrections are the norm; early retirement, golden parachutes, and lateral assignments are routine. Furthermore, overcoming barriers and roadblocks can be horrendous. As a result, many corporate climbers stop climbing; even the best and the brightest lapse into apathy. While this holds true for everyone who dares to test these tricky waters, the black corporate achiever is cast afloat with the most limited provisions.

In their early years, many black executives were belittled. For example, in the late 1960s, with degree in hand, Frito-Lay's Lloyd Ward was greeted with derision during an interview when he tried to convince a college recruiter that a black man could achieve and prosper in the corporate arena. "Sorry, you're too early," Ward was told by an indifferent personnel manager. "Come back in twenty years," the man said. Unyielding, this serenely confident college grad fired back, "Sir, will that be in the morning or the afternoon?"

Just imagine the type of skepticism that was aimed her way when Linda Baker Keene decided to make her move in the personal care division of Gillette. The whispers behind her back; ignored by her peers in staff meetings; and the combined burdens of sexism and racism were laid at her feet. But every day of meeting sorrow makes the life more grand. Somehow, some way, this black woman with a Harvard MBA would rise above it. Before the final page was turned, Vice-President for Market Development would be written by her name. Kraft Foods' Paula Sneed, Sun Microsystems' Dorothy Terrell, and Coca-Cola's Carolyn Baldwin have similar stories to tell. All started from scratch, without influence or connections.

WHO MAKES IT UP THE CORPORATE LADDER AND WHY

In 1992, I came to Clark Atlanta University in Atlanta, Georgia, as a professor in the School of Business Administration and director of the newly created Center of Entrepreneurship. Here, I gained access to a remarkably gifted and diverse group of business students, alumni, and visiting luminaries. As in my earlier search for the formula for achievement among black entrepreneurs, an idea began to take hold. I turned my sights to the essence of leadership and the pursuit of excellence. I sought out individuals who could provide answers to the question: Who makes it up the corporate ladder and why? I shifted my focus to members of one of the most elite clubs in the nation—the top one hundred senior-level corporate executives in Black America. Because little practical material exists, my approach to the research was similar to the methods I followed in *Think and Grow Rich: A Black Choice.* To begin the search, I cast a broad net looking for men and women of power and influence. Because the goal of this research was to uncover a number of candidates, I collected names and data from many sources: *Black Enterprise, BusinessWeek, Forbes,* and *Fortune* magazines, human resource specialists, executive recruiters, business schools, professional organizations, and, most prominent, the Washington, D.C.–based Executive Leadership Council. The eventual choice of participants was a decidedly nonstatistical, subjective judgment call. In some cases the choice of candidates was obvious. No matter the criteria—position, industry, bottom-line impact, or compensation—by any measure these individuals had to be included. On the other hand, as my fieldwork progressed, names were added that had not emerged from the initial screening process.

THE EXECUTIVE PROFILE—
WHAT IT TELLS YOU

These individuals are, by definition, successful. They have achieved highly visible and responsible positions at the nation's most prominent corporations and financial institutions. These findings offer an overview of the goals, attitudes, and range of experience of these executives, as well as examining how their motivations and priorities shaped their career paths. But how does each individual define success? Surprisingly, not in monetary terms or in terms of title or prestige. Instead, in the corporate arena, executives consider themselves successful when they have obtained the ability to effect change and the capacity to enjoy their work.

The composite black executive is a forty-six-year-old college graduate (27 percent are female), who has been with his or her present employer less than ten years. He or she bears the title "vice-president," and, more often than not, holds an MBA degree. In terms of compensation, he or she broke the $100,000 barrier at or before age forty. Their current annual compensation is $200,000. A few are millionaires. Their career moves have been motivated by a desire for increased responsibility and challenge; one-third aspire to the top job in the firm. Most of their career has been spent within marketing and sales, pitching some of the country's most competitive products. They work between fifty-five and sixty-two hours a week and take two weeks vacation a year. They consider themselves liberal to moderate on social issues and moderate to conservative on fiscal matters. He or she belongs to several organizations, choosing to devote his or her time to the National Association for the Advancement of Colored People (NAACP), the Urban League, 100 Black Men, or 100 Black Women. Their combined net worth would position them as thirty-third on the *Black Enterprise* list of top one hundred black-owned firms.*

But this tells only part of the story. I wish to emphasize data that most people overlook. A common belief exists that there are indeed qualities that lead some to the top of their fields, whereas others struggle along in the middle of the pack. If this is true, what is the secret formula for success that lies hidden in the personality of those who achieve it? In this case, the answer may be worth thousands of dollars—maybe even

* For complete survey findings, see the Kimbro Executive Profile on p. 311. To obtain a copy of the Kimbro Executive Profile, send your request to The P. Kimbro Group, Decatur, Georgia 30034.

millions. When asked to evaluate which factor was most important to their career, it is astonishing how uniformly these business leaders replied: "Hard work."

BLESSED ARE THOSE WHO HAVE FOUND THEIR WORK

Let's face it. Whenever men and women on the move are asked for their key to success and they reply, "Hard work!" we usually respond in a cynical fashion, wondering what the *real* secret is behind their good fortune. Was it a lucky break, a rich uncle, or knowing the right person at the right time that accounted for their rise to the top? Questions like this may comfort our sagging egos, but they also blind us from the truth—and the truth, in most cases, is that peak performers do achieve their objectives through hard work.

But you work hard, too, don't you? And yet, you don't frequently dine out or travel exclusively first-class or vacation in your Caribbean summer home. Your definition of hard work probably means forty to fifty hours a week of your best effort. Well, when these high achievers say "hard work," they mean working at top capacity for sixty to seventy hours or more, each week, loving their work until it becomes a driving passion, and devoting their waking hours to thinking, planning, and striving toward goals that others consider impossible. By hard work, they mean nothing less than total commitment. You will never be promoted until you become overqualified for your present position.

Those who envy the star performers in any field should realize that, across the entire galaxy of achievement, the stars are those who do not idly wish for success. They give their dedication, their singleness of purpose, their days and nights, weeks, months, and years to an unceasing struggle for greater proficiency. And when the talent they have so painstakingly cultivated for so long begins to bloom, others, who had the same amount of time, the same opportunity, the same freedom, come up and say, "I'd give anything to be able to do what you're doing, to have the things you have."

Why not complete your mission? Why not fulfill your dream? Do you apply the same standards of diligence and excellence that you expect from other areas of your life? The greatest results in life are usually attained by simple means and the exercise of ordinary qualities. With enough effort and hard work, everyone can be great at something.

6
The Greatest Secret:

You Are
Already Rich!

- **Words of Wisdom and Wealth**

- **Is Money Important?**

- **The Nine Disciplines of Wealth**

- **Will You Master Money or Will Money Master You?**

The history of civilization shows that no people can well rise to a
high degree of mental or even moral excellence without wealth. A
people uniformly poor and compelled to struggle for barely a
physical existence will be dependent and despised by their
neighbors and will finally despise themselves.
—FREDERICK DOUGLASS

'Tis the mind that makes the body rich.
—SHAKESPEARE

Money doesn't make you different.
It makes your circumstances different.
—MALCOLM FORBES

I'll show you what pride can do; I'll show you what money can do.
But most important, I'll show you what pride and money
can do together.
—MARCUS GARVEY

The Lord is my shepherd; I shall not want.
—PSALMS 23:1

In all my writing and speeches throughout the years, I am forever re-minding my audiences that, like the laws of nature, the true principles of wealth have been with us for thousands of years. They have never changed! Unfortunately, we're living in an age that seems to be traveling faster than the speed of light. We're all looking for fast answers to our problems, easy, quick-fix solutions. This futile search for the philoso-phers' stone that will magically transform our daily efforts into trunks of gold has blinded us to the old laws that have always worked and always will. Even though they're right under our nose, we no longer recognize them. And, so, they have become "secrets."

WORDS OF WISDOM AND WEALTH

From the earliest writings of humanity, we know that the human race has been comprised of the "haves" and the "have-nots." Since my days as an impressionable college student, I've been obsessed with the desire to know what invisible barrier separates these groups. Being a have-not, I wanted to know why so few of my race managed to climb among the ranks of the wealthy, particularly in a country where success is available to anyone who comes calling.

For example, when reviewing the United States Statistical Abstract, I discovered that fewer than 3 percent of black males sixty-five years of age and older boast incomes of $75,000 a year. Moreover, more than 60 percent of African Americans have incomes under $50,000 a year, and nearly 75 percent maintain incomes between $5,000 and $50,000. To-day, the majority of men and women launch their working careers in their twenties. These individuals are fortunate to live in a free world—the most open society on the face of the earth. They have better than forty years to make the grade financially. Yet, according to the data, only one out of ten does so. Why?

Conduct your own survey. Stroll through your neighborhood and ask your neighbors the following questions: What are you doing to increase your current income? and How much money will you be worth at age sixty-five? Canvass your community—ask fifty men and women, a hun-dred, a thousand, everyone that you know—until you are completely convinced that the reason people don't earn more money, and the rea-son so few are financially stable as they approach retirement, is that they seldom, if ever, engage in any constructive thinking on either sub-ject. To prove this, ask yourself the same thought-provoking questions. Prior to reading this lesson, what were *your* plans for increasing your income? How much do *you* want to earn? And how much money have *you* decided to be worth by age sixty-five?

The answer is simple. People who earn impressive incomes are not lucky, nor do they have a monopoly on talent or ideas. Nor are they endowed with more brains than their friends or neighbors. Most individuals who earn handsome incomes began in the same fashion as you and I. The only difference between those who earn large incomes and those who don't is that the financially well-off *decided* to earn more money. They made a conscious decision to make their lives better financially. It's that simple! The individual who never decides to earn more money never will. Begin now to rid yourself of any excuses as well as the erroneous thinking that suggests that the wealthy are "special," or "smarter," or "get all the breaks." We are all self-made; however, only the wealthy will admit it.

Many individuals date their discovery to the key to wealth and prosperity from some dramatic experience. I know this to be true in my case. During my many years of trials and heartbreak, I recall the advice given to me by W. Clement Stone as I sought to create my fortune. Throughout our relationship, he took on the role of the teacher and I, the student. During one of my tougher moments, I visited with him in his richly paneled executive office, where Mr. Stone explained one of life's least understood secrets. "When you've earned a lot of money—and you will—never forget the cause of your wealth. If you do, you will neglect your greatest power." At the time, I was confused as to what he meant, but I eventually grasped the meaning of the message.

I have made it a point to question every topflight businessperson that I have met. I have taken enough notes to fill a good-size garage in an attempt to draw a composite picture of Black America's wealthy and financially independent. I talked to the old and the young; male and female; educated and uneducated. Entrepreneurs, corporate executives, senior-level cabinet members—high-achieving men and women of all types. I felt like a voyeur as I peered into the lives of those who had such a profound influence upon my life. By their own actions, all of these individuals proved what is possible to accomplish when you have clarity of purpose, a labor of love backed by outstanding sales skills, and an indefatigable commitment to providing more and better service than that which is expected. To say the least, this was a far cry from what I expected to hear concerning the creation of wealth and success.

Like a transfixed scientist on the brink of some earth-shattering discovery, I absorbed everything that I learned. I distilled the formula down to its bare essence, and like the great African American chemist Dr.

Percy Julian, I was left with a substance of incredible power. Upon examination, this radiating, life-changing formula of personal wealth and independence wasn't really new. In fact, it has been known to mankind for thousands of years.

No matter whom I interviewed, I paid extremely close attention to their remarks about money, wealth, and prosperity. Fortunately, I kept the audiotapes and notes that revealed their wisdom, advice, and anecdotes on this most important subject. Focused, candid, and oh-so-wise, these men and women all shared the same philosophy. Deeply embedded in all the processes and the principles leading to a life of abundance and fulfillment lies one element—the cause of wealth. Have you discovered it? Only you can answer that. Here's a clue: There is a way to become wealthy without ever increasing your income, and it's easier than you think!

WEALTH CAN BE FOUND IN IDEAS . . .

"I may not know what wealth is, but I certainly know how to get it," said John Johnson, founder of Johnson Publications. Here's a man who was rocked in the cradle of poverty but eventually made his mark. He has lifted the consciousness of an entire race. "And it isn't what most people think. Wealth isn't a fancy car, or fancy clothes, or a spacious home. It won't be found within any material possessions. Wealth is located in *you,* the individual, within *your* heart. It can only be attained by pursuing your dreams."

Oh, the power of one great idea. It can truly change the face of the world! One grand idea or vision can be the turning point in your life, and you should not, must not, walk away from this challenge. Never allow the dawn of a new day to greet you without a dream! "Forget needs and wants," Wally Amos advises. "The key is creativity and imagination. Wealth is not something 'out there,' in the external, but it's something 'in here,' in the internal. It's dependent on universal principles and a higher consciousness. You will never be given a dream without the tools to reach that dream."

Maxima founder and CEO Joshua Smith related his feelings from one of his darker moments as he dared to build a $40-million high-tech firm. "For damn near two years I did nothing but crystallize my goals and objectives. I had no steady income, my bills were piling up, and, to say the least, my lifestyle was out of sorts. I knew I had a plan that could drastically offer software services to companies that had neither the manpower nor the hardware to keep pace with a changing business environment. But until the day arrived when I could deploy all my efforts and introduce my services to a waiting public, life was one big hassle.

"Was I hurting? No question. Was I broke? Most definitely. Was I discouraged? Yes, many times. But was I poor? No! Because poverty is a state of mind. It's a negative force that numbs the body and drains the spirit. As I look back, I can now see how wealth is brought into being by concentration: a tremendous desire to make something happen, to keep moving forward, to stay true to your course and fight for your dreams."

Great wealth calls for concentration, singleness of purpose, one unwavering aim. To drift from day to day is easy. No skill is required, no effort or pain. On the other hand, to set goals for a day or a week or a month, and to obtain those objectives, is never easy. All wealthy men and women have been noted for their power of concentration, which makes them oblivious to trivial pursuits. Don King, the fight promoter and showman, chose the right metaphor to convey his point. "Wealth is a by-product of one's thinking. I can't make you wealthy by giving you a handout, but I can put you on the road to prosperity by teaching you what I know." He then gave me a stunning new version of Benjamin Mays's oft-used quote. "Not to reach one's goals is not nearly as bad as having no goal to reach."

"And what are your goals?" I interrupted.

"To become America's first black billionaire," he fired back.

"How are going to do that?" I asked.

"I just told you," his emotion obviously spilling over. "By hanging around billionaires, learning all they know."

. . . AND IN WORK . . .

To many, work is unfulfilling. The great majority think they would be happier doing something else. To almost everyone, the day of choice arrives. What career? What shall my life's work be? If your instinct and your heart ask for carpentry, be a carpenter; if for medicine, be a physician. Choose one vocation or calling and master it in all details. Sleep by it, swear by it, and work for it; and, with a firm choice and resolute will, you cannot help but succeed. "Wealth is most likely to appear when you are totally engaged in doing something you enjoy," Percy Sutton explains. "One of the things I discovered throughout my career is that wealth usually comes to those who are immersed in a labor of love. It's only when the individual forgets his problems and shortcomings, and pours himself wholeheartedly into reaching his objective, that wealth will eventually make its appearance."

Wealth is not acquired, as many people believe, by chance or speculation, but by the daily practice of industry, frugality, and toil. The individual who relies upon these means will rarely be found destitute. There
is one towering pillar of wealth that dwarfs all others. It is certain to be
included in every list of affirmations on creating a better life for centuries to come, and yet most of mankind will reject it, again and again,
as too difficult. Wealth, fame, and fortune will be yours, eventually, if you
determine to render more and better service than you are paid to do.
"Many of my race hate the rich," Herman Russell says with a tinge of bitterness. "They don't understand the role that hard work plays in success. Too frequently, we idolize celebrities or those who make succeeding look easy. There's no magical formula—achieving anything
worthwhile is tough. Just as diamonds do not look like diamonds in
their rough form, wealth takes on a much different appearance in its
early stages. People need to know the value of work, the completion of
a difficult task, and the just rewards it brings." Money is what you receive when you help someone else achieve his or her goal.

. . . AND IN ADDING VALUE

"The key to wealth," Ernesta Procope says, "is to add value. Successful
entrepreneurs take an average, mundane product and add value. Look at
McDonald's. Ray Kroc certainly didn't invent the hamburger, but he
combined service, quality, and convenience and made a routine product
into something highly marketable."

Ernesta was just a babe in the insurance industry when she made a
bold and, some said at the time, outlandish move. As cofounder and
president of the largest black-owned insurance brokerage firm in the
country, she has journeyed and prospered in an environment where no
black man—let alone a black woman—has ever set foot. For twenty-five
years her firm, the E. G. Bowman Company, was headquartered in Bed-
ford-Stuyvesant, a squalid Brooklyn, New York, ghetto. During this period, the enterprise grew from a tiny home-and-car insurer with three
employees to a company with a staff of forty, among them several black
CPCUs (chartered property and casualty underwriters), well-creden-
tialed professionals who would make the industry's pacesetters most
envious. With a list of accounts that includes top Fortune 500 firms, Procope felt that if her company was to develop and truly flourish, she
needed to move it to the industry's financial hub—Wall Street.

Procope's business acuity was developed and nurtured by her parents, West Indian immigrants who settled in Brooklyn during the 1910s
and imparted ambition, drive, and wisdom to Ernesta and her three

brothers. These qualities obviously spilled over into other areas. At age thirteen, she had studied piano seriously enough to be showcased at New York's Carnegie Hall. After completing high school, she attended Brooklyn College as a music major, but left to marry Albin Bowman, a Brooklyn real estate investor. At his insistence, she studied and passed the state exam for insurance brokers in 1950 to help support him in the business. Four years later, her husband died, and she resisted any temptation to sell out.

Procope based her strategy upon long-term planning, providing a quality service, boundless energy, and an insistence upon personal excellence. "Over the years we have had loads of challenges. This industry has not flung its doors wide open to train, encourage, or welcome black professionals. The predominantly white male composition can be daunting. But like any product or service, you cannot wait for others to pave the way. You overwhelm prejudice and discrimination with excellence and effort." Her words are not just philosophical, they're practical.

YOU MUST GIVE TO GET

If you want to get more out of life, you must give more to life. No one can be truly rich without enriching the lives of others. Money is like a refreshing mountain stream. When it spills its way through the meadow, it turns everything in its path vibrant and green. But once obstructed, the stream and the valley dry up; the flowers wither and die. So, too, with the money we possess. While it flows and freely circulates, it blesses many. But when the circulation is halted by hoarding, squandering, or abuse, money becomes a curse. The heart hardens, peace is compromised, and noble aims become misguided.

Strong-willed, opinionated, and passionate about her work, Cathy Hughes has built a media empire that consists of eight radio stations worth more than $50 million. Her accomplishments would be considered noteworthy for any broadcaster, but for an African American woman in an industry where few of her gender and race survive, they are even more remarkable. From a truly humble beginning—as a single parent and without a dime—Hughes has managed to push, prod, and elbow her way to the table. When asked to offer her views on wealth, she mentions words like "hope" and "opportunity." "Wealth and economic empowerment is the key to everything," she explained. "Billie Holiday was right: 'God bless the child who's got his own.' But wealth doesn't mean a thing if it doesn't translate into opportunities for others."

IS MONEY IMPORTANT?

Money is one of mankind's greatest tools. It is a tangible substance wrestled from intangible ideas. It is like any other resource or commodity, neither good nor bad, neither sinful nor sacred. Unlike other resources, however, it evolves from the thought processes of the individual, from his or her flow of ideas. Money is an instrument, a standard, that can be used for both good and evil, by the rich and the not so rich, by the wise and not so wise. Whether used within or outside the context of money, wealth is a basic human desire. The pursuit of wealth—say what you may—is not only legitimate but a duty!

There's something wrong with our thinking when we, children of a king, mope about in this pilgrimage of life like sheep hounded by a pack of wolves. There's something wrong when we, who have inherited infinite supply, are scrounging about for our daily bread; when we, who are dogged by fear and anxiety, let peace elude us; when we allow our lives to be preoccupied with limit and less; when we take little because we demand little. There's something wrong when we spill our cups that runneth over. It is impossible for God's creation and likeness to reflect failure or poverty. Humanity's Divine image reflects prosperity, riches that are royal, abundance that never fails, and plenty that can never grow less.

If men and women are to be Men and Women, and their fortune is created by legitimate efforts, it will increase their power and multiply their supply. In their struggle to attain wealth, if they are careful to guard against any negative influences, money will improve their judgment, increase their wisdom, enhance their character, uplift the race, and promote independence. Without independence, they cannot truly be men and women. They cannot do their best work with poverty clutching at their heels. They cannot reach a higher calling when they are only a day's march ahead of lack and want. Money means shoes for bare feet; it means clothing for the naked; it means education for the illiterate. It means a chance for opportunity and a life of peace. And although money may not buy you happiness, neither will poverty. Because poverty can't buy a thing!

Amway supersalesman George Halsey is living proof. "Wealth," he explains, "holds the promise of personal freedom." After spending a day with him at his home and office, I caught a whiff of what he meant by "peace of mind." Halsey comes and goes as he pleases. Money is no object. Work, which does not adequately describe what he does, and leisure are so intertwined in his life as to be indiscernible. For him, the average workday is a holiday on earth. There is no office to go to. He eats when his body tells him to, not at a prescribed hour of the day. There is no rush-hour traffic to navigate. A suit and tie are completely out of character for him, and he answers to no one. His work is to share his unique networking opportunity, just as others shared it with him.

What will humanity do to satisfy this all-absorbing passion for riches? Everybody and everything thirsts for the almighty dollar. Pride seeks it. What else besides pride can render power, position, and influence to those who possess it? Vanity yearns for it. What other force could make a status-hungry people purchase fine clothing, sumptuous housing, fancy cars, and a host of material possessions that they cannot afford to buy? Love hopes for it. What loving parent doesn't want the best for his or her children? The church prays for it. Don't you hear it every Sunday: Send me your tithes and offerings? And even death gropes for it. After all, who wants to die poor? Money has many uses that work best when kept in the heart and not in the head. Listen carefully: Money is very important!

PURSUING WEALTH WAS HIS DUTY

La-Van Hawkins grew up poor as a church mouse but has always been intoxicated with the smell of success. At age ten, he sold candy and soft drinks from his mother's apartment in Chicago's Cabrini Green, a three-mile stretch of housing projects, one of the toughest in the city. His father died a year later, a victim of alcoholism, forcing La-Van to help provide for his family. As a result, he withdrew from the private high school he was attending on scholarship to work in his uncle's fast-food restaurant. He was barely thirteen years old.

The job provided him with a needed outlet. With an inner drive to succeed, he quickly rose through the ranks. "Fast food was fun for me," Hawkins recalls. "It gave me a chance to channel my energy. I look up and say thank God for my uncle, because he definitely gave me a new appreciation for life. He instilled in me the idea that—if you're willing to work hard, get in and roll up your sleeves—your color doesn't matter. Anyone can succeed."

Five years later, as a supervisor at the same restaurant, he caught the eye of a Kentucky Fried Chicken executive who offered him a $500 bonus to become an area manager. In eleven years with KFC, he reached regional vice-president status, supervising more than 650 stores. Hawkins was twenty-eight years old, earning $275,000 a year. Four years later, he was pried away from KFC by an offer from multimillionaire Texas oilman T. Boone Pickens to become operating partner for BoJangles Fried Chicken. Today, La-Van Hawkins's Inner City Foods owns more than two dozen Checkers restaurants, a Florida-based fast-food firm, with sales exceeding $30 million.

"Is money important?" I questioned. Listen to his reply.

"Money is very important for what it can do and provide. Money in the form of jobs can rebuild a community; money in the form of scholarships can educate a people; and money in the form of profits can build institutions. Yes, money is extremely important."

USE THE SAME WEALTH-PRODUCING FORMULA THAT OTHERS HAVE USED

When J. Bruce Llewellyn made his foray into the world of commerce, he mortgaged everything he owned—a house, a car, modest assets, and even his clothing. This move got him a $3-million loan, which he invested in a chain of grocery stores—but not before the lender warned: "I guarantee, if this doesn't work out, it's going to hurt you a lot more than it does me." That was 1969. Today, Llewellyn can laugh about that veiled threat. It wouldn't be the last time he has used a bit of guts and a unique moneymaking formula to launch even bigger deals.

Raised in White Plains, New York, Llewellyn's Jamaican-born parents, like countless other immigrants, came to the United States in search of opportunity. His father found work as a Linotype operator with the once prominent *New York Herald Tribune,* while his mother cared for him and a younger sister. Llewellyn's parents were believers in hard work, in America, and in individual initiative. Together, they evoked racial pride and imparted a competitive spirit in their children. Their son still recites a dictum drilled by his father: "You must work twice as hard to get half as far."

In 1981, Llewellyn decided it was time to seriously march toward his dream of operating a beverage bottling plant. The timing was perfect. That year, Jesse Jackson and Operation PUSH had called for a boycott of all Coca-Cola products. Consumption data had indicated that black Americans accounted for nearly one-third of the entire soft drink market and spent more than $300 million on Coke products alone. The ban forced the bottler to agree to increase its minority participation. Two years later, Llewellyn, basketball great Julius Erving, and actor Bill Cosby together purchased a 36 percent share in a Coca-Cola bottling plant in New York—only one of eight black operators to be chosen.

As the company's single largest shareholder, Llewellyn sat on the board and became chairman of its subsidiary, the Philadelphia Coca-Cola Bottling Company. By the mid-1980s, Llewellyn got the chance to buy the entire Philadelphia bottling operations. He and Erving converted their Coca-Cola shares, obtained loans from several lending institutions, and paid $80 million toward buyout costs for the company. To help bolster sales and market share, Llewellyn added new routes and more trucks, and hustled for increased exposure. The result: The plant is now Coke's eighth largest operation. Sales have since topped $300 million.

How did he do it? "Every day Black America stands aghast at the accomplishments of other ethnic groups," Llewellyn says. "These groups are driven to save, to invest, to risk, and to formulate capital—not consume it. They share common values that further their business expansion. What I've done is no big deal. I've just repeated the same wealth-producing formula."

Here is a man who has earned millions, who knows that we live in an abundant universe filled with ideas flowing through time and space. It is up to each of us to take what we need out of this flow. There is an abundance of ideas that we can use to create more riches in our life. If you think about it, money is an idea in action. The universe always says yes. If we stand in the flow of life and say that there isn't enough, or I can't have, or I'm not able to, then the flow passes us by. The current is always moving. People hoard money, worship money, covet it, hide it, and even steal it, which springs from a belief that if they do, prosperity will find its way to their door. This misguided behavior goes against the flow.

We can all be wealthy. Wealth is, to a large extent, a state of mind. Each of us has the human urge for the best that life has to offer. You desire economic security, which money alone can provide. You may desire an outlet for your talents in order that you may experience the joy of creating your own riches. Some seek the easy way to wealth, hoping to find it without giving anything in return. Mistakenly, this, too, is a common desire. But it is a desire I hope to modify. If I have uncovered anything during the course of my research, I've found there's no such thing as something for nothing. There's only one sure road to wealth—a path that anyone can travel.

WE NEED A CHANGE OF THINKING

Wise men, since the beginning of time, have been telling us that all we achieve, or fail to achieve, is the direct result of our thoughts. James Allen, the English writer and author of *As a Man Thinketh,* told us that good thoughts bear good fruit and bad thoughts bear bad fruit. Ralph Waldo Emerson concurred. He wrote, "A man becomes what he thinks about most of the time." The Roman emperor Marcus Aurelius taught us that our life is what our thoughts make it: good or bad, triumphant or hopeless. In 600 B.C., Buddha, the Eastern spiritual teacher, wrote, "All that we are is the result of what we have thought. The mind is everything. What we think, we become."

The way to be great is to *know* that you are great; and to *know* is to *think;* and to *think* is to master your thoughts and emotions—to *raise your consciousness.* It is what you know in your heart that determines what you express in your world. If you believe these great writers and philosophers, then you know that if you belittle your talents and gifts, you are doomed to failure. If you question your ability, the world will quickly accept your evaluation. And, if you constantly dwell on thoughts of lack or limit, unfortunately, this, too, will define your life. Over time, you create the mental equivalent of your innermost convictions about yourself and what is possible for you. In other words, you need not be sick. You need not be distraught. You need only to lift your thoughts and rise above those conditions or imperfections that may impede your progress. Granted, you may not be able to choose your circumstances, but you *can* choose your thoughts, which will eventually *shape* your circumstances.

As I studied the wealthy, I was struck by a common knowledge that each seemed to share: Each possessed a "prosperity consciousness" in addition to an unshakeable belief in his or her ability to overcome obstacles. This mind-set seemed to offer them powers unavailable to ordinary individuals. They set high standards and achieved lofty goals, often in the face of overwhelming odds and in defiance of the predictions of those around them. But it all started with a prosperity consciousness.

THE POOR WILL ALWAYS BE AMONG YOU

Ultimately, a human being is wealthy not because of what he has, but because of what he *knows.* What he has, he can lose through disaster, obsolescence, or theft. What he knows, he can never lose unless he loses life itself. Thus, his real wealth is a characteristic of his thinking, not any physical assets. The continuous unfolding of ideas and knowledge is the principal cause of society's ability to progressively do more with less. It was the internal combustion engine that gave value to oil, not the other way around. And it is the semiconductor industry that is making a treasure out of our most plentiful and inexpensive resource—sand—which in turn fuels the information society. "High" should be seen in terms of consciousness, not in terms of technology. Wherever we turn, physical toil is being traded in for mental effort.

Yet we hear that ubiquitous locution "The rich get richer and the poor get poorer." Worse still, society is cajoled into believing the poor are poor simply because they have no money. A popular solution suggests that alleviating poverty is quite simple: Just get money into the hands of the poor. If that were true, society could eliminate poverty by distributing money equally to all its citizens. At various points in their development, the entrepreneurs within this study were broke. If the poor are poor because they have no money, then these entrepreneurs would be considered poor—just as poor as the millions of Americans who fall below the poverty line. Yet each was motivated, eager, teachable, focused, and was more than willing to serve. Now compare this man or woman to his or her impoverished counterpart who lives within life's recesses. Chances are he or she lives life at the margins, with no skills, no training, and worse yet, no motivation.

Although both groups have no money, only one is poor; the other has unlimited wealth potential. By merely giving each an allotted sum of money, the chances are that over the course of a career, one would remain poor, while the other would increase his wealth potential still more. In case it has gone unnoticed, wealth, in large measure, means thinking big and starting small. Its price is huge and may not be for the faint of heart. And it is most likely to occur when passion and effort meet.

YOU NEED NOT BE POOR!

Black America, we need not be poor; no one needs to beg for soup and sympathy. The belief in limitations—the conviction that we cannot rise out of our environment, that we are the victims of circumstances—has dampened our spirit, dulled our senses, and caused untold tragic failures. Until we erase "can't" and "deprived" and "disadvantaged" and "underclass" and "impoverished" from our vocabulary, prosperity will never come calling. Enough! The truth of the matter is that we are not inferior and we are wealthy! However, if we believe in inferiority, we will assume an inferior status; if we think poor, we will behave poor. This is universal law. We have control over our fate, over our destiny. Our prosperity is unlimited—*if* we dare to unleash the power of positive-thought consciousness. We must cast our nets on the "right" side. Not in terms of direction or proximity, but in terms of our collective attitudes and thinking.

What if Madame C. J. Walker had given in to the naysayers of her day?

Network marketing and modes of distribution would never be taught in the nation's top business schools—theories that she developed. Suppose Berry Gordy had listened to his broke friends on that assembly-line floor, who said he was wasting his time and money on a handful of songs? There would be no Smokey; there would be no Stevie; there would be no Jackson—Janet or Michael! I shudder to think what would have happened if Booker T. Washington had lost faith and confidence in himself after he had expended his last dollar in his bid to elevate his race. Imagine, if he could cast down his bucket and come up from slavery, then, in terms of wealth, we must start where we are and raise up our consciousness.

THE NINE DISCIPLINES OF WEALTH

How is wealth created and maintained by seemingly "average" men and women with no special skills or talents? What do the wealthy do on a consistent basis? What disciplines have they developed or do they follow that allow them to achieve their dreams? Over the past decade, I have been exposed to the best and the brightest. I have interviewed many wealthy people. I have read countless books on money and capital—its creation and growth. And I have found one thing to be certain of those who control vast resources: They don't allow money to master them—they master money! These individuals take certain actions and follow consistent routines that allow them to create and maintain considerable wealth. They plan, dream, save, invest, and give in a never-ending cycle of financial prosperity. To drive the point home, they utilize the Nine Disciplines of Wealth.

1. *Clarity.* Clarity is defined as "a vision for life; the ability to determine exactly what you want." The men and women of this study possess the ability to set clear, well-defined goals as well as to formulate plans for the achievement of those goals. Many have developed the mindset that allows them to tune out distractions and give absolute attention to their top priorities. Clarity is the "master skill" of success that unleashes the power of goals. Clarity unlocks the door to wealth, happiness, high self-esteem, and the accompanying feelings of pride, satisfaction, and success. Clarity is essential for those who seek financial independence.

2. *Finding the right vocation.* The wealthy chase the dream—not the rainbow. They are driven more by the prospects of success and enjoyment than by money. When you are passionately engaged in your

work, it feels natural and right. You feel alive and capable of extraordinary things. Your imagination opens up and you find a steady stream of new ideas, better ways of feeding your vocation. On the other hand, if you lack passion for your chosen field, you are losing money. Because, as it turns out, your work is more likely to make you wealthy than any investment or any business opportunity to which you are only halfheartedly attracted.

Matthew 6:21: "Where your treasure is, there your heart will be also." Successful people regard material rewards as a by-product, not a goal, of success. They do what they love to do; they work "near the heart of things"; they "discover their right voice." Those that I have observed found a labor of love; an area of excellence; something they love doing; a field in which they became completely absorbed and engaged. An area in which they can become proficient. What is striking is that many within this study talk about their work in the same manner that others describe a hobby. Each was willing to pay any price, to go any distance, to invest his or her time to find the correct vocation. They know that if you seek your dream—if you do what you love—the money will follow.

3. *Superior sales skills.* These skills require the ability to influence, persuade, and motivate others to use your products or services; the ability to interact effectively, convey ideas and thoughts in a positive manner. The millionaires I have interviewed possess high levels of ambition, and they pattern their behavior after leaders in their field. They view themselves as thoroughly prepared, completely competent sales professionals tough enough to deal with any rejection, capable of overcoming any objection, and caring enough to help others attain their goals.

4. *The ability to execute ideas.* Any successful plan or mission has two essential elements—conception and execution. Without a successful linkage of the two, the plan fails. Those who succeed know that society pays for results, not effort. Moreover, execution is so crucial to achievement that it can be considered not simply an important factor but the foundation upon which all hopes and visions are built. At some point during their careers, these men and women discovered that the marketplace became more enthused *after* they proved their ideas, not before. Therefore, they moved forward and willingly took charge of implementing their bold plans. They grab hold of any situation and rely upon their own ability to carry them to financial success. Consistent, dependable execution is the hallmark to greatness.

5. *Persistence.* Self-made millionaires are realistic enough to expect challenges and setbacks. Further, they do not become disappointed, discouraged, or depressed by difficulties or temporary defeat. They resolve in advance that they will never give up. Typically, they see opportunities in adversity or the seed of an equivalent benefit. They find promise where others find pessimism. Nothing in the world will take the place of persistence. The courage to persist in the face of adversity and disappointment is a key quality that guarantees success.

6. *A dedication to lifelong learning.* Surprisingly, education is not required for great financial achievement. Several of the multimillionaires within this study never ventured past the tenth grade. Though I found these men and women to be no more gifted than others throughout society, each had developed an insatiable desire for knowledge and information. They stand out because they had taken the time to prepare, to read and study, to develop their full potential to a level considerably above average. Having a commitment to wealth means becoming a student of wealth. They live by this maxim: *If you wish to be successful, study success; if you wish to be happy, study happiness; if you desire great wealth, study the acquisition of wealth.* They read, read, and read. It's their curiosity that propels them forward. Education involved both learning of the new and unlearning of the old. Regardless of their educational background, they remain teachable. They simply *have* to know. Each views learning as a lifelong process.

7. *Service.* People will make you rich or keep you broke, depending on the way you serve them. You should decide at the outset, if millionaireship is your goal, that you're going to make people—inside the organization and out—your primary concern. Millionaires realize the value of service. "Your rewards in life will be in direct proportion to your service," I was told. Each of us is here to serve others. Service is the price you pay for the space you occupy—and everyone can serve.

8. *Spirituality.* The majority of millionaires maintain a close personal relationship with their Creator and a belief that the Almighty has a plan for their life. Divine guidance, rather than religion, dogma, or doctrine, seems to make a difference in achieving grand objectives. A faith provides inner strength on a consistent basis. As one interviewee stated, "If you have the faith, God certainly has the power." The majority nurture their belief system through daily prayer and affirmation. Those surveyed went on to say that, to succeed, entrepre-

neurial hopefuls should "work hard, be honest in all business dealings, and trust in the Lord with all your heart and soul." An African
proverb states, "Pray to God, but row for the shore."

9. *Savings.* More than talent, intellect, education, or skill, the habit of
saving is the key to amassing a fortune. The philosophy of the
wealthy versus the poor is this: The rich invest their money and
spend what's left; the poor *spend* their money and *invest* what's left.
"Pay yourself first," I was admonished. "If you can't save at least ten
percent of your income, the seeds of greatness aren't in you." The
habit of thrift not only opens the door to opportunity but is a safe-
guard against our own weaknesses—the tendency to scatter our
earnings. The saving of money so often means the saving of the individual. Some of the shrewdest businessmen and -women I know
believe that thrift is a character trait well worth developing. They
cherish their savings and abhor debt. "Slow and steady wins the
race," John Rogers of Ariel Capital Management attests. Maxima's
Joshua Smith agrees: "If it's on your back, it's not in the bank. And if
it's on your ass, it's not an asset!" Those who understand interest,
earn it; those who don't, pay it. The lesson is clear: If you do nothing
but change the way you manage your current income, it could
change your life. It's not what you earn that makes you wealthy, it's
what you keep!

HOW ONE MAN DEVELOPED A MILLIONAIRE'S MENTALITY

Arthur G. Gaston arrived in Birmingham the grandson of a slave from
Demopolis, a southern Alabama town. He insists that Birmingham is a
better place now due to his involvement and that of other concerned
citizens. Gaston directs a massive business empire that he built despite
Birmingham's history of rampant bigotry.

Gaston's life spans nearly a century. Lincoln had signed the Emanci-
pation Proclamation twenty-eight years before his birth, and only four
decades after slavery, Gaston was in business. A multimillionaire, he's a
hero in the classic American mold—a true rags-to-riches story. As a
twelve-year-old, Gaston picked pounds of cotton for pennies a day. But
as the decade of the 1990s continues, this diminutive black man is now
board chairman and president of at least ten businesses worth more
than $40 million. His vast financial holdings include an insurance com-
pany, a business college, several motels, a realty and investment firm,
two nursing homes, a mortuary, three cemeteries, and a radio station—
all of which provide more than fifteen hundred jobs.

Despite his enduring optimism and relentless ability to persevere, Gaston's road to wealth was choked with hardships. "Blacks were lynched in Demopolis in those days for the most trivial of reasons," Gaston remembers. "It was not the kind of place where you'd find many black role models." But Gaston looked hard and found people worthy of emulation. His grandparents built the log cabin where he was born. They were slaves who became sharecroppers after the Civil War. His mother was a domestic, but he scarcely remembers his father, who died during his childhood.

After moving to Birmingham, Gaston attended the Carrie Tuggle Institute—a school for black children run by Carrie Tuggle, an ex-slave and a strict disciplinarian. Though Gaston's formal schooling ended with the tenth grade, the institute's highest class, its founder taught him all she could about life and success. "Miss Tuggle taught us to never give up on our dreams. 'Keep planning, keep saving, do for self,' she would say. 'You cannot fight and beg the same man. You must build your own.' " Able-bodied and eager to work, Gaston soon learned what was expected of him. He was confronted with the realization that blacks earned their living with their backs and little else.

> Miss Tuggle taught us to never give up on our dreams. "Keep planning, keep saving," she would say. "You can't fight and beg the same man. You must build your own."
>
> —Arthur G. Gaston

A Key Moment Arrives

Gaston's pursuit of wealth and comfort exposed him to a world he knew little about. He took a job in a steel mill for "hardly nothing" but never gave up hope of striking out on his own. "I'd constantly search for a break, a spark, an idea. One day, after watching my white supervisor read the *Wall Street Journal,* I began to read it, too. I enjoyed the success stories telling of fame and fortune. This was the first time I had ever seen the word 'millionaire' in print. Almost instinctively, I knew what I wanted."

To supplement a meager income, Gaston sold peanuts and box lunches and loaned money to less frugal coworkers. In 1921, his minor enterprise gave way to the Booker T. Washington Burial Society. This society eventually grew into the Booker T. Washington Insurance Company, which today has nearly $44 million in assets. Since the 1940s, Gaston has wielded power and influence in Birmingham's black and white communities. Routinely, blacks would line up for hours outside his office, where he offered financial and personal advice like a local godfather. They would listen intently, captivated by Gaston's penetrating insights. His advice was based upon the same wealth-creating formula given to him by his teacher decades ago:

- Save a portion of all you earn. Delay gratification—spend less, save more. Pay yourself first. Compound interest is a moneymaking tool, so use it.
- Establish a reputation at a bank or save at a reputable institution.
- Don't lose money. A man who can't afford to lose money has no business gambling.
- Never borrow anything you can't pay back.
- Respect others, regardless of their social or economic position.
- Specialize; find a need and fill it. Successful businesses are built on the needs of others.
- Once you launch your business, keep good books and hire the best people you can find.

The dramatic story of big business that you have just read is a perfect illustration of the skills and mind-set of a man who claimed great wealth among his possessions. Gaston, like others in his class, fought hard for every inch of ground he covered. He was frugal, clear in his purpose, and sought to serve. He settled upon a chosen profession and was a firm believer in continued personal development. These were the traits that served him best. Each of us, whether we realize it or not, has the same opportunity to employ these qualities. Few individuals know how to properly utilize their earnings. We can earn it, hoard it, spend it, save it, waste it, or worship it. But to deal with it wisely, as a means to an end, is an education worth its weight in gold. As the Master instructed, "What is a man profited, if he shall gain the whole world, and lose his own soul?"

"Power comes from accumulated wealth," Gaston asserts. "What I've done, anybody can do, provided he or she has the will to achieve, has a clear idea of what he wants, and is able to subject himself to the rigors and discipline that wealth demands. It's a rule—just like a rule of nature. Managing what you make is more important than how much you make."

Poverty has no place for the man or woman who adheres to Gaston's philosophy. His distinction lies not in his monetary success, but in his tremendous achievement in self-understanding. He has tried, practiced, and proved the principles of wealth and prosperity. There's no magic formula; there are no secret tenets. These steps call for no extra effort; they call for no personal sacrifice. Yet these principles are so earth-shaking in their scope and power that it may be difficult for the uninitiated to comprehend. Moreover, to apply them calls for no formal education. There is simply the willingness to listen, to learn, and to understand that accumulation of money cannot be left to chance, good fortune, or luck.

SAVINGS MEANS POWER!

It is by the mysterious power of savings that your resources grow; that the loaf is multiplied, that little becomes much, that scattered fragments grow to unity, and that out of nothing comes the miracle of something. Such disciplined habits of thrift will enable anyone to surprise the world with his or her gifts, even if he or she is poor. "Societies which live entirely from hand to mouth never make much progress," wrote Orison Swett Marden, a nineteenth-century inspirational writer. "Comfort and independence abide with those who can postpone their desires. Savings means power!"

"Learn early in life to say, 'I can't afford it,' " Benjamin Franklin suggested. "It is an indication of power, courage, character."

"We are ruined," writes Arthur Willis Colton, a nineteenth-century novelist, "not by what we really want, but by what we *think* we want. Therefore, never search for your wants; if they truly are wants, they will come home in search of you. For he that buys what he does not want will soon want what he cannot buy."

Frederick Douglass, the great abolitionist, examined the minutest expenditures of his family, even as he toiled on the docks of the Potomac. He knew that without thrift and frugality none could be rich, and with it no one need be poor.

"Take the road less traveled," Percy Sutton counseled. "When choosing between sacrifice and instant gratification, always choose sacrifice."

Saving is the first great principle of success. Saving paves the way for happiness and contentment. Saving increases the stock and value of he who saves. Saving sustains and preserves the highest welfare of the race.

By saving even a small portion of your earnings, it will strengthen the will, and it will brighten the spirit. Recall the advice given to you by J. Bruce Llewellyn and A. G. Gaston, two of the wealthiest men in the country: "Formulate capital—don't consume it"; "save a portion of everything that you earn." There is no mystery regarding their rise to fortune.

If you doubt that each of us could benefit by increasing our knowledge of saving and investment, the following story should be enlightening. Sarah Louise and A. Elizabeth Delany, 106 and 104 years old, took the reading public by storm with their surprise best-seller, *Having Our Say: The Delany Sisters' First 100 Years.* Born in 1889 and 1891 respectively, the second and third of ten children, they grew up in Raleigh, North Carolina. Their father, who was born into slavery, became America's first elected black Episcopal bishop. His daughters, after they moved to Harlem during World War I, were among the first African American women professionals in New York City—Sarah as a schoolteacher and Annie as a dentist. After the publication of their book, the sisters became international celebrities.

The personal accounts of two centenarians—black women who have seen their share of triumph and disappointment, love and hatred—is dramatic enough. Their message will be read by hundreds of thousands. However, this is not the point I wish to emphasize. I call your attention to something far more important. Though great effort has been made to protect their privacy, an admirer wrote and asked for their keys to financial success. They responded with seven steps on how to handle money. "Anyone who lives for money," Annie explains, "is surely missing the best things in life. There's an old saying, 'Money is useful, but don't let it use you.' " Study and underscore their words and notations. It can point you to a way of life that may have seemed beyond your reach:

The Delany Sisters' Seven Ways to Handle Money

1. When it comes to money, keep your mouth shut.
2. Cut back on your possessions. The more you own, the more time you waste taking care of things.
3. Don't spend what you don't have. Forget credit cards—they are the Devil's work!
4. Don't live above your income. If your income goes down, your spending must go down.
5. Out of every dollar, give the first ten cents to the Lord, the second ten cents to the bank for hard times, and keep the rest—but you'd better spend it wisely.
6. Once you put your hard-earned money in the bank, leave it there!

Smart people invest it, and then they'll always have some to fool
with.

7. Teach your children to save money from day one. Give your child an
    allowance so he or she can practice responsibility. A child who
    doesn't learn thrift at home will have money trouble all her life.

"WE CAN DRIVE THE BUS ANYPLACE WE DAMN WELL PLEASE!"

S. B. Fuller could hardly contain his excitement. He had seen what all
entrepreneurs call "a window of opportunity," and he was determined
to pry it open. He rushed into Dr. King's makeshift offices in downtown
Montgomery and exclaimed, "Martin, we've won—the boycott has
worked. No one is riding the bus!" For nearly a century, local whites had
controlled Montgomery, Alabama, an economic mecca during the
1950s. From this cradle of the Confederacy, a wellspring of business activity and prosperity flourished that included iron, textiles, and transportation, while nearly half of its inhabitants suffered physical and economic abuse. By 1957, a young Baptist minister from neighboring
Atlanta, Georgia, Martin Luther King, was vaulted into national prominence when he sought to correct a host of injustices. Thus, the Montgomery bus boycott was born. Dr. King's stride toward freedom carried
a message that Black America openly embraced. Thanks, in part, to his
urging, "Fifty thousand Negroes were willing to substitute tired feet for
tired souls, and walk the streets of Montgomery until the walls of segregation were finally battered by the forces of justice."

In short order, the boycott took its effect, and the numbers did not go
unnoticed. For months, Fuller, an astute businessman who was twice
King's age with a net worth in the millions, studied bus routes, city
maps, and the records of comparable Northern carriers. Black pa-
trons—the city's largest consumer group—had made their point. The
savvy tycoon saw an enterprise on its knees in a tight money pinch and
he stood ready to solve the firm's problems in the manner he knew
best. All Fuller had to do was to follow up his hunch with hard numbers, sales and expense projections, and sell his idea to King and his
staff. A piece of cake? Not hardly.

With data in hand, Fuller ran up the steps leading to the pastor's
study, blurting out, "Martin, we've got them just where we want them.
The city has got to sell!"

King sat back, shocked, without the slightest idea what his visitor was
talking about. Without stopping to catch his breath, Fuller continued.
"Man, I've looked at this thing from every possible angle and I'm telling

you, the bus line is hurting. Go ask A.G." A.G., of course, was Arthur G. Gaston, the black insurance and banking whiz—and master visionary. Gaston took a liking to Fuller's bold plans. "We know they've got to sell," he continued. "We'll call Atlanta and Chicago, put the finances together, and buy them out. Then we can drive the bus anyplace we damn well please!" Unfortunately, in the late 1950s, economic empowerment was not the focus of the struggle. At this critical juncture in history, black leadership said, "But . . ."

WILL YOU MASTER MONEY OR WILL MONEY MASTER YOU?

You now have an understanding of the fundamentals of wealth and prosperity. It should be encouraging to observe that each discipline is well within reach of anyone who wants to embrace it. It is by this method that poverty can be transformed into abundance. Begin now to change your habits and alter your thinking regarding wealth. Make a commitment to do whatever it takes to apply the *greatest secret* in your life. To be poor and to have developed an aversion for poverty is a positive step toward experiencing great wealth. Still, if your thoughts are allowed to go unchecked and you entertain ideas of lack or limit, you may be blind to those opportunities that can alter your life for the better. As you continue to read, please remember, those who fail to understand their history are doomed to repeat it.

Unfortunately, 98 percent of the population are too busy with the day-to-day tasks of trying to earn a living to ever make any real progress toward their vision of financial independence. Most people work hard all their lives, yet fail to develop the habit of spending less than they earn. Sadly, even in a country known for its level of opportunity, most men and women will probably never achieve a lifestyle of financial freedom.

We, as African Americans, live in the wealthiest country the universe has known. Sometimes it's easy to lose perspective—to forget that 25 percent of the world's population lives on less than $200 a year and that 90 million people throughout the world live on less than $75 a year. For the majority of us, food, clothing, and shelter are relatively accessible and in abundance. In the United States, poverty is defined as a family of four living at or below $18,000 a year. And yet, tragically, many hard-working, deserving people spend their entire lives with their shoulder to the wheel only to end up financial failures. In a country and a world where opportunity is unlimited, role models are abundant, and information free-flowing, far too many people fail to achieve financial freedom or financial independence. Yet most of us could be incredibly wealthy and live our dreams if we just followed several simple disciplines. Tod Barnhart, in his book *The Five Rituals of Wealth,* shares the following tale.

One day, in 400 B.C., the Greek philosopher Socrates and a student walked through a marketplace in Athens. Socrates, the wise teacher, browsed among the merchants, stopping at each stand to compliment the shopkeepers on their wares. Ironically, he never bought a thing. His pupil, noticing the philosopher's actions, questioned why he loved to frequent the market but never purchased any items. Socrates replied, "I'm always amazed to see just how many things there are that I don't need." So many times people manage their money in a way that prevents them from appreciating the true level of wealth that they already possess. They buy and spend, and many times commit their hard-earned dollars to everyone else, never keeping any for themselves. The problem is they forget to make themselves just as important as those who are competing for their dollars. In essence, they give all their economic power away.

THE LAND OF MILK AND HONEY

One cold, dark night, as a traveler was crossing a dry riverbed, a mysterious voice in the night ordered him to halt. "Get off your camel," the voice said. So the man did. The voice then commanded, "Pick up some gravel from the riverbed." The man picked up the gravel. Then the voice said, "Now mount and ride on. In the morning you'll be both pleased and disappointed." As the sun rose, the rider looked at what he had gathered and discovered that it was not a handful of pebbles as he had thought—but a handful of gleaming gems! As the voice had indicated, he was both pleased and disappointed: pleased he had collected a few precious jewels, and disappointed he had not collected more.

Like most fables, this story is based on human nature and has special meaning for those fortunate enough to live in this land of opportunity, where too many of us resemble the traveler who is both glad and sorry.

Imagine a country with a per-capita income slightly more than that of western Europe and considerably higher than the per-capita income of Asia, Africa, and Latin America combined. Imagine further, a country where half of its 15 million households own an automobile, which is one-third more than in the former Soviet states, and more cars than in Asia, Africa, and Latin America together. Furthermore, imagine a country where one out of sixteen households owns two cars, and one out of one hundred owns three or more.

In this land of prosperity, 52 percent of the households own their homes, and 80 percent of these homes are equipped with two television sets, which is twice the number of sets that can be found in France or Italy and four times as many as in Sweden. These families have more members earning college degrees than the total student enrollment in England, Italy, and most of Europe. Even among the poorest of the poor, the majority have air-conditioning, a microwave, and twice as much living space as the average Japanese and four times as much space as the average Russian.

Where is this country? you might ask. Surely, you would love to live there. Does it really exist? Yes, it does! It's Black America and the black consumer market.* Each year 32 million black Americans spend billions—$350 billion in 1995—on goods and services. As early as 1969, Black America's cumulative GNP made it the ninth wealthiest nation in the free world—equivalent to the GNP of Canada or Australia and larger than both Israel's and South Africa's. Black Americans are wealthier and better educated than any other blacks worldwide. From New York to California, nothing elicits as much interest on Wall Street as what Black America buys with its enormous wealth. But like our weary traveler, there are some concerns. Consider these trends:

• The 1990 Census Bureau found that the median black family income was only 60 percent of the white median income—where it has been since the mid-1960s. However, East Indians, Koreans, Chinese, Japanese, and West Indian immigrants are carving their niche in the U.S. economy and creating great wealth along the way. Today, 47 of every 1,000 East Indian and Korean Americans earn $100,000 a year, while only 15 of every 1,000 whites earn that much.

• Currently, 49 of every 1,000 U.S. workers are self-employed. Although more than 65 of every 1,000 Asian Americans are self-employed, only 9 out of every 1,000 blacks are. While blacks constitute 12 percent of the population, black businesses account for less than 1 percent of all business revenues.

• The total assets of black banks nationwide rests at a minuscule $1.61 billion, less than 0.1 percent of the total. As the twentieth century nears its end, there are still major metropolitan markets where blacks

---

* For Black America's consumption patterns, see African American Consumption Patterns, 1993–95, on p. 325.

have yet to penetrate the banking industry. For example, Los Angeles and New York City together operate only one black-owned savings and loan, and no black banks. Contrast this with Miami, where Hispanics control thirty banks.

• According to the Federal Reserve, other ethnic groups tend to be more loyal to merchants of their own kind. Capital within the Chinese community circulates there five or six times among other Chinese entrepreneurs before leaving the ethnic enclave. With blacks, money earned in the community usually leaves within minutes. From 1969 to 1994, the proportion of black income spent with black-owned businesses dropped from 13.5 percent to 7 percent.

• West Indians and Africans, nearly 10 percent of the new immigrants, have surpassed the living standard of native American blacks. Furthermore, black West Indians earn significantly more than the average white American and are better educated than their white counterpart.

• The U.S. Census Bureau claims that nearly 2 million Americans are of millionaire status. However, there are only 90,000 blacks who earn more than $75,000 per year.

So what's the answer? You need only look around. As you do, think for a moment. Are the most successful people you know those with the highest intellect or talents? Are the wealthiest—those who live life to the fullest and partake in the finest that life has to offer—the brightest, the smartest, or the most gifted? If you think they are, I dare to disagree. Wealth comes to the man and woman who sees and uses his or her *potential* for wealth. Chances are these men and women made a decision—a decision to set priorities; to pay themselves first; to keep their economic power for their own benefit.

Individual millionaires consume very little of what they create. Society assumes that the wealthy wear expensive clothing and live in sumptuous housing. Many people who are leveraged to the hilt do, but not true millionaires. The most successful are more likely to wear a Seiko or a Timex than a Rolex, to be as comfortable with clothes off the rack as high-end designer fashions, to drive a Chrysler or a Ford rather than a Mercedes or a BMW, to dine at home with their spouse as opposed to eating out, and to pay cash rather than bankrolling VISA or American Express. "It never fails," says T. M. Alexander, a paragon of frugality. "The folks I hire look better, smell better, and eat better than I do, and I pay their salary! The only thing that stands between them and poverty is their weekly paychecks. If someone looks wealthy, the odds are he isn't."

The Creator made you a creature who can think for yourself, who can believe and achieve in whatever you wish to accomplish. Do less than this and you cannot possibly fulfill your glorious humanity. The mind of mankind is filled with powers to be used—not to be neglected. Either these powers are utilized—and the benefits of their use shared with others—or we incur the penalties for ignoring these gifts.

For example, if you were in need of a house, and you possessed the lot, the materials, and the know-how to construct the house and yet neglected to build the house, you would understand your penalty as you sat in the cold and rain. Too many of us do not use our power to gather in the wealth that lies around us. As a result, we are penalized by poverty, misery, and worry—and we blame everyone but ourselves.

FAILURE TO APPLY THE GREATEST SECRET

Phil Knight was a mediocre miler in college. His best time for the event was four minutes and thirteen seconds. Knight had trained under the watchful eye of Bill Bowerman, the renowned University of Oregon track coach. During the late 1950s, Bowerman's training techniques placed little-known Eugene, Oregon, on the map when, year after year, he turned out a bevy of world-record-setting long-distance runners. In an effort to improve the times of his athletes, he toyed with running shoes. Their improvement became his silent passion. The innovative coach had theorized that slicing even an ounce off a runner's cleats might just prove the critical difference between winning and losing.

While completing an MBA at Stanford University, Phil Knight wrote a research paper based on his theory that the Japanese could do for athletic shoes what they had done for cameras. Convinced by his ideas, Knight took off for Japan, hoping to corner the domestic rights for Tiger running shoes. Upon returning home, he shared samples with his ex-coach as they made plans to set up shop. In 1964, Knight and Bowerman each scraped up $500 and formed the Blue Ribbon Sports Company, sole U.S. distributor of Tiger equipment. Strapped for cash, Knight placed their small inventory in his father-in-law's basement and peddled his wares at night and on the weekends to high school athletic teams. By year's end, sales had approached $8,000, hardly enough for him to justify quitting his full-time accounting job. But Knight's dreams rested on larger goals. He knew he was a big fish in a small pond. The sport shoe market was new, wide open, and seemingly inexhaustible.

Up to this point, Adidas, a West German corporation, had been the innovator in athletic equipment and, later, ancillary apparel. Although the European firm had set the standard that subsequently was followed by most of its competitors, it had drastically misjudged the potential and opportunity of the 1970 athletic boom. Even U.S. manufacturers like Converse and Keds were caught napping. Knight and Bowerman could hardly sit still. The next year, they gambled everything and decided to go after a larger share of the American market by developing their own shoe.

Bowerman, ever the tinkerer, fashioned a waffle iron and urethane rubber together to produce a more durable, cushioned sole. The new "waffle sole" proved popular and exceeded expectations. Pushing full blast, they contracted much of the work abroad to mostly Asian factories, adopted the "swoosh" logo, and called their product Nike, after the Greek goddess of victory. In 1980, Nike went public, shooting Knight's net worth to $300 million. Bowerman, who had long since retired, sold most of his stock and opted for a more relaxed lifestyle far removed from corporate boardrooms and shoe wars.

CHANGE THE COLOR OF YOUR THINKING!

Phil Knight and Bill Bowerman saw what those of a lesser vision didn't see and rode the crest of a booming industry. But the athletic shoe market is still booming, propped up by black dollars. More than a handful of the entrepreneurs I spoke with questioned, and even displayed displeasure, as to why some budding black businessman or -woman doesn't go after the same market that was, and is, so lucrative to Knight and Bowerman.

"What's the problem?" one of the entrepreneurs in this study snapped. "We've held on too long to that old saw about us being twice as good and only moving half as far. If those black corporate types and would-be entrepreneurs really believed they were twice as good, then why don't they leave those safe, cushy jobs to form their own firms and gain the full benefits of their wisdom and superiority?"

Another spoke undaunted and without discomfort. "In a population of 30 million, and a shoe market somewhere in the billions of dollars, I refuse to believe that not a single black businessman or -woman will step forward. We are just throwing money away."

One entrepreneurial stalwart was just as perturbed. He ruefully summarized a deeper internal problem: the lack of black support for black businesses. "There is another type of black-on-black violence taking place on America's streets," he said testily. "These acts of aggression are just as deadly and just as much a waste of human potential. But the media never airs it and very few within the race bother to address it. I'm talking about middle-class blacks who have turned their backs on small, black businessmen and -women fighting for survival." He went on to add that Black America has the primary responsibility of developing its own economic power base the way other groups have done in the past.

"Do you think America likes the Japanese better than us? Hell no! They are forced to deal with the Japanese because of their economic muscle. The Japanese harbor a strong bias for their race. They pool their funds, support their institutions, learn everything they can, and utilize Japanese resources first. Fifty years ago, they came to this country without a quarter. No one would do business with them. Did they march or picket or pass a civil rights bill? No. They stared corporate America in the face and snarled, 'You can run but you can't hide.' The next thing you know, they bought major stakes in every city of importance in the nation.

"Furthermore," he added, "they could care less if some company ever hired them. If something isn't quite to their liking, they just go in and buy huge shares of the enterprise in question. Look at Universal Studios, Columbia Pictures, and IBM. They analyze every challenge from a purely economic point of view. They think in terms of business first and politics never. As a matter of fact, their economics is their politics."

Lastly, another interviewee who insisted upon anonymity sat back in his creaky old swivel chair shaking his head in disbelief. "As a people we're three times the size of Sweden and damn near three times as wealthy. The Swedes produce a car and sell it across the globe. We don't even make a lousy pair of gym shoes. Why sugarcoat the truth? Though we can't change the color of our skin, we can sure change the color of our thinking."

A QUESTION FROM A WHITE LIBERAL TO BLACK LEADERS

Not long ago I received a letter from a minister who had read a *New York Times* article in which I was quoted extensively on success and wealth. After reading my comments he felt compelled to write, entitling his letter "A Question from a White Liberal to Black Leaders." It read, in part:

August 15, 1995
RE: A Question from a White Liberal to Black Leaders

Dear Dr. Kimbro:
Instead of holding out the tin cup to Washington, D.C., a futile gesture these days, why hasn't your race organized the cash assets of black celebrities,

mainly athletes and entertainers? Why is it that Arabs, Koreans, and other immigrants barely off the boat, unable to speak the language, often dominate the retail trade, including the vital food stores in long settled black communities?

No capital? We don't buy that anymore. Your celebrities' annual salaries and bonuses run into the hundreds of millions combined. Why no summit meetings of these rich and powerful African Americans where they could pool their resources to help their struggling brothers and sisters? Why not this real grass roots, down home affirmative action? Today, in our inner cities, there are many thousands of black youths literally dying for lack of a job in black owned and operated stores while they endlessly, mindlessly dribble a basketball dreaming of the NBA.

Many Americans, rightly or wrongly, themselves hard pressed, feel that Black America must now look to its own boot straps to effect its economic revolution. White liberals like myself applauded in 1954 when the all white Supreme Court, in the Brown decision, started the educational revolution. We marched with King in Selma and Washington, D.C. We marched and worked with Dr. King for the political revolution under Lyndon Johnson. But we cannot and will not fund and operate stores offering life necessities in black communities when there is money and ability enough within them. Your economic revolution must come from within. If Black America fails to galvanize its resources and enhance its own economic development, it will miss a unique point in history—one that it may not be able to capture again.

How blind we are! In the midst of it all—the wealthiest country on the face of the earth. How we underestimate everything. How we search high and low for a king to serve, before whom to fall on our knees in abject subjection. Someone—anyone other than ourselves—to provide us with answers and solutions. "Tell us what to do!" we shout. "Show us the way—we are helpless without you." We can no longer say: "Why don't they do something?" Instead, we must say: "Here's what I am doing to solve the problem." This letter is a reveille call to individual action. Each of us must be willing to take responsibility for the manner in which we spend, consume, and direct our assets. Greatness is in the man and the woman or nowhere. The golden opportunity we seek lies within ourselves: "Behold, I have set before you an open door which no man can shut."

No matter who you are—regardless of your race or background—if you truly wish to change the color of your thinking, from want to wealth, from survival to success, then you must make it a point to apply the Nine Disciplines of Wealth in your life. Make a decision to apply the *greatest secret* in your affairs. Remember, wealth is not an amount, but a habit—an act, an idea, a discovery, an attitude. Wealth is an attitude that fuels the desire to become a person of deep value and achievement; an attitude that provides you with a constant sense of joy; an attitude that allows you to be happy with what you have as you pursue what you want. Wealth flows from the fully developed mind regardless of the size of the bank account. Clarify your thinking today; find your true vocation today; hone your sales skills today; serve today; read and study today; and begin to save 10 percent of your earnings *today*. Begin to spot and seize opportunities wherever and whenever they exist.

When you realize that you do not need to look outside yourself for your needs; that the source of all supply, the Divine spring that will quench any thirst, lies within, then you shall not want. You need only to dip deep into your consciousness to tap into infinite supply. When you have faith enough in all that has been written to spend your last dollar with the same confidence and assurance that you would if you had thousands more, then you have grasped the *greatest secret*.

7
The Greatest Victory:

Triumph of the Human Spirit

- **The School of Hard Knocks**

- **Four Steps to Attain the Greatest Victory**

- **Who Is Holding You Back?**

The harder the conflict, the more glorious the triumph.
What we obtain too cheap, we esteem too lightly;
'tis dearness only that gives everything its value.
—THOMAS PAINE

The good things of prosperity are to be wished;
but the good things that belong to adversity are to be admired.
—SENECA

When your feet are so tired that you have to shuffle back to the
center of the ring, fight one more round. When your arms are so
tired that you can hardly lift your hands to come on guard, fight
one more round. When your nose is bleeding and your eyes are
black and you are so tired that you wish your opponent would
crack you on the jaw and put you out to sleep, fight one more
round. Remember, the man who always fights one more round is
never whipped.
—JAMES J. CORBETT

Again, I rise!
—MAYA ANGELOU

What is it about the human psyche that gives us the power to hold on? What catalyst, what force, what intangible energy, allows one to succeed where hundreds dropped in their tracks? We hear a great deal of talk about genius, talent, intellect, personality, vision, and courage playing a large part in one's success. Yes, it's true, all of these factors are important elements. Yet the possession of any or all of these traits, unaccompanied by the *greatest victory,* will not ensure success. What power trounces tragedy, devastates defeat, conquers chaos, routs ruin, and brushes aside misfortune? What makes you so strong?

There's a quality of personality that the truly great possess, no matter how they differ otherwise. Call it a sense of quiet assurance, but never mistake it for lack of backbone. It's that low-key attitude of command, based on self-knowledge, that effectively says, "I've been tried in some tough situations, and I've passed the tests. I know who I am. There's no need to impress anyone else with regard to my own importance." Life comes equipped with hazard and pain, though we may try to escape these maladies. We search for a smooth path, for comfort and security, for cheering friends and unbroken success. But the Creator ordains storms and disasters, hostilities and sufferings, and the grand question of whether or not we shall reach our objectives, in spite of these challenges, rests within the heart and soul of the Divine. What makes you so strong?

Many people whom we consider great have overcome incredible struggles. More than a few have seen everything go up in smoke. Some have endured disease, loss of family and friends, homelessness, bankruptcy, bouts of depression bordering on suicide, or accidents so horrific it seems a miracle the victims survived. All have danced with disaster. Yet it isn't the tragedy that forms the essence of a great comeback; it's the individual's tenacity, perseverance, will to win, and the triumph of the human spirit. If you lack this trait by nature, you must cultivate it. With it, you can succeed, you can make difficulties easier, you can make opposition give way, you can force doubt and hesitancy to yield to confidence and assurance.

How many centuries of justice would it take to produce a Martin Luther King? As blessed as fairness is, it could never craft a Jackie Robinson. Few knew Barbara Jordan until the great weight of discrimination and sexism showed on her face. It was poverty that made Clara Hale rich. Decades of wealth couldn't create a single Fannie Lou Hamer. Perhaps Nat Turner and Denmark Vesey would have never been known to history had it not been for slavery. And, as unfortunate as it was, it took death, not life, to call forth Myrlie Evers. When you challenge the human spirit, you demand the best.

HE NEVER LET DEAFNESS STAND
IN THE WAY OF HIS DREAM

Kenny Walker, aged five, was playing with his six-year-old brother, Gus, near their Denver home. "What's that funny-looking thing in your ear, kid?" a neighborhood boy yelled at Kenny. Kenny didn't answer. He didn't even know he was being taunted about the hearing aid he had just been fitted for. But Gus knew.

"You deaf?" the bully teased. "I'm talking to you!"

Clenching his fists, Gus felt his heart pound. "He's deaf. Leave him alone."

"He's deaf, all right. Deaf and dumb!" In a moment, punches were flying, and Gus and the antagonist were rolling on the ground.

In 1969, when he was two, Kenny Walker had contracted spinal meningitis. After a week of high fever and suffering, he survived—but he had lost his hearing. Times were tough for his parents, Julia and Fred Walker, and their six children, who lived in Crane, a tiny Texas town. When marital difficulties caused the parents to separate, Kenny's mother, a cafeteria worker, moved to Denver, where her son could receive special instruction in sign language, lipreading, and speech therapy.

School wasn't easy for the shy boy. Even with his hearing aid, he could barely pick up the sound of his own voice. Hoping to help, Alice Avstreih, an instructor for the hearing-impaired, took Kenny to speech therapy twice a week after school. She could see him struggling—his inability to communicate and all the changes in his young life had built up great frustration in him. Imprisoned by his handicap, he tried to speak, but the sounds were garbled. Suddenly he began crying; then came screams of rage. The tantrums recurred periodically for months before Kenny settled down and poured himself into academics and sports.

Kenny enjoyed basketball, but the sport he loved most was football. Neighborhood boys spent hours playing a rough, freewheeling game in the street. When other children learned that their playmate was deaf, they always chose him last, underestimating his ability. In time, he learned to compensate for his impediment with almost supernatural alertness. During a game, he instinctively seemed to know where everyone was going and what they were doing. His Saturday afternoons were spent watching college football games on television. For Kenny, the team that made the biggest impression wore scarlet and cream with the letter "N" on their helmets. "That's the team I'm going to play for," he decided, "the University of Nebraska."

"Don't Be a Quitter!"

On the playing field and in the classroom, Kenny gave his all. One season he led his junior high basketball team from last place to the league championship, and as a high school freshman he made the honor roll, too. But the cost of raising her family in Denver gradually got beyond his mother. She decided to move back to Crane. For Kenny, the change was traumatic. He had many deaf friends in Denver, but Crane had no deaf community. In that small western town tucked near the panhandle, he found himself working twice as hard as his classmates just to stay even. As a result, Kenny languished, turning inward, refusing to allow anyone into his world. Gus saw the shift in behavior and insisted that his brother associate with normal kids. When Kenny became discouraged, as he did from time to time, his older brother talked tough. "No one is going to feel sorry for you," he insisted. "Your deafness can't prevent you from doing anything you want to do. Don't be a quitter!"

Kenny glared at his brother before making a silent vow. "After much thought and soul-searching," he recalls, "I was determined to overcome all obstacles. What I lacked in physical abilities, I would make up for with an iron will." By his senior year, Kenny added fifteen pounds of muscle to his six-three, two-hundred-pound frame. He became a lightning-fast defensive end who averaged more than a dozen tackles per game. He made all-state in football *and* basketball, and, as a result, southwestern powerhouse football programs came calling—Texas A&M, Baylor, and the University of Oklahoma. Julia Walker asked high school football coach Rickey White to help select a school that would be best for her son.

"I want to go to Nebraska," Kenny announced.

"Nebraska hasn't contacted us," his coach shot back.

"I want to go to Nebraska," he repeated, as though that settled the matter. Coach White stared at his prized athlete, then picked up the phone and called Nebraska's recruiting coordinator. The university's offensive-line coach, Milt Tenopir, happened to be nearby, in the middle of a recruiting trip. Two hours later, he was in White's office viewing films of Kenny. Tenopir watched three or four plays and turned off the projector. White braced himself, thinking Tenopir had decided his trip had been a waste of time. "Can I use the phone?" the coach asked.

Excitedly, the coach called Nebraska's recruiting coordinator. "This kid can play!" Tenopir told him. "Let's sign him."

"If You Need Help, Help Yourself!"

In Lincoln, home to the Nebraska Cornhuskers football team, Kenny was met by sign-language interpreter Mimi Mann from the university's handicapped services office. Soon after that, he accepted a scholarship, and, at the request of the athletic department, Mann agreed to make a five-year commitment to be Kenny's interpreter.

Mann, however, didn't know a thing about football. Defensive-line coach Charlie McBride gave her a playbook and long hours of instruction. She and Kenny developed five hundred sign-language signals so that he could understand instantly what the coaches wanted him to do. At first, not all the coaches or fans thought Kenny would make it. After two years at Nebraska, the pressure was so great that he was ready to give up. Longing for the closeness of his family, he decided to visit Gus, who was then in the army, stationed at Fort Knox, Kentucky.

"I've been doing my best," Kenny told his brother after arriving, "but I'm not doing well, and besides I'm having a hard time with my studies. I might even fail. I'm considering dropping out." He loved children, though, and Kenny told his brother, "I'd like to be a schoolteacher for deaf kids."

"A teacher needs a college education," Gus snapped, "so forget about dropping out of school. You've got to give it your best shot." Kenny spent a month with Gus and returned to Lincoln rejuvenated. That fall, he played with a passion and soon found himself the focus of national media attention. By his senior year, Kenny had become a dominating defensive end. One day near the end of the season, an emotional Charlie McBride walked onto the practice field and said, "Kenny, you've made All-America." His coach was in tears. Kenny was incredulous. He was the first deaf player ever to win the honor. Then UPI named him its Big Eight Conference Defensive Player of the Year.

But clearly, the high point of his collegiate career arrived the last week of the regular season. It had become a tradition for each senior player to be introduced in recognition of his final game. As each player runs onto the field, fans shout and cheer. Before Kenny's final appearance, local media as well as the university's sports information office engaged in a conspiracy. The *Omaha World Herald,* a statewide newspaper, illustrated the sign-language symbol of an ovation: stand holding your hands above your head, fingers spread, then wave both hands side to side. Both Kenny's interpreter and his mother, who had come to see him play, made sure that he didn't see the newspaper that morning. They had wanted the gesture to be a complete surprise. That afternoon, Kenny stood in the stadium tunnel as one senior after another ran onto the field to thunderous applause. He could feel the vibrations in his shoulder pads. Then it was his turn. Butterflies in his stomach, he jogged out—but felt no vibrations at all. Puzzled, he stopped, looked up and around the huge stadium. More than 76,000 fans were standing for him, silently signing an ovation in his language. Kenny stood humbled and overjoyed at the center of this silent, rhythmic dance of affection. Then turning around the stadium, he signed to the fans, "I love you."

In April 1991, Kenny Walker was drafted by his old hometown team, the Denver Broncos, and became the first black deaf player in NFL history. What makes him so strong? you may ask. What are the qualities that enabled him to triumph over the bleakest circumstances, over his physical disabilities, transcending the pain that embitters others? Call it what you will—determination, persistence, desire, perseverance, confidence, an iron will, true grit, or the God force—but whatever it is, there's no substitute for it!

What makes Kenny Walker so strong, and what will strengthen your resolve as you dare to scale the slippery slope of success? Kenny Walker knows. He shared the answer with a group of hearing-impaired elementary school children after arriving in Denver. Standing before the students, he signed, "Don't feel discouraged or disappointed that you are deaf. If you need help, help yourself!"

THE SCHOOL OF HARD KNOCKS

The best tools receive their temper from fire, their edge from grinding; the noblest characters are developed in a similar way. The harder the diamond, the more brilliant the sparkle, and the greater the friction necessary to bring it out. Only its own dust is hard enough to make this most precious stone reveal its full beauty. From an aimless, idle, and useless soul, opposition also calls out powers and virtues otherwise unknown and unsuspected. Many times greatness will not make its entrance until adversity has paved the way. The prison, for example, has aroused the slumbering fire in many a noble mind. *The Philosophies and Opinions of Marcus Garvey* made its appearance while its author stood trial in New York. A cold, damp prison cell would be the platform from which a famed Muslim minister would come full circle: from Malcolm Little to Malcolm X. Solitary confinement steeled Nelson Mandela. What did not kill him made him stronger—and even his enemies were forced to agree—it was a long walk to freedom. And one spring day, written in the sweltering heat of injustice, the world received the "Letter from a Birmingham Jail." In it, we were told, it's much more important to be a human being than to be either black or white.

When the Creator wants to educate a man or woman, He does not send His star pupil to the academy of social graces, but rather, He enrolls the candidate in the school of hard knocks. We are not aware of the power within us until we face great adversity, a Goliath that must be conquered. As soon as the young eagle can fly, the seasoned birds thrust it out and tear the bark and leaves from its nest. This rough-and-tumble treatment of the tiny creature molds it and shapes it, permitting it to become the bold king of birds, fierce and hardened as it pursues its prey. At this point, it is fit to become the symbol of a nation. Men and women who are bound out, crowded out, kicked out, forced out, and kept out usually "turn out," while those who do not have these "dis"-advantages frequently fail to "come out." The world admires the man or woman who never flinches from unexpected difficulties, who calmly, patiently, and courageously grapples with his or her fate; who dies, if need be, at his or her post. Clear grit always commands respect.

Adversity has its advantages. It will help you decide what you really believe. Through the pit and the dungeon, Joseph came to the throne. It was the belly of a whale that provided Jonah with the altar to preach his greatest sermon. Under the yoke of colonialism, Jomo Kenyatta rose to lead a people to recapture their greatness. On the picket lines, Dorothy Height marched toward her date with destiny. Because she sang in the cancer ward, Minnie Riperton died with a song in her heart. Once an astonishing blend of power and speed, for nearly three years Bo Jackson absorbed the pain of a shattered hip that cut short his baseball and football careers. One of the paintings that made Romare Bearden famous rested on his easel for more than five years.

Susan Taylor, alone and with no money, no car, and barely a step ahead of her creditors, owing thousands more than she possessed, believed in herself when no one else would. She got in tune with the infinite and made her own way when she could not find one that already existed.

Carol Moseley Braun, sprung from a despised and disdained race, without opportunity, pushed her way up through the classes until she stood toe-to-toe, eye-to-eye with the scions of political and social power. Scoffed, ridiculed, and rebuffed on the U.S. Senate floor, she simply said, "The day will come when all of America will hear me!" Oh, the triumphs of the indomitable spirit!

In Revelation it is written: "He that overcometh, I will give him to sit down with me on my throne." Ernest Hemingway said that the world breaks all of us, and we grow stronger in the broken places. "Our strength," Emerson insisted, "grows out of weakness. Not until we are pricked and stung and sorely shot at, awakens the indignation which arms itself with secret forces. The world is no longer clay, but rather iron in the hands of its workers. Men and women have got to hammer out a place for themselves by steady and rugged blows." Adversity is the breeding ground for miracles.

"Never despair," wrote the philosopher and writer Edmund Burke. "But if you do, work on in despair."

"If you only knock long enough and loud enough at the gate," Longfellow advised, "you are sure to wake up somebody." Samuel Johnson, the early American college president agreed: "Few things are impossible to diligence. Great works are performed not by strength, but perseverance."

Fowell Buxton, a nineteenth-century English abolitionist, said in one of his emotionally charged lectures, "The longer I live the more certain I am that the great difference between men and women, between the feeble and the powerful, the great and the insignificant is energy—invincible determination—a purpose once fixed, and then death or victory."

Don't let me ever hear you use the word 'impossible.' If I've learned anything over the course of my career, there's no such thing as impossible. Overnight the impossible may not be possible. But over time, the impossible certainly becomes possible.

—Earl Graves

"He who is silent," wrote Swiss philosopher Henri Amiel more than a century ago, "he who does not advance falls back. He who stops is overwhelmed, outdistanced, crushed. He who ceases to grow becomes smaller. He who leaves off, gives up. The condition of standing still is the beginning of the end."

But *Black Enterprise* founder Earl Graves may have said it best. "Don't let me ever hear you use the word 'impossible,' " Graves admonished. "If I've learned anything over the course of my career, there's no such thing as impossible. Overnight the impossible may not be possible. But over time, the impossible certainly becomes possible!"

We are often told that life is a journey. Teachers and philosophers use the phrase incessantly, and you can hear it in a number of motivational talks: Life is a journey! It sounds so practical, so simplistic. Yet it means that we must struggle tooth and nail, and work years upon end to claim success. Champions are rarely chosen from the ranks of the unscarred.

THE GREATEST CHALLENGE

In 1978, Alicia Paige confronted the three most obvious truths about her life: she was black, female, and by her own choosing, out of work. Compounding these matters was that, after working thirty-five years within a number of library systems, she had had enough. Avon, Massachusetts, the city where she was employed, was caught in a spending freeze, trying to compensate for past economic sins. The city had tried to stave off fiscal disaster by using a series of constraining guidelines that had turned a once pleasant career into sheer torture. And, as if this was not enough, Paige faced other heartbreaks: A sixteen-year marriage dissolved and her only sister died. She was worn down, both mentally and physically. To take her mind off her personal tragedies, she did the only thing she knew how to do: She threw herself into the task at hand.

Paige loved books and enjoyed helping others, an apparent offshoot of her upbringing, which had stressed education. Her parents were West Indian immigrants who thought the road to success was paved with academics and effort. Her father had the greatest impact. Though his sixth-grade education didn't take him beyond a job as a janitor, she admired his work ethic. "He worked from five in the morning to ten at night to provide as best he could," she remembers. "For that, I will always be grateful."

As part of her routine duties as head cataloger for a suburban library branch, Paige secured books and journals through the statewide interlibrary loan system. Though it was a useful service to its borrowers, the process was cumbersome—"a heap of paperwork to keep up with"—and proved more of a hassle than anything else. Users wanted books yesterday, and librarians had no idea as to the general availability of requested materials. Paige brainstormed. Wouldn't it be nice, she thought, if all our library holdings were computerized on one easily accessible database? She thought each library in the system should have a CRT interconnected to statewide archives by phone. Designing such a program and inputting the necessary data would be quite a chore, but, in the long run, an efficient time-saver.

Paige shared her ideas with coworkers, who thought her dream was a bit far-fetched. "If it could be done," one rationalized, "someone would have certainly done it." "And besides," another scoffed, "you're a librarian—what do you know about computers?"

With her ingrained ladylike shyness, her first inclination was to agree. But she continued to mull the idea over. "They're right. What do I know about computers?" However, as the days wore on, she shrugged off her critics. Her restless energy, her vision, wouldn't die. At age fifty-seven, she held a torch to her future. Her once orderly life was about to encounter massive change.

Her Dream Wouldn't Die

After witnessing the degree of her commitment, two older brothers urged her to press forward. Though their words of inspiration were uplifting, they were completely caught off guard for what happened next. Paige burned every bridge. She quit her job and wrote a sketchy proposal. Unaware of federal assistance programs and refusing to borrow money, she sold her three-bedroom home and threw the $60,000 profit behind her company, which she ambitiously named Computer Engineering Associates. "It was all or nothing, and I knew if the business did not prosper, and quickly, I'd go under. It was an eerie feeling." Breathing a sigh of relief, she then adds with no exaggeration, "I never thought of just a small business. I thought, if I was going to start a company, I might as well go big. I always had a vision of where my enterprise was going to go."

With a freshly printed brochure and a handful of business cards, Paige turned to her former employer—the public library system—in hope of selling her services. But times were tight, and businesses—government included—were retrenching. Not only did the recession have Avon, Massachusetts, backpedaling, but the entire metro area was stapled to a sputtering economy. There were few listeners and definitely no buyers. Moreover, during her many conversations with would-be clients, and despite the high-tech hyperbole, each confirmed what she already knew— at best she had a layperson's knowledge of information systems. No client in his right mind would contract with a consultant who knew less than he did about computer systems. "So what if I had no experience with telecommunications or running a business?" she said, recalling her feelings at the time. "You don't have to know how to make steel to own a steel mill. I was confident I had a good idea." Paige knew she could learn from others.

One Hurdle at a Time

For the next eighteen months, Paige developed a steep learning curve. She scrambled to close the loop in her level of expertise. Seven days a week, virtually twenty-four hours a day, when she wasn't peddling her idea, her nose was stuck in a book related to computing, programming, or both. To free up her time, she combed for a secretary to handle light correspondence and anchor her office, a one-room storefront on Avon's main strip. But an ad in a local newspaper netted a brainy high-tech standout instead, who was looking for fresh opportunities. Stanley Zavatsky, a former vice-president of a computer firm, believed in her ideas and asked to join her team. Paige leveled with him. "I told him I couldn't afford to pay him one-tenth of what he was used to earning. He smiled and said he wasn't looking for a salary. So in a matter of minutes we hammered out a deal. He put in a few grand. I, in turn, sold him twenty percent of the business."

Paige and Zavatsky complement each other well. He's a deep thinker, a bit of an introvert, and can iron out the toughest problems associated with automated data processing. The energetic Paige, on the other hand, meshes well with prospective clients. Where she is lacking in experience and know-how, he's a real whiz. Together, they scrapped the plan of automating library systems and opted for a full-blown, full-service computer support company instead. Paige caught a glimpse of the big picture and assembled a highly technical staff: a mathematician, a systems analyst, and a programmer. She and her partner transformed CEA into a firm that could troubleshoot, perform feasibility studies, link computer systems, and custom-design programs with a personalized touch.

Moreover, she's never been shy about keeping her business afloat. CEA's success, she now realized, depended on qualifying for the federal 8(a) program that helps black-owned businesses bid for government and military contracts. Hoping to be added to its bidding list, she bombarded the government with 25,000 pieces of mail, and as a backup, even contacted Massachusetts Senator Paul Tsongas. For all her effort, she received a lukewarm response.

Angry that she was being overlooked, Paige played out a hunch. She and an associate, John Solomon, drove to neighboring Hanscom Air

Force Base in Bedford to introduce her firm. There, they met with Field Commander Jim Stansberry, a two-star general pushing for a third star. General Stansberry was receptive but blunt. He gave Paige a classified list of contract officers and a warning: "We'll give you a chance, but if you fall short of the terms of any agreement, I'll personally see to it that your company never gets another piece of government business again." Paige forced a smile, collected her papers, and shook Stansberry's hand. Somewhat confident, she and Solomon were headed out of the commander's office when his phone rang. On the end of the line was one of Stansberry's subordinates in West Germany, with bad news: An 8(a) supplier had botched a cable linkup job. To complicate matters, the project was running grossly overbudget and behind schedule. Solomon, who had watched quietly, saw the commander's heart sink with every word. While the general jotted down the particulars, Solomon gave Paige a slight belt to the ribs and murmured, "We can do the work."

Stansberry overheard his remark and blinked hard. "What did you say?"

Solomon straightened his tie, peered at a quizzical Paige, and replied, "I said we can do the work, sir." This was the breakthrough Paige had desperately sought.

Stansberry told his caller he would solve the problem and hung up the phone. He then turned his full attention back to his visitors and told them what the job entailed. As Paige read the spec sheet, she wouldn't commit until her team saw the job in question firsthand. When asked about the coy move, she would later reply, "So many 8(a) firms say they can do everything. Well, obviously, this one couldn't. If I don't feel comfortable that we can complete a project, I don't sign on, no matter how much I need the business." In the following weeks, Paige sent two of her staff to Germany for an assessment. In a few days they called with good news. Not only could CEA do the work, but they could complete the job within the original time frame.

"I Was Tougher Than I Thought"

Less than three months later, Paige beamed as an ecstatic General Stansberry read their report. And, to top it all off, by completing the project underbudget, she hand-delivered a $37,000 check made payable to the U.S. Air Force—a mixture of naïveté and savvy that delighted military brass more accustomed to cost overruns. "In this business, that is almost unheard-of," she admits. "Standard operating procedure is to take whatever you can lay your hands on. Because of my openness and honesty, I was poor-mouthed by my competitors. They questioned my sanity and made remarks like, 'Paige, you must be crazy. You're a small businessman, you need all the money you can get.' I just said, 'I want you to know that I'm in business to succeed. And for your information, I am neither small nor am I a businessman!' "

Paige is used to doing battle for what she believes in. And her story has a deeper message. "That gesture brought us an additional $7 million in business. We became known throughout the government as the company that gives back change. Far too many entrepreneurs lose dollars while watching dimes."

Paige's big gamble on CEA is now paying off, in terms of both profits and recognition. In 1986, she accepted the Small Business Administration's Award for Excellence. Her company now employs thirty-three programmers and technicians who custom-design software and databases for select clients. No longer reliant on the government or its 8(a) program, CEA has customers that include GTE, Raytheon, RCA, Goodyear Tire & Rubber, Pillsbury, American Express, and Westinghouse. At last count, her firm was about to exceed $10 million in revenues.

With the lean years behind, Paige took a moment to reflect. She was on the verge of tears as she recounted her enormous gamble. "I spent the first four years hanging on by my fingernails. The experience was riveting. I really don't know when things started to turn around. You work hard, you're in the midst of things, when suddenly, you look—and you're standing in a pool of liquid gold. Tenacity is what I've learned about myself. I found out that I was tougher than I thought."

Few stories are this dramatic: A fifty-seven-year-old black woman with little knowledge or prior experience in an industry soaked with competition bet the ranch on herself and won. Determination is part of her success. But she also drew upon faith and ingenuity when she had nothing else left. In enterprise, as in technology, the single vision prevails; consensus gives way to the man or woman who is willing to succeed. And a warm embrace of what is truly possible doesn't hurt. The story of Alicia Paige proves again—as if proof were still necessary—that progress and achievement are the result of grit and diligence.

FOUR STEPS TO ATTAIN THE GREATEST VICTORY

Greatness, it seems, harbors heroes—resilient and resourceful—in every corner. One of the first lessons of life is to learn how to wrestle victory from defeat, to transform shattered dreams into plans of action. When faced with humiliation and disaster, it takes mental toughness and stamina to sit by and watch your hopes fall from grace. It takes everything you can muster to search through the wreckage and ruins for the elements of future conquests. Yet this measures the difference between those who succeed and those who fail. You cannot measure an individual by his or her failures, but rather by what he or she makes of them.

Many people seem to think that ambition is a quality born within; that it is not susceptible to improvement; that it is something thrust upon us that will guide itself. But it is a passion that responds to cultivation and requires constant care and attention. Society watches a child's first failure with deep interest. It is the index of his or her life, the measure of his capacity. The mere fact of his failure doesn't generate much concern, but how did he digest defeat? Was he discouraged; numbed when it all turned to ashes? Rocked to his knees, did he drift out of sight? Did he slip the noose around his neck and blame others for his misfortune? Did he conclude that he had made a mistake in his calling and dabble in something else? Or did he come roaring back armed with a new outlook and breathe new life into his goals? You don't drown by falling into the water—you drown by staying there.

When the prizes of life shall be awarded by the Supreme Judge, who knows our weaknesses and frailties, the distance we have run, the weights we have carried, the handicaps we have endured, all will be taken into account. Not the distance of our race, but rather the obstacles we have overcome, will decide the prize. The beleaguered soul who has plodded along against unknown temptations, the poor woman who has buried her sorrows within her heart and managed her weary way through life, those who have suffered abuse in silence, and those who have gone unrecognized or despised by their fellow runners will receive the greater gift.

Here are four steps by which you can secure your *greatest victory*. Each step will work, regardless of your level of education or self-esteem. As these steps become the cultivated habits of your daily life, they will enable you to face every challenge with a deeper sense of purpose in yourself and your abilities.

STEP 1
DECIDE WHAT LIMITATIONS YOU WILL ACCEPT

There are two common errors that can devastate your ability to succeed. First, it is a mistake to assume that all limits are self-imposed; second, it is equally foolish and self-defeating to knuckle under to self-imposed limits. Surviving the odds involves choosing which limitations you will accept and which you will resist. People who drive themselves against their natural limitations tend to become frustrated and embittered. They hold unrealistic ideals to which they try to measure up, often becoming square pegs in round holes. They rob the world of what they could do best because they spend their lives trying to do what they can only do poorly or not at all. Constant failure beats them down, and they lose all semblance of confidence and determination. These individuals expend their energies chasing what is really an impossible dream. Your first step to attaining your *greatest victory* is to determine what limits are truly limits versus those that are self-imposed.

Tiny, physically impaired, and in constant pain, Fanniedell Peeples is a mighty hero to the staff, families, and young patients at Detroit's Children's Hospital. Since 1983, this seventy-two-year-old black woman has been a tireless volunteer at the hospital, logging thousands of dedicated hours without pay.

Peep, as she is affectionately called, is there each morning in the surgical waiting room, offering support and comfort to all who cross her path. She is in the nursery holding sick and terminally ill infants who have no one else to cuddle them. She is with pediatric patients, uplifting each child with words of encouragement and a beaming smile. She hands out library books, gives tours, and holds daily prayer sessions. And for all her good work, day in and day out, she gets a free meal in the hospital cafeteria.

Born with acute scoliosis, curvature of the spine, Peep realized at a young age that what she couldn't accomplish with good looks and physical abilities she could achieve with a powerful spirit. Although she was raised in foster homes from the time she entered grade school, Peep was an honor student, received a scholarship to Lincoln University in Missouri, where she was named Most Likely to Succeed, and graduated valedictorian of her class.

When she was only a teenager, fate took hold. Peep underwent fifteen grueling operations, was confined to a body cast, and then, without any money or family support, she cared for herself for ten lonely years. Finally, despite disabling back pain, kidney, lung, and heart problems, arthritis, and other ailments, she decided just to "get on with life." Peep found a way to help herself by extending a helping hand to others. As a result, her generosity has earned her a share of fame. Articles about her special gifts have appeared in national magazines, and she has received two personal White House commendations. In the evening, Peep returns home to her cozy little apartment, paid in part with a small monthly Social Security check. Her fortitude and strength have propelled her through another day—a day in which she accepts physical limits but conquers those of the mind and spirit. Each day she makes a difference in her life as well as the lives of others.

Are you tired of allowing circumstances to define your life? Are you tired of having people tell you what you can or cannot do, or what you should or must do? Perhaps you were brought up in an environment that taught limitation, that accentuated the negative—particularly your mistakes and shortcomings. Yet I know that within you something has told you that you *can* make it—that you can survive and succeed in spite of the difficulties. Surroundings that others deem unfavorable cannot prevent the unfolding of your powers. Here's the key: *You can have anything you want if you will only develop a consciousness to obtain it.* Now is the time to go beyond what "they" say. Now is the time to be sick and tired of being sick and tired. Program your dreams into your subconscious, then say yes to life. Life, in turn, will say yes to you.

> God grant me the serenity to accept
> the things I cannot change;
> The courage to change the things I can change;
> And the wisdom to know the difference.

This old prayer has helped more people sort out where they should place the thrust of their efforts and concerns than any of us can imagine.

STEP 2
FOCUS ATTENTION ON YOUR GREATEST STRENGTHS

All achievers have learned the secret of concentrated energy. They are in touch with their inner resources and have discovered what they can do best—what they believe is worth giving their best to accomplish. And they have learned to channel their energies into a single purpose. "Always lead with your strong suit" has become their personal affirmation.

Greg Baranco shifted his college major from premed to business because he was determined to play to his strengths: preparation and persistence. In his native hometown of Baton Rouge, Louisiana, he dropped in on the general sales manager of Audubon Ford, a high-volume south-eastern car dealership. He was determined to tear a hole in the new-car market big enough to fit his dreams. He swallowed hard, stuck out his hand, and uttered the words he had practiced for weeks: "Hi, I'm Greg Baranco, and I like to sell cars."

"How many times do I have to tell you?" the manager fumed. "We are not hiring any more salesmen!" Baranco, barely twenty-one years old and impeccably dressed, had been calling on the same hapless sales manager every day. Most prospective job seekers would have turned to Jell-O by now or knocked on someone else's door. But Baranco smiled warmly, shook the man's hand just as he had done the day before, and left yet another résumé. He was willing to pay the price for success. As he left the showroom floor, he had already made up his mind to come back first thing the next morning.

It took the manager nearly a month before he agreed to give the eager upstart a thirty-day trial. Baranco came in with a full head of steam—and struck out again and again. Three weeks elapsed before he managed to close his first deal: He convinced his sister to buy a car from him. Then, in the final week, he experienced the *greatest victory.* He averaged nearly a car a day, which convinced the manager to keep him on. Six months later, he had broken every sales record at the dealership. A few years later, Baranco took the entrepreneurial plunge and launched the Baranco Automotive Group, which, with $70 million in annual sales, is now among the top black-owned car retailers in the nation.

What makes Greg Baranco keep pushing to the front? His words ring in the ears of all those who aspire. "The golden opportunity that you seek lies within yourself. I only know of one road to success and that's the trail marked by persistence."

As you learn to concentrate on your strengths, and on what you can do well, you will feel your self-confidence and inborn abilities rising up within you. For example, the sports world stands in agreement that the one quality that made heavyweight boxing champ Muhammad Ali nearly unbeatable was that he always made his opponent fight his fight. Ali would "float like a butterfly and sting like a bee." Beneath the poetry and self-adoration lay a great fighter who knew what he could do best and stuck to it. No wonder he made far more powerful fighters believe he was "The Greatest."

Take the second step to overcoming the odds: Make the world fight your fight. Focus attention on your greatest strengths.

STEP 3
ADOPT A POSITIVE MENTAL ATTITUDE
AND SEEK OUT POSITIVE PEOPLE

There are two types of people throughout the world: positive people and negative people. Whether you are an optimist or a pessimist, the future lies in your hands, and yours alone. If you want to be joyful, enthusiastic, and excited about life, you can be, regardless of your circumstances.

The first rule of developing a positive mental attitude is: *Act positively, and you will become positive!* You can't *think* your way into *acting* positively, but you can *act* your way into *thinking* positive. Welcome every morning with a smile. Look on the new day as another special gift from the Creator, another golden opportunity to complete what you were unable to finish the day before. Be a self-starter. Allow your first hour to set the tone of success and positive action that is certain to echo through your entire day. Today will never happen again. Don't waste it with a false start or no start at all. You were not born to fail. Keep your mind uncluttered. Practice ridding your mind of all negative, self-defeating thoughts; discipline your mind to work for you. Make it do what you want it to do, when you want it to do it.

The second part of this rule suggests that you must seek out and associate with other positive individuals. Take a look at the people in your life that are telling you "It cannot be done," "There's no way," "No one has ever done this before." Are you allowing these individuals to determine whether *you* are capable of reaching your goals or not? In essence, are you giving your power away to others? If you are, make a decision to reclaim that power. What kind of people do you surround yourself with in your business? Are they men and women who are always searching for reasons why some things can't be done, or are you surrounding yourself with people who find solutions? Be very careful when choosing the kind of people with whom you associate, because whether you realize it or not, they strongly influence your life. Their negativity becomes contagious—in your office, in your relationships, in your family and your business. People who believe that things *can't* be done will set out to prove themselves right. But men and women who know things *can* be done go out and make it happen.

As you begin to spend time with like-minded people—positive, upbeat men and women—they will reinforce your attitudes about life. Greet everyone you meet with love and laughter, be gentle, kind, and courteous toward friend and foe. People who respect themselves and their abilities help nurture your capabilities and your self-esteem. So if misery loves company, don't be a part of it. Spend your time with those from whom you can draw strength and whom you can support in return. Those who do not increase you will inevitably *decrease* you.

Lee Haney was bodybuilding's Mr. Olympia for eight consecutive years. At five feet eleven, 245 pounds, with a thirty-one-inch waist and less than 5 percent body fat, Haney has set the standard for the sport. Since 1983, his dominance has been numbing. Haney lives in Atlanta, Georgia, where he trains housewives, corporate executives, and Olympic hopefuls. One of his prize pupils, Evander Holyfield, who has won boxing's most coveted prize—the heavyweight title—confesses, "Lee makes *me* feel small. He is totally awesome."

Though "totally awesome" may aptly describe Haney's outward appearance, it is also a catchy tag line that represents the business side of Mr. Olympia, which is just as expansive. Haney's mastery has earned him a string of sponsors, an exercise show on ESPN, a mail-order company that pitches nutritional products, a library of workout videos, two aerobic and weight training gyms, with plans to open more, and a signature line of sportswear. Like his predecessor Arnold Schwarzenegger, Haney has parlayed his enormous biceps into a one-man conglomerate that earns more than $2 million per year.

Success, however, came anything but easy for a poor, black kid from Spartanburg, South Carolina. Haney was raised in an environment where the work ethic was wielded like a sledgehammer. His mother was a domestic and his father drove spikes for a railroad, and later eighteen-wheelers across the country, when he wasn't drilling his son on the rudiments of success. "My parents told me that no one was ever going to give me a thing," Haney recalls. "That I better be prepared to work hard for whatever I wanted." These words would sustain him as he fought for his place in history.

As a teenager, Haney squeezed a string of part-time jobs into an already crowded schedule that included schoolwork and letters in three sports. During his senior year, he showed promise as a speedy high school tailback and held hopes of college and maybe professional football, until he broke both legs during a routine scrimmage. His coach assured him the quickest way back to the gridiron was through the weight room. Haney took his advice and blasted forward.

As Haney's body began to develop and take shape, so, too, did his competitive spirit. In 1979, Haney won the Teenage Mr. America competition. Two years later, he made a name for himself by sweeping the

Junior Mr. America, the American Nationals, and the Mr. Universe titles. He was twenty-two years old, fast reaching his peak in a sport packed with seasoned pros. Despite his success, he was still dissatisfied. Haney's period of crystallization came at the close of 1982. His face a picture of intense concentration, he vividly describes what was going through his mind.

"I attended a party with some friends when I stood up and announced that I would win next year's Mr. Olympia. To this day, I don't know why I made such an outlandish statement, but I said it. There wasn't a soul in the room who believed me."

Haney's words were no idle boast as he would seize every opportunity to disprove his naysayers. A nearly naked ambition led him to seek the wisdom of the ages. While training on the West Coast, he sought out Lou Ferrigno (the Incredible Hulk), Frank Zane, Ben and Joe Weider, and other bodybuilding greats, before returning to Spartanburg renewed, mentally refreshed, and fully aware of what was required of him. "They all emphasized the same thing," Haney reflected. "Attitude!"

In true Rocky fashion, he sold damn near everything he owned from his modestly furnished apartment but a bed, clothing, and other bare essentials, and took up residence on the second floor of a battered neighborhood gym. Here, Haney would undertake a life that could only be described as stoic monasticism. From this vantage point, he would view his world. The next year would consist of nothing more than eating, sleeping, and pumping iron. "Some bodybuilders go to Southern California for inspiration," Haney reflected. "I looked within and found all the inspiration I needed. I became very particular about whom I associated with and what I allowed to occupy my mind. Attitude was everything."

Haney's magic moment arrived in 1984, when he became the youngest ever to win the Mr. Olympia title. And seven years later, he still rested atop the heap, a precarious spot for anyone in any sport or discipline. Today, he oversees his empire from a vastly different reference point, opting to flex his muscles in the business world as well. What Haney really wants to be is a role model for similar self-initiated men and women, to lead by example. He says that whatever he has earned means nothing if he cannot show others how they, too, can reach their goals. Above all else, he seeks to inspire. "I guess it all goes back to four basic principles that have anchored my life and helped me master the moment."

- *Faith.* "Whatever you attain in life will be based upon your faith; be willing to take risks. You cannot discover new oceans unless you have the courage to lose sight of the shore."

- *Vision.* "Don't be afraid to dream big dreams. Take advantage of what this country has to offer. Get a dream, and then lock onto it with intensified focus."
- *Information.* "Seek knowledge. You may not have all the answers, but someone does. In 1983, I had no idea how I was going to reach my goal of Mr. Olympia, but I sought the counsel of those who had gone before me."
- *Attitude.* "You must develop an attitude that lifts your sights from the ordinary to the extraordinary. You must develop an attitude that gives you hope, that inspires you to attempt the impossible, that challenges you to grow. A winning attitude is the world's most desperate need. There are no hopeless situations, only people who think hopelessly. The only way you can lose in life is to defeat yourself mentally first."

Your own self-doubts or the opinions of others can often stifle your abilities and any possibility of achievement. Self-confidence is often little more than a feeling, deep down in the pit of your stomach, that you can do something that reason says is impossible. But, as you respond positively to that feeling, it grows and grows until it reaches full bloom in concrete action.

STEP 4
MAKE A STRONG COMMITMENT TO REACH YOUR FULL POTENTIAL AS A HUMAN BEING

If you are to reach your full potential, you must cultivate the creative urges within you and respond to the sensitivity that cries out for expression. The greatest enemy of your creative powers is smug complacency—being satisfied with less than what you are capable of doing. You must find positive ways to express your individuality. Robert Holland, president and CEO of Ben & Jerry's, paraphrases an old ditty: "Be who you is, 'cause when you ain't who you is, you is who you ain't." In other words, people who accept themselves are not preoccupied with what others think about them. They are willing to express those traits and inner feelings that give them their uniqueness, without an undue regard for what anyone else thinks. People with strong positive self-images are satisfied to be themselves, regardless of what others think, say, or do.

The human mind, coupled with an indomitable spirit and a physical body, is capable of creating in a way that is unknown anywhere in the universe. Even when the physical body is limited in certain key areas, the human mind and spirit can break free to carve out success in the most amazing ways. But you must face one of life's most difficult questions: Who is holding you back?

WHO IS HOLDING YOU BACK?

When you were younger, did you possess grand dreams, great ambitions to write or to paint, to start a business, or to master another field? Most of us did. In fact, if we are truly honest with ourselves, most of us still cherish these dreams, but we excuse ourselves on the basis of other commitments: I have my job to do; I would love to write a novel, but I lack the resources; I would love to launch my own business, but I can't leave my current employer; or we come up with some other excuse for not fulfilling our hopes and desires. Most of the barriers that keep us from realizing our full potential are artificial. They are imposed on us by circumstances or by other people. *Artificial* limitations include our age (we're "too" young or "too" old), empty pockets, past failures, the short-sightedness of those around us, lack of education, and fears and doubts. The *real* limitations that rob us of our freedom to make the best of what we have, and of what we are, spring from the way we see ourselves and the world around us. Our attitudes hold us back from becoming all that we were created to be. A negative outlook on life, procrastination, inflexibility, self-pity, worry, laziness, lack of self-discipline, and bad habits—all are limitations to what we can become.

How many of our youth are weighted down with poverty and low self-esteem, with parents who never found purpose or direction in *their* lives? How many young men and women slip through the cracks of potential greatness because they are hampered by a negative attitude, life-threatening surroundings, and no hope? How many are delayed in the race of life because of their race, because no one believes in them, because no one encourages, uplifts, or loves them? How many are weakened for the journey because no one took the time to insist upon discipline, demand commitment, and delay instant gratification? How many are forced to hobble along because they were raised on the crutches of self-pity? How many have to feel their way to the goal because they have been blinded by ignorance and a lack of ambition?

Achieving men and women have always been those who have relentlessly made a strong commitment to reach their potential. Victory spoke from his face and expressed itself in his manner even when Frederick Douglass walked barefoot in the snow, half-starved and thinly clad. Bonnie St. John put grit in place of an artificial limb and became Black

America's most celebrated Special Olympics skier. A date with destiny sustained Hannibal, who charged into battle with only one eye. Kwame Nkrumah, asked by his countrymen what he would do after four or five years if Ghana did not gain its independence, replied, "There is no alternative but to keep pounding away." And for more than three decades, George Washington Carver held on to his dream of enriching the depleted soil of the southern United States as he perfected the many uses of the peanut.

What a sublime patience Dr. Charles Drew demonstrated as he examined the circulation and properties of blood. Labeled a harebrained impostor by his colleagues, nearly a quarter century would pass before his great discovery was honored by the medical profession.

If impossibilities ever existed, they should have been found in the life of Dr. Georgia L. McMurray—but she has yet to find them! Dr. McMurray, who has been stricken with Charcot-Marie-Tooth atrophy, a congenital degenerative disease that has left her completely paralyzed, is one of the nation's top educators. From her motorized wheelchair, she continues her research and remains committed to championing the causes of young adults, particularly teenage mothers. Dr. McMurray's remarkable life proves that a physical challenge of any kind—whether an early pregnancy or a rare disease—need not be a limitation to achievement.

Who is holding you back? The victorious attitude is that element of character that enables an individual to clutch his or her aim with an iron grip and keep the needle of his purpose pointing to the star of his hope. Through sunshine and storm, through pleasant weather and foul, with a leaky ship or with a crew in mutiny, it perseveres; in fact, nothing but death can subdue it, and it dies still struggling.

THEY TOLD HIM IT COULDN'T BE DONE

Like many others before him, Melvin McCoy of Memphis, Tennessee, was told that it couldn't be done. People said that his "backpack" invention, the M.U.L.E.—a multipurpose uniaxial-litter device, a cross between a standard backpack and a Native American travois—would not work, that he would not be able to walk across America without vehicle support because of the equipment necessary for such a journey. With no background in engineering, and never having spent a night out of doors, McCoy perfected his design and, with his dog Buddy as his constant companion, began his Walk Across America in January 1993, beginning in Newport Beach, California. Three thousand miles later—on September 15, 1993—he reached his destination of Cape Helopen

State Park in Lewes, Delaware. "I lived eight months out under the stars," McCoy says with stoic determination. "I encountered blizzards, tornadoes, detours due to floodwaters, a sprained ankle, and the loss of forty pounds." But, in the spirit of the African American explorer Matthew Henson, McCoy pressed on, undaunted. "I wanted to prove that it could be done!"

Who is holding you back? Think about Steveland Morris Hardaway, whom Motown Records renamed "Little Stevie Wonder." Born blind to a single mother of five in Saginaw, Michigan, Stevie Wonder never let sightlessness hold him back. He put a dream in place of his eyes and carved out an illustrious musical career. At two, Stevie was creating music with spoons; at four, he could play the harmonica. He moved on to the drums, and by the age of eight, he was composing tunes on the piano. Discovered by Ron White, one of Smokey Robinson's Miracles, Wonder was signed by Motown when he was twelve. From his first hit, "Fingertips," the young musician was a phenomenon, racking up one pop hit after another. As he matured—and dropped "Little" from his name—he adapted music to the changing times. He has written songs supporting a variety of causes including AIDS research, sickle-cell anemia, world hunger, and the end of apartheid. One of his most popular songs, "Happy Birthday," was part of Wonder's campaign to designate Dr. Martin Luther King, Jr.'s birthday as a national holiday. Though he may have lost his sight, Stevie Wonder never lost his vision. He remains a vigilant optimist. "I believe this is God's island," he says, "and ultimately He will make it right."

"IF THOU WOULD ONLY BELIEVE"

Do you find yourself bound in some way and do you think, "Oh no, not with my shortcomings. I'll never be able to do what I want to do." Do you think of yourself as physically or mentally challenged? Do you see yourself doomed to a marginal existence? Do you feel chained to your limitations? If so, consider the following analogy. Have you ever gone to the circus and noticed that huge elephants are held in check by only a small wooden stake while much younger elephants are kept at bay by a deep-set metal stake and iron chains? Try as they may to free themselves, the baby elephants push and pull to break the chains that bind them. If the stake is driven far enough into the ground and the chain is strong enough to withstand their efforts to escape, the young elephants won't be able to budge. Eventually, the day will arrive when the creature will cease to pull and tug. At this moment, the metal stake is replaced with a wooden spike, because the elephant has now been conditioned to believe that it cannot escape. In a similar fashion, by creating limitations through our own erroneous belief system, we mimic the older elephant. We become limited not by reality, but by reality as we perceive it.

Think again about the treasured ambitions locked up in your soul. Look again at the excuse you have used to prevent yourself from fulfilling your dreams. See it for the false belief that it really is. Cast it aside and resolve to express your creative desires through your own creative activity. This is a task that only you can do. No one else can hold you back.

Of the terms that best describe humanity's challenges, "self-defeating" is perhaps the most appropriate. The aim of all the great teachers was to awaken mankind to its self-defeating behavior. Henry David Thoreau said it quite cleverly: "As long as a man stands in his own way, everything seems to be in his way." In other words, the greatest obstacle on our path to greatness is ourselves. How to apply the power that lies within us to move that obstacle is a question of considerable importance.

People say they want to grow and assume life's responsibilities, but, subconsciously, what they really wish is to remain a child. They are not willing to embrace change. Instead, they offer countless excuses and reasons as to why they continually fall short of the mark. The way out of this maze of self-defeating behavior is through the virtue of commitment. Commitment is the willingness to do whatever it takes to obtain your heart's desires. A true commitment is a heartfelt promise to yourself from which you will not retreat. Many people hold dreams and good intentions, but few are willing to make the commitment necessary for their attainment.

As fate will have it, at some point in your life you will face a moment of truth. No matter how noble your purpose, how clear your vision, or how positive your attitude, what you have envisioned for your future will remain only a dream, a fantasy, unless you are willing to take a stand—to be committed. Now would be a good time to review your goals and statement of purpose and ask yourself: How badly do I want to reach my objectives? How strongly do I desire those goals?

Commitment influences behavior, and behavior determines results. If you are committed to your health, you will exercise and consume food that nourishes your body. If you are committed to your family, you will love, provide, and spend quality time with each family member. If you are committed to your vocation and career, you will continually seek ways to improve the quality of your work. Each of us is challenged by the words of Benjamin Disraeli, the English writer and prime minister, who wrote, "Nothing can withstand the power of the human will if it is willing to stake its very existence to the extent of its purpose."

Begin now to commit to your dreams, to a vision, to a higher purpose. Cast aside all debilitating excuses. If you believe that someone or something outside of yourself is the cause of your problems, you will continually search outside of yourself for the solution. In order to find the answers to your needs, and to overcome any limitations, begin now by looking at yourself in a new way, which will in turn cause you to see the world and its events in an optimistic light. The outer world is often a reproduction of the inner world. This is the starting point of all success. It's time for you to grow up.

No one can solve your problems but you. No one can overcome your limitations but you. Government cannot make you successful. Only you can do that. No other group or race can provide you with peace of mind and happiness. Only you can do that. Nobody else can care for or nurture your family. Only you can do that. No organization or legislation can remove the blight or cynicism from your communities. Only you can do that. Nobody can turn your life around for the better. Only you can do that. It is time for each of us—you and me—to grow up!

THERE ARE NO LIMITATIONS!

Once you begin to practice the principles in this chapter, they will allow you to develop a positive, "can do" belief system. This in turn will produce results that will supply the outlook that permits you to grow even more. There are no limitations! The only limitation is the limitation within your mind. For example, have you ever driven your car with the emergency brake on? The emergency brake represents fear, worry, procrastination, and poor self-esteem. Needless to say, you can still reach your goals with all these unworkable beliefs, just as you can arrive at your destination with the emergency brake intact. But it is much easier to just let go and release your brake—your misconceptions, superstitions, negative thinking, and preconceived notions. It is much easier to reach your goals if you will release anything and everything that does not support your efforts.

What makes the great great? Throughout this chapter, you've been reminded once again of your potential for success. That is your destiny. Remember, you can have anything you desire if you will give up the belief that you cannot possess it.

8
The Greatest Need:

Prayer

- **The Breath of God**

- **The Power of Prayer**

- **Six Mental Shifts for Greater Spiritual Awareness**

- **Watching and Waiting, Looking Above**

- **Ancient Secrets**

Lord, make me an instrument of your peace. Where there is hatred let me sow love; where there is injury, pardon; where there is doubt, faith; where there is despair, hope; where there is darkness, light; and where there is sadness, joy.
—St. Francis of Assisi

Every step toward progress is a step more spiritual.
—Mary Baker Eddy

Let us pray . . .
—David

Life is fragile . . . handle with prayer.
—A Bumper Sticker

Here is the key to the power to transform your life. Here is your passport to success, your visa to happiness and well-being, your hidden guide for human progress. This very day you may exercise a special privilege which, if you avail yourself of it, will completely alter your life. This privilege is yours regardless of the mistakes you may have made in the past. You possess this privilege now, this very moment, of making a new start, a fresh beginning by turning away from your old limiting thoughts and beliefs, to exercising your inherent birthright.

We who live today stand at the portal of a vast reservoir of human development, slowly accumulated through the many long struggling generations of the past. We are the heirs of all that has ever been accomplished, all that humanity has ever done to improve itself and the world in which we live. We are the heirs of all that mankind has ever dreamed, thought, fought and died for—all that humanity has eloquently written or expressed. But today, we still hunger for our greatest need.

When millions are troubled, uncertain and confused, this need takes on a new and vital importance. There has never been a time when our brothers and sisters were more desperately in need of faith, hope, courage, peace of mind—of standards and ideals by which to live. There has never been a time or moment during the course of history when humanity didn't need something to cling to, something on which to build; something enduring and everlasting; something to secure us to the floor as we face the stiff winds of change; something that will provide firm structure to fragile lives.

But where in the staggering wealth of ideas and ideals that have been laid before us can we find exactly the help, the guidance, and the inspiration we sorely need? Where in the thousands upon thousands of books, papers, and records which preserve and transmit the best that mankind has ever written or spoken are we likely to find the words that can mean most to us now, that can have the greatest impact and influence on our daily lives? Where, among the old classic favorites—from the *Analects* of Confucius and the *Meditations* of Marcus Aurelius; from the *Ethics* of Aristotle and the *Confessions* of Saint Augustine; from the *Dialogues* of Plato and Cicero's *De Officiis;* from the sacred Bhagavad-Gita and the Upanishads, and the Koran, Talmud, and Bible—can we find the answers we seek?

How, from the long shining caravan of the great—Mohammed, Buddha, Seneca, Saint Paul, Horace, Dante, Goethe, Voltaire, Shakespeare, Gandhi, and King, can we hear the words of inspiration that will provide us with food for our journey? Where, among the rich grains of wisdom and philosophy that have survived through the centuries, can we find the solution to meet the challenge of the times? Who or what will provide us the light for our many lamps?

WHAT IS THE GREATEST NEED?

The world's needs are many. For most it is money, for others it is health, and yet all yearn for happiness, fame, and fortune. But the greatest need is not contingent upon material possessions, and it can rarely be found in the opinions of others. The highest thoughts are those least dependent upon language. When people are profoundly moved, they do not necessarily speak with the eloquence of literature. What we humans need, rather than mere beauty, are thoughts that breathe and words that burn—words that have the power to ease the heart and lift the spirit; to encourage and sustain; to give hope, faith, and consolation; words for the worried, the ailing, the bereaved, the physically challenged and the emotionally disturbed; words that speak to our condition. We need thoughts that knock at the gates of the soul, that have the ability to solve each and every problem. We need a power that comes from within and recognizes no such reality as a permanent barrier. We need a force that converts defeat into a challenge to greater effort. We need a catalyst that will remove self-imposed limitations such as doubt and fear. We need the God factor that will bring forth fresh opportunities for individual achievement which need not be burdened by yesterday's failures. When thoughts of peace and harmony rise to pierce the soul, we carefully turn them over in our minds and cling to them with all diligence. What is the *greatest need? The greatest need is for prayer.*

THE BREATH OF GOD

There are vast records of men and women who in times of distress prayed for guidance and wisdom, for faith and hearts of steel. In their hour of pain and peril, they turned to the "On High" and earnestly sought help. And such prayer always brought solace. When we pray, we link ourselves with the inexhaustible power that spins the universe. We humbly ask that a part of this power be apportioned to our needs. Even in asking, our human deficiencies are filled and we arise strengthened and renewed. Only in prayer do we achieve that complete and harmonious assembly of body, mind, and spirit that gives the frail human reed its unshakeable strength.

But what is prayer? Prayer is a source of power that at best most of us have only a cursory understanding. Prayer is the heart's sincerest desire. Prayer is the direct application of the dynamic power of the universe. Prayer is a daily appointment with God. "Prayer," it has been written, "is the breath of God." Prayer is not only worship, it is an invisible emanation of humanity's spirit—the most powerful form of energy that one can create. If you make a habit of sincere prayer and "seek His face," your life will be profoundly altered. Prayer places its indelible stamp upon our thoughts and actions. Prayer is a force as real as terrestrial gravity; it's the only power that overcomes the laws of nature. In open defiance of medical science, prayer restores health where all else has failed. Prayer heals the wounds of sorrow and disappointment regardless of their cause. Countless men and women have been lifted out of disease, placed beyond the grips of poverty, and released from the clutches of despair by the serene power of prayer. These acts have been termed miracles. But a constant, hidden miracle takes place in the hearts and minds of individuals who have discovered that prayer supplies them with a steady flow of sustaining power in their daily lives. Prayer quickens the soul and stirs the spirit. The most meaningful life is one that rests on prayer.

BLESSED ASSURANCE

Prayer favors no race, color, or creed; nor is it bound by any sort of religion, ecclesiastical tradition, organized doctrine or dogma. Prayer recognizes no precedent, follows no hard-and-fast rules. Prayer makes kings and queens of the humblest men and women. Prayer transcends all human experience, all education, all knowledge available to mankind. And its only fixed price is that of an unyielding faith—an active applied faith. When we "touch the hem of His garment," when we feel the thrill of the great central force that comes from the heart of truth, we shall no longer doubt, no longer hesitate, no longer be satisfied with the superficial, the material. When the soul consumes its daily bread, when it feels the thrill of the infinite pulse, it no longer is content with mediocrity.

When we realize that we are Divine, when we see that we are a part of the everlasting principle that is the very essence of reality, nothing can throw us off balance. We will realize that we are a part of a great cause and that we were made to dominate and not be dominated. As a result, we will rise to meet every situation. Our peace will not be disturbed. We will soon discover that we are centered in the everlasting truth; a sense that we are in touch with the power that made and upholds the universe. Ours becomes a sense of security and peace. When we awaken in the morning, refreshed and renewed, we feel that we have been drawn "nearer to the cross"; that we have passed the physical and have come into the presence of an infinite force, an infinite life. We have been born again. To some, life has a price tag; but life is priceless. Humanity will never attain its highest power until it learns the power of prayer.

THE POWER OF PRAYER

Many who have achieved the mantle of greatness, oddly enough, cannot account for their accomplishments. They cannot explain why they had implicit confidence, nor are they able to identify the factors that resulted in their success. But they are aware that *something within* got a glimpse of their dormant power and possibilities. Ironically, when they could not see a ray of light, something else urged them to hold on; that, in spite of appearances, their dreams and hopes would prove true. It told them so because they had been in communication with the Divine. They had passed the bounds of the limited and had entered the domain of the limitless.

When we exercise the power of prayer, we are stimulating and increasing the strength of the very resources that enable us to do the thing we have set out to do. It is through prayer that the uncertain is cleared away as we come into oneness with the Blessed One. It is through prayer that we succeed in spite of the odds, that we experience our greatest victories. We cannot escape tough times—we cannot avoid the inevitable—but prayer prepares the way. It is through prayer that we make a life, not just a living. It is through prayer that we uncover our true nature. It is through prayer that we move from mess to miracle. It is through prayer that we are placed in touch with the infinite—a new way to unbounded possibilities, limitless power. It is through prayer that we destroy the greatest enemies of achievement—fear and doubt. Prayer is the miracle worker of the ages; it removes any obstacle that impedes our progress. Prayer enables us to shout through tears, to dance through pain. It is through prayer that we will complete our mission— the conviction to realize our life's calling. Thoughts are forces, and the constant affirmation of our inherent right and will to succeed will change inhospitable conditions to those more favorable. If we resolve upon success with energy and determination, we will eventually create a success consciousness that will literally force our desires to come to bear.

There are times when misfortune and tragedy might overtake us; moments when we experience reversals in our careers, when sickness and disease attack our bodies, when we can only see midnight at midday. It is prayer that sees us through. And how do we expedite this process? By kneeling down to stand up. Through the power of prayer. Prayer is the doorway to destiny!

CALM SEAS IN A STORM OF CONFUSION

An ocean liner was caught in a terrible storm. It seemed that at any moment the seaworthy vessel would capsize. As one of the passengers sought safety, he saw a small child sitting in the middle of the ship's dining room, playing with a toy, seemingly oblivious to the chaos and confusion around him. Frantically, the passenger ran up to him and screamed, "You'd better put on your life vest and find your parents. We're in the middle of a storm!"

The little boy looked up at the stranger and calmly replied, "Thank you, mister, but I'm not worried. My daddy is the captain of the ship."

There are people who question how you can keep on believing when everything is turning against you. There may be some who wonder how you can hold your head high when your world is crashing all around. There may be a few who ask how you can keep smiling when you're going through one of the toughest storms in your life. In one word: prayer. Prayer enables us to believe the unbelievable and achieve the impossible. It is prayer that makes men and women gods, whose will must be obeyed. Prayer changes lives. Prayer has transformed sighs into songs; gloom into glory; burdens into blessings; sadness into gladness; and tragedy into triumph. Few people realize how much prayer has to do with success. The great majority never seem to think that it is a creative force. Yet prayer is not only a real power but one of the greatest resources known to mankind. In fact, our deeds will be in direct proportion to the intensity and persistence of our discipline to pray. Show me a high achiever and I will show you a man or woman who makes prayer a part of his or her life. No prayer, no achievement. All-absorbing prayer, remarkable achievement. Prayer is not something we do to the Creator, but to ourselves. It is not a position, but a disposition; it is not asking, but knowing. It is not the words, but the feeling. Though we may leave this place, we need not leave His presence. Prayer is the willingness to talk with God.

Prayer is the cornerstone to fame and fortune. The creative principle, the law of achievement, does not vary any more than the law of gravity. The Creator cannot fulfill your desire in any other way, no more than He can make the sun turn from its course in the heavens. Here lies the difference between the person who lives by chance and circumstance—

"the blind leading the blind"—and the individual who believes in his destiny, who possesses the committed prayer life, who has unquestioned faith in his mission, who believes that he is a part of the Divine plan and that he rests in the current of the spiritual flow. The greatest minds of all ages have drawn their strength from the invisible source; from their vital connection with the power that creates and works through each of us.

PRAYER, ACTION, WORK

It's not important to understand how prayer works—only that it does. It is a matter of record. There are many mysteries in the cosmos that we may never understand, but we do know that there are certain universal laws that always apply. Through the power of prayer, we can use those laws to direct our own lives into positive, productive channels. Please note, however, that prayer is participatory, not passive. It isn't enough to ask for guidance, you must take action. Anything worth praying for is worth working for. The success cycle is *prayer, action, work!* You can achieve any goal you set for yourself by following this cycle.

If your prayers go unanswered, it is because they are not backed by faith and effort. The invisible is made visible by two mighty instruments—prayer and work. Your prayers go unheeded because you don't truly believe you will receive or because you fail to back your request with the necessary effort to turn dreams into reality. To earnestly pray for desires and not work for them is a mockery. To ask the everlasting Father to give us that which we seek but are too lazy to strive for is begging. In response to our prayers, we receive our universal supply. But if you think your stumbling blocks will be removed, or your wishes realized without lifting a finger, you may pray until kingdom come without ever receiving an answer. Prayer without faith is of no avail; and *faith without work is dead.*

RETURN TO THE SOURCE

"I and the Father are one!"

"I am the vine, ye are the branches."

We are as closely united to each other, and all to the Father, as are the branches to the tree. When we are conscious of our union, of our partnership with the infinite, we feel an added power, just as the branch feels the force of the life currents flowing into it from the vine.

Our individual strength comes from our conscious contact with Omnipotence. Each human being is like a drop of water in the ocean: interconnected in every way. We are not independent. We cannot work alone. Consciously or unconsciously, each individual is a part of those around him. He is touched by other drops of water on every side, and his existence and success are largely dependent upon his interconnectedness with his fellow human beings. Even if a drop of the ocean could separate itself from the mass and try to live its own life in its own way, it would soon cease to exist as a drop. It takes reinforcement and association to provide strength and power. Once again, the process by which we all interconnect with our Maker is prayer.

As long as we know and pursue the "true idea" and live within the sunlight of the Creator's spirit and the "right mental attitude," all of our possibilities are open, all of our channels are free, all of our powers are wondrously alive. Our minds are activated, accentuated, elevated, and we can live and walk in the light and power that streams to us and through us. But when we walk in the shadows of dismal doubt, damp denial, dumb disbelief, discouraging dismay, depressing despair, we droop and drop. Our possibilities are closed, our channels are clogged, our powers are diminished, our hopes are frustrated, our minds are dead and dull, and we are tragically cut short. Like a sunflower hidden from the sun, we close and dry up. And when we get in that condition, the only answer we can give to life's demands and love's obligation is to say "I can't."

I can't find a job; I can't finish high school; I can't go to college; I can't pass my courses; I can't stand my boss; I can't stand the racism; I can't let go of a bad habit; I can't stop drinking; I can't stop smoking; I can't lose this excess weight; I can't shake this cold; I can't be the person I ought to be; I can't do what is expected of me; I can't love my wife; I can't respect my husband; I can't understand my parents; I can't communicate with my children!

I can't. I can't. I can't! That's all you can say when you're living outside of the sunlight of God's amazing power, when you're living beyond the source of all goodness.

"If only things would change," you cry. What is it that changes things? Wishing, or dreaming, or hoping? Can you expect circumstances to change while you merely sit down and *wish* them to change? How long would it take to construct a house if you only sat on a pile of bricks and *hoped* that the foundation would go up? Wishing and dreaming do not amount to much unless they are backed by sweat, discipline, determination, and prayer. But it is prayer that truly changes things.

If you have failed to reach a new spiritual high, if you are unable to stand tall against the forces of fear and doubt, maybe—just maybe—

your God is too small. It is only when you can accept infinity, boundless without dimension, timeless throughout eternity, holy beyond reverence, and know that you, in some spiritual way, play a role—only then can you stand tall. In prayer, yours is a life that can never be forfeited. Through prayer, you can experience a power that can never be exhausted. Thanks to prayer, you will be a victor who can never be defeated. And, as soon as you pray, your joy can never be diminished.

LET US PRAY

The call to prayer is heard throughout all languages by every form of religion. "Pray about it" is common advice to the troubled heart. "Prayer changes things" and "The family that prays together stays together" are popular slogans stressing the importance of prayer. But what do we mean by prayer?

A study of prayer in various denominations reveals how far humanity has strayed from the true idea. We find prayers of flattery, whereby we expect a jealous God to be moved by praise. There are pleading and begging prayers intended to coax a miracle from a reluctant God. There are educated and vain prayers, where those who ask are hoping that, if they pray long enough and eloquently enough, an apparently inattentive God may be impressed and respond. In many cases, prayer has been reduced to a sacramental ritual performed only by those "trained in the word." Thus, the typical prayer begs and pleads, is couched in pious language, is carefully intoned and vainly repetitious. Unfortunately, this process leaves the multitudes thirsty with a heightened sense of frustration and an absence of any real sense of communion.

Many of us have been trapped in a religion steeped in superstition and doctrine that has left the faithful in deeper bondage than if the participant would have turned a deaf ear. How easy it is to fall into the practice of reciting rote prayers that leave the heart unchanged. We blindly worship the symbols and forsake the spiritual truths that lie behind them. We have deluded ourselves by believing that outward acts can take the place of interior changes in thought, feeling, and consciousness. How easy it is to voice the phrase "prayer changes things." Prayer does not change things unless it first changes our attitude and state of mind. We can never alter the Creator's attitude toward us. We can only change our attitude toward Him. The sincerest prayer may be the longing of the heart to cultivate a talent or the intense desire to be of greater service. Whatever we envision and struggle to attain is a genuine prayer.

You are a thinking being, and your mind is the connecting link between you and the Creator. The Almighty is spirit and "they that worship Him must worship in spirit and truth." This is the key to the *greatest need.* Prayer is not a matter of words or outer forms, but an awareness of consciousness, right-directed, spiritually guided positive thinking! Your personal transformation comes from knowing deep within that each and every human being is far more than a physical body, and that the essence of being human includes the ability to think and feel, to possess a higher consciousness, and to know that there is an intelligence engaging the entire universe. You are able to tap into that invisible part of you, to use your mind in any manner that you choose, and to recognize that this is your essential humanity. Your humanness—soul, pure and perfect—is not a form or body at all, but something infinitely more Divine. So before you changed your friends; before you changed your clothes; before you changed your name; before you changed your place of worship; and before you changed your mind—you were an idea in the mind of God. You are still a soul with a body rather than a body with a soul. You are not a human being having a spiritual experience, but rather a spiritual being having a human experience.

SIX MENTAL SHIFTS FOR GREATER SPIRITUAL AWARENESS

When you understand the truth about life and the source of your being, about who you are, where you come from, where you are going, and what God is, you are *free!* Free from all preconceived notions, free from the ways of the world. You experience wholeness. You achieve a breakthrough to a new spiritual awareness. However, there are essential elements—mental "shifts"—that must be understood to experience an ever-increasing spiritual awareness. They can be considered steps toward personal fulfillment. Take them up, one by one, and incorporate them into your daily life. You must shift from one state of mind to a higher one.

FEAR TO FAITH

A shift from fear to faith is a shift from outer to inner, from worrying about the circumstances around you to a calm, quiet inner awareness that the Creator "is in His glory and all is right with the world." The great enemy of happiness and achievement is, and always has been, fear—fear of failure, fear of rejection, fear of criticism, fear of poor health, fear of not measuring up to the expectations of others, and so on. When we are fearful, we become tense and uptight. As a result, our mental faculties shut down. We do and say things that under normal conditions we would never say. But when we increase our faith and turn our problems over to a higher power, miraculously, everything seems to take care of itself. We begin to "lay up our treasures in heaven." We recognize that God is our source of supply; "He is sufficient unto today." We become conscious of our strengths more so than our weaknesses.

Faith was the great characteristic of the Master. The word was constantly on his lips: "According to thy faith be it unto you"; "Thy faith has made thee whole"; "Thy faith has saved thee." Faith believes; doubt fears. Faith creates; doubt destroys. Faith opens the door to all things desirable in life; doubt closes it. Faith excites and arouses our creative forces. It cracks open the door of ability. Faith is the Divine messenger sent to guide men and women blinded by doubt and trepidation. The individual who cannot see the Designer behind the design, who does not see Infinite Intelligence behind all creation, cannot possess the sublime faith that buoys up great achievement. No one can rise higher than his or her faith. We have within us every moment of our lives the potential for greatness. Suffering builds character, character builds faith, and faith will prove itself in the end!

HOPE TO BELIEF

Hope is the raw material with which you build success. Hope crystallizes into faith, faith into determination, and determination into action. Hope springs eternal from your imagination, from your dreams of a better world, a better life, a better tomorrow. But throughout all the mystical teachings, the keynote to harmony has been "Do you believe?" The world is full of people who are hoping and praying that things turn out okay. But belief, according to the philosopher William James, *creates the actual fact.* The Bible states the same proposition this way: "According to your faith [belief] it is done unto you." To put it another way, you do not necessarily believe what you see but you *see* what you believe. When you develop a deep-seated belief or conviction that you will obtain your desires, you activate forces and powers that pull you toward your goals and your goals toward you. Whereas hope may uplift, regenerate, and inspire, belief becomes your reality. We walk, talk, and interact with others in a manner consistent with our beliefs.

A teacher asked a young boy, "Can you play a musical instrument?"

"I don't know," the child replied. "I never tried." In a way, many of us are like that young student. We're not aware of our full capabilities. We shouldn't be so quick to sell ourselves short. We should refuse to accept limitations on our potential. Studies have revealed that we can do far more than we've ever realized. There is always a strong case made for maintaining hope that will contribute to our life's purpose. However, if you are to win in the end, this dimmer of hope must grow into belief.

DOUBTING TO TRUSTING

The perfect order of the universe always operates as a law of right action. This perfect right action governs the seasons as they change from fall to winter, spring to summer. It is why the day is always followed by night. It explains why we can go through difficult times and be grateful for the lessons we have gleaned from our experiences; why we trust that life gets better as it goes on. This is the natural process of the universe. Life is a part of this spiritual trust. You are guardian and administrator of your trust. It is your responsibility to guard and ensure its safety.

The best way to complete your assignment is to allow yourself to be led by Infinite Intelligence—the still, small voice. Trust it. Place your full and unwavering confidence in it: "Trust in the Lord with all thine heart . . . and it shall direct thy paths." Rid yourself of doubt. Doubt blinds us to all types of possibilities. Continue to move from doubt to trust. When you trust in a higher power, when you claim your spiritual unity with the infinite to direct your life, you are empowering the most capable and benevolent tool. The key to peace and plenty is to allow yourself to be guided by spiritual power. Trust in it.

ANGER AND BLAME TO
FORGIVING AND FORGETTING

The most important principle of spiritual development is the principle of forgiveness. Our natural tendency is to always blame others when things don't work out. Guilt, blame, and judgment go hand in hand. But we break free from the bondage of guilt and blame by practicing the law of forgiveness in everything we do. As long as we continue to judge others, we will be enslaved to negative emotions and preoccupied with assessing blame. Judging others opens the door to a negative mental attitude as well as blame. It has been written, "Judge not, that you be not judged. For with what judgment you judge, you will be judged; and with the same measure you use, it will be measured back to you."

Nearly all negative emotions depend on the catalyst of blame for their existence. Once you stop blaming, you shut off the flow of negativity. You become positive and accepting. Your consciousness takes on a new aura. Forgiving others is the key to the kingdom of heaven. When you stop blaming, judging, and condemning others, you begin forgiving and forgetting any transgression that may have been done to you. You experience a feeling of release and happiness. You free yourself from any negativity that others may have caused. Failure to do so may give someone else the power over your emotions. You can't forgive while holding a grudge. Usually, the very thought of past indiscretions may set you off on an emotional roller coaster. By constantly blessing and forgiving those in question, you break your connection to negative emotion. You are now able to turn the other cheek, to turn your consciousness to higher and better thoughts. It's time to let go and let God.

FRANTIC ACTIVITY TO MEDITATION

You may speak to the Creator in your words and thoughts, but He answers you in the silence that you allow. When you sit perfectly quietly still in meditation, you open yourself up to receive the answers to the mysteries of life: "Be still, and know that I am God."

When we plug a battery into a charger, it doesn't indicate how much it needs recharging. It simply and quietly accepts the inflow of energy. In the same manner, when we pray, the Creator tells us we should go into the depths of our being and shut out the concerns of the world: "When you pray, go into your room, and when you have shut your door, pray to your Father who is in the secret place; and your Father who sees in secret will reward you openly."

Men and women begin to become great when they listen. As we grow in understanding of the truth of our relationship with God, as we begin to see ourselves in the light of our divinity, prayer becomes an experience in the silence. In solitude, we should center our thoughts on the perfect outcome of every situation and circumstance in our lives. During meditation, fears dissipate. We enter a state of restful alertness. Like the battery that needs recharging, we can now tap into the flow of positive energy.

Take up the practice of meditation. Sit quietly and concentrate on the desires of your heart. Think about your goals, dreams, aspirations, and challenges with complete confidence that the answers you seek will come when you are ready to receive them. Your job is to become patient and in a position to receive your good.

MAKING A LIVING TO
MAKING A DIFFERENCE

The truly successful in all walks of life focus more on making a difference than on making money. They're more concerned with practicing the presence of God than being caught up with the ways of the world. Spiritual development is the most important activity that you can do. As you develop spiritually, you begin to live by grace. Life is growth and unfoldment. The average person lives his life from the outside in. He is constantly caught in the web of frustration when he allows his level of consciousness to be determined by what people think, say, or do. He becomes little more than a barometer of worldly events. But when he centers his being on thoughts from above, he is not "conformed to this world; he is transformed by the renewing of his mind." This individual becomes the "salt of the earth." Making an impact on the lives of his brothers and sisters is now of tantamount importance.

Nathaniel Hawthorne, the nineteenth-century American novelist, warned us that it is much easier to capture a butterfly than to grasp that elusive feeling called happiness. "Happiness," he wrote, "when it comes in this world, comes incidentally. Make it the object of pursuit and it will lead you on a wild-goose chase and never be attained."

Happiness that endures, lies within. Waste no time and effort searching for peace, contentment, and joy in a world locked in materialism. There is no happiness in having or in getting, but only in giving. So reach out. Share. Love. Hug. If society is in trouble today, it is not because of the wrath of God. It is due to the darkness in the minds of men and women. The kingdom of heaven is still within, and "the mind that was in Christ Jesus" is available to each of us. Move toward making a difference by working out your own salvation.

WATCHING AND WAITING, LOOKING ABOVE

Men and women who have left their mark on the world know the value of a prayer-filled life. They obey the voice, the God urge within, which not only leads but lifts the race to greater heights. Prayer led them through the wilderness of doubt. Prayer told them that they could proceed safely even in the dark, when little or no light was visible. Prayer put them in touch with the infinite; it is the truth of their being. Without this essential trait, there would be a great lack or longing in their lives. If each of us could grasp this superb truth, the oneness with the creative principle of the universe, it would transform the race.

This is the manner in which you can live life to your spiritual advantage. Prayer is of the utmost importance. Find time in your life for daily prayer and meditation. Place your attitudes, thoughts, and deeds on par with God truths. There is one place in which each of us will return after our physical death. We are all one family in God, created by the Almighty: "In Him we live and have our being."

Put aside your thoughts of nationality and begin to think in terms of humanity. Dismiss any thoughts of "my religion" and think in terms of spirituality and the unity of mankind. A hearty prayer life is the essential ingredient to survival—your survival in life eternal. The life which is lived on earth is but a small part of your being. Your reality lies within the spirit. It is the spirit which is made in the image and likeness of God. Appreciate the beauty in this world and strive to do your part to care for humanity. Lift as you climb; obey the call of the Almighty through prayer. Pray for your brothers and sisters. Pray for those who curse and spite you. Pray for peace to be in the hearts and minds of men and women. Pray with your heart and soul. Pray in your rising up and in your lying down; in your going out and in your coming in. But pray!

"Speak the word and my servant shall be healed," the centurion said to the Christ. "You only need to say it and it will be done so." Though they were divided by culture and religion, they were united by prayer. And when the Roman guard returned home, he found his servant healed. When he asked at what hour the slave had begun to improve, the soldier was told it was the seventh hour—the very time of day he had requested of the Christ. There's power in the blood.

George Washington Carver once remarked, "My prayers seem to be more of an attitude than anything else. I indulge in no lip service but ask the great God silently, daily, and throughout the day to permit me to speak to Him. I ask for wisdom, understanding, and strength to carry out His will. As a result, I am asking and receiving all the time."

Nothing contributes more to good health than a strong will and spirit. Spirit braces the body, enabling it to endure hardships, disappointments, and disease. Fear frequently trips the robust, but the quiet reverence of prayer administers the magic potion. No regimen of drugs can coax as much healing as a single ray of hope. God never made His work for man alone to mend.

In 1993, Ben Vereen celebrated two key moments in his life: his birthday—the anniversary of his entry into this world—and the day he came close to leaving it. In June of that year, Vereen was hit by a car as he walked along a dark stretch of the Pacific Coast Highway. For the next three weeks, in the intensive-care unit at UCLA, he lay motionless, suffering from severe internal injuries as well as a fractured right leg. He entered the hospital in a coma, barely breathing. A tracheotomy saved his life but left a hole in his windpipe. When he finally regained consciousness, the thought that he would ever sing and dance again seemed remote. Yet less than a year later, the award-winning entertainer was back on Broadway, headlining in *Jelly's Last Jam* and amazing audiences with his stamina. What was the Divine remedy that soothed his ailments and restored his soul? By no other means could his health have been restored so completely and so quickly. He revealed his spiritual nature and shared his secret during a Sunday morning church service.

"After the doctors had done all they could do," Vereen recalls, "I knew that I could only ask for God to put His angels to work. When we pray, we open a Divine channel. Sometimes we can't see what God is already giving us, but we must have faith. If we claim His word, we know that His power will prevail. It's amazing what you can see with your eyes closed."

Prayer will steady the heart and strengthen the will; it will give force to the thought and courage to the hand until what was only a possibility becomes a reality. So deep are the scars of segregation that, even to this day when retired judge and Harvard professor A. Leon Higginbotham reflects upon that mountaintop called separate and equal, he dries an eye. When asked how his race survived this most bitter period of American history, he quoted the words of his forefathers and -mothers, and said, "Lord! My soul looks back and wonders how we got over."

Five days a week you can observe success in action by tuning into *The Oprah Winfrey Show.* This program, the highest-rated talk show in television history, earned an estimated $40 million for its host in the mid-1990s. Besides owning the production company that produces this show, Winfrey's Harpo Productions also owns the studio where the show is taped. In addition, Winfrey has diversified her business by purchasing a restaurant, producing an off-Broadway play, and making films and other television programs. Barely forty, Oprah came to her success with characteristics that society routinely categorizes as obstacles: She's black and female. She frequently shares her experiences in the course of her program and tells viewers about her own personal growth and setbacks. Yet Oprah credits her personal philosophy as the secret of her success, reminding her audience that inner beliefs and attitudes are as important as hard work.

"The Bible has taught us, metaphysics has taught us, myth has taught us," she points out, "that if you get into the flow, if you do what you're supposed to do, you'll be rewarded with riches you've never imagined. What I have received is the natural order of things. You would be shocked as to what you can accomplish when you rid yourself of the slave mentality."

How does one get into the flow of the universe? How do you receive the natural order of things? How do you rid yourself of the slave mentality? By giving the soul expression; by seeking oneness with the Divine; by sharing the power of the wonderful counselor; by a willingness to follow the voice of your soul. By prayer!

"On some cases," Deborah Hyde confesses, "I will not go into the operating room until I get down on my knees and pray." As only one of four black female neurosurgeons in the country, each day Dr. Hyde advances her profession and her spirit with skilled hands and an obedient heart. Her career has been built upon prayer. "I believe God uses me. I feel I'm an instrument, and I try so hard to be deserving."

He's a showstopper, a tough act to follow. Denzel Washington is at the top of his game. His presence draws hordes of admirers to theaters around the globe to view his films. As one of Hollywood's top-grossing leading men, Washington is among a small cadre of actors who can write their own ticket. Over the course of a twenty-year career, he has earned an Academy Award and several Oscar nominations for his memorable character portrayals. Female readers of a major magazine listed him as the man they would most like to spend an evening with. Yet this says nothing about the texture and the fabric of the man. After arriving in South Africa, the first leg of a four-week vacation, Washington immediately set out to St. George's Cathedral in Cape Town, where he would renew his wedding vows. The son of a beautician mother and a minister father, he has an ongoing conversation with God. "The Lord has blessed me with a beautiful wife and family," he openly shared, "and I intend to keep my part of the bargain."

If she said it once, she said it a million times:

God is my health, I cannot be sick;
God is my strength, unfailing quick;
God is my all, I know no fear,
Since God and love and Truth are here.

As a college student in Houston, Texas, Dr. Barbara King, pastor of one of the largest churches in the nation, overcame a life-threatening bout with tuberculosis. Frail and weak but up to the task, she was cleared to resume her studies after spending four years in a sanitarium. During her ordeal, Dr. Barbara, as she is affectionately called, had come to the following spiritual awakening: "The answer to our prayers lies within. They are answered by obeying spiritual laws—those closest to the soul. Test me, if you must—but just pray in truth and see if the chorus of the heavens rings loud and clear!" It's no secret that the Creator gives us the ingredients for our daily bread, but He expects us to do the baking.

Though urban radio claimed it as a best-selling hit single, Curtis Mayfield's "We're Moving on Up" was more than a rallying cry or a call to honor African American history and culture. Call it Top 40, call it rhythm and blues, call it what you may, but it was a prayer for deliverance and empowerment. It was this bead on the rosary that gave form and definition to a new consciousness of unity and pride. There is barely a bar in the music that doesn't preach, "Yes, Lord!"

When an individual catches a glimpse of the enormous power locked within his nature, he will never doubt again. His faith is established, and he will never rest until he brings out all that he has to offer. "My 'secret,' " says the pizza mogul Herman Cain, "is my belief in Almighty God! There's never been a time in my life when He didn't bring me through. It's not that I'm so great—it's just that the God in me is greater."

> My "secret" is my belief in Almighty God! He receives all the glory in everything I do and in every success I've achieved. It's not that I'm so great—it's just that the God in me is greater.
>
> —Herman Cain

There is a Divine voice within us which only speaks when all other voices are hushed. It only renders its message in the silence. Carol Gist, when asked how she managed to capture the Miss USA crown, the first African American woman to do so, simply turned her eyes toward the sky.

Paula Abdul has loads of talent, but talent alone could not secure her a spot on the cheerleading squad at the University of California-Northridge. When she was told by her teammates that she was out of her element, she sank to her knees. But she didn't stay there long. "God hath not giveth the spirit of fear." Oh, you know the rest of the story. Today, she is one of Hollywood's rising choreographers. It was grace that lifted her.

Straight As at Yale could not guarantee a Rhodes Scholarship, but prayer did! "We have many impressive candidates," was the response given to Kurt Schmoke by the admissions committee. "We'll let you know." One of the youngest in his class and the only black applicant, Schmoke returned to his Baltimore home and did what we all do in times of crisis—he praised His holy name! As the future mayor of the nation's thirteenth largest city, during a follow-up interview, Schmoke stepped to the front with the confidence of one who belonged there. It wasn't long before his ability was recognized and his place conceded. Prayer was the raw material from which he carved his career.

Prayer has been the power that has moved mountains, that has fought battles and shifted men and women of note to higher planes of thought and life. It has been the fundamental principle of human achievement and personal development. Even in the world of professional sports, prayer plays a role.

Hidden beneath the mud-crusted face mask and soiled jersey of the Green Bay Packers lies the indomitable spirit of the man teammates reverently call "the Minister of Defense." Physically gifted and worshiped by thousands, All-Pro defensive tackle Reggie White, however, worships someone else. At the conclusion of each game—win, lose, or tie—White can be found at the fifty-yard line holding hands with other believers basking in God's word. When narrow-minded league officials tried to end his weekly demonstration, the ordained Baptist minister leaned upon the scriptures, quoting Revelation: "And they overcame him by the blood of the lamb and by the word of their testimony."

And who could ever forget? Michael Jordan, who has been called "the most exciting player in NBA history," has shown that the game can be played in a manner that no one before him imagined. During seventeen agonizing and painful months, millions of basketball fans around the world had wished for it, hoped for it, and even prayed for it. And just when it appeared their prayers had fallen on deaf ears, on March 18, 1995, their answer came in a two-word statement: "I'm back!" With that long-awaited announcement, Jordan—already immortalized in bronze outside the arena where he had captured his glory—began his storied comeback.

Millions of individuals attempt to extract honey from the hive of life without getting stung. Marc Antony sought happiness in love; Brutus in glory; Caesar in dominion. Are the rich and wise the happiest? The wealthy experience the best that life has to offer. But wealth alone has no power to produce success. The educated can impress with their depth and breadth of knowledge. But scholarship alone cannot deliver peace of mind. The cultured and refined can wine and dine with kings and queens. But sooner or later, even the vain are left thirsting for something more fulfilling. Contentment consists not in adding to your treasure house, but in subtracting your desires. It is only when men and women turn from the ways of the world and march on to Zion that they experience true happiness.

Give me the man or woman who sees righteousness in his cause, who believes there is a remedy for every wrong, a purpose for every soul; the man or woman who sees the best in everyone, who sees beauty and hope where others see ugliness and disgust. Give me the man or woman who believes in the ultimate triumph of truth over error, of harmony over discord, of love over hate, of purity over vice, of light over darkness, of life over death. Give me the man and woman of God!

As a teacher, Thomas A. Fleming knows it takes special skills to make all children feel valued, especially if the students are caught in a vicious cycle of abuse, neglect, failure, drugs, and crime. "But with prayer," Fleming attests, "all things are possible.

"I've seen this principle work in my life," he continues, reciting the scriptures. "I tell my students that, if they can internalize the optimism of the gospel, if they can see the stars instead of the mud in their lives, they can reach their dreams." Each day he continues to provide a beacon of hope as he walks into his classroom to teach kids few believe in—juvenile offenders.

Fleming can openly relate. He has known the bitter taste of poverty, racism, and illiteracy. And like these children, at one point in his life, he, too, was on a downward spiral. In 1950, as a seventeen-year-old running with a tough crowd in inner-city Detroit, Fleming was barely literate. He had lost all interest in school and had dropped out. He then lied his way into the National Guard to escape the long arm of the law. He never knew his father, and the searing agony of raising a child with no resources became too much for his mother to bear.

It would be years before he would know it, but Fleming did have a force for good in his life. He was raised and nurtured by the love and faith of Carrie and Gordon Starks, his grandparents. Although his grandfather could not read and his grandmother had only a third-grade education, they taught their grandson about the power of prayer. "My grandmother was a big part of my life," Fleming remembers. "She was the spiritual core of our family. She told me to have faith in God's word and to trust His promises. 'Son,' my grandmother advised, 'whenever you're in trouble, read your Bible and pray.' " It would be a while, however, before her counsel would take hold. And then something happened!

After joining the National Guard, Fleming served with the occupation troops in Germany. He had grown accustomed to European hospitality and decided to frequent his favorite French pub. The next morning he woke up as he did so many times before—hung over from a drinking binge, broke from gambling his money away, and barely able to dress for inspection. Fearing for his health and hoping to keep his job, he decided to change. Recalling his grandmother's advice, he picked up a government-issue New Testament, only to discover that he could barely read! His comprehension was poor at best.

"At that moment, I realized I was illiterate. Frightened and in a panic, I sought out the base chaplain. Unfortunately, he couldn't help me. I then found a Bible study group that met weekly on the base. Trying to disguise my embarrassment, I leveled with them. With open hearts they agreed to help me. Their warm gesture altered the direction of my life." With their tutoring, Fleming learned to read as a whole new world burst forth. The first book he read by himself was the Gospel of Mark.

After his tour ended, Fleming returned home and found work in an automobile plant on the assembly-line floor. Armed with an insatiable desire to learn, he earned a high school equivalency diploma at night, and eventually graduated from Detroit Bible College several years later with a bachelor's degree in religious education. In 1968, he received a master of arts degree in special education from Eastern Michigan University. For the next twenty years, Fleming would go back to his roots and teach in the most challenging classroom in the country—the United States juvenile corrections system. His students are juvenile detention inmates in Ann Arbor, Michigan. And like their teacher many years before, many of them can neither read nor write.

Over the years, Fleming has developed a number of effective methods for reaching troubled youths. In his "reading laboratory," he becomes his students' stenographer as they enhance their vocabulary and comprehension skills. This personal attention encourages initiative as students eventually desire to learn on their own. Moreover, Fleming always connects the world of knowledge with the hidden world of values. For example, when explaining economics and the history of capitalism, Fleming will prod his class to question whether the nation's wealth creators used their money wisely and ethically. "Were they responsible to the rest of humanity?" he quizzes. "Were they their brothers' and sisters' keepers?" He desperately wants his students to understand the role that values and purpose play in their lives. "We are not here just to receive gifts," he instructs, "but to also be givers."

Perhaps the secret of Fleming's success is that he never gives up on a student, just as his grandparents never gave up on him. His faith inspires his pupils to have faith in themselves, perhaps for the first time in their young lives. "I see a light in these kids," he says. "By God's grace, I can see the innocence and beauty inside. So many have an emptiness at the core of their being, a hunger that can only be met by truth and love. Without faith in a higher power, they can never know happiness and success."

Fleming's words have reached thousands, and to each he teaches the same life-changing lesson he learned as a youth: Whenever you're in trouble, read your Bible and pray. In 1992, thanks in part to his grandmother's wisdom, he was chosen from more than 2 million elementary and secondary public school teachers as the National Teacher of the Year. Among other civic and business leaders, Fleming received a crystal apple, indicative of educational excellence, from President George Bush during a White House ceremony.

It is important to note that Thomas Fleming started life with few advantages. Though poverty and obscurity may have impeded his progress, a solid faith and the power of prayer made him equal to the task. There is an immense difference between the chances of the individual who begins with truth and understanding, with the Almighty on his lips as well as in his heart, and the man or woman with no relationship with God. There is no grander sight than the person down on bended knee.

ANCIENT SECRETS

There is nothing more thrilling or instructive than the wisdom that is contained in the great spiritual books: the Koran; the Bhagavad-Gita, the sacred book of the East; the Upanishad, the sacred book of ancient India; the *Analects* of Confucius; the Dhammapada, which contains the moral teachings of Buddha; the Talmud and the Torah, great books of the Jewish faith; and the Holy Bible. Throughout history, humanity has been moved to action by the knowledge and principles found on the pages of these scriptural guides. At the core of each book are universal laws of abundance and supply that govern the universe. These laws are spiritual guideposts that exist on a grand cosmic scale. All that is good, all that is bountiful and beautiful, all that has been or ever will be, emanates from these pages. They are the fountain from which achievement, both great and small, flows forth. Anyone with ordinary intelligence can understand the message of peace, prosperity, and happiness that is incorporated within these books.

For centuries, organized religion, specifically clergy and laypeople, have written about, rhapsodized, and openly discussed these life-changing ideas. Unfortunately, much of their dialogue and teachings has been enshrouded and couched in mystique and misinterpretation. As a result, the deeper, inner, spiritual meaning of the words and deeds of the Creator leaves followers confused and unable to separate the wheat from the chaff. We often quote scripture with our lips but not our minds. The great powers hidden behind the words have been lost upon "human ears." In order to understand their full meaning, it is necessary to go behind the words. We must search for the inner meaning of the message.

Since our Maker blew breath into Adam, mankind has been on a spiritual journey and quest for knowledge and understanding. Collectively, we have been through hills and valleys, experiences with elements of both heaven and hell. Through it all, humanity has survived with an inner strength and conviction in the absolute, unconditional power and presence of God. The greatest challenge today is to provide mankind with truth and wisdom that enables us to discover the power within. The following story clearly illustrates this point.

Many centuries ago, an African king sent his son to the temple to study under one of the tribe's great spiritual leaders. Because the prince was to succeed his father as king, the wise old sage was charged with teaching the boy the basics of success, abundance, and prosperity. When the prince arrived at the temple gates, the master sent him alone deep into the forest surrounding the village. After several months of introspection, the prince returned to the temple to describe all that he had heard.

"What did you hear, my son?" the old man asked.

"Master," the prince replied energetically, "I could hear the birds chirping, the owls hooting, the leaves rustle, the bees buzzing, and the whistling of the wind."

When the young boy had finished, his teacher was visibly upset. Not receiving the answer that he wanted, he instructed the prince to visit the forest again. "Go back," he urged, "and this time, listen more intently—to *all the sounds* within the forest." The young warrior was puzzled by the old man's request. Had he not discerned every sound already?

For days and nights on end, the boy sat motionless in the woods unable to detect any other sounds. Then one morning, as he sat silently beneath the sun, the prince began to discern faint sounds unlike those he had ever heard before. The more acutely he listened, the clearer the noises became. A feeling of enlightenment eveloped his being. He reflected, "These must be the sounds the master wished me to discern."

When the prince returned to the temple, the old man asked what he had heard. "Master," he responded, "when I listened more closely, I could hear the unheard—the sounds of the flowers opening, the sound of the sun warming the earth, and the sound of the grass drinking the morning dew."

The wise old sage nodded in agreement. "To hear the unheard," he remarked, "is a necessary discipline for achievement. For only when an individual has learned to listen closely with his or her inner ear, to spiritually discern and translate all that is being said or communicated, will he or she be able to uncover the ancient secrets to success, prosperity, and happiness."

As you advance in your quest for greater spiritual awareness, read the parables and take in the lessons of truth contained within each great book. Listen. Listen intently. Listen to all the sounds and voices. Discern and translate these words of wisdom with an inner ear, with a higher consciousness of spiritual renewal. Each book is a metaphysical textbook, a manual for the growth of the soul. Each word, subject, and story, whether true or allegorical, looks at all questions from the broadest possible point of view. It is written, "The letter killeth but the spirit gives life." The goal of each message is not to confuse or to confine the reader, but to regenerate, to develop the soul, to become a witness. When properly interpreted, you will discover that you are the dancer and the dance, the creator and the creation, and peace and prosperity are merely yours for the asking. As you study the following samples from the Bible, you, too, will be empowered to hear all the voices within God's kingdom.

THE INNER VOICES OF PRAYER

Blessed are the poor in spirit: for theirs is the kingdom of heaven.

Most religious teachings identify poverty as a virtue: Suffer patiently through your poverty, for in some future heaven you will have your reward. Unfortunately, this is a gross misunderstanding. To be "poor in spirit or pride" means to be empty of the desire to exercise your personal will in the quest for self-realization. You cannot storm the gates of heaven. You cannot achieve an understanding of God through intellect alone. "Blessed are the poor in pride." Blessed are those who can relinquish the attempt to understand intellectually, who accept the full meaning of spirit as a little child. Blessed are those who are teachable, open-minded, receptive to the truth, and who let go of all preconceived opinions. In other words, before you can actually understand what is being taught, you must be teachable; you must be "poor in spirit or pride"; you must be willing to say, "I don't know the answer, but I am willing to learn."

So the last will be first and the first will be last.

Once again, if we try to comprehend this statement from a human standpoint, we'll miss the full meaning that lies within the promise. Ours is a society that judges the world by appearances. We see things not as they are, but as we are. We live under a consciousness that says, "Until I see the physical, until I feel and touch the actual, I won't believe it."

"I'll believe it when I see it," say the cynics of the day. However, such cannot be the case. In our lives, everything happens to us twice: first the "inner," then the "outer"; first the "thought," then the "thing"; first the "mental," then the "physical." Remember, your greatest source of power lies within your imagination. Let us affirm one meaning of this biblical statement: The physical that you have placed first, put last; and the mental that you have placed last, put first. In other words, start with the dream, the vision, begin to imagine. And as you do, you will create. The time for thinkers has come!

The kingdom of heaven is within.

Heaven is not some faraway state—the reward of years of tribulation. Heaven is right here—here and now! In the original Greek text, the word used for "heaven" is *ouranos,* meaning "expansion." In other words, a state of being where you can grow, multiply, and increase. This interpretation is strengthened by the Master's own description of heaven.

"The kingdom of heaven," he taught, "is like to a grain of mustard seed, which a man took, and sowed in his field: which indeed is the least of all seeds: but when it is grown, it is the greatest among herbs, and becometh a tree, so that the birds of the air come and lodge in the branches thereof.

"The kingdom of heaven," he continued, "is like unto leaven, which a woman took, and hid in three measures of meal, till the whole was leavened."

What is the property of a mustard seed? It spreads—a single seed will grow into a tree, a single tree will produce enough seeds to plant an entire field. And what is the property of leaven or yeast? It expands—in a single night it can expand a hundred times in size. So when Christ determined that heaven was within, he meant just what he said—the power to multiply our happiness, to increase our good, to expand all our needs, lies within each of us.

Thou shalt not steal.

You can never possess anything that you have failed to possess through consciousness. Our possessions and gifts first come to us through an outpouring of thoughts. You and only you know of specific desires and needs that eventually transform into material possessions. For example, where does *your* dream house dwell? Where does *your* perfect job exist? When did you catch a glimpse of *your* future car? At this point, you might keep in mind that beleaguered souls steal all the time. People steal cars, money, jewelry. History is replete, unfortunately, with examples where theft was attempted and sometimes thought successful until it was weighed on the scales of God's justice. To attempt to take something without nurturing the correct thinking or consciousness to which it truly belongs is mental theft. And the physical manifestation will simply not come to pass. We cannot keep something for which we do not have the consciousness to correspond. We must gain our possessions mentally before we gain them physically. This is one of the fundamental laws of being. "Thou shalt not steal" because you *cannot* steal! The sooner we grasp this spiritual truth, the sooner we will abandon the selfish notion of something for nothing, and begin to develop the consciousness that leads to enduring possessions and fulfillment.

Thou anointest my head with oil.

Throughout the ages, oil has been used as a demonstration of gladness, praise, and thanksgiving. Many of us were taught that angels were routinely sent to bless and pray over souls, anointing bodies with oil in the process. While this may indeed be true, oil holds another use—as a lubricant to reduce friction, to ease tension, to smooth transition. Whereas the starting point of prosperity is a prosperity consciousness, many times it is easier said than done to think plentiful as you experience want. At this key moment, all that stands between you and your desires is the ability to "anoint your head with oil," to shift from ideas of pain and limit to peace and abundance; to move your thoughts smoothly, easily, without tension and hassle from despair to hope. Words of inspiration, prayer, and spiritual encounters can provide the oil by which we can smooth this transition.

**For whosoever will save his life shall lose it, and
whosoever will lose his life for my sake shall find it.**

This is the principle of action and reaction, give and receive. Call it karma, call it cause and effect, call it the law of compensation, this is the fundamental truth of life, and a most needed realization for all who would live life effectively. We must *give up that which we want.* If we want love, we must give love; if we want kindness, we must give kindness. If you're unemployed and searching for work, help someone else in his or her quest for employment. Many of the country's most profitable executive search firms began in this manner. If poverty is clutching at your heels, don't spend every dime or consume whatever comes by your hand. Start with your meager supply and simply "give up" a portion to savings and investment. It will only be a matter of time before your acts of discipline and faith will be rewarded. If you are hungry, don't consume the bread that others may offer out of kindness. Break it up mentally. Plant it into the seed of abundance. If you give it up and allow the seasons of life to harvest vast fields of grain, you won't be hungry much longer. There is never a time when you can't find some way to start the giving flow, which in turn will open the way to receiving your good.

A PRAYER THAT REALLY WORKS

Prayer is the secret of the ages, the true foundation of all human greatness. Prayer is the greatest need and the core value of exceptional people. The unique characteristic of prayer is that you can fill your life by deciding to pray. It demands nothing of you, only that you celebrate the spiritual part of yourself. What I am describing is the process of knowing that everything is going to work out because you are "born of the spirit—washed in His blood." Let these ideas in and simply see where they lead. As you do, allow your soul to rest upon the moving words of Marian Wright Edelman, founder of the Children's Defense Fund. They deserve to be read slowly and prayerfully:

O God of beggar, beaten, abused, neglected, homeless
AIDS, drug, and hunger-ravaged children,
Of children who are emotionally and physically and mentally
    fragile, and of children who rebel and ridicule, torment and
    taunt,
Help us to love and respect and protect them all.

O God of children of destiny and of despair, of war and of peace,
Of disfigured, diseased, and dying children,
Of children without hope and of children with hope to spare
    and to share,
Help us to love and respect and protect them all.

9
The Greatest Story Ever Told:

Leaving a Legacy

- **What Does It Take to Become a Legend?**

- **Living in the Now!**

- **Yes, You Too Can Make a Difference**

- **A New Definition of Greatness**

- **It's Time to Fly!**

It matters not how strait the gate,
How charged with punishment the scroll,
I am the master of my fate;
I am the captain of my soul.
—WILLIAM ERNEST HENLEY

I hear and think. I see and I remember. I do and I know.
—CONFUCIUS

Lives of great men all remind us
We can make our lives sublime,
And, departing, leave behind us
Footprints on the sands of time.
—HENRY WADSWORTH LONGFELLOW

Well done beats well said.
—ANONYMOUS

Oseola McCarty never sought publicity, fame, or fortune. She never owned a car, nor, until recently, did she have an air conditioner—which she only turns on for guests. She still lives in the modest frame house in Hattiesburg, Mississippi, that an uncle left her nearly fifty years ago. She never married or had children. Her life is filled with "nevers." She never watches television; she never ventured out of the South; and she never raises her voice much above a whisper. Miss Oseola, as she is known to those who are closest to her, walks wherever she goes, pulling a shopping cart to the nearest grocery store. All she ever really wanted was an education—but it was not to be. After dropping out of school in the sixth grade to care for an elderly aunt, McCarty spent the rest of her life washing and ironing the clothes of well-to-do neighbors in her small southern town, living within her means and saving every cent.

As a child McCarty carried burdens that would have staggered many adults. Amazingly, she can't recall not working. For more than seventy years, her days followed a simple routine: She rose with the sun, drew water from a hydrant, and lit a fire under a huge black pot to boil white cotton garments, then scrubbed each item by hand before draping them across one hundred feet of line to dry. Her day ended as it had begun—rinsing delicates, then meticulously ironing every piece, pressing razor-sharp creases in the process. Initially, she charged only fifty cents a bundle—a week's worth of laundry for a family of four—but eventually the fee rose to ten dollars, still not all that much. She worked religiously—day in and day out.

All she ever had was her work, which she saw as a blessing. Some of her neighbors, however, saw little redeeming value. Openly criticized by other blacks who berated her for "washing them white folks' dirty drawers" and by affluent whites who considered her "just a poor ol' washerwoman who lived alone," she held close to her family, a few special friends, and her church. With a bundle of soiled clothes not far away, the silver-haired McCarty kept to her chores and found a way to be of service.

"Since I was a child, I've been working," says the fragile little woman with a smile big enough for everyone. "We'd get up early. When we'd get all our work and cleaning up in the house done, then we'd go out to the washhouse and start our day. We didn't have no washing machine, so we had to wash everything by hand. We scrubbed them all and throw 'em over into the wash pot and boil them, boil 'em 'til the clothes get yellow gold, and then take 'em out and rinse 'em, and you have some pretty white clothes hangin' up on your line."

In the mid-1960s, McCarty bought an automatic washer and dryer but in a fit of frustration gave both away. After using them once, she found them miserably insufficient. "The washing machine didn't rinse enough," she says, disappointed, "and the dryer turned the whites yellow."

As the days became years, Oseola never got sick and she spent next to nothing. She does not mind that her tiny black-and-white television set receives only one channel—she's too busy reading her tattered Bible, bound together with Scotch tape to keep Corinthians from falling out. From her vantage point, life has been good. She has few needs and even fewer complaints. But now the years have taken their toll. Over the past fifteen years, all her immediate family died. Her movements are slow now, since arthritis has left her hands stiff and numb. McCarty misses more Sundays than she would like at Friendship Baptist Church. For the first time in nearly eighty years, her independence is threatened. After finding a good doctor and a caring lawyer, she finally retired.

"My hand was swollen up so bad that it was pitiful," Oseola remembers. "It was my arthritis. It was all in this hand. That's the one I iron with. That's when I decided to make out my will."

And Then the Phone Rang

"Miss McCarty," the voice from the phone said in a soft, apologetic tone, "have you given any consideration as to what you want done with your money? I mean, in the event of your passing. I hate to bring up the subject, but bank policy states that we address the issue with all of our customers in circumstances similar to yours."

The tiny woman's heart began beating just a bit faster. Her banker's question had given her the perfect opening that she had been silently praying about. Secretly, she had hoped to make a difference. Without skipping a beat, she gave a response that would inspire a nation and crush stereotypes throughout the South.

"Yes, I have," she replied, leaning forward, staring at her hand. "I want ten percent to go to my relatives. I want another ten percent to go to my church. And I want the rest to go to the university."

"The university?" the banker questioned.

"That's right. The school right here in town—Southern Mississippi. I want the money to go to some child who needs it. I'm too old to get an education, but now they can."

As a young woman in her twenties, McCarty began the diligent habit of saving, living frugally, and refusing to withdraw any interest. Every week she deposited half her earnings. As a result, her nickels and dimes grew—from passbook savings to Christmas Club accounts to savings bonds to certificates of deposit, and, eventually, to a money market account. Only her banker knew that while McCarty was elbow-deep in soapy water, she was knee-deep in cash, having squirreled away a small fortune—more than $250,000. "When I made my money every week, I'd take out so much for groceries and so much for bills, and then put the rest in the bank. I didn't know the difference between a savings account and CDs, those things that get high interest. But I try to deal with people who *do* know."

The Oseola McCarty Scholarship Fund bears the name of a woman who, with little money and less education, believes the solution to any problem can be found in hard work and the Bible. Her generosity has stirred the soul of a nation. When her donation was announced—the largest single gift by an African American to a Mississippi university—Oseola McCarty, the washerwoman, rose from obscurity to celebrity status in only a few short days. The national media picked up the story and she was featured on NBC, CNN, ABC, and Black Entertainment Television and in the *New York Times, Washington Post, Newsweek,* and *People* magazine. Her extraordinary act of selflessness created a domino effect on the hearts and pocketbooks of people far and wide. From New York to California, people have pledged to match her contribution.

"It's more blessed to give than to receive," McCarty said quietly, quoting her beloved Bible. "When I leave this world, I can't carry nothing away from here. I live where I want to live. I couldn't drive a car if I had one. This is what I planned to do. Years ago, my race couldn't go to that college. But now they can.

"I can't do everything," she continued, "but I can do something to help somebody. And what I can do I will do. The only thing that I regret is that I didn't have more to give."

> It's more blessed to give than to receive. When I leave this world, I can't carry nothing away from here. The only thing that I regret is that I didn't have more to give.
>
> —Oseola McCarty

Recognition hasn't changed McCarty one bit. She still works harder than most and never asks others to do something she hasn't done or wouldn't do for herself. She is as comfortable with the President and celebrities as she is with common folk. She still clings to the values that lie near and dear to her heart as she quietly goes about performing acts of kindness and generosity, sharing the wealth that she has earned, while helping others to achieve levels of success they never dreamed possible. Unfazed by it all, she still sits in her little frame house, blocks from the college, and patiently greets reporters and business and civic leaders who line up outside her door. She truly answers to a higher calling. Many ask the same question she hears over and over: Why didn't you spend the money on yourself? "I *am* spending it on myself," she replies with the sweetest of smiles.

As you study Oseola McCarty's life, read about it not with envy, but with joy and anticipation. The principles she practiced, the success qualities she developed, are yours for the taking. The keys to her greatness—and that of many others—are contained within these pages. You need only to grasp them and apply them in your own life.

WHAT DOES IT TAKE TO BECOME A LEGEND?

We all want to leave something behind to mark our time on earth: our children, our work, the impressions we made on those who knew us. Our Creator hides a high ideal in every human soul—the desire to continue to live in the hearts of mankind long after our time has passed. People with legacies are rich in values that endure, in qualities that can never be lost. These rare gifts provide contentment and harmony within the soul. Such men and women are labeled "legends." In their own special way, they conquer the world. They combat difficulty diligently; they sustain misfortune bravely; they endure poverty and injustice nobly; and they encounter disappointment courageously. But most important, they . . .

- Find peace and happiness by helping others.
- Hate no one, are envious of no one, but love and respect all.
- Pray daily, not for more riches, but for greater wisdom with which to recognize, embrace, and enjoy the wealth they already possess.
- Ask no favors of anyone except the privilege of sharing their blessings.

- Are on good terms with their conscience, which therefore guides them in everything they do.

In spite of any obstacles, they manage to leave a legacy and lift humanity from groveling pursuits to the achievement of great and noble deeds. We can hear their voices:

"Higher!" they instruct. Each of us can do more with the resources we have been given. "Higher yet!" they insist. No matter the opposition you face or the discouragements that might overtake you, continue to rise. "Higher still!" Drudgery cannot disgust you, obstacles cannot discourage you, labor cannot stagger you. Persist no matter what comes or what goes. "And even higher!" until you have reached the apex of your calling. To grow higher, deeper, wider, as the years go on; to conquer difficulties and acquire more and give more; to feel all faculties unfolding and truth descending into the soul—this makes life worth living. Complete this task and the young and old will unite to give you honor. This is the greatest story ever told.

Every individual needs the inspiration of a grand mission to lift him or her above the pettiness and triteness of ordinary life. Some great undertaking with an element of heroism, of which the very thought quickens the blood and fires the soul, awakens the spirit and gives significance to life—this is an essential condition of greatness. No one can be called great without this purpose of mind, without some grand design to be carried out. Steadfast application, passion—the glue of the soul—characterizes the well-spent life. It made Romare Bearden a great painter; Carter G. Woodson a great historian; Marva Collins a great teacher; Benjamin O. Davis a great general; Ann Fudge a great manager; Ernestine Dillard a great singer; Eddie Robinson a great coach; Ed Bradley a great journalist; and Johnnie Colemon a great preacher.

What urged them on? It is the same "something" that pushed Hannibal across the Alps, that delivered Sojourner Truth to freedom, and that drove Ernie Green to endure years of hardship and strife in order to desegregate Arkansas' public schools.

How you live your life and what you do with it shapes not only your own future but also that of the world. Our world has been profoundly influenced by the thoughts, beliefs, and actions of all who have walked this planet. History is created not only by those whose names are revered and celebrated but also by the infamous and unknown. All who have lived have carved out, in some way, their own special niche. It doesn't matter whether or not as individuals we rank among the famous. What does matter is that each of us blazes a trail for others to follow.

With 5 billion of us around the globe, it might be difficult to believe that there could be a special mission for each of our lives. Yes, it is easy to feel insignificant among the multitudes. But nothing will have a more positive effect on your level of accomplishment, fulfillment, and happiness than the belief and understanding that you do bring to humanity something unique that no one else can offer. The most important thought that you can ever hold is: *Your life matters.* YOU are worth the effort it takes to succeed! Greatness, as defined upon these pages, is worth the trouble, the effort, the commitment, the time, and the dedication. Perhaps the most splendid success of all is the constant striving to surpass oneself. Let's face it, we are not all cut out to be straight-A students or brain surgeons or chief executive officers in corporate America. But we are all designed to make the most of the talents, skills, and intelligence we do possess. True greatness is a melding of success, wealth, self-satisfaction with service to others, rich friendships, and the ability to enjoy all the fruits of this life.

BUILDING A MASTERPIECE

Apelles, the ancient Greek artist, was considered to be the greatest painter of his day. The old master had hoped to leave a legacy, the one thing that would separate his name from the many. Four centuries before the birth of Christ, this skilled craftsman traveled the globe searching for subjects that would inspire his final masterpiece. He sought to paint a portrait of the perfect woman. This was to be his grand design.

Enchanted wherever he turned, Apelles observed the finest points of the world's most beautiful women. In Asia, he noticed a nose here and an eye there; in the Mediterranean, he thought the mouth to be ideal. In Africa, he was intoxicated with the graceful curves and body structure of African women. By combining the most striking features of his subjects—individual lines of beauty—Apelles completed a breathtaking work of art. This great artist knew that all the elements of beauty and radiance could not be found in one person. He knew, too, that some of the most perfect features would be found in women who never thought of themselves as beautiful. It was not a portrait, but a composite, a combination of features, that would allow Apelles to leave his testimony.

Like this Greek artist, for many years I, too, have been in quest of the elements of the grand, virtuous man and woman—the individual that society labels "great." As I embarked upon this journey, I knew from the start that it would be difficult to find any one person who embodied every quality of greatness; a person who could combine in perfect degree all the traits of success. Nevertheless, like this renowned painter, I decided to single out specific strengths prevalent in scores of candidates which, if placed together, would shape an individual worthy of emulation. Eventually, I came upon the object of my search. I found a Bill Pinkney, illustrative of undaunted purpose; a Chucky Mullins, marked by heroic courage; a Dr. Reatha Clark King, a prime example of grit overcoming all obstacles; and an Alicia Paige, pronouncing that the quick grasping of opportunities leads to noble achievement.

I have interviewed men and women in various vocations hoping to uncover the secret of their success, the reasons for their advancement. These varied life stories offer us the brick and mortar for constructing the composite character of the great man and the great woman—one that combines the best virtues and qualities, whose imitation will help ensure a useful, productive, and honored life. I have attempted to drive home every precept and lesson with stirring and inspiring tales of great lives which clearly demonstrate that each of us is the architect of our own fortunes, and which will negate the excuses used by far too many who believe they have no chance in life. I have tried to teach that those who dare to leave their mark must be greater than the books they write, than the patients they treat, than the goods they sell, than the cause they plead in the courts—that leaving a legacy is above all titles and is greater than any profession.

Granted, we cannot all create those things of beauty that fill the heart of humanity with a perpetual joy. But we can all do something to enhance the sum of human happiness, to make the world better, to advance the state of human progress. It is better to be born blind than not to see the true glory of life.

LIVING IN THE NOW!

Time is your most precious possession—and the hands of time move swiftly onward. Fasten this warning deep into your mind, not for sorrow's sake, but to remind yourself that today may be all you have. Now is the time for you to move forward. Now is the time for you to stand up and be counted. The ground is now ready for you to plant the seeds of a new vision, one that will bear only the finest fruit. It is time to focus on what you want, to turn your dreams into realities so that you are able to spend your life in the manner in which you desire. *It is later than you think.*

Too many of us waste our years waiting for better times in the future or reflecting upon better times in the past, instead of working for better times in the present. If only we could have lived in better times. If only we lived with better people or had better parents. If only we lived in a better home or under better conditions. If only we had better schooling, better opportunities, or better resources. If, if, if! Tomorrow, tomorrow, tomorrow!

The problem with waiting until tomorrow is that when it finally arrives, it is called today. Today is yesterday's tomorrow. The question is what did we do with *yesterday's* opportunity? All too often we waste tomorrow as we wasted yesterday, and as we are wasting today. All that could have been accomplished can easily elude us, despite our intentions, until we inevitably discover that the things that *might have been* have slipped from our embrace a single, unused day at a time. Each of us must pause frequently to remind ourselves that the clock is ticking. The same clock that began to tick from the moment we drew our first breath will also someday cease. The only moment in which we live our lives is now. We may pretend that we live in the past, or we may imagine that we live in the future, but the only moment we can ever live is this very moment—the *now!*

Today is always here; yesterday is gone; and tomorrow never comes. Time offers opportunity but demands a sense of urgency. Now is the time. This is the place. You are the one!

Those who leave a legacy of achievement master the art of living in the now—the ability to make each moment count. Here are their tips.

- First, they accept each moment as a gift to be received with joy.
- Second, they use each moment to maximum advantage.
- Third, they are bent on making a contribution to humanity.
- Fourth, they learn from their mistakes.
- Fifth, they concentrate all their efforts on the task at hand.
- Sixth, they plan for the future rather than fretting over the past.
- Seventh, they simply refuse to allow the weight of an unpleasant circumstance to encumber their thoughts or objectives.

What separates "the greatest story ever told" from a marginal existence? Those who leave their mark are in love with life as well as with the possibilities of what it means to be human.

HE SHARES A SPECIAL MESSAGE
WITH HIS STUDENTS

In the fall of 1932, Howard Thurman was offered a teaching post in the School of Religion at Howard University, a position he held for several years. Dr. Thurman had a genius for teaching and was widely recognized as one of the nation's outstanding educators. In 1953, *Life* magazine listed him as one of the twelve greatest preachers of the twentieth century. Today his words still have the power to command and inspire; and, in these anxious times, when many have lost faith in the future and in their own abilities, his message is perhaps more comforting than ever. Thousands of young men and women came under his influence. Many went on to achieve honors and distinction in their adult lives. He sowed the seeds that bred generations of activists who tore down ancient walls of oppression. Times have changed enormously in the intervening years, and Dr. Thurman has since passed away. But he left us a rich legacy that is as vibrant and alive today as it was more than sixty years ago. Ironically, of all his lectures in the dim old Rankin Chapel on the District of Columbia campus, his greatest lesson is known only by a few.

"What is the greatest possession that one can claim?" Dr. Thurman probed his philosophy students. After a brief deliberation, one of his prize pupils answered.

"Faith! Nothing is more important than faith in God." Thurman said nothing as he searched the class for another answer.

"I know," a young man said as he thumbed through a book. "It's got to be a kind and gentle heart—you've said so yourself—what this world needs is more compassion."

"Health!" another classmate shot back. "Without your health you have nothing."

And still another hand rose in the back of the class. "How about companionship, Professor Thurman? I would hate to live in this world alone—everyone needs a friend."

"I disagree," still another interjected. "Without money you have nothing."

Dr. Thurman strolled the aisles and remained quiet. Sensing his consternation, the students fell silent. He grew visibly upset and decided not to push the issue any further. With no one now bold enough to offer a solution, Thurman asked the class to imagine a world void of dreamers. To drive home his point, he then took the remaining moments of class time to share one of his many life experiences.

"I was born in Daytona, Florida," he began, leaning against a desk. "Daytona was a small town except in the winter when such notables as the Rockefellers and the Gambles came south for the season. The city was completely segregated and provided no schooling for colored children beyond the seventh grade. Because of my hunger to learn and grow, the principal at the colored elementary school offered to tutor me, using eighth-grade lessons. This was my chance to break free and I was determined to make the most of it. A short period later, I passed an eighth-grade examination and was given permission to attend high school—nearly one hundred miles away!"

Thurman continued his story, his students perched on the edge of their seats. "My parents were very poor. Nonetheless, they managed to enroll me in a church-supported high school in Jacksonville—one of only three that Negroes could attend in the entire state. There, I lived with a cousin, working at night to pay for my room and board.

"My plan to finish high school, and eventually go to college, was nearly derailed. Before boarding the train to Jacksonville, I had packed an old borrowed trunk with no lock or handles, roped it securely, and said my good-byes. The clerk at the railroad station refused to accept my luggage as baggage. I was forced to ship it as freight at an additional charge. But having spent my last dollar for a ticket, I cried in frustration on the station steps. And I would have remained there if it weren't for the warm gesture of a complete stranger. A black man dressed in overalls asked me what was wrong. When I told him of my dilemma, he stepped up to the ticket counter, paid the freight charge, and handed me the receipt.

"He said, 'If you're trying to get out of this damn town to get an education, the least I can do is help you.' Then without another word, he disappeared. I never learned the man's name, nor did I ever see him again. This complete stranger helped shape my life."

After several thought-provoking moments, Dr. Thurman looked into his students' questioning eyes and moved to the heart of the issue. He closed with these words: "There should be something in a person's life greater than his vocation; more grand than material possessions or wealth; higher than genius; more enduring than fame. Here lies your greatest challenge as well as your most compelling duty. Whoever uplifts civilization is rich though he die penniless, and future generations will erect his monument. No matter who you are, no matter the odds, regardless of what lies in your path, you must leave your mark—you must tell future generations that you were here!"

Howard Thurman was correct. There exists within each of us a longing to leave our mark, some proof that we were indeed here. We need to know that our lives were important, that somehow our *being* mattered. Our legacy of achievement has value far beyond any monetary figure. It ennobles the human condition by demonstrating the power of the human spirit to overcome tribulations in the pursuit of a dream. And today there are thousands of men and women whose lives stand as examples to those who seek to be successful. Whether working for ourselves or employed by others, each of us has a contribution that only we can make. The key is for us to find our own path—our purpose for living—and follow it.

It doesn't matter whether we possess the genius of a Howard Thurman or a mere hope for the future, like that stranger who decided to make a difference. Each has made a contribution to humanity and deserves to be admired. But beyond admiration lies respect. Both are models for what we seek—to create something of value, to accomplish something worthwhile. We can attempt to stifle this innate human desire, but we cannot escape it. As humans we are distinguished and defined by it: Force him to shine your shoes and he becomes a James Brown; place her in a wheelchair and she becomes Barbara Jordan; confine him to a prison cell and I'll show you a Nelson Mandela; spit in his face and you have a Marcus Garvey; tell her she can't write and I'll show you an Alice Walker; tell her she can't lead and she becomes Myrlie Evers; blind him and he becomes Stevie Wonder; rape her and she turns into an Oprah Winfrey; disobey his orders and I'll show you a Colin Powell; conceal his history and he becomes an Alex Haley; write him off as another fatherless black male and he turns into a Ben Carson; and deny them an adequate education and they become an Oseola McCarty and a Howard Thurman.

YES, YOU TOO CAN MAKE A DIFFERENCE

On September 2, 1992, shortly after the Los Angeles riots that followed the Rodney King jury verdict, Crenshaw High School students of all races came together to discuss how they could restore their ravaged community. At first, the idea was simple: to create a community garden that would bring life back to one of the city's most battered neighborhoods while offering the students hands-on science experience. They

296 Dennis P. Kimbro

planted flowers, herbs, squash, collard greens, and other vegetables. A colorful mural soon appeared on the high school's back wall, with a brown hand reaching toward a white one. In the middle of South-Central L.A., an oasis bloomed. The students donated some of the produce to needy families and sold the rest at local farmers' markets. But they also realized that the garden was about more than simply feeding the needy—it was about ownership: business ownership. Together, with science teacher Tammy Bird and volunteer business consultant Melinda McMullen, the students set up shop. They called their struggling enterprise Food From the 'Hood.

But it wasn't easy. The school had neither a strong science program nor resources to spare. Brimming with enthusiasm, Bird, a biology teacher and the school's volleyball coach, relinquished her coaching duties to devote more time to the project. McMullen, a former public relations executive, had never been to the inner city. After viewing the garden firsthand, she recalled thinking to herself: "The riots weren't about gardening. They were about economics." She suggested that the students sell the produce to develop a scholarship fund, but after the first year they had netted only $600. "To be successful," McMullen shared, "we knew the students had to raise cash. We wanted to empower them by giving each a stake in the results of their efforts. That's when the group decided on the next logical extension."

Since the garden was full of lettuce and herbs, why not make the stuff that goes on top? Besides, they thought, if actor Paul Newman could market a salad dressing with profits going to more than four hundred charities worldwide, why couldn't Food From the 'Hood sell a dressing that helps kids help themselves?

Bent on making a contribution, everyone played a role. Students worked in the garden—after school, during free periods, and on weekends. Duties were divided and assigned; no task was too menial. Some answered the phone, some wrote copy and prepared promotional materials. Others filed papers in the company's makeshift school office, which until recently was a science lab. The remaining "owners" beat the pavement, handing out samples and pitching their product at neighborhood stores. Every aspect of the business, including all company-related decisions—from weeding the garden to producing labels—was handled by students. And their ideas kept sprouting.

And to Think It All Started with a Patch of Land

For six months, Bird's biology class tested various recipes. They literally concocted hundreds of formulas that were sent to a food chemist for further analysis. Meanwhile their efforts began to attract high-profile support. Norris Bernstein, a wily entrepreneur and founder of Bernstein's salad dressings, provided marketing and distribution advice. The Long Beach native said he had been searching for a way to make a contribution after the disturbance. "When I heard about Food From the 'Hood, I knew this was my chance to get involved."

Next, a minority-owned investment banking firm, Luther Smith & Small, helped the young owners draft a business plan and nail down financial projections. Under the leadership of Sy Hare, a senior vice-president, the students authored a plan that was designed to generate enough profit to support each owner in his or her quest for a college education. The final pieces of the project were set in place when the kids from Crenshaw met with grocery executives and a food broker, who offered tips on shelf space and market segmentation. Impressed with the taste and the quality of the product, and everyone's level of preparation and commitment, retailers began to sign on. "If any product has the potential to make it," said Harold Rudnik, senior vice-president of Vons, a Los Angeles–based supermarket chain, "this one does. New products don't need huge ad and sales campaigns to be considered winners. Excellence and service play a big role, too."

Two years to the week after the nation's costliest riots demoralized a country, seeds of hope had not only sprouted but had begun to blossom. Sweet Adelaide Enterprises, an area-based packer, began producing and shipping twelve-ounce bottles of Straight out the Garden, an all-natural creamy Italian salad dressing, to local stores. With each shipment came a new attitude.

"Never in our wildest dreams did we expect to have corporate offices in three weeks and two thousand bottles of salad dressing in four months," said Maurice McNeely, a founding student-owner and member of the board of directors. "With teamwork, dedication, and the right attitude, anything is possible." His business partner, Ketric Jenkins, agrees. "Originally, I had not planned to go to college, but Food From the 'Hood is making a way. Over the course of the year I've changed, the neighborhood has changed. I think we all have changed." What started as a small vegetable plot has now bloomed into a thriving business that wholesales salad dressing to more than two thousand stores in Southern California, including Albertson's and Lucky, the two largest supermarket chains in the state.

Today the far-flung enterprise is expanding full bore, fueled by hard work and the need to make a contribution. With the launch of their first product behind them, the buzz around the South-Central office is changing. Now you hear talk of "line extensions" and "brand management"—not exactly the hip-hop slang of your typical high school student. By all accounts, the business is on schedule to surpass $300,000 in sales, which will fund a bevy of scholarships. At last count, ten of the fifteen seniors were accepted at four-year institutions—a remarkable record for a predominantly black inner-city public school where many never graduate.

But more important than the money is the sense of accomplishment and the source of pride that have grown out of the students' involvement. "We've shown that a group of inner-city kids can make a difference," says Crenshaw freshman Terrie Smith. And their efforts have struck a nerve. They have received inquiries from across the country regarding additional opportunities. A New York high school has expressed a desire to franchise Crenshaw's logo and business plan with the hopes of producing applesauce. There's also talk regarding a much-needed mentor program as well as college preparatory workshops. Clearly, these young men and women are leaving their mark.

What was once an overgrown corner of an abandoned football field has now been transformed into a lush green learning center. It may not be history's biggest victory garden, but we cannot underestimate the size of the victory. "We all try to help each other," Jaynell Grayson confesses. And who should know better than she? An A student throughout her high school career, Grayson never knew her father, and her mother has been incarcerated most of Jaynell's life. Nonetheless, this motivated eighteen-year-old attends Boston's Babson College on academic scholarship. Food From the 'Hood has transformed her life. "What comes from that garden is inspiration," says one of the volunteers. "It's not that these kids are special. It's that they wanted to *do* something special."

WILL YOU DO SOMETHING SPECIAL?

What will *you* do? Will *you* do something special . . . something great? To *be* what you are and to *become* what you are capable of becoming is the secret to leaving your legacy. This is the secret to your greatness. No one can cheat you out of an honorable life unless you cheat yourself. There can be no better resolution. An ancient parable illustrates this point.

Centuries ago, there existed the tiny kingdom of Phrygia. Its sole claim to fame rested on an antique wagon in one of the courtyards. The relic was fastened to a yoke by a sturdy hitch called the Gordian knot. It was prophesied that whoever untied the knot would conquer the world. But for more than one hundred years, the knot defied all efforts of kings and queens. One day, a newly crowned ruler, Alexander of Macedonia, journeyed to Phrygia to test his fate. At the appointed time, the courtyard was full of excitement and swarmed with curious, though skeptical onlookers. All others had failed, so surely this test would be beyond the abilities of this young king. But Alexander would not be denied his true place in history. Armed with nothing but belief and the desire to take his true place among the world's greatest leaders, he drew his sword and sliced the knot in two.

Many times, people search for solutions to their challenges outside of themselves. It is no secret that, when confronted with difficulties, human nature will send us looking high and low, far and wide, for anyone who can solve our problems for us. When the average man or woman desires something great, he or she begins to look for others to help him or her acquire it. What we must recognize, however, is that what we need has already been given to us. The solution to every problem is at hand. We need only to cut the knot that binds us to our difficulties in order to experience our own individual greatness.

Millions of people struggle all the days of their lives with no stronger urge than that of acquiring the necessities of life—food, shelter, and clothing. Now and then someone will step out of the masses and demand of himself or herself, and of the world, more than a mere living. He is determined to leave a legacy—a solid faith in his mission—the rooted belief that *this is the one thing* to which he has been called. Look about you and you will see that the world's greatest are those who rose up and refused to be victimized by anything less than their destiny. This calling lured Hannibal to the Alps. This desire for something better impelled Dr. Carver to the laboratory. This urge drove Matthew Henson to the north pole, induced Thurgood Marshall to the courts, and drew T. D. Jakes to the pulpit.

Kwesi Mfume, former chair of the Congressional Black Caucus, was asked by a colleague why he chose to relinquish a safe seat in Congress to lead the struggling NAACP. To which Mfume quietly replied: "I learned at an early age that life is a short commodity. You have to do all you can when you can."

Ronald McNair's whole heart was buried in the stars. As a mission specialist aboard the ill-fated space shuttle *Challenger,* McNair was a trailblazer who sought to extend the world's frontiers. "I can't think of anything else," he confessed. These would be the same stars that would devour him.

DON'T AIM LOW!

Take stock of yourself. What is the special mark that only you can inscribe? Are you among those who say "I can" and "It will be done," or do you fall into the "what if" category at the very moment others may be accomplishing it? You must dream bigger than your predicament; you must aspire higher than your circumstances; you must imagine bolder than your surroundings. Don't aim low—someone might follow you. Don't aim low—you might hit your target. Don't aim low—you might waste your life!

At some point in life, we all become keenly aware that we choose the path that we hope will lead to our true destiny. The first building block from which we shape the outcome of our lives is the process of moving with definiteness and purpose toward our goals. If you do not yet know what you desire from life, if it is still a hazy, altering, unnamed goal, reread the first chapter of this book. You should earnestly seek to define your objectives. Without a purpose, without adequate plans for the fulfillment of your destiny, your mind is bound to the negative habit patterns of failure. Successful men and women are those who set clear, specific goals replete with timetables and the means by which they expect to achieve them. Now is the time to open your mind and set it free; free to discover the added power of a mind that knows no boundaries. Only if you have an open mind can you grasp the full impact of the first rule of greatness: *Whatever the mind can conceive and believe, it can achieve.*

The person blessed with an open mind can perform miracles in business, industry, and other professions while those chained to the negativity around them are shouting "impossible." The person who closes his mind to new ideas, concepts, and experiences enslaves his or her own personality. A closed mind is a sign of a static personality. It allows progress to pass it by, and it fails to grasp the opportunities progress offers. An open mind, on the other hand, requires courage, integrity, and faith—in yourself, your fellow human beings, and the Creator, who laid out a pattern of progress for you and His universe. When you open your mind, you give your imagination freedom to act on your behalf. You utilize the gift of vision.

Right now, while it is fresh in your mind, write down a clear outline stating the desires of your heart—specifically, your purpose for living. Include a statement of the most important objective you wish to accomplish. Write a description of your chosen occupation, business, or profession. Do not be too modest in your description, but do define all the reasons why you believe you are entitled to such an objective. Also focus on the income you desire and, just as specifically, what you intend to give to earn this income. This is important. Your subconscious mind will not violate natural laws, and a request for something for nothing would only end in defeat. What do you want? Name it and it is yours. Love? Money? Recognition? Happiness? Or do you wish to make the world a better place in which to live?

We cannot help but notice the two parallel themes that border all of life. First, you can achieve as much as you desire, providing you are willing to combine your God-given abilities with knowledge and are determined to pay the price for success. Second, there is no success without a purpose. The goal of life is to find your life's purpose and thus light the path for future generations toward the treasures that really matter—peace of mind, loving relationships, and personal fulfillment.

A NEW DEFINITION OF GREATNESS

To bring out your best, you must adopt a new attitude toward success. No matter who you are, there has to be more to accomplishment than fame or fortune. It has been written, "You don't sing to get to the end of the song." The same applies to your destiny: You don't tolerate the trials and tribulations of goal attainment just to finish or to complete the race. Of course, we all like to do our best, to succeed, to set new personal marks. Our performances provide a handy gauge of self-improvement, and the recognition we receive is rewarding. But too many of those who scale the mountain called success suffocate their enjoyment of personal accomplishment by overemphasizing the importance of monetary goals and positional power. About all this does is build up tension and anxiety, which stifles individual performance, thus creating barriers to your objectives, to say nothing of how such negative attitudes diminish the fun and enjoyment of striving for a goal.

What makes the great great? True greatness is an expanding transformation that begins within: *Success is the progressive realization of a worthy goal or ideal.* Give this some serious thought. No amount of fame or fortune, wealth or recognition, will ever bring you true success, or happiness for that matter. Greatness is a journey that begins with you, in you. If you are not enjoying your life at this moment, with what you have accumulated, with your current state of consciousness, you will not appreciate nor will you enjoy any new or different conditions or relationships that you may experience in the future. Nothing outside of ourselves has the power to bestow happiness or fulfillment on us. What determines the quality of our lives is our choice to be fulfilled, based on how we think and how we view ourselves. Let me warn you: If you are an individual who needs more in order to feel complete, then you will still feel incomplete no matter how great the possessions that grace has bestowed upon you.

Success is more than wealth! If you have arrived at your destiny through wealth alone, there's a question that will be asked that you cannot evade: In what manner was your fortune gained? Some people build as cathedrals are built: the foundation finished, but the moldings that soar toward the heavens, the turrets and spires, forever incomplete. "Such builders will never dwell in the house of the Lord." If your money was not earned through character, decency, and integrity, you have not succeeded. If your bank account is stained with the blood of the poor or the unfortunate, you have not succeeded. If you dashed the hopes and dreams of others, you have not succeeded. If your wealth has made others poor or buried the opportunities of your fellow human beings; if your wealth shortens the lives of others or smothers the rights of others; if your riches were gained in an occupation that kills, that poisons the spirit, that denigrates or stunts the morality of others, you have not succeeded. Greatness will forever be denied. It would benefit you deeply to analyze the following story.

THE GREATEST PERSON IN THE LAND

There was a wealthy old man who lived in the valley. He was more than graciously endowed with vast possessions. Among his most treasured gifts was a stately mansion that overlooked the scenic valley. But there was an emptiness in his spirit. He lived alone without family or friends or spiritual foundation, surrounded only by his priceless fortune. In the guest quarters of his estate lived a servant, John, and his family. John was a simple man with modest needs and desires but deeply spiritual. The Creator's presence was a reality in his life witnessed by his employer, who late at night would see John and his family devotedly in prayer.

One morning the wealthy landlord was looking over his holdings. As he gazed over his domain, he said to himself, "It's all mine." Just then the doorbell rang. At the bottom of the steps he found John, his humble servant.

"What's the matter?" he asked. "Are the animals okay?"

John looked embarrassed. "Yes, sir," he replied. "Everything is fine. Hmmm, sir, could I have a word with you?" John was invited onto the plush carpet in the den.

"Sir," John said hesitantly, "last night I had a dream, and in it a voice told me that the greatest man in the valley would die the next night. I felt compelled to tell you. I apologize if I disturbed you."

"Go back to your work and forget it," said the lord. "I won't have anything to do with such childish superstition."

John still looked uneasy. "The dream was quite vivid," he continued, "and the message was that the greatest man in the land would die at midnight. I just had to tell you."

The landowner quickly dismissed him, but his servant's words distracted him so much that he visited his doctor that day. His physician examined him from head to toe, pronounced him fit as a fiddle, and said that he'd give him another twenty-five years. The old baron was relieved, but a lingering doubt caused him to invite his doctor to dinner that evening. Together, they enjoyed a hearty meal and shortly after eleven-thirty, the physician prepared to leave. When his host asked him to remain for a nightcap, he agreed. Eventually, when midnight passed and they still reminisced about old times, the wealthy old man muttered to his guest, "Silly old John. Upset my whole day—him and his stupid dreams." He then bade good night to his friend.

No sooner was the tycoon in bed than he heard the doorbell ring. It was twelve-thirty. At the bottom of the steps he found a grief-stricken child who he knew was John's youngest daughter.

"Sir," she said, looking at him through her tears, "my mother sent me to tell you that my father just died." The old man froze. It was suddenly made clear to him who was the greatest person in the land.

Please understand that I am not contending that the accumulation of material wealth and possessions is evil. Having attained wealth after impoverished beginnings, I delight in the harvest that has come from having made a great deal of money. It is satisfying and fulfilling. I am proud of my accomplishments and do not feel apologetic for being able to purchase whatever I choose as a result of my labors. What I am referring to is the ability to live life at a higher degree of consciousness that is the result of this spiritual journey. If we are to become great, we too must dedicate ourselves to the same values that guided the life of this humble servant—among others God, family, and work.

True greatness is an inward journey that, to some degree, should blend nine core qualities: peace of mind, character, courage, commitment, discipline, faith, perseverance, worthy goals and ideals, and, the most important, love. Success of this magnitude is priceless. Finer than any precious jewel, rarer than any crown or kingdom, more adorning than any royal robe. This is the fabric of true success, and weaving it is the noblest task on earth! Success is not about striving, it's about arriving.

Those who master their destiny share many qualities, none of which are determined by society's definition of success—an explanation that centers on fame and fortune alone. Their path remains crystal-clear. How many of these statements describe your principles and values? Those who've tasted this vintage wine of success:

- Have the courage to risk failure and realize that setbacks are lessons to learn from.
- Lose the ability to blame others for the circumstances of their lives.
- Develop their strengths and manage their weaknesses.
- Know that labels are unnecessary. They see the true divinity—the brotherhood and sisterhood of humanity.
- Continually look for ways to express love.
- Are visionaries and dream of those things that haven't been and believe they are possible.
- Tap into a higher consciousness to master their destiny; they go "within" as they deal "without."
- Commit to personal excellence.
- Say "I can."

IT'S TIME TO FLY!

To the German pilots who battled them in the skies over Europe in World War II, they were the *Schwartze Vogelmenschen,* the Black Birdmen. To their comrades and the white pilots who would not fly with them, they were the "Red Tails" because of the color they painted the rear of their P-51 Mustang fighters. But to the crews of the Allied bombers, the black pilots known as the Tuskegee Airmen were heroes and saviors. Flying more than 15,000 sorties and 1,500 missions, the segregated fighter squadrons, whose pilots trained in Tuskegee, Alabama, never lost a bomber they were escorting, a record that can be claimed by no other unit. And, yet, it is doubtful there would have been any Tuskegee Airmen were it not for the single-minded persistence and courage of one man. In August 1940, Charles Alfred "Chief" Anderson— arguably the most important figure in black aviation—came to

Tuskegee to train pilots. He was the most qualified black pilot of the day.

Though he trained countless others on the fundamentals of flight, the first person Anderson taught to fly was himself. Born in Bryn Mawr, Pennsylvania, and yearning for wings from the age of eight, he first took to the skies in 1928. Regarded as a kook by blacks and whites alike, Chief could find no one who would teach a black boy to fly. So he hung out at airfields, in an openly racist climate, closely watching white pilots and eavesdropping on their shoptalk. He took copious notes, recording variables, measurements, wind speeds—anything that would help him secure his dream.

"Other pilots would talk around the hangar about tailspins and 360-degree turns," Anderson remembers, "but when I'd walk up to listen, they would quickly change the subject. So I had to figure out things for myself."

Chief was fearless in tackling assignments that would terrify others. He coaxed loans out of a few close friends and purchased his own plane—a $2,500 Velie Monocoupe. On a small private strip near his hometown, with clipboard notes in one hand and the throttle in the other, Chief sat nervously in the cockpit of the aircraft, his heart racing faster than the engine. Compromising his own safety, this pioneer would attempt his first takeoffs and landings alone. Turning the pages of his flight plan, Anderson was clearly in his element. He stared at the controls and recited the code phrases.

Fuel? Check . . .

Oil pressure? Check . . .

Altimeter? Check . . .

Tachometer? Check.

Finally he was ready—or at least he thought he was. Anderson sent up a quick prayer, pulled back on the wheel, and whispered, "I guess it's time to fly." Banking sharply to the right, Anderson swooped back over a verdant carpet of piney woods and farms in eastern Pennsylvania, and eventually, his aircraft came coasting down. A man who rarely talks about himself, Chief remembers his maiden voyage as no big deal.

"I never gave it much thought. In those days, it was taboo for blacks to fly, but if you had access to a plane, you could learn to use it. Flying was something I had wanted to do since I was a child. Did it take faith? You bet. Courage? I guess. But I was determined. To me, flying is like breathing."

Word of Anderson's achievements spread, and along with it, his reputation. Soon he began preparing for a commercial license, studying meteorology and engine mechanics on his own. In 1933, Chief and an associate, Dr. Albert Forsythe, made their first showcase flight, a transcontinental jaunt from Atlantic City to Los Angeles. The flight, the first round-trip cross-country effort by blacks, was made in a 95-horsepower Fairchild, far from state-of-the-art. The two men did it without navigational instruments, a radio, or even parachutes. Airborne, they puzzled out their locations with a Rand McNally road map until it blew away. Poor lighting at night forced them to hold a flashlight out the window. Even so, they arrived at a Los Angeles airport in two and a half days to a mostly black crowd of two thousand, proudly applauding.

The next year, Forsythe and Anderson embarked on their Pan-American Goodwill Tour around the Caribbean. In another small plane, christened the *Booker T. Washington,* the two fliers took off from Miami in November 1934. They arrived at their first stop, in the Bahamas, after dark. No plane had ever landed in Nassau before, so throngs surged into the road when they heard an engine in the sky. Anderson made a couple of passes overhead before people realized they had to get out of the way. Then a double wall of cars lined the main thoroughfare, shining their headlights to simulate a landing strip. Their flight together—enthusiastically reported in the newspapers—dealt the last blow to the U.S. Army's exclusion of blacks from the Air Corps. Within a month, the first training of black military pilots began.

"The Tuskegee Experiment," as the Pentagon referred to the training of black pilots at Alabama, produced a corps of well-trained, dedicated, and disciplined fliers who more than held their own in combat. Some of these young men had college backgrounds, some had already established professional careers, and a few were well-to-do, but all were highly motivated, possessed of impeccable character with a burning desire to fly. All would be held to the highest standards of their mentor and teacher, and only the best of the best would earn their silver wings.

"It was an experiment designed to fail," Chief says with sudden tears. "The program started with just twelve blacks, shoddy equipment, and absolutely no funding. We were asked to do the impossible." Thanks to fate, Anderson and his charges completed their mission.

"Performance Is the Measure of Merit"

Dr. Frederick Patterson, then president of Tuskegee Institute, tried desperately to persuade the federal government to use blacks as combat pilots. Though America's armed forces were critically short of pilots when war was looming in Europe and the Pacific, a War Department report concluded that "Negroes have neither the intelligence nor the discipline to fly airplanes." Eleanor Roosevelt helped dispel that racist sentiment. In March 1941, she visited Tuskegee while her husband, President Franklin Roosevelt, stricken with polio, rested at Warm Springs, Georgia. When she arrived at Moton Field, a single-runway airstrip surrounded by marshes and pine trees, she announced she was going to fly with Chief Anderson.

Chief recalls the First Lady's security scrambling for telephones to reach the President so he could talk her out of a foolish stunt. "She was going to do what she damned well pleased," Anderson says. An aging photograph of that historic moment shows a smiling Mrs. Roosevelt sitting behind a self-assured Chief Anderson before takeoff. He took her on a forty-minute aerial tour in his Piper Cub as they talked about a number of things, not the least of which was black pilots.

"She told me, 'I've always heard that colored people can't fly. But I see them flying all around here.' I'm sure when she went back she said to the President: 'Franklin, I was down there and flew with one of those boys. We've got to do something about letting them fly.' Because ten days later, we got word that the program was funded."

At eighty-five, Alfred "Chief" Anderson still haunts this airfield, a scrap of asphalt pinned between an interstate highway and a mosaic of corn and cotton fields. He has been flying for sixty-one years and has logged more than 57,000 flight hours—second highest in the world. Under his tutelage, many of Black America's best and brightest have met with honor and acclaim. "He taught me the value of self-reliance and responsibility," said Daniel "Chappie" James, the second black to rise to the rank of general in the U.S. Air Force. Benjamin O. Davis, Jr., the first black to graduate from West Point, couldn't agree more. "To think something is impossible makes it so. Chief taught us to stand on our own in the face of all opposition," General Davis remembers. "He was somebody we could look up to."

In 1990, Anderson was inducted into the Gallery of Iron Eagles, an international society that recognizes those who have made the greatest contributions in the field of flight. Though he has received hundreds of awards and citations, none was more fitting. His name in now enshrined with the likes of Charles Lindbergh, Chuck Yeager, and Amelia Earhart. He has been a positive influence on countless people whose lives he has touched. By believing in them, he has helped others to believe in themselves. But most important, Chief has pointed the way to legendary greatness.

"In the annals of black history, Chief Anderson's place is secured," says Colonel Roosevelt Lewis, a Vietnam veteran and one of his star pupils. "But in the realm of achievement he stands alone at center stage. Though ridiculed and scorned, he seemed destined for greatness. He is a living legend. Chief demonstrated that out of simple beginnings each of us can carve something glorious. A man of few words, his favorite saying is, 'Performance is the measure of merit.' He taught the science of flying but he instructed us on the art of living. Now each of us can fly as high as we wish—in life as well as the skies.'"

HOW HIGH WILL *YOU* FLY?

Your future, like a block of pure marble, stands untouched before you. In your abilities, talents, and gifts, you hold the chisel and mallet. The dramatic story of Chief Anderson's persistence and fierce determination is a perfect illustration. The world has the right to expect a work of art. You have been given freedom, opportunity, and life—the greatest gift of all! What will you hammer out? Given the resources at your command, society expects you to be a refining, uplifting force in your community; an inspiration to those trapped by poverty and ignorance; a man or woman of character and distinction. Great advantages bring great responsibilities. Will you shatter the block into an unsightly piece of stone; or will you call out a monument of grace and beauty, a symbol to future generations that will tell the story of the man or woman who flew with eagles?

You have been superbly equipped. You have been entrusted with godlike gifts, and now you have been commissioned to do something far from the ordinary—to leave a legacy. You've been given the instructions; your hand is on the throttle. How high will you rise? How high will you fly?

WHAT WILL BE SAID ABOUT YOU?

When it's all said and done, what will others say about you? What does it all come down to?

We sweat and labor to find our place. We take ourselves so seriously, overreacting to the insignificant events of each passing day. Then, finally, even for the kindest and the wisest among us, upon our death all these experiences fade into history and our lives are summarized in a twenty-minute speech and a moment of silence. It hardly seems worth the effort. But, when your moment comes, because it surely will, what will be said about you? How will others describe your moment on earth? Did you give it your all? Did you do your best? Did you scatter flowers as you walked this path? Did you?

Did you utilize your talents, those gifts at birth so endowed to you by God Almighty . . .

Did you develop a burning desire that is required of all achievement . . .

Did you stand up for the rights of others against the undesirable influence and threats of enemies . . .

Did you work faithfully and make the best of your opportunities . . .

Did you save your money so that you could pay your way in this world and yet be generous to those in need . . . Did you master money or did you allow money to master you . . .

Did you bathe each day in the golden glow of enthusiasm . . .

Did you render more and better service than that which you were paid for . . .

Did you love your fellow human beings without regard to race, creed, or color . . .

Did you forgive and forget those that may have harmed you . . .

Did you accept full responsibility for the successes as well as the failures in your life . . .

Did you seek the seed of triumph in every adversity . . .

Did you share yourself with others without expecting reward or payment in return . . .

Did you abide by the Golden Rule . . .

Did you know the greatest blessing: *peace.*

Did you know the greatest obstacle: *ignorance.*

Did you know the greatest challenge: *understanding.*

Did you know the greatest mistake: *conformity.*

Did you know the greatest race: *the human race.*

Did you know the greatest strength: *faith.*

Did you know the greatest weakness: *pride.*

Did you know the greatest day: *today.*

Did you know the greatest word: *thanks.*

Did you know the greatest among us: *whoever serves.*

Did you know the greatest message: *hope.*

Did you know the greatest of these: *love.*

Did you pray . . .

Did you do your best . . .

Did you remember the Great Commission?

WHEN THE STUDENT IS READY, THE TEACHER APPEARS!

You now hold in your hands the keys that will assure your own greatness. Apply all that you have learned. With these ideas, you can experience peace and abundance far beyond your fondest dreams. Furthermore, these virtues will bring you a wealth of happiness. Do you believe in the magic of those words?

By itself, this message alone can change the world! Just think, society spends its days seeking peace and fulfillment, only to secure limited results. Why? Infinite Intelligence provided the means by which humanity could possess peace of mind, and gave every individual access to these means. Why, then, do some go through life imprisoned in a jail of their making—the jail of ignorance, the jail of poverty, the jail of fear—when the key that would free them is within their reach? Each of us is born free and equal. We may not walk the road of life with the same amount of wealth or opportunity immediately available to us, but each of us can go to the source of all wealth, personal fulfillment, and happiness. The answers to these questions will jump to life *if* you are ready to receive them. What a blessing it would be if each of us could truthfully say, "I am the master of my fate; I am the captain of my soul."

But mastery is always a matter of *choice*. From this day forth, you are invited to become the master of your life. Will you accept the invitation? I must warn you, it won't be easy. Succeeding never is. Answer "yes," and you will set yourself apart by marching toward your true destiny. When that occurs, you will be poised instead of tense, confident instead of confused, and bold instead of timid. You will begin to explore places where no other man or woman has ever gone before. You will experience your infinite possibilities. Answer "no," and you may turn your back on your destiny—the rich legacy that life has set aside for you. But *you must choose*. Are you willing to pay the price and extract the secrets hidden within these pages? The choice is yours . . . and yours alone.

> Somebody said that it couldn't be done,
> But he with a chuckle replied
> That maybe it couldn't, but he would be one
> Who wouldn't say so till he'd tried.
> So he buckled right in with the trace of a grin
> On his face. If he worried he hid it.
> He started to sing as he tackled the thing
> That couldn't be done, *and he did it!*
>   —EDGAR A. GUEST

The Kimbro
Executive Profile

African American executives have made such remarkable strides in both their professional and personal lives that today they are beginning to exercise a range of choices that appeared to be unthinkable nearly a decade ago. Over the past twenty years, black corporate climbers have moved steadily up the ladder within the largest U.S. corporations, earning greater compensation, influence, and status, and pushing the "glass ceiling" ever higher until today it blocks only the route to the very top.

The Kimbro Executive Profile is a snapshot of America's top 100 black managers. Talented, gifted, and self-motivated, this 1995 survey paints a picture of a select group worthy of emulation. Through their responses, these executives provide a clear and consistent view of how leadership, management, and personal effectiveness should be defined. But, most important, it offers solid documentation as to who makes it up the corporate ladder and why.

- **What is your current title?**
Chief Financial Officer	1
Executive Vice-President	4
Senior Vice-President	12
Vice-President	54
Director	16
Other	13

- **Which of the following categories best describes your company?**
SERVICES	70
Banking	5
Health care	9
Food/beverage	15
Energy	12
High-tech/communications	12
Financial	3
Insurance	3
Real estate	1
Entertainment	5
Other	5

MANUFACTURING	30
Industrial	4
Automotive	3
Consumer goods	17
Transportation	3
Construction	3

- **How many years have you been employed by your current employer?**

5 and under	31
6-10	21
11-15	16
16-20	11
21-25	11
26-30	5
Over 30	5

- **Age**

Under 40	17
40-45	25
46-50	28
51-55	21
56-60	7
61-65	2
Over 65	0

- **Gender**

Male	73
Female	27

- **Marital status**

Married	77
Single	10
Divorced	10
Separated	0
Widowed	3

- **Number of children**

0	22
1	23
2	42
3	7

4	3
5	2
6	1
More than 6	0

- **Political affiliation**

Republican	2
Democrat	66
Independent	30
Other	2

- **On social issues, do you consider yourself . . .**

Conservative	6
Moderate	58
Liberal	36

- **On fiscal issues, do you consider yourself . . .**

Conservative	35
Moderate	58
Liberal	7

- **How many different companies have you worked for during your career?**

1	14
2	25
3	22
4	19
5	11
6 or more	9

- **If you have worked for more than one company, what was the most important factor in your decision to change jobs? [Multiple responses were allowed.]**

Increased responsibility	30
More challenge	15
Better compensation	26
Faster advancement	18
Favorable location	4
Quality of life	7

- **Do you expect to change companies in the future?**
Yes	54
No	46

- **What would motivate you to move to another firm?**
Increased responsibility	29
More challenge	23
Better compensation	21
Faster advancement	9
Favorable location	4
Quality of life	14

- **How many times have you relocated with your present employer?**
None	70
1	14
2	7
3	2
4	2
5	2
6	1
7 or more	2

- **Have you ever refused to relocate?**
Yes	18
No	82

- **If "yes," did it have a negative effect on your career?**
Yes	22
No	78

- **Have you ever been transferred overseas during your career?**
Yes	15
No	85

- **If "yes," what was the length of your assignment (in years)?**
0	11
1	22
2	33
3	23
4	0
5	0

| 6 | 0 |
| 7 or more | 11 |

- **Have you ever taken a leave of absence?**

| Yes | 17 |
| No | 83 |

- **What was the reason for taking a leave of absence?**

Education	31
Family	15
Public service	8
Health	46

- **What is your current functional area?**

General management	43
Finance/accounting	8
Engineering	10
Marketing/sales	16
Personnel/HR	16
Production/manufacturing	3
International	0
Other	4

- **In which functional area did you begin your career?**

General management	22
Finance/accounting	11
Engineering	7
Marketing/sales	33
Personnel/HR	18
Production/manufacturing	9
International	0

- **In which functional area have you spent most of your career?**

General management	43
Finance/accounting	15
Engineering	0
Marketing/sales	22
Personnel/HR	14
Production/manufacturing	5
International	1

- **Which functional area do you believe is currently the fastest route to the top?**

General management	30
Finance/accounting	17
Engineering	2
Marketing/sales	35
Personnel/HR	0
Production/manufacturing	3
International	13

- **What is the highest position to which you aspire?**

CEO	38
Present position	13
Own a business	42
Other	7

- **In your present assignment, are you satisfied with your current level of responsibility?**

Yes	55
No	45

- **If you were starting over, what career would you pursue?**

Same career	56
Different career	19
Entrepreneurship	23
Other	2

- **If you were financially independent, would you continue in your present position?**

Yes	32
No	68

- **When do you plan to retire?**

Before age 60	41
60–65	41
66–70	5
Work as long as possible	13

- **How important are the following characteristics in enhancing an executive's chances for success? [Multiple responses were allowed. Figures show percent of respondents reporting as "most important."]**

Ability to make decisions	71
Integrity	56
Desire for responsibility	24
Hard work	69
Ambition	26
Vision	48
Securing a mentor	36
Concern for the bottom line	41
Concern for people	41
Creativity	36
Loyalty	11
Risk taking	48
Aggressiveness	26
Visibility	36

- **How would you define success?**

Ability to effect change	39
Enjoying your work	9
Power and influence	19
Recognition	6
Position	5
Money	12
Social status	2
Other	8

- **At what age did you make the major breakthrough that placed you on the path to success?**

21–25	3
26–30	34
31–35	41
36–40	15
41–45	6
46–50	1
Over 50	0

- **What factors were involved in your career turning point? [Multiple responses were allowed.]**

Different functional responsibility	12
Improving bottom line	11
Switching companies	16
Taking on a high-risk project	26
Aligning with the right people	17
Launching a new product	3
Concern for people	5
Luck	7
Other	3

- **What do you perceive as the principal threat to your present career?**

Blocked by incumbents	13
Merger/reorganization	17
Slow-growth industry	13
Superiors	16
Race	17
Gender	6
Education	1
Age	4
Health	3
Other	10

- **Present base salary**

Less than $100,000	8
$101–150,000	31
$151–200,000	22
$201–250,000	20
$251–300,000	11
$301–400,000	3
$401–500,000	5

- **At what age did you reach $100,000 in base salary?**

35 and under	27
36–40	32
41–45	32
46–50	8
51–55	1
Over 55	0

- **Chart your career path in terms of salary and age. [Average age reported.]**

COMPENSATION	AGE
Less than $25,000	21
$26-50,000	26
$51-100,000	35
$101-150,000	45
$151-200,000	46
$201-250,000	50
$251-300,000	51+
$301-400,000	51+
Over $400,000	51+

- **Last bonus received**

Less than $25,000	25
$26-50,000	41
$51-75,000	13
$76-100,000	6
$101-150,000	4
$151-200,000	11
Over $200,000	0

- **Level of education**

No college degree	4
College degree	96

- **Undergraduate major. [Percent of those with undergraduate degrees.]**

Business/accounting	28
Engineering	14
Economics	13
Social sciences	31
Math/sciences	7
Humanities/art/philosophy	7

- **Graduate degree. [Number reported is percent of degrees.]**

M.B.A.	56
LL.B./J.D.	8
Ph.D.	5
M.A.	7
M.S.	12
M.S.E.	2
Other	10

- **Name of graduate school. [Twenty-eight respondents listed one school.]**

Harvard	11
Wharton	5
Northwestern	2
Yale	2

- **Which factor was most important to your career?**

Hard work	44
Desire	24
Having a mentor	21
Networking	6
Other	5

- **Which three characteristics will be most important to executives in the year 2000?**

Creativity	27
Ability to make decisions	26
Vision	31
Networking	9
Education	7
Loyalty	0

- **How many days have you spent out of town on business within the last twelve months?**

Less than 10	4
10–20	18
21–30	16
31–40	14
41–50	17
51–75	14
76–100	10
101–125	4
More than 126	3

- **How many hours do you usually work per week?**

40–45	1
46–50	12
51–55	25
56–60	37
61–65	14
66–70	8
More than 70	3

- **How many vacation days have you taken within the last twelve months?**

5 and under	4
6–10	19
11–15	34
16–20	28
21–25	7
More than 25	7

- **Which of your parents did you live with during your childhood?**

Both	79
Mother only	19
Father only	0
Neither	2

- **Father's occupation**

Managerial	9
Blue-collar	43
Professional/technical	13
Entrepreneur	13
Menial	11
Other	11

- **Mother's occupation**

Managerial	4
Blue-collar	20
Professional/technical	27
Entrepreneur	4
Menial	14
Other	31

- **Does your spouse work?**

Yes	56
No	35
Part-time	9

- **Spouse's occupation**

Managerial	29
Blue-collar	0
Professional/technical	44
Entrepreneur	11
Other	16

- **What percent of your family income is earned by your spouse?**

0	38
1–5	11
6–10	11
11–20	9
More than 20	31

- **Which were you of the following?**

First child	40
Youngest child	15
Only child	6
Middle child	39

- **Where did you spend most of your childhood?**

REGION

Northeast	38
Southeast	21
Midwest	25
Southwest	4
West	5
Other	7

LOCALE

Urban	68
Suburban	25
Rural	7

- **Which clubs or organizations do you belong to?**

Professional organization	32
Country club	8
Private club	12
Health club	17
Nonprofit board	21
Other	10

- **Are you a member of these organizations? [Some belong to more than one.]**

NAACP	47
Urban League	33
100 Black Men	16
100 Black Women	4

- **Greek organizations**

Alpha Kappa Alpha	0
Delta Sigma Theta	7
Sigma Gamma Rho	0
Omega Psi Phi	23
Alpha Phi Alpha	40
Kappa Alpha Psi	27
Zeta Phi Beta	0
Phi Beta Sigma	3

- **Do you sit on any company's board?**

Yes	34
No	66

- **If "yes," on how many?**

1	64
2	28
3	4
4	4
5	0
More than 5	0

- **Do you believe your successor will be African American?**

Yes	13
No	87

- **Do you believe your successor will be African American female?**

Yes	10
No	90

- **What impact does mentorship have on a successful corporate career?**

Very important	90
Important	10
Not important	0

- **Are you a mentor to other African American corporate climbers?**

Yes	99
No	1

- **In your opinion, did you sacrifice or compromise values in order to advance in your career?**

Yes	17
No	83

- **Type of books most often read**

Motivational/self-help	25
Business	36
Biography/history	12
Mystery	11
Religious/spiritual	4

- **The most important public policy issues facing African Americans are (ranked from 1, most important, to 5, least important):***

Improving education	29
Maintenance of the family unit	47
Entrepreneurship/economic development	21
Race relations	17
Reducing crime	19

* Data were weighted most important to least important. The data read as follows: 47 percent ranked "maintenance of the family unit" as most important public policy issue; 29 percent ranked "improving education" as second most important issue; 21 percent ranked "entrepreneurship and economic development" as third most important; 19 percent ranked "reducing crime" as fourth most important; and 17 percent ranked "race relations" as fifth most important.

African American Consumption Patterns, 1993–95

- Black Americans constitute 12 percent of the total U.S. population and are responsible for the following consumption statistics.
  36 percent of hair conditioners
  32 percent of malt liquors
  30 percent of movie theater tickets
  28 percent of readership of *GQ* magazine
  25–35 percent of barbecue sauce, baby formula, detergent, potato chips, salt, pasta, toothpaste, and household cleaners
  22 percent of rice
  20 percent of Scotch whisky
  20 percent of portable television sets
  20 percent of Hasbro, Mattel, and Kenner toys
  17 percent of coin-operated washing machines
  17 percent of the *National Enquirer*
  16 percent of orange juice
  15 percent of tobacco products
  12 percent of Japanese automobiles

- Black females, who constitute 6 percent of the population, consume 15 percent ($600 million) of the $4-billion cosmetic market (mostly to Maybelline); spend 23 percent more on shoes than the population at large; and consume 26 percent more perfume than any other ethnic group of females.
- Black males aged thirteen to twenty-four, who constitute less than 3 percent of the population, purchase 10 percent of the $12-billion athletic shoe market and more than 20 percent of Nike shoes; 55 percent of Starter jacket sales ($283 million in 1993) are linked to inner-city buyers.
- Black Americans spend $6 billion per year on soft drinks and more than $500 million on McDonald's fast foods and are twice as likely as whites to own an Audi, BMW, or Mercedes-Benz.

Data were gathered from the U.S. Department of Commerce, *Black Enterprise, Essence, Target Market News,* Urban Marketing Institute, and Clark Atlanta University School of Business.